An Examined Life

ALSO BY KARAN SINGH

Varied Rhythms: Essays & Poems, 1960

Shadow and Sunlight: Dogri Folk Songs, 1962

Prophet of Indian Nationalism: The Political Thought of Sri Aurobindo Ghosh, 1963

Post-Independence Generation: Challenge and Response, 1966

Contemporary Essays, 1971

Population, Poverty and the Future of India, 1975

In Defence of Religion, 1978

Religions of India, 1983

One Man's World, 1986

Bridge to Immortality: The Mundaka Upanishad, 1987

Humanity at the Crossroads: With Professor Daisaku Ikeda, 1988

Autobiography, 1989

Essays on Hinduism, 1990

Brief Sojourn, 1991

Hymn to Shiva and Other Poems, 1991

The Mountain of Shiva: A Novel, 1994

India and the World, 1995

Hinduism: The Eternal Religion, 1999

As I See It: The Karan Singh Reader, 2001

Vedanta, 2004

Jammu & Kashmir, 1949–64: Select Correspondence with Jawaharlal Nehru, 2006

Kashmir and Beyond, 1966–84: Select Correspondence with Indira Gandhi, 2011

Meetings with Remarkable Women, 2014

Triveni: Essays, Poems and a Novella, 2014

An Examined Life

Essays and Reflections by

Karan Singh

Edited by

RAGHAV VERMA

HarperCollins *Publishers* India

First published India by
HarperCollins *Publishers* in 2019
An imprint of HarperCollins Publishers
HarperCollins *Publishers* India, Cyber City, Building 10-A, Gurugram, Haryana-122002
India
www.harpercollins.co.in

2 4 6 8 10 9 7 5 3 1

P-ISBN: 9789353570231
E-ISBN: 9789353570248

Typeset in 11/14.2 Minion Pro at
Manipal Digital Systems, Manipal

Printed and bound at
Manipal Technologies Limited, Manipal

*

HarperCollins *Publishers*, Macken House, 39/40 Mayor Street Upper, Dublin 1, D01
C9W8, Ireland

To
My two gurus: Pandit Jawaharlal Nehru,
Dr Sarvepalli Radhakrishnan, and

Plato: 'The unexamined life
is not worth living.'

Contents

Foreword

There will be no end to the troubles of states, or of humanity itself, till philosophers become kings in this world, or till those we now call kings and rulers really and truly become philosophers, and political power and philosophy thus come into the same hands.

—Plato

I AM DELIGHTED TO present the new collection of Karan Singh's writings. Suitably titled *An Examined Life*, it offers a look inside the rich mind of the politician and the scholar.

Karan Singh has been a good friend and a guiding light to the Indian National Congress movement. It is a rare occasion in the history of a nation to encounter a personality like him, someone who was born into a royal family but has lead his entire life for the cause of strengthening democracy.

A man of letters, he carries deep knowledge of the Upanishads and has given immense importance to the cultural and constitutional values of India throughout his long personal and political life. His poems and essays make for a thoughtful read, and his farewell speech in the Rajya Sabha is progressive and carries ideas worthy of being espoused. An inspiring statesman and a cultural icon, he is the last of the legion from the great Nehruvian era.

A man of ineffable grace and dignity, Karan Singh and his writings have a lot to teach the young readers about the importance of culture and learning to live in harmony with each other. I congratulate the editor of this volume, Raghav Verma, for the insightful conversation with him and HarperCollins India for bringing this intelligent edition as we celebrate seventy years of his public life.

I hope the readers will find this book as fascinating as I did.

Manmohan Singh
New Delhi
15 April 2019

Preface

ON 20 JUNE 2019, I complete seventy years in public life, having been appointed regent of Jammu and Kashmir by my father way back in 1949. These seventy years have been a fascinating journey that has taken me literally across the world. I also started writing soon thereafter and my first series of articles on a visit to Amarnath was published by the *Hindustan Times* in 1953. So, for sixty-seven years I have been writing on diverse topics: politics (having been in the Indian parliament for forty years—ten of them as cabinet minister); political science (my PhD in Delhi University was on the political thought of Sri Aurobindo); wildlife conservation (as chairman of the Indian Board for Wildlife for several years during which I was responsible for getting the national animal of India changed from lion to tiger); environment (having been on the Indian delegation to the first UN conference on human environment in Stockholm in 1972); Hinduism (based on the universal principles of Vedanta as articulated in the Upanishads, and not on narrow, exclusivist thinking); the interfaith movement (as chairman of the Temple of Understanding for forty years); a novel set in Kashmir; a book of poems; meetings with remarkable women and so on.

There are also travelogues from when my wife and I travelled to the ends of the earth: from the heights of Machu Picchu to the great Ayers Rock in the heart of the Australian continent; from the Norwegian fjords down to lake Nahuel Hüapi in Bariloche, Argentina; from the islands of Kauai in

Hawaii all the way across the ocean to Fiji; from the magnificent Hindu temple of Angkor Vat in Cambodia to the great Buddhist Borobudur in Indonesia; not to speak of extensive travel within India itself, from the splendid Himalayas in the north to Kanyakumari in the south where three great oceans meet at the feet of Mother India.

While in public life, I never stopped reading or writing. I have always had a fascination for books; even as a young boy my greatest joy was when my father gave me ten rupees to visit Raina's Book Depot near the Polo Ground in Srinagar. I have been buying books for many decades now and have also been given many, including a valuable tranche of rare books inherited from my father. Numbering almost 25,000, these books are now housed in the Amar Mahal Museum and Library that my wife and I set up in Jammu in 1974.

These experiences and writings constitute a vast archive, and it was suggested by family and close friends that a good selection from all the genres could usefully be chosen for publishing. Over numerous meetings, this anthology has been compiled and edited by Raghav Verma and published by HarperCollins. I take pleasure in presenting this book to the general public in the hope that readers will find in it something of interest and perhaps even inspiration.

I must thank my good friend Shashi Tharoor for his perceptive introduction to this volume, as also former prime minister Manmohan Singh for kindly writing the foreword. Thanks are due to my editor Raghav Verma for his long and painstaking scholarly work on this book.

Karan Singh
New Delhi
9 March 2019

Introduction

KARAN SINGH IS A legend of our contemporary political history. I've heard of him since I was old enough to take an interest in politics. From following his work as a minister when I was a college student and now to have known him and worked with him as a close colleague and friend, and to chair the Parliamentary External Affairs Committee with him as its senior member, has been a rare privilege. And to my delight, we share our day and month of birth, which adds to the sense of affinity I have for this remarkable man.

When India was transforming itself on its way to independence from the perils of British Raj, Karan Singh was born on 9 March 1931 in Cannes, France to Maharaja Hari Singh and Maharani Tara Devi of Jammu and Kashmir. When his son was six, Maharaja Hari Singh decided to send him to live in a separate establishment under the care of a British guardian, with two companions, to groom him into various princely talents for the next five years, whereupon at age eleven he went to study at the Doon School.

India was still burning in the horrific flames of Partition, when in October 1947 Maharaja Hari Singh had to sign the Instrument of Accession of Jammu and Kashmir to India in return for aid to secure its borders from a violent invasion by tribals who would be ancestors of present-day Taliban. As a result of contestations with the popular Kashmiri leader Sheikh Abdullah and in hope of a successful plebiscite, Maharaja Hari

Singh went on to live in Bombay, appointing his son as regent of the state of Jammu and Kashmir in 1949.

At the age of eighteen, Karan Singh embarked on an exceptional political life among the populace of Jammu and Kashmir as the youngest head of the state that India would ever see. It also makes him the only person from the historic Nehruvian age to have worked closely with all the prime ministers of independent India, as he mentions in his farewell speech to Parliament in 2018.

Emerging from the colonial ghosts and mired in the aftermath of Partition, India's long and difficult transition from a motley collection of princely states to a free republic has also been a political and personal transition for Karan Singh. His political ascent did not stop him from evolving personally. His keen interest in academic scholarship in political philosophy continued to pursue its course along with making critical decisions of state policy at a young age. When a life is lived amidst constant rigorous philosophical and spiritual inquiry, with faith and not apostasy, a path to enlightenment is inevitable.

Seventy years on, Karan Singh is a living, breathing history of India and a cultural icon. He added a unique character to decades of parliamentary discourse by moving away from the conventional outlook of the typical Indian politician, by standing up for issues and leading by example in speaking out for core constitutional values. Even if that involved public disagreements with his own party president—not as a renegade but with an unmatched professional ethics of constructive politics.

He is a man of astonishing erudition, extremely well versed in the Sanskrit texts and particularly the spiritual readings of our culture. My own book *Why I Am A Hindu* is in many parts influenced by, and at time quotes directly from, his sterling scholarship on the subject, including an excellent translation of the works of Mirabai, which became an integral part and an invaluable addition to the arguments in my book. Of course, he very graciously allowed me to do so and subsequently launched the book in New Delhi a few months later.

He has also had an inimitable political career in which he has served in a number of vital portfolios in successive governments, going back to the days of Indira Gandhi. In his over half a century-long innings in national politics, Singh also served as a Member of Parliament for a remarkable forty years in eight terms, spent equally between the Lok Sabha and the

Rajya Sabha. He has served as head of state as well as the governor in his own state and subsequently as minister in New Delhi, and is in many ways considered by many like me as the best president India never had.

His grace and civility are all too uncommon in today's politics. A man of great culture and refinement, Karan Singh is an individual whom I am privileged to introduce.

This book is a remarkable narrative of an astonishing life.

Shashi Tharoor
New Delhi
24 April 2019

An Interview with Karan Singh

RAGHAV VERMA: I would like to start at the very beginning. What are your initial memories of reading different books and literatures?

KARAN SINGH: I have had an affinity for books throughout my life. Ever since I was little, I used to read children's books and I loved going to book shops and buying books. My father would give me ten rupees to go to the Raina Book Depot in Srinagar, which was a great delight. When I went to Doon [a boarding school in Dehradun] I started reading more extensively. I remember reading many of the P.G. Wodehouse novels, the Sherlock Holmes and Scarlet Pimpernel series, and I loved the classics: *War and Peace, A Tale of Two Cities, The Three Musketeers.* I subsequently moved to more serious reading: books on philosophy and politics by Plato, Bertrand Russell, Aldous Huxley, Vivekananda, the Arthurian novels by Mary Stewart and the Cretan novels of Mary Renault are some of my favourites. In poetry, I love Yeats, Wordsworth, Sri Aurobindo, Gurudev Tagore, Robert Frost in English; Ghalib, Faiz and Iqbal in Urdu, Dinkar and Tulsidas in Hindi.

RAGHAV VERMA: Was it largely the English language or did you read in other languages as well?

KARAN SINGH: Almost entirely English. I just had the English books, but then I moved on to Indian poets writing in English.

RAGHAV VERMA: What was the climate of reading books then?

KARAN SINGH: In those days, we did not have the internet and computers, so reading books was the only way you could increase your knowledge, and therefore it was a very conducive atmosphere. At school also, we were encouraged to go to the library and read in the spare time. When I came home, I had my own books.

RAGHAV VERMA: As a child, you did not stay with your parents.

KARAN SINGH: I had a rather curious childhood. For the first five years, I was with my mother, and at six my father organized for me to live separately with two companions under a British guardian. He felt, perhaps rightly, that had I continued to live with my mother in the palace I would be thoroughly spoilt. Therefore, it was decided that I needed to be brought up with some discipline. Our guardians were good people, so there were three of us living in a separate establishment.

RAGHAV VERMA: Were you spoilt anyway?

KARAN SINGH: Oh, no! My father was very sure about that. He made clear I was to not get any special treatment. I could meet my mother thrice a week and my father once a week.

I had to spend a lot of time developing different skills, such as horse riding and music. I had to go riding every morning with the bodyguard cavalry. I had private tutors: the British guardians and an Indian tutor. This was the setup till I was eleven, five years from the age of six. After that, I went to Doon. The whole structure—of living with a guardian in a separate establishment—changed with boarding school, and I would stay with my parents when I went home for holidays.

RAGHAV VERMA: When did you start writing and what did you write about?

KARAN SINGH: We had to write a lot of essays in school. I had a very good teacher who taught us English, V. Siddharthacharry[1]. I enjoyed the early process of learning to structure my essays. When I came home after finishing school at eighteen, I started writing extensively.

RAGHAV VERMA: I read your notes on Aristotle, Hegel, Kant and continental philosophy—twenty-nine notebooks.

KARAN SINGH: The notes at Amar Mahal that you must have read are from my preparation for my master's degree at Delhi University.

I liked to be meticulous. Initially, I read a lot on western philosophy but also made notes on the administration and constitutions of different nations and civilizations.

RAGHAV VERMA: What led to your interest in philosophy?

KARAN SINGH: I came to philosophy first through Plato. I was very interested in Plato, the person and his works.

[*The*] *Republic* is a much larger work. I was fascinated particularly by his *Symposium.* It is a beautiful work with Plato's signature dialogues and the speech on Socrates, Aristophanes and others. I read the history of western philosophy and eventually moved to Indian philosophy.

RAGHAV VERMA: Why this shift?

KARAN SINGH: I think generally a quest for knowledge. Also, the discovery and realization that we have a tremendously rich heritage which nobody seems to know about. At least in my family or where I lived, people were not even remotely interested in the study of the Upanishads. Once I started reading, it just became my philosophy and way of life.

RAGHAV VERMA: Was it purely academic or also a spiritual quest?

KARAN SINGH: It was a bit of both. I started with Indian philosophy as an academic would, as I wrote my doctoral thesis on the political thought of Sri Aurobindo, who combined spirituality and public life. Later, Vivekananda became, as it were, my spiritual idol. These were the two people who influenced me in my later reading and writing.

RAGHAV VERMA: Did you have idols?

KARAN SINGH: I have two of these spiritual gurus (Swami Vivekananda and Sri Aurobindo) whom I did not meet. I also had two living gurus in Jawaharlal Nehru for politics and Dr Radhakrishnan for philosophy.

In my spiritual quest, I have had a whole spectrum of spiritual gurus; a Shakta guru who was a Kashmiri pandit, a Vaishnava guru who was an Englishman, a Shaiva guru who was an American, a Sufi guru who was Muslim, a Kriya yoga guru who is from Kerala. So, I have been blessed with a number of gurus and teachings around the world.

RAGHAV VERMA: Did you receive formal training in Hinduism from any particular school of thought?

KARAN SINGH: No. At home, we did our normal prayers and I did my own readings and discoveries. I took more to the Upanishads rather than the Puranas. The Upanishads are the quintessential texts on Hinduism, reflecting the wisdom and thoughts of enlightened seers. The Puranas go into various kinds of stories and myths which are fascinating but less attractive to me.

RAGHAV VERMA: What about this cyclic change after every eighteen years in your life?

KARAN SINGH: It's just a coincidence, not all the time. The first eighteen years I lived a private life. At the age of eighteen, I was appointed regent by my father, then elected as Sadar-i-Riyasat for three terms and later became the governor of the state of Jammu and Kashmir. This covered eighteen years from 1949. At the age of thirty-six, I joined Mrs (Indira) Gandhi's cabinet and remained a member of the Lok Sabha for the next eighteen years until 1984.

RAGHAV VERMA: What are your memories of Partition?

KARAN SINGH: Partition tore India into three pieces. Disaster struck. There was East Pakistan, there was West Pakistan, and there was the rest of India. Millions of people were uprooted from their houses, tens of thousands massacred on both sides. It was one of the greatest mass migrations and killings in human history. People today do not realize the tremendous trauma of Partition, whose negative vibrations continue to haunt us even today.

RAGHAV VERMA: How was Jammu and Kashmir affected by Partition?

KARAN SINGH: Jammu and Kashmir, although not part of British India and not formally partitioned, could not escape this tremendous historical process. The result was that until Partition my father had not yet acceded either to India or Pakistan. Then in the third week of October 1947, there was a tribal invasion from Pakistan. They attacked and were taking over vast areas of the state.

After the attack, the state was being overrun by the invaders despite the brave defence by the state forces. They were spread out thinly across the whole state, but they put up a fierce defence. Brigadier Rajinder Singh, for example, held up the raiders for forty-eight hours, fighting to the last man and the last bullet and thus gaining time for the Srinagar airport to be saved by the Indian army. At that stage, my father appealed to India for aid, and India said it could only help if Jammu and Kashmir were a part of it. So, my father signed the Instrument of Accession.

RAGHAV VERMA: Later when you took over as regent of the state, was it a political necessity or to keep the family legacy?

KARAN SINGH: There is a complex background to that. After the 1947 accession to India, Jawaharlal Nehru insisted that power in the state of Jammu and Kashmir be handed over to Sheikh Abdullah, who was then the leader of the National Conference, which was supporting the accession to India. However, he was also a close personal friend of his. It was my father who signed the Instrument of Accession—without him it would not have happened.

Once he signed the document the inevitable transition had to come—as was happening all over the country—from monarchy to democracy. For a year or so, I was not well and went to America [USA] to receive medical treatment. By the time I returned in early '49, there was growing tension between my father and Sheikh Abdullah. Sheikh Abdullah was a powerful Kashmiri leader, but very anti-Dogra. His whole movement had been against the Dogra maharaja. My father represented the old order and Sheikh Abdullah represented the new power equations. Remember, at the time, a plebiscite was very much in the air. People hardly remember that the plebiscite was actually agreed upon and a plebiscite administrator had been appointed by the United Nations. Admiral Chester W. Nimitz of the US Navy was appointed as the plebiscite administrator. But who was going to win the plebiscite? Panditji thought that it was Sheikh Abdullah. But then Sheikh Abdullah said that he could not win the plebiscite as long as Maharaja Hari Singh was there.

RAGHAV VERMA: The exile as a result?

KARAN SINGH: Yes. Sardar Patel asked my parents to stay out of the state for a while. My mother was more gregarious than my father; she would go to the temples, to the refugee camps, and she was in many ways better known and more popular. Sheikh Abdullah insisted that both must go. That was when my father, in his capacity as maharaja, appointed me regent.

RAGHAV VERMA: And moved to Bombay?

KARAN SINGH: Moved to Bombay, where his favourite pastime was horse racing. He was a great patron of the turf and had an excellent string of horses. He also had started a stud farm in Nagbani near Jammu. He never went back to his beloved state and passed away in 1961 at the age of sixty-six. Two years later they abolished the monarchy. It was just a formality but it had to be done. The Constituent Assembly created the post of an elective Sadar-i-Riyasat in the new Constitution, to which I was appointed. That was where another conflict came to be. Many people in Jammu were not happy that I should become Sadar-i-Riyasat.

RAGHAV VERMA: There are different political interpretations over whether Kashmir is a part of the Indian state or not, or in what capacity. You raised the issue in Parliament and asked us to introspect, calling for a ban on using pellet guns after the deaths of sixty citizens in the Valley and thousands injured at the hands of the state. But you also placed in front of your parliamentary colleagues the uncomfortable but critical fact of 'limited accession'. Tell us about that.

KARAN SINGH: There is huge ignorance in our country about this. They consider Jammu and Kashmir to be just like any other state. The Instrument of Accession that my father signed was exactly the same as the ones all the other rulers signed, on that there is no question. But what happened after that was that all the other rulers, thanks to Sardar Patel and V.P. Menon, signed merger agreements, whereby they integrated their territories with India. But in J&K there was no such agreement. There was a war still going on and half of the state had already fallen under Pakistan's control. So, our relationship with the rest of India was governed by the Instrument of Accession but, more importantly, by Article 370, granting a special autonomous status to Jammu and Kashmir.

We have to remember that accession is complete but the state has not merged. There is a lot of confusion when people of the Valley talk of autonomy; critics say that they are talking of independence. That is not true. Autonomy is not independence. Autonomy is living with the fact that we have not merged. How much power to retain and how much power to give to the Indian government has been the real political question for Jammu and Kashmir.

RAGHAV VERMA: What would be the contemporary political interpretation of that limited accession? Does it still hold true? Because the mass narrative, as you said, has been made to believe otherwise.

KARAN SINGH: It is there. It is still there legally. It is operative. The state still uses the Ranbir Penal Code[2] instead of the Indian Penal Code.

RAGHAV VERMA: The current political discourse seems bent on erasing any nuance and claims complete integration rather than to recognize the truth of its special status.

KARAN SINGH: The right wing seems to resent that Jammu and Kashmir carries a special status, different from other states. This has always surprised me. We are a great country, we should be large-hearted. Jammu and Kashmir came into India under complex and difficult circumstances. Now, after all these years, to ask why it holds a special position is baffling. It will always be special because it was born out of a special historical event and subsequent political developments. In England, they have all sorts of different governing systems, like in the Jersey Island, Scotland and Ireland. Hong Kong is, for example, governed by the principle of 'one country, two systems'. We should feel so lucky that Jammu and Kashmir, a Muslim-majority state, became a part of India despite the religion-led Partition. Cherish that; relish that; honour that.

On the other hand, what has happened from the time of 1947 till today is, a great deal of autonomy has been eroded. A large number of items from the Union list have been extended to J&K. But this idea to get rid of the last shred of autonomy is not justified, although opinion on this is sharply divided in the three regions of Kashmir, Jammu and Ladakh.

RAGHAV VERMA: From 1952 onwards, you wrote consistently to then prime minister Jawaharlal Nehru about J&K's changing relationship with the Indian government, but the growing conflicts in the state changed the conversation.

KARAN SINGH: What I used to largely write and talk to Pandit Nehru was of course about the state's changing relationship with the government. But what I particularly would call his attention to was on the specific regional problems that were far more complex than the news headlines portrayed. There is a common misconception when people ask me about Kashmir.

RAGHAV VERMA: What is this misconception?

KARAN SINGH: There is no such state as Kashmir. It is Jammu *and* Kashmir, the state for which my father signed the Instrument of Accession and which my ancestors built. We conquered Ladakh, we conquered Gilgit–Baltistan. It was a Dogra empire. This needs to be understood historically. Jammu–Kashmir was never an integrated state. We kept these regions together for a century. This was an empire[3] larger than the size of England. The area was about 84,000 square miles and very diverse. There was Gilgit–Baltistan in Central Asia; then the regions Ladakh, Kargil and Leh were an extension of the Tibetan culture. There was the Kashmir valley and then there was Jammu, essentially a Dogra area. When the UN-sponsored ceasefire came into effect on 1 January 1948, a fifth region was created: Mirpur–Muzaffarabad, in effect the Punjabi-Pahadi Muslim region.

Of the five regions, Gilgit–Baltistan are under Pakistan's control, from which they have leased thousands of square miles to China. Over half of the state area is with them. With India remains the rest, with three regions—Kashmir, Jammu and Leh. To say that Jammu, Kashmir and Ladakh are as diverse as Kerala, Gujarat and Assam may be an overstatement, but they are very different: culturally, linguistically, administratively and historically. So, it was important for me to acknowledge all parts of the state, especially when writing to Prime Minister Nehru stressing that while Kashmir is important and in the eye of the storm, we cannot ignore Jammu and Ladakh.

RAGHAV VERMA: While Kashmir has suffered excess militarization, do you think historically because of its turbulent politics, the regions of Jammu and Ladakh have been affected too?

KARAN SINGH: Yes, because of Kashmir's central position the concentration has been on the Valley, and other regions have been comparatively neglected, even to this day. That is why even if you look at the politics of J&K, you will find different aspirations . The Kashmiris want freedom; people of Jammu want to emerge out of the shadow of Kashmir's over-politicization; and Ladakhis want access to basic amenities to begin with.

RAGHAV VERMA: How was it like being appointed the head of state just as you attained maturity?

KARAN SINGH: It was very difficult, but it was also exciting and challenging. I was young and idealistic. I felt the need to be committed to the responsibility. At eighteen, suddenly to be pitchforked to talk and work with stalwarts such as Jawaharlal Nehru and Sardar Patel was unnerving. I used to write detailed letters and kept giving my own views which were not necessarily the views of the J&K government. Regardless of what the government felt, whether it was Sheikh Mohammed Abdullah or Bakshi Ghulam Mohammad, I considered it my duty to keep the centre informed of my views as I saw the truth, about facts and facets which may not have been available to them. It was great privilege too. I think, I managed reasonably well over these eighteen years as the head of state.

RAGHAV VERMA: How was your relationship with Jawaharlal Nehru and when did you first meet him?

KARAN SINGH: He was my guru. I first met him in 1947 when I was in bed with an orthopaedic condition. By the time I came back from the States and became the regent, and subsequently Sadar-i-Riyasat, we were in direct contact constantly, through correspondence and meetings, and I had his guidance and support at all times.

RAGHAV VERMA: Any memories of other luminaries from pre-independent India?

KARAN SINGH: I had a historic opportunity to meet Mahatma Gandhi when he visited my father in Srinagar in June 1947. Only my parents were to meet him, but I insisted on being present. He sat with us for about an hour, with all of us listening respectfully. There is now a plaque recording the meeting, on the tree under which we met him in the palace lawns. I met B.R. Ambedkar once when he came as the law minister. Sardar Patel invited me as his guest in Dehradun and I spent over a fortnight with him in June 1949. He was very ill and was looked after by his daughter Maniben Patel.

I owe a great debt to Sardar Patel. Had it not been for him, I would have spent my entire life on a wheelchair. He used to come to meet my father in Jammu. When he saw me in that condition, he insisted that my father send me to America immediately for treatment, and so I spent an entire year in hospital before walking again. Later, I could play tennis and badminton and have since walked all my life.

RAGHAV VERMA: I ask because I wanted your view on the contemporary polity of India. While the generation of Nehru, Patel and Ambedkar brought a revolutionary democratic constitution to the Indian Union after the country was partitioned, today citizens are forced to prove their patriotism or risk being called anti-national.

KARAN SINGH: I think it's very unfortunate that people of India should be made to prove their patriotism. Except, of course, those groups that do not believe in the Constitution and resort to violence.

RAGHAV VERMA: Not just in India but across the world. Recently, French president Emmanuel Macron said in the presence of world leaders, 'Patriotism is the exact opposite of nationalism. Nationalism is its betrayal.' But the truth is that across western countries a far-right nationalistic movement is rapidly spreading.

KARAN SINGH: This raises a broader question, between nationalism and the global society. Interestingly, many of our leaders transcended nationalism. Rabindranath Tagore wrote very clearly that nationalism has its limitations. Sri Aurobindo, the prophet of Indian nationalism, towards the end of his life in 1950 wrote that nationalism had run its course and needed to be transcended. Even Mahatma Gandhi was not only talking of India but universal humanism. So, all the great thinkers of pre-Independence and even our ancient sages preached *vasudhaiva kutumbakam*, the concept of the world as one family. Indians have the philosophical concept of a global society. Also, there's a difference between patriotism and chauvinism. Patriotism is when everybody is expected to love their country. But the chauvinism we are seeing today is a hostile and possessive sort of attitude where anyone who is slightly critical of the government gets vile abuse and is accused of being an anti-national. That is unfortunate. Citizens are being asked to prove their nationalism and patriotism, but why should they have to? Unless they have publicly resorted to violence or done something that challenges the very basis of the Indian state, it is unconstitutional to do so.

RAGHAV VERMA: But the term ant-national is now so loosely used.

KARAN SINGH: It's very loosely used and frequently heard. Now if you say that the Pakistani cricket team batted very well, you are against the nation! We must have a sense of balance in our speech. We must gain a sense of proportion as to what extent things could be said. Every third person is being accused of being anti-national these days. This is unacceptable. '*Tum hi kaho ki yeh andaz-e-guftugu kya hai.*'[4]

RAGHAV VERMA: In your farewell speech to Parliament, you refer to critical debates of Hiren Mukherjee, Madhu Limaye and Nath Pai. Those confrontational parliamentary debates, I assume, would easily be termed anti-national in today's political climate.

KARAN SINGH: Maybe, because many of those political heavyweights were sharp and bitter but also substantial and responsible. Those were great debates in those days. As I said in my farewell, the Indian parliament has changed a lot but not for the better. The quality of speeches has deteriorated and the whole atmosphere of parliamentary discourse and discipline has been disturbed.

RAGHAV VERMA: It is not just limited to nationalism. We are also asked to prove our Hinduism. Who is a better or worse Hindu? As if there are no other ethnicities to debate.

KARAN SINGH: That is also laughable. Who is a better Hindu?—there aren't any degrees made by the god. How can one judge who is a better Hindu or even a better human being?

RAGHAV VERMA: How can such a big and diverse country like India have a singular identity?

KARAN SINGH: I found it very strange and stupid that a BJP spokesperson asked for Rahul's [Gandhi] gotra. Although he caved in to the demand, the question itself was inconsequential. Hinduism at its best is Vedanta. It's an extremely broad, inclusive and enlightened worldview where we believe that the divine resides in the heart of every human being.

RAGHAV VERMA: You said in your 1965 essay on Hinduism: 'Not all Indians are Hindus and not all Hindus are Indians.' Does it matter to you who is a better Hindu?

KARAN SINGH: A Hindu is somebody who is born Hindu and continues their religion, or people who may not have been born Hindu but are attracted to its philosophy and therefore follow many aspects of its culture. There are no certificates for that.

RAGHAV VERMA: We are living in times where there is rampant Hindu extremism channelled through Hindutva.

KARAN SINGH: We should not be fundamentalist in our beliefs. It is really more a semantic problem. Hindutva is now being propagated by people who are chauvinistic Hindus; this is an unfortunate dichotomy.

RAGHAV VERMA: What is the fundamental difference between Hinduism and Hindutva?

KARAN SINGH: There's a political difference that's obvious. The Hindu right wing has officially adopted what they call Hindutva. I don't think any of them have got on to any spiritual level.

RAGHAV VERMA: There are other consequences that are brought on by Hindutva. For instance, apart from religious intolerance there are other freedoms of citizens that are being curbed. You wrote and publicly supported the LGBTQ community in 2009, when India was still struggling to come to terms with it. But the present climate is hostile and there are brazen attacks on fundamental freedoms, such as what to wear, eat, read, think and express.

KARAN SINGH: Thank goodness the obnoxious Section 377 criminalizing the entire queer community has at last been knocked down. It was long overdue. To talk about this business of dictating to others what one should eat or what one should wear and how and where to worship and whom is trivializing Hinduism.

RAGHAV VERMA: The symbolism of Hindutva used by political parties have also led to violent communal attacks across nation, many just staged as an excuse to hurt minorities and further enforce the symbolism.

KARAN SINGH: These attacks—I believe you are talking about cow vigilantism—lead only to violence and innocent people dying. It is abhorrent and unacceptable.

RAGHAV VERMA: Dissent solidifies democracy. But when a government uses its power and institutions to directly shut down any voice that questions and criticizes it, from students to journalists, writers and artists, what new precedents are being set?

KARAN SINGH: That does seem to be the case with the current government. I don't know about the entirety of the press; I know there are many good people still out there who haven't given up. As far as the printed word is concerned, some newspapers seem fairly balanced and often critical. It is the television channels that have created havoc in the minds of the masses. There are some channels that are blatantly partisan.

Among the English-language channels, with an exception of one or two maybe, almost all of them are leaning towards the ruling dispensation, which is not good for the future. It is all right to be partisan in your arguments but to constantly distort facts of the happenings on the ground every day, in order to portray a situation in a certain light, is not correct. Sadly, that is what is happening.

RAGHAV VERMA: Do you think it affects the idea of justice?

KARAN SINGH: In a way it does. The mob culture is often a gift of prime-time television. On the other hand, there is the power of positive TV; take the Jessica Lal case for example. Had it not been for its reportage, the killers would have never been caught. So, it has the capacity to work both ways.

RAGHAV VERMA: One could say, fear in the press is a danger to democracy.

KARAN SINGH: That's again a broader question. I'm not sure if there's an immediate danger. The only time democracy was definitely in danger was during the Emergency. After that, there have been ups and down. In a way, democracy is always in danger. It is never permanently established; we have to keep it going. It is a question of value and degree. But we have to keep working towards ensuring democratic processes in our institutions and political system.

RAGHAV VERMA: One would say it's a different kind of socio-capital emergency, where our public institutions have not been effective lately. Attacks on universities, dissent within the CBI and RBI and so on.

KARAN SINGH: Yes, that's very unfortunate. The CBI is our highest police investigation agency. Both the top cops were at loggerheads with each other and were asked to leave suddenly. The RBI and government have also had sharp differences. And constant attacks on institutions like Jawaharlal Nehru University and Banaras Hindu University. These universities are tremendously important for the health of our nation. It does not help a democracy when institutions fail. Democracy is not just the parliament. There are financial institutions, public universities, the justice system and the Supreme Court itself. Remember when the four Supreme Court judges came out in an unprecedented move to make a public statement. So, all the great institutions in our country are clearly under tremendous pressure.

RAGHAV VERMA: We have also seen a surge of anti-intellectualism.

KARAN SINGH: I think it is true in a way. Whenever there's a rise in populism, based particularly on religion or caste, it tends to be more dogmatic than self-reflective. It automatically becomes unthinking, anti-intellectual. So, when you write a rational, nuanced article about any such issue, it doesn't go well with those aligning with the contemporary populism.

RAGHAV VERMA: Some have paid the price through their lives. Take, for instance, the deaths of those critical of the government, the recent case being Gauri Lankesh in Bengaluru.

KARAN SINGH: Those are, of course, very bad cases. They were actually murdered because they were anti-Hindutva rationalists. In their writings they attacked some deity or belief. If we start bumping off our writers, then we hark back to an era of fascism. The killings of rationalists Narendra Dabholkar, M.M. Kalburgi, Govind Pansare and Gauri Lankesh are very disturbing and must stop. In a different context, Shujaat Bukhari, a good Kashmiri journalist, was killed for not towing the separatist line.

RAGHAV VERMA: And we stop that by a change of government?

KARAN SINGH: That's one of the good ways. If there's one majoritarian group that's very powerful in a democracy, we need an alternative group, an alternative coalition to counter it. We have been talking several facets of democracy. There's one very remarkable thing about democracy: It has a self-correcting mechanism. I have lived through the Emergency; in fact, I was in Mrs Indira Gandhi's cabinet during the time.

RAGHAV VERMA: Yet you had the freedom to advise your prime minister to resign.

KARAN SINGH: Yes, and I was also the only minister from the party who won the election afterwards. Everyone else in north India was wiped out. The self-correcting measures had come into play. The Janata Party came in and the government was swept away, but then they made such a mess of things that Indira Gandhi came back just three years later with an astounding victory. So, I am still hopeful that the self-correcting mechanisms within our democracy will continue to work. This will include new people, new movements, new ideas to adjust to the flow of time. What I found disturbing is the statement by Amit Shah, the president of the ruling party, who said, from what I read in the papers, that if the BJP wins the next election they will remain in power for fifty years. What does that mean—ten general elections or no elections at all?

RAGHAV VERMA: Like the Chinese premier?

KARAN SINGH: Something like that. I don't know what he [Shah] exactly meant. It didn't receive much attention, but I immediately caught the psyche and thought behind the wish for eternal power over a democratic nation. If he were to say that Modi is good for the next two terms, that's justified in a democratic political system. But to say that they will rule for fifty years, what does that mean?

RAGHAV VERMA: Wouldn't that require fundamental changes in our Constitution?

KARAN SINGH: That's what one could read into it. That's why I am concerned. That's why I am talking about it and this question has remained with me. It is not a good sign and certainly not responsible speech.

RAGHAV VERMA: What's your real take on it? Would India, or any democracy for that matter, survive such political attempts to change its social fabric forever?

KARAN SINGH: I am concerned, but hopeful. I have great faith in democracy and the capacity of our institutions to survive. I have even greater faith in the collective wisdom of the people of India. The collective wisdom always rises to the occasion during crisis. It might be worrisome on many levels but not a hopeless situation. Individually people may be living on the margins, suffering the burden of poverty or policies or suppression, but collectively the Indian civilization's values of inclusiveness and constitutionalism will prevail.

RAGHAV VERMA: Is there something still uniting us even in such polarized times?

KARAN SINGH: Yes. As Iqbal said in the famous poem 'Tarana-i-Hindi':

> कुछ बात है कि हस्ती मिटती नहीं हमारी
> सदियों रहा है दुश्मन दौर-ए-ज़माँ हमारा।

> There is something about our civilization for it does not get erased,
> Even though, for centuries, the time cycle of the world has been our enemy.

We have something in us, in our people that whatever the turbulence we always come back to a steady state. I hope that it will happen again and 'we shall overcome'.

RAGHAV VERMA: Where does one start?

KARAN SINGH: We start with ourselves. To put all the blame on any government, present or past, is easy—as if the citizens are free of sins. The corrupt and the criminal are also among them as well as from the political class. As individuals, we are the ones who make our society and vote for our politicians. But we are also the ones who can hold the powerful accountable and change the course of our times.

RAGHAV VERMA: But the polity is the machine that drives both the people and the resources.

KARAN SINGH: It does. Therefore, it depends on us whether we look into history to learn, or inject the present and future with anger and hatred for each other. We need to educate the public too. Young people particularly get swayed by the mob culture—they need to realize that there are certain norms in a democracy that you cannot break. While all freedoms are essential, no freedom is absolute. An ignorant comment is made by someone and a fire erupts somewhere. There's constant harm done to public property. So much youth wasted on violence. Someone should tell them, you [the youth] are breaking your own resources, which are not easy to build in the first place. So, this violent disposition among people today over any little incident and they go berserk. It sometimes feels like a mass neurosis, everybody waiting for something to happen. We have got to go back to sanity, to our civilizational values of tolerance, of inclusiveness, of living in religious and cultural harmony with each other despite all our differences.

RAGHAV VERMA: How does one go back to a time that has never existed? A time of sanity where one can think, read, eat, wear, love and work in harmony without fearing for one's life. How do we produce that time?

KARAN SINGH: We can do that by first trying to understand an ethos of life that sustains co-existence. Our civilizational value is inclusiveness. We have flaws as well, but our strengths are of accepting diversities, not being afraid or repulsed by them. To maintain respect for oneself and the other. Respecting different traditions, of living, of praying, of any sort of culture however strange it may seem to us. This is something that at least I have always followed in my personal life.

> एकम सत्य, विप्रा: बहुधा वदन्ति
>
> The Truth is one, the wise call it by many names.
>
> —The *Rig Veda*

It's all there, we have just forgotten it. It's not like we have to invent it. It is just hiding in different books. We have to revisit these great ideas and make them come alive for us. That is where the intellectuals have to come in. The Upanishadic tradition, the Vivekananda tradition and the Radhakrishnan tradition, if followed honestly, can illuminate our path.

RAGHAV VERMA: Surely, the Upanishads did not intend to polarize religious identities.

KARAN SINGH: They are meant to bring everyone together. The Upanishads are the essence of the Vedas. They accept and recommend pluralism. They ask fundamental questions of us, of nature, of self, like any good philosophy should do, to make us more reflective and less prejudiced and judgemental of each other. The difficulty is to get the message of harmony across to the people and communities across villages and cities. Our education system, both formal and informal learnings, need to take some responsibility and contain the polarization of the minds.

RAGHAV VERMA: You seem hopeful.

KARAN SINGH: I have never been pessimistic about India. I am concerned but not hopeless about democracy. I am aware that we are facing great challenges. I have lived through the partition of British India. The challenges then were much more complex than they are today. The country was torn apart and no one knew where to start. There was chaos and bloodshed. Today, we have a structure of law, administration and justice. Some institutions are beginning to wobble, which is a pity, but they will make a comeback soon. Maybe my hope is overcoming my realism, but we cannot afford the luxury of pessimism, especially in these times. A lot of intellectuals and youths throw up their hands in despair seeing the corruption and violence all around them. The moment you throw up your hands, you are adding to the confusion. Whatever you can do for the good at an individual or a societal level, you must do, however little it may seem.

RAGHAV VERMA: Whom do you identify more with at this time—Karan Singh as a nationalist politician or Karan Singh as a cultural icon?

KARAN SINGH: The latter, I would say. But with seventy years in public life I have inevitably been involved in politics. I like to look upon myself as a global citizen. All of us have multiple identities. I am a Dogra, that's a small community in north India that founded the state of Jammu and Kashmir, based mainly in Jammu and Himachal. So, I am ethnically a Dogra.

When I tell people I am not Kashmiri, they look at me bewildered. Our family ruled Kashmir, but I am not an ethnic Kashmiri. I am a Dogra and my language is Dogri. That's one identity. The second identity is, I am from Jammu and Kashmir, which my ancestors built and my father ruled. That is my regional identity and the language Urdu. In my religious identity, I am a Hindu. When you are born as a Hindu, you are inevitably born into a caste whether you like it or not. So, as a Rajput we grew up hearing tales of bravery of Rana Pratap, Chhatrapati Shivaji, General Zorawar Singh. My national identity is Indian. My spiritual identity is of the Vedanta and the language is Sanskrit. And for my global identity the language is English because, like it or not, that is the language of the global society. I have all of these identities within me, as do all of us. If you can create a centre strong enough around which you can integrate these identities, then it does not matter how many concentric circles there are, so long as the centre remains firm. It's when the centre shifts, when you are confused about your identity, that's when you get nervous and become neurotic. I believe, we have a spiritual centre around which all our identities can revolve. All of these identities are dear to me.

RAGHAV VERMA: What do you look forward to now?

KARAN SINGH: Now, I just have to deepen my awareness. One has to carry on evolving. There's a saying, 'You don't grow old. When you stop growing, you become old.' I always try to keep my mind clear and forward-thinking. I've never looked back, in anger or in regret.

RAGHAV VERMA: No regrets?

KARAN SINGH: I've made some mistakes, like everyone else, politically and personally, and I have paid for them. But I am over that. I have no regrets.

RAGHAV VERMA: What is the lesson you would like to share?

KARAN SINGH: Never lose hope. Always have confidence in your positive self, in your constitutional and civilizational values. Totally abjure violence. Violence is the singular, most self-destructive thing in one's life, whether in speech or in action. But most importantly, when intended. Try and see if you can live your life without hostility but with humility. Do your best and keep the faith. May the force be with you.

The infant prince: Karan Singh, Srinagar

Karan Singh presiding over Jammu and Kashmir University's first convocation as chancellor, with PM Jawaharlal Nehru, in 1949

Karan Singh on his wedding day, 5 March 1950

Maharaja Hari Singh (third from the left) leading his son's wedding procession

Regent and chancellor, Srinagar

Karan Singh flanked by Edwina Mountbatten and Indira Gandhi along with Yasho Rajya Lakshmi, Sheikh Abdullah and Jawaharlal Nehru at Chushul airport in Ladakh, 1951

Karan Singh on his graduation day at Jammu and Kashmir University, 1952. He recalls presenting degrees to graduating students as chancellor of the university and stepping down from the podium to receive his from Dr S. Radhakrishnan, vice president of India, along with Rajkumari Amrit Kaur and C.D. Deshmukh.

Karan Singh taking oath of office of Sadar-i-Riyasat from J&K's chief justice Wazir Janki Nath in 1952

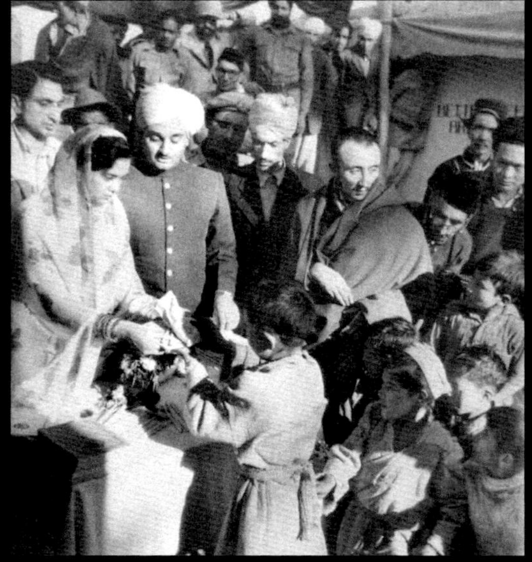

Yasho Rajya Lakshmi and Karan Singh in Leh, with Kushok Bakula, head lama of Ladakh

Jawaharlal Nehru on a tour of Srinagar with Karan Singh and Sheikh Abdullah

Prime Minister Jawaharlal Nehru with Karan Singh and Bakshi Ghulam Mohammad in Srinagar

Governors' and rajpramukhs' conference in Delhi, February 1955

Karan Singh, with his wife Yasho, London 1956 (portrait by Dorothy Wilding)

Karan Singh with a young Dalai Lama and Jawaharlal Nehru in New Delhi, 1956

Karan Singh, Yasho Rajya Lakshmi, Indira Gandhi and a young Sanjay at Karan Mahal, Srinagar

Karan Singh at a meeting with N.S. Khrushchev in the Kremlin, Moscow. He was joined by Yasho and ambassador K.P.S. Menon and his wife

Karan Singh with Major General Rajinder Singh Sparrow (left) atop an Indian tank in Sialkot, during the 1965 war

Karan Singh as chancellor of Banaras Hindu University, presenting an honorary doctorate

With Indira Gandhi and Ghulam Mohammed Sadiq, chief minister of Jammu and Kashmir

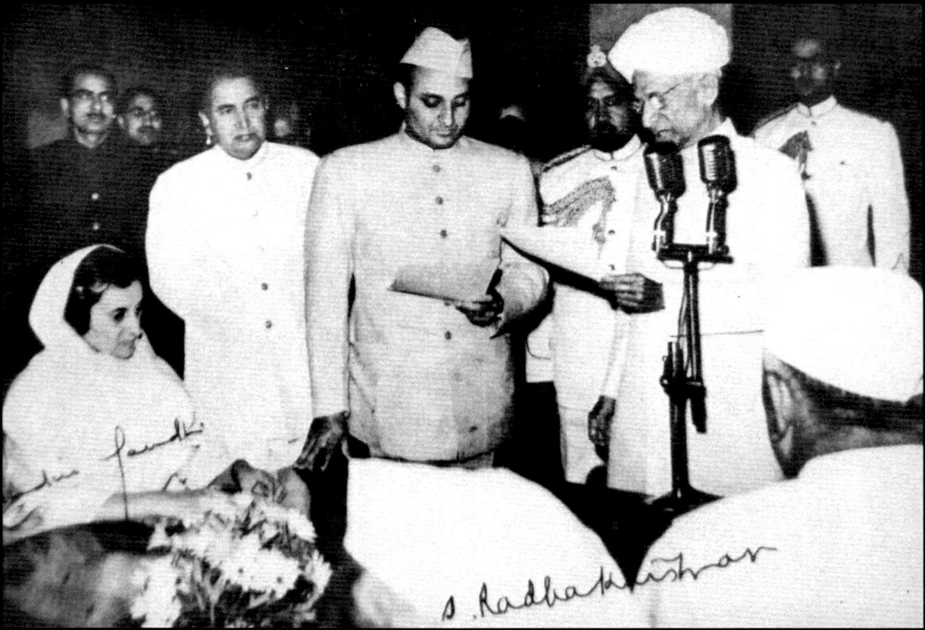

Karan Singh taking the oath of minister for tourism and civil aviation from President Dr S. Radhakrishnan at the age of 36, the youngest cabinet minister in India

All images courtesy of Amar Mahal Museum Archiv

‘I Believe’

1

I believe that man, still in an intermediate stage between the animal and the divine, can raise himself to a higher plane of being if he makes a conscious and dedicated effort to do so; and there can be no nobler endeavour than this aspiration towards divinity. I believe that each human being born on this planet, or for that matter anywhere else in the limitless cosmos, carries within himself an unquenchable spark of divinity. Our true destiny, as human beings, revolves around the fanning of this spark into the smokeless flame of spiritual realization.

2

I believe that all political, economic and social activities should have as their ultimate goal the fostering of this divinity within each individual. Scientific and technological developments are ultimately counterproductive if they do not lead us towards this end.

3

I believe that, at their highest, all religions are so many different paths leading to the same goal, the ineffable and indescribable union between the human and the divine; that mystics of all religious persuasions have realized and preached essentially the same doctrine of human love and divine communion; and that strife and hatred in the name of religion are therefore the antithesis of spirituality and a gross slur on the name of humanity.

4

I believe that India, with its unique heritage stretching back to the dawn of civilization, has a special role to play in fostering a society which would support this process of evolution. In a world torn by violence and hatred I believe that India can play a crucial role in leading humanity towards a new equilibrium between wealth and wisdom, of having and being. I believe that we must work for political integration, economic growth, social transformation and a secular democracy not merely as ends in themselves but because this combination can best provide the framework within which the people of our ancient land can fulfil their destiny.

5

I believe that as long as millions go without the basic necessities of civilized existence it is utterly unreal to talk to them about things of the spirit, and that the basic material needs of man must be satisfied as a foundation for further spiritual growth. I believe that this can be achieved only when we succeed in motivating the people of India to put in several decades of hard, disciplined effort for the production of wealth and simultaneously adopt policies to ensure that the wealth so produced is distributed fairly to all sections of society. I believe that this can be achieved not by propagating the bitter doctrine of implacable class warfare but, rather, by trying to involve the nation as a whole in the mighty effort required to break the poverty barrier that still persists around us.

6

I believe that politics will always be turbulent because that is the nature of politics, as it is the nature of the sun to be hot and water to be wet, and that we must face boldly the battle of life into which we find ourselves precipitated. I believe that, approached in the right spirit, political activity can be a powerful instrument for human transformation and can thus contribute substantially to the broader goals that lie before the human race.

7

I believe that we must, therefore, protect this planet from wanton despoliation and blatant exploitation in the name of progress, that we must conserve its atmosphere and water, its forests and wildlife, from the destruction they are facing as a result of increasing urbanization and industrialization.

8

I believe that life is necessarily a mosaic of joy and sorrow, of pleasure and pain, of failure and success, of shadow and sunlight; that we must accept these dualities as a necessary stage in our spiritual progress until we are able to transcend them; and that each experience can be a valuable means for inner growth, unpleasant situations often affording greater opportunities for development than superficially pleasant ones.

9

I believe that love and friendship constitute the surest bonds in a world where everything is constantly changing, and that these should be cherished whenever and wherever they are found. I believe that the creation of beauty through music and poetry, the fine arts and architecture is a central function of civilization and must be encouraged so that increasingly large sections of society can derive the intangible but extremely valuable benefits that flow therefrom, so that we can be led from the outer beauty of form to the inner beauty of spirit. I believe, further, that our system of education should be designed to inculcate in the young an awareness of the primacy of spirit, without in any way belittling the importance of the material foundations upon which any dynamic civilization must rest.

10

I believe that while each one of us owes a deep debt to the country of our origin, as members of the human race we also owe a wider loyalty to the planet that has nurtured our kind for millions of years.

11

I believe that death is a natural and necessary corollary to life, and must be accepted in a positive manner rather than with fear and dread. I believe that death of the body merely marks another step in the long journey of the pilgrim soul towards its final destination, and that man must shake off the superstitious dread that he has with regard to this essential and inescapable phenomenon. One of Lord Shiva's appellations is Mahakaleshwar, the lord of death, and when He is ready, so am I.

12

I believe, finally, that a divine destiny pervades the cosmos, a destiny not distant and remote but one in which, in some mysterious way, each one of us is actively involved. I believe that the most effective means of fulfilling that destiny is a combination of active outer involvement in furthering human welfare and intense inner striving to reach the goal of spiritual realization. I believe, thus, that the most eloquent prayer that has ever been evolved is one that has resounded in India down through the corridors of time since the dawn of our civilization:

From illusion lead me unto Reality,
From darkness lead me unto Light,
From death lead me unto Immortality.
—Pavamana Mantra, *Brihadaranyaka Upanishad*

From *I Believe: A Philosophy for the Global Society*, 2012

Dialogue with Daisaku Ikeda

The Wisdom of the Orient and the Future of Humanity

1. Modern Civilization

IKEDA: All of the major problems facing modern civilization—the threat of nuclear war, exhaustion of Earth's natural resources, environmental pollution, moral degeneration, and so on—contain elements jeopardizing the continued existence of humanity. Although it is true that, at present, the industrialized nations are most seriously affected by these concerns, if the developing nations pursue material prosperity as their forerunners have done, they too will sooner or later have to confront at least some of the same problems. In other words, these problems affect all humanity.

Since these problems are man-made, and therefore different from natural disasters, their solutions necessitate fundamental alterations in our way of living. This in turn demands a profound spiritual revolution that will change our interpretation of ourselves and our surroundings. This is where oriental thought, which stresses the spiritual instead of the material aspects of human experience, becomes increasingly significant.

I am a Buddhist and you are a Hindu, and our religions differ in certain philosophical aspects. Nonetheless, both came into existence in India. And I believe that certain elements of Buddhist thought have been incorporated into and passed down by Hinduism.

Buddhism teaches that the three poisons of greed, anger and folly sully human life. Greed causes the desolation of nature and thus brings about such disasters as famine. Anger is the source of altercation and war, and folly causes both physical and mental illness. While teaching that these three poisons exist, Buddhism prescribes ways to purify life of them.

I am certain that such Buddhist teachings as these contain the key to the problems confronting humankind today. As a Hindu, how do you interpret the role of eastern spiritual civilization in dealing with the difficulties we now face?

KARAN SINGH: Mankind today is facing an unprecedented ecological crisis. As a result of rapacious exploitation over the last century, the biosphere has been gravely damaged. A nuclear holocaust would be the ultimate pollutant, destroying not only the human race, but also most other species on this planet. Today it is necessary to remind ourselves that nature cannot be destroyed without mankind ultimately destroying itself.

The curious notion prevalent in the West that the human race is in some way divinely endowed with sovereignty over nature—a notion that gives licence to destroy and pollute indiscriminately—is directly antithetical to the eastern world view. Both Hinduism and Buddhism share the belief that mankind is a part of nature and that human welfare cannot be looked upon in isolation from the welfare of all beings. A purely anthropocentric view is unacceptable to us; we believe that all creation is divine, and this is repeatedly stressed in the Vedas and Upanishads as well as in many Buddhist texts, including the Lotus Sutra.

IKEDA: I would be interested to know whether there is a Hindu teaching corresponding to the Buddhist doctrine of the three poisons, which I mentioned earlier.

KARAN SINGH: Hinduism teaches what are called the five major distortions—lust, anger, avarice, delusion and pride—which are largely responsible for the disasters that mankind has inflicted upon this planet. We share the view that these poisons can be eradicated only through individual effort and prolonged inner discipline. Unfortunately, governments magnify individual distortions a million times, making their resolution extremely difficult.

IKEDA: Yes, that is true. And this is the reason why, instead of allowing themselves to remain confined to their own special fields of interest, people of religion must find ways to apply their principles in actual politics and economics.

KARAN SINGH: It is my view that the eastern spiritual heritage can go a long way towards helping to solve the major problems facing mankind, providing the principles upon which it is based are widely accepted. Jawaharlal Nehru's Five Principles of Peaceful Coexistence (Panchsheel) and repeated declarations by the Non-Aligned Movement (NAM) that insist on the importance of renouncing the use of force in settling bilateral disputes reflect the eastern attitude towards such problems.

It is necessary for us to work on two levels. Individually, we must strive to reduce the effect of the so-called poisons within our own consciousness and in our daily activities. Collectively, we must strive for a just and fair world based on friendship and mutual respect. The key concept must be the unity of the planet Earth, which, in our traditions, is looked upon not merely as a mass of soil, stone and water, but also as a spiritual entity, the Mother that has nurtured consciousness for billions of years from the slime of the primeval ocean to the present human condition.

2. The West Turning Eastward

IKEDA: Although some people disparage it as a fad limited to a small number of eccentrics, the recent popularity of yoga, the Hare Krishna religion and Zen Buddhism among young people in the West strikes me as clear indication of interest in oriental culture. As long as this interest fails to take root in ordinary living, however, it remains nothing but a hobby or a diversion lacking the power to work changes in the fundamental social and civilizational structure. And what we need today is not a mere diversion, but something capable of revolutionizing that fundamental structure.

The peoples of the West seem to have reached a point where they are questioning their own ways of thinking and living on the most basic level. What is your opinion of the current interest in things oriental among young Westerners? How would you characterize a spiritual civilization that is capable of offering leadership in matters related to actual, material living?

KARAN SINGH: The widespread revulsion in the West against the crass materialism that has dominated their civilization for many centuries has resulted in a considerable movement towards eastern religion and philosophy. This is no longer a fad; a large number of people—young and old—are now turning towards yoga, Zen Buddhism and other eastern religious traditions. During my travels in the West over the past few years I have been greatly struck by the extent of this movement.

It is important to keep in mind, however, that the question is really no longer one of East or West but one of a new global dimension. Mankind today is in a transition as fundamental as the earlier ones from nomadic to agricultural, from agricultural to industrial, and from industrial to post-industrial civilization. Science and technology have triggered revolutions in so many spheres, particularly communications and information technology, that, in our own lifetime, the world has been transformed into a global village. Unfortunately, there has been no commensurate transformation in consciousness, hence the dangerous gap between the emergence of a global society and its acceptance by the majority.

IKEDA: You are correct. Though the world is fated to be a communality, individual units within it remain isolated and plot war. It is as if people in a small room were threatening each other with explosives. The oriental concept that all beings should mutually assist each other can be useful in alleviating the tension generated by this situation.

KARAN SINGH: A significant number of people throughout the world strongly feel the pressure of the future and strive in their own ways to respond to our situation. The whole New Consciousness movement in North America and Europe bears testimony to this. Actually, consisting of dozens of individual groups, this movement owes a great deal to eastern philosophy. The strange thing is that the East itself, which might have been expected to spearhead this transition to global consciousness, seems to have got mired in essentially western value systems and goals.

IKEDA: Practical affairs must be taken into consideration if a philosophy is to help people find new paths of thought and action. Although some forms of Buddhism can be accused of ignoring suffering in the present world and of demonstrating concern solely with post-mortem paradise, the teachings of the Lotus Sutra provide a way of revolution for the self and for all of society.

KARAN SINGH: To be valid and effective, a philosophy cannot neglect the material side of life. Hinduism is quite clear on this issue. It postulates four goals of life—dharma, the framework of moral and spiritual values; *artha*, material progress and well-being; kama, sensual enjoyment; and, finally, moksha, liberation. It can thus be seen that both material and sensual aspects are given due importance, provided always that they fall within the road framework of Dharma and, ultimately, are transcended in Moksha.

3. The Lotus Sutra and Gautama Buddha's True Intentions

IKEDA: Since it was first compiled in India, I feel certain that you have had some exposure to the Lotus Sutra, the Buddhist scripture in which I put my faith, and which was revered by the founder of Nichiren Buddhism, Nichiren Daishonin (1222–82), who described himself as its practitioner. I should now like to centre our discussion on this sutra because I believe it contains truth that can help us solve the problems currently confronting humanity.

KARAN SINGH: Clearly, the Lotus Sutra is not a text that can be grasped easily, because it uses a wealth of imagery and expository techniques that must be understood before the deeper meaning of the Sutra becomes apparent.

IKEDA: Yes, as a matter of fact, the sutra itself contains a comment to the effect that it is the most difficult to believe and the most difficult to understand of all sutras that have been or will be expounded. In the early fifth century, Kumarajiva, of whom we have already spoken, translated the text from Sanskrit into Chinese. Its Sanskrit title is *Saddharma Pundarika Sutra;* and its Chinese title in Kumarajiva's version is *Miao Fa Lian Hua Jing,* the Japanese reading of which is *Myoho Renge Kyo,* or the Sutra of the

Lotus of the Wonderful Law. And, as the title suggests, the wonderful law is not easy to understand.

Though parts of it were compiled shortly after the death of Gautama Buddha, the bulk of the Lotus Sutra came into being five centuries later, at a time when, according to some scholars, an organized body devoted to its teachings may already have existed.

As you know, the Hinayana Buddhists, who stressed monastic discipline, were opposed by the Mahayanists, whose teachings can be thought to emphasize salvation for the many. While recognizing the validity of both their approaches, the Lotus Sutra insists that everything is governed by one vast, all-inclusive truth and that rivalry between Hinayana and Mahayana should cease. Although some people have viewed the Lotus Sutra as exclusivist because of the way it rejects the idea of two separate, valid teachings, the principles contained in it are found in the so-called primitive teachings; at least, it can be said that the fundamental doctrines were the ones expounded by Gautama Buddha himself. The use of the word sutra in the title indicates that it is one of the Buddha's teachings.

KARAN SINGH: The word sutra in Hindu tradition means thread, the bare essentials of an exposition, memorized and handed down from generation to generation. The brevity and cryptic nature of such Hindu sutras as Panini's Vyakarana treatise or Patanjali's *Yoga Sutras* make them easy to remember. Each teacher explained the sutra in detail; and some of their commentaries, called *bhashyas,* are important for an understanding of the texts. Thus, the greatest Hindu philosopher—Adi Shankaracharya, who is believed to have been born in 788 of the common era—wrote commentaries on various key Vedic texts, which themselves became classics. The Lotus Sutra, however, is a long and complex text that lends itself poorly to memorization.

IKEDA: The Lotus Sutra consists of passages of poetry, or *gathas*, interspersed with sections of prose usually of roughly the same content as the verse passages. It is thought that the *gathas* were transmitted by memory and that the prose sections, which contain commentaries and descriptions of human conditions as well, were added when the sutra was given written form.

Incidentally, the Chinese character used to write *jing*, for sutra, in the title means thread; more specifically, the vertical thread, or the warp, in woven fabric, and is used in the names of such venerable, pre-Buddhist Chinese texts as the *Yijing* (The Book of Changes) and the *Shijing* (The Book of Songs). After the introduction of Buddhism into China, this character was used to translate the word sutra.

The lotus, of course, has a very ancient tradition in India.

KARAN SINGH: In the Hindu tradition, the lotus has diverse spiritual significances. At the esoteric level, individual consciousness itself is often envisaged as an unfolding lotus; and the chakras, or centres, which are activated with the rise of the kundalini power, are described as lotuses with a varying number of petals. In Hindu mythology and iconography, the lotus is equally important. It is seated upon the lotus growing from Vishnu's navel that Brahma creates the universe. Again, the great goddess of grace and prosperity, Mahalakshmi, is depicted standing upon a lotus and holding a lotus in each of her hands.

To Hindus, the lotus represents the manifestation of the divine and symbolizes purity and tenderness. Such of the oldest Hindu scriptures as the Vedas and Samhitas are replete with mention of the lotus as the seat or pedestal of Hindu gods and goddesses. Sanskrit poets used the lotus as an emblem of beauty to which they compared the faces of their heroes and heroines. The lotus also entered the art and literature of other India-born religions like Buddhism and Jainism. With the spread of Buddhism outside India, the use of the lotus as an ornament in religious art extended to Sri Lanka, Burma, Nepal, Tibet, China, Indonesia and Japan.

IKEDA: Although in Chinese, Korean and Japanese art, too, the form of the lotus blossom is frequently used as a pedestal on which stand or sit various Buddhas and other figures from the Buddhist pantheon, the true significance of the flower is much more profound.

First, it is the famous symbol of the Lotus Sutra itself, in which it stands not merely for a divine nature, but also for the principle of the essential oneness of the life force of the unenlightened sentient being and the enlightened Buddha. As the lotus blossom beats within itself its own fruit in the form of seeds, so the sentient being contains within himself the possibility of attaining Buddhahood in his current form.

In addition, though it grows in muddy waters, the lotus puts forth flowers of immaculate beauty, and the plant represents the Buddha who, while living in the world of delusion, remains undefiled by it.

KARAN SINGH: The same symbolism is effectively used to illustrate the way a Hindu sage lives in this world. It is born from the mud—hence one of its Sanskrit names, *pankaj*—and lives in the water but remains detached and unaffected by its environment. Though in water, a lotus flower is always dry; Hindu texts urge that we all live in this mortal world (samsara) in such a way that, while fully involved in its activities, we remain unsullied by the dirt around us.

The Lotus Sutra is one of the most popular Buddhist texts in East Asia, particularly in Japan, and is a pre-eminent scripture of the Mahayana philosophy. In India, the *Dhammapada* is generally better known as a definitive Buddhist text, but of late the Lotus Sutra seems to be gaining popularity. After commencing this dialogue, I have had occasion to look through the sutra; even on first acquaintance, it impresses me as a truly remarkable body of teachings expressed in eloquent and vivid imagery. In its original Sanskrit, a language of unparalleled majesty, it must be even more impressive than in translation.

IKEDA: I dare say that is true. But I should like to make a point about the nature of the content of the sutra. Teaching that all sentient beings can attain Buddhahood, it embraces all humanity and is thoroughly egalitarian. It severely refutes Mahayana teachings denying the possibility of Buddhahood by means of both vehicles—Hinayana and Mahayana. In addition to rejecting the discrimination of the caste system in society at large, it eliminates discrimination between Hinayana and Mahayana within the Buddhist Order itself. Although some people have criticized it as exclusivist, it must be remembered that, while rejecting discriminatory teachings, the Lotus Sutra is completely egalitarian where human beings are concerned.

KARAN SINGH: Nonetheless, it does explain the conflict and controversy that seem to have surrounded the followers of this sutra, symbolized in a most dramatic fashion in the life of your great saint Nichiren Daishonin. His tempestuous career, full of trials and tribulations, is a remarkable saga.

IKEDA: Gautama Buddha denied the supreme universal truth as taught by the Brahmins, but also denied the teachings of the so-called six unorthodox teachers who opposed Brahmanism too. Looking hard at the actualities of human life, Gautama Buddha saw only inconstancy and void (sunyata), which led him to turn from both the orthodox and the unorthodox teachings of his day. It must be said, however, that the word sunyata does not imply nihilism but, as the primitive Buddhist texts repeatedly point out and as is made even clearer in the Lotus Sutra itself, stands for a middle way between being and non-being. I believe that the generosity and middle-way teachings of the Lotus Sutra represent Gautama Buddha's true approach. Nichiren Daishonin can be said to have manifested in his own life the truth revealed in the Lotus Sutra.

KARAN SINGH: You mention the word sunyata. This is indeed one of the most enigmatic and perplexing words in Buddhist philosophy. Etymologically it is derived from the root *sui* which means 'to swell, to expand'. Curiously enough, the word Brahman is derived from the root *brh* which also means 'to swell, to expand'. This parallel is striking, because on the question of the ultimate reality hinge the whole basis of Hindu and Buddhist philosophies. Your view that sunyata implies a middle way between being and non-being stands halfway between the concept of nihilism and the Hindu concept of Brahman, described in the *Mundaka Upanishad* as, 'That which is shining, causes everything to shine; the light that illuminates the universe.'

IKEDA: Nichiren Daishonin manifested the truth of the Lotus Sutra in the form of *Nam Myoho Renge Kyo*. In relation to the *Mundaka Upanishad*, which you have mentioned, the Daishonin taught that everything, including all Buddhas, bodhisattvas, heavenly beings, and even mortal sentient beings in such states as those of hell and ravenous beasts manifest their true and noble forms when illuminated by the light of the Wondrous Law. In other words, when they are fundamentally based in the Wondrous Law, all things in the universe, including human desires and greed, manifest their good aspects.

4. The Treasure Tower and the Dignity of Life

IKEDA: Although its initial part is set on the ground on Vulture Peak, the central section of the Lotus Sutra is a magnificent ceremony that occurs suspended in the air. A great assembly floats above ground to hear the teachings before a splendid treasure tower made of the seven precious substances, said to be as tall as the radius of the earth is long.

As you have said, the sutras skilfully employ metaphor to make profound meanings easy to understand. And this apparently impossible assembly in the air and the vast treasure tower have a very deep significance.

Nichiren Daishonin has said that the treasure tower is the Mystic Law itself. No doubt, at the time of the compilation of the Lotus Sutra, the idea of erecting stupas to house relics of Gautama Buddha as objects of faith still persisted. Consequently, the appearance of the treasure tower, which is in the form of such a stupa, is not unexpected. The meaning of the tower in this instance, however, is different. The Lotus Sutra makes mention of erecting towers to house copies of the sutra itself. In other words, emphasis is placed, not on the physical remains of the body of Gautama Buddha, but on the record of the teachings contained in the sutra.

This interpretation clarifies the meaning of the magnificent incredible tower and the ceremony suspended in the air. This part of the sutra proclaims the eternal life of the Buddha. In this instance, Gautama Buddha is not the historical Gautama Buddha but the Buddha of ultimate truth. It is therefore necessary for his teachings to be presented suspended in air, in clear distinction from those of the Gautama Buddha of history, who was subject to the limitations of time and space. The participation in the ceremony of the Tathagata Abundant Treasures and of emanation Buddhas from all quarters of the universe symbolizes the universal nature of Gautama Buddha's teachings, which are boundless in terms of both time and space.

The ceremony of the treasure tower is an expression of respect for the dignity of life, an issue of supreme importance in all ages. We must make constant, unflagging efforts to realize the dignity not only of our own lives but also of all other life forms, and to act in a way reflecting that realization.

Distinct from the historical personage of the same name, the Gautama Buddha who enters the treasure tower symbolizes the Buddha nature inherent in all sentient beings. This is why the Lotus Sutra stresses the nature of the tower, not as a container of relics but as a receptacle of sutras. It is not the individual Gautama Buddha, but the universal truth he represents, that is great. This truth pervades the universe and is the Buddha nature in all sentient beings.

And, if we translate this dazzling assembly into the terms of ordinary life, we must interpret the innumerable emanation Buddhas too as representations of the Buddha nature. The splendour of the tower can be viewed as the splendour of the universal force of life—it is so magnificent as to be compared in size with the whole earth itself.

Nichiren Daishonin drew a parallel between the seven precious substances used in the tower and the following acts of human faith: hearing the Law, believing and keeping it, abiding by the precepts, meditation, diligence, joyful giving and repentance. Human beings manifest supreme value when engaged in these practical activities in the pursuit of Enlightenment.

KARAN SINGH: The amazing description of the assembly in space in the Lotus Sutra is indeed fascinating. It reminds me of the great Vishvarupa Darshan—Vision of the World Form—which Lord Krishna reveals to Arjuna on the battlefield of Kurukshetra, and which represents the most dramatic portion of Hinduism's best-known text, the Bhagavadgita. Like the assembly, the Gita's vision is of the resplendent, multifarious universe in all its bewildering diversity unified in the form of a great spiritual revelation. Indeed, a comparative study of the Bhagavadgita and the Lotus Sutra could yield much valuable material.

Such unique phenomena as the assembly in space or the world form can be interpreted on different levels. There is the intellectual interpretation, like the one you have given regarding the assembly and the tower. This is important, especially for the rational and intellectual elements, in our consciousness. Then there is a symbolic interpretation, whereby each of the substances making up the tower can be compared with certain virtues and each of its levels can be taken as representing various aspects of the teaching. Such creative symbology can often throw unexpected light on aspects of the teaching that might not be immediately available in a purely rational interpretation. There is yet another way of viewing these phenomena: to look upon them as states of inner consciousness or, better still, as expressions of enhanced states of consciousness. Great teachers like Krishna or the Buddha have the capacity to transmute the normal waking consciousness of their disciples into realms of dazzling beauty and majesty. These interpretations are by no means mutually exclusive; human consciousness has many levels of awareness, and great texts such as the Bhagavadgita and the Lotus Sutra operate on several levels simultaneously.

In your remarks regarding the assembly in space and the vast treasure tower, you say that the message is that all sentient beings possess inherent Buddhahood in the form of the Buddha nature and can come to understand universal truth, which is Life itself. As a Hindu I would be quite prepared to accept this, interpreting Buddhahood as the light of the all-pervasive Brahman and Buddha nature as the undying Atman within each individual.

IKEDA: In all ages, awakening to the value and dignity of life, which is expressed by the assembly in space and the great treasure tower in the Lotus Sutra, is a matter of utmost concern for all humanity. Of course, ceaseless efforts must be expended in the name of respect for not only one's own individual life, but for all other life forms as well.

While claiming to honour the dignity of life, modern civilization is often so strongly governed by desire and impulse that, in our highly organized society, the individual human life tends to be reduced to a minor part in a great machine. I am firmly convinced that, under such circumstances, the respect for life set forth in the chapter on the treasure tower in the Lotus Sutra and efforts to awaken people to the need to honour life's dignity are of the greatest significance.

KARAN SINGH: I am in full agreement with you regarding the danger of the individual's being steamrolled in present social and political organizations. In our own century we have seen how collectives of different kinds—economic, social and political—have reduced millions of human beings to mere ciphers in the name of what is claimed to be the larger interest. It is here that the Hindu–Buddhist view of the dignity of the individual is significant. In the Upanishads, human beings are referred to as children of immortality, implying that each individual has the right to develop his or her inner consciousness until it bursts into the glory of spiritual realization. Hence each individual is precious and unique, and his individual dignity must be respected.

5. Significance of the Eternal Life of the Buddha

IKEDA: The eternal life of the Buddha, a highly distinctive concept of the Lotus Sutra, cannot be understood apart from the ancient Indian doctrine of transmigration, or samsara. In Buddhist doctrine, the serene state of nirvana is liberation from this cycle. In contrast to the modern idea that rebirth into this world is desirable and filled with hope, ancient Indians found life an aggregation of sufferings and sorrows into which rebirth was anything but welcome. And for this reason, they longed to break the chain of transmigration.

KARAN SINGH: The concept of rebirth over vast periods of time until the soul finally attains moksha, or liberation, is a fundamental tenet of Hinduism. Samsara is looked upon as a state to be transcended, not because it is necessarily full of suffering as we understand it but because worldly pleasures cannot last.

IKEDA: In other words, the state of samsara must be overcome to attain liberation (moksha), the condition that may be referred to as nirvana.

A Buddha is one who has escaped to nirvana. If this is so, however, the Lotus Sutra teaching to the effect that Gautama Buddha has been a Buddha since the infinite past runs counter to the teaching of nirvana, for if a Buddha has broken from the chain of transmigrations why should he be born again as a human being into this mortal world, as Gautama Buddha was?

The concept of the eternal existence of the Buddha, therefore, was a reversal of approach towards the idea of transmigration, which, instead of being something to escape from, becomes desirable truth to be welcomed. In this respect, the Lotus Sutra is by far more positive in outlook than other sutras.

KARAN SINGH: It is important to remember that, in the Hindu view, the period between births in this world is spent either in pleasant or in unpleasant states according to one's own karma. Good karma gains good after-death states and favourable rebirth conditions, but the Upanishads are insistent that even the most ecstatic heavenly enjoyments are evanescent and fleeting when viewed in the longer time span. It is for this reason that the cycle of birth and death is to be transcended. There is, however, less emphasis in Hinduism on suffering than there is in Buddhism: the Buddha postulated his entire philosophy on the assumption that life is nothing but suffering, *dukha*, while Hinduism holds that the essence of life is bliss, ananda.

IKEDA: The astronomical figures used to represent infinity in the Lotus Sutra—and especially frequent in the latter half—signify that, by this stage of the text, the Buddha is no longer the historical person Gautama Buddha, who was born in India, but is Gautama Buddha as a manifestation of eternal Buddhahood. In other words, emphasis has shifted from the finite, historical Gautama Buddha to the infinite, true Gautama Buddha. The doctrine of the eternal life span of Gautama Buddha indicates that he is himself an eternal Buddha and that the Buddha nature exists infinitely and is accessible to all sentient beings. In other words, the Buddha is not a creator-god exercising sway over humanity, but is an infinite, ubiquitous Buddha nature existing in all beings.

This is a source of great hope for people born into the world after Gautama Buddha's death and unable, therefore, ever to come into direct contact with him. But if the Buddha is truly an entity demonstrating compassion equally to all sentient beings, his life force must be eternal and immutable. By demonstrating that such is indeed the case, the Lotus Sutra enables sentient beings born after Gautama Buddha's death to make not only the revealed truth but also this compassionate entity their mainstay.

KARAN SINGH: The concept of the eternal nature of the Buddha is a very striking one and reminds us of the great declaration by Lord Krishna in the tenth and eleventh chapters of the Bhagavadgita. Considering the manner in which the Buddha is shown in the Lotus Sutra as transcending space and time and encompassing a whole range of beings, from the celestial to the subhuman, and of all ages from the distant past into the illimitable future, it is quite clear that the sutra represents the Buddha no longer as the historical person Prince Siddhartha, but as a symbol of the eternal Buddhahood. If life is to have any meaning, the divine principle must transcend time and space and be reflected within all beings.

The issue of a being who has transcended birth and death, like the Buddha, poses the question you raise: why was he born at all if he had already achieved liberation? The answer to this question is that, once he attained illumination, he became what one would call a *jivanmukta,* and his *future* births would take place only as a result of a deliberate act of his own will. The purpose of his being reborn is to save people. This brings us one of the most important contributions of Buddhist thought: the concept of the Bodhisattva, a great being who, having achieved nirvana, turns his back on ultimate bliss and, instead of merging into the great ocean of light, takes upon himself the burden of serving humanity by sweetening the bitter sea of sorrow. There is a similar concept in the Upanishads, but Buddhism highlighted this aspect, which emerges as one of the most impressive features of the Lotus Sutra.

IKEDA: The Indian prince, Siddhartha was a partial manifestation of the eternal Buddha; as is set forth in the Lotus Sutra, bodhisattvas who emerge from within the earth itself appear in this wicked world to save sentient beings after the death of Gautama Buddha.

In addition to being the fundamental source of all things in the universe, the eternal Buddha nature exists in the life of each sentient being. The Lotus Sutra stresses this universality. Tracing the existence of the Buddha to the infinitely distant past simultaneously clarifies the Buddha nature's spatial boundlessness. Furthermore, showing that the Buddha, who was formerly considered distant and isolated, actually abides within all sentient beings has a limitlessly elevating effect on humanity.

The Buddha cannot be truly universal unless he exists within sentient beings. And such a universal existence is precisely what the Lotus Sutra emphasizes. Its view of the Buddha is infinite in terms of both time and space. And making the holy and distant Buddha a living entity within sentient beings elevates us all to infinite heights.

KARAN SINGH: What you call the Buddha nature is what we in Hinduism call the personified aspect of the Brahman, the Great Being that stands behind all manifestations and that descends in human form from time to time in order to spread the spiritual dharma. Both in Hinduism and Buddhism there are predictions that in the present cycle, or yuga, there will be one final such manifestation before a major catastrophe destroys the world—the Kalki avatar, or Maitreya Buddha.

IKEDA: While recognizing the eternal nature of life, Westerners posit a final judgement, after which will follow either unending bliss in heaven or unending torment in hell. Unwilling to accept this myth-like interpretation of existence after death, however, modern human beings tend to fall into the belief that life is a one-time affair, at the conclusion of which comes only nothingness. I consider this attitude a fundamental threat to respect for the dignity of life.

KARAN SINGH: With regard to the Semitic notion of a single life followed by an infinitely long period in heaven, hell or purgatory until a final judgement 'at the end of time', I agree with you that this seems to be a most unsatisfactory position. It gives enough time for neither the fulfilment of karma, nor the flowering of spiritual realization within the individual. I often liken the idea of a single life with a child being sent to school for only one day but being expected to cover a full educational course in that day. Further, the Semitic position offers no acceptable explanation for the immense diversity of the human condition, in which millions wallow in dirt and poverty while others live off the fat of the land.

IKEDA: I agree entirely. Only in the light of a philosophy positing eternally repeated existences, in which karma is worked out on the basis of the law of cause and effect, is it possible to explain the apparently inexplicable disparity in human conditions. In addition, it is important to remember that, instead of being helplessly bound to fate, we are endowed with the great power to challenge and alter our karma. While limited by the same desires and instincts as other animals, human beings have and must cultivate the will power, reason and ethical sense to overcome those restrictions.

6. The Buddha Land and the Cosmos

IKEDA: The Lotus Sutra mentions the assembling of emanation Buddhas from all quarters of the universe to hear the teachings. This raises several very interesting points.

First, this means that Buddhas exist in the three worlds of the past, present and future, and in all directions; that is, they are ubiquitous in terms of space and infinite in terms of time. In other words, a limitless number of Buddhas inhabit a limitless number of worlds. This means that the world we human beings inhabit is in no way unique but merely one of an immense number of worlds. The view of the cosmos represented by this approach is vastly different from those of most religions, which assume that this world, the planet Earth, is the only world there is and that it has its own heaven, which is likewise unique.

KARAN SINGH: Although the teaching found in the Lotus Sutra symbolizes the universality of the Buddha's teachings, the concept of an infinite number of universes—*anantakoti brahmanda*—is deeply rooted in the Vedas and was also adopted in Buddhism. The term *brahmanda* means the universal egg. And, indeed, seen in a photograph, the Milky Way in cosmic space looks like a huge egg. Hindu cosmology is most beautifully portrayed in the great figure of Shiva Nataraja, the lord of the cosmic dance. In one hand he holds the drum, which symbolizes the creative power of the world, impelled by which millions of universes spring into existence without end. In another hand he holds the fire, which symbolizes the destruction of these worlds. With a third hand he preserves creation and comforts his worshippers, while with the fourth he points towards his upraised foot as indicating the path of salvation from this cycle of creation, preservation and destruction. The dancing figure is surrounded by a nimbus, which symbolizes the cosmic dimension.

In much of Buddhist iconography, these myriad universes are represented in various ways, and therefore I would not say that the concept of an infinity of worlds is confined to the Lotus Sutra.

IKEDA: I see; however, in the Lotus Sutra, the aim is not to expound this view of the cosmos but to set forth the eternal and universal nature of the Law and the Buddha's greatness. Explaining the space–time limitlessness of the Buddha world implies that, since truth is universal, enlightenment to it, too, has no space–time limitations. This can be interpreted as a statement to the effect that the Law is always the fundamental source of Buddhism.

KARAN SINGH: The Hindu view is that there have been in the past, not only in this solar system but also in millions of other worlds, an infinite number of divine manifestations and that there will be infinitely more in the future. Until recently this view was laughed out by western philosophers, but now that radio astronomy has shown that there are hundreds of millions of stars in our own Milky Way and hundreds of millions of galaxies in the observed universe, scientists are beginning to look upon our tradition with greater respect.

IKEDA: Advances in the natural and physical sciences are making it apparent that the views of the world, the cosmos and matter based on oriental philosophy and religion are closer to the truth than many of the ideas here-to-fore held in the West. This is true partly because, since oriental religions are much less dogmatic than Judaism and Christianity, it has been possible in the East to take a more objective view of the world. Of course, many aspects of oriental thought on these matters have been very shallow.

KARAN SINGH: On the other hand, many deserve to be re-evaluated by science. A persisting, curiously conservative body of opinion stubbornly insists that the tiny speck of dust that we call Earth is the only place where human consciousness has evolved or to which the divine has descended, but this view is so absurdly egocentric that it will be unable to hold the field much longer. It is to be hoped that, by the end of the century, this attitude will have become as outmoded as that of the flat-earth society.

IKEDA: I believe that philosophical and religious truth has as much universal applicability and communality as the fundamental truths elucidated by the sciences. The countless emanation Buddhas, who have come to the assembly from the infinites of time and space, bear witness to the truth of the teachings of the Lotus Sutra and thereby indicate that this truth is universally applicable. Consequently, I feel certain that beings as sophisticated as, or possibly, human beings inhabiting other worlds in cosmic space would at least fundamentally agree with the law of cause and effect in life and with its ethical ramifications.

KARAN SINGH: It is, of course, a moot point as to whether exactly the same law would be applicable in all these millions of worlds. Certainly, as you say, the law of cause and effect, or karma, would seem to be universal. It is just possible that, because of our intellectual limitations, we tend to project our present knowledge and concepts on the universal scale. Let us remember that what were once called 'immutable laws' governing the behaviour of matter break down when the scale becomes either extremely small or extremely large. It is quite possible that some orders of beings may exist who are free from the law of karma, just as the law of gravity, which appears immutable on this planet in fact ceases to function outside the gravitational sphere.

7. Reinterpreting Delusion

IKEDA: A major teaching of the Lotus Sutra holds that delusion and wisdom are actually one and the same thing. By delusion *(klesha)* is meant those things that cause suffering and pain to the human mind; that is, desires. In contrast to the Hinayana insistence that we must strive to divest ourselves of them, the Lotus Sutra teaches that we should convert desires into enlightenment and wisdom. The *Samantabhadra Meditation Sutra*, or the Sutra of Meditation on Bodhisattva Universal Virtue, regarded as the concluding section of the Threefold Lotus Sutra, comments on not breaking with delusion and the five desires. Most ancient Indian philosophy, including pre-Buddhist Brahmanism, regards delusion as an evil.

Gautama Buddha was enlightened to the truth that all things in the universe are interdependent and rely on each other for existence. This is why Buddhist philosophy teaches that, to the maximum of our abilities, we human beings should make every effort to repay all other things for the good we enjoy from them; this means that we should love all things. Doing so is especially important in times like our own.

KARAN SINGH: I find the approach of the Lotus Sutra in this regard to be creative and compassionate. Instead of stressing the sinful nature of man, as some of the great world religions tend to do, the Lotus Sutra is a great declaration of faith in the inherent goodness of human beings. We must, however, admit that delusions or, rather, ignorance can cause havoc. In Hinduism the concept revolves around ignorance (*avidya*) rather than sin (*papa*). The great eighth-century Hindu philosopher Shankaracharya holds that, when the divine knowledge is born within the human psyche, ignorance is automatically dispelled just as darkness disappears with the rising of the sun. The awareness of our limitations and a determination to overcome them are an essential feature of the spiritual quest, and the interpretation of the Lotus Sutra in this regard is indeed a positive one.

As far as our individual delusions are concerned, once we have realized that they *are* delusions, the problem resolves itself. But the real difficulty arises when people refuse to accept that they are deluded. There is a saying in India that it is possible to wake someone who is sleeping, but it is impossible to wake someone who is pretending that he is asleep, because, however much we may shake him, he will refuse to open his eyes. This is the attitude of those who consider themselves wise, when in fact they are mired in ignorance. Of such does the Upanishad speak when it describes 'the blind leading the blind'.

IKEDA: Unbridled desires—or delusions—may be considered reprehensible when they hinder the absolute harmony that should prevail in the world. Instead of attempting to make repayment to other life forms for their help, however, human beings allow their own ugly, selfish desires to exploit and harm them. This is an example of disrupting universal harmony. Moreover, because of the law of cause and effect, acts of this kind inevitably rebound on the perpetrator. In other words, they are a source of suffering for human beings and for all other forms of life.

If correctly used, however, human desires can be oriented towards compassion for the life forces of other living forms and towards the preservation of universal harmony.

The Lotus Sutra's assertion that delusion (desire) and wisdom are one can be interpreted in the following way. While it can become an evil force destructive of the universal harmony, human delusion can, if founded in a higher wisdom, contribute to the preservation and strengthening of that harmony. In other words, it is possible in this light to take a positive view of humanity.

The Lotus Sutra teaches that, instead of allowing ourselves to be swayed by delusion and its associated desires and instinctive impulses, we should strive to develop ourselves into independent, tough-willed human beings capable of wisely using our own delusions and desires in the correct way. This seems to me to be the most important issue facing humanity.

KARAN SINGH: Another way of viewing this problem, which could be called the evolutionary approach, has been brilliantly expounded in recent times by the great Indian philosopher and yogi Sri Aurobindo. In his powerful and dynamic philosophic structure, the key concept is the evolution of human consciousness. According to him, man today, though at the peak of the evolutionary pyramid on this planet, has by no means reached ultimate growth. He is in fact an intermediate creature, somewhere halfway between the animal and the divine consciousness, and his spiritual destiny lies in taking the next evolutionary step from the mental to the supramental level. He says, this step alone can really enable the individual to overcome delusion and get a correct insight into reality. The method of this transformation, which he calls Integral Yoga, has been worked out by him in great detail and is expounded in his numerous works, including *Life Divine, The Synthesis of Yoga* and *Essays on the Gita.*

From the Christian point of view, a somewhat similar exercise was undertaken by the great Jesuit philosopher Teilhard de Chardin, whose major work *The Phenomenon of Man* was, significantly enough, proscribed by the Roman Catholic Church and published only after his passing away. I mention these evolutionary philosophers because their approach has a direct bearing on the problem of mental delusion. While certainly one must take a compassionate view about delusions, it must be quite clear that the inner quest seeks to overcome, not perpetuate, them.

8. Reincarnation and the Dignity of Life

IKEDA: Although it is probably universally accepted that respect for the dignity of life ought to be the foundation of society, peoples in the East and the West take different views of the object of that respect. Acting on the basis of the Old Testament teaching that man was the ultimate creation of God, who was given sway over all other creatures, Westerners generally consider human life worthy of maximum respect. The oriental tradition, on the other hand—and it is especially strong in India—is that human beings ought to live in harmony with all other life forms. In both China and Japan, animals are customarily deified or feared for the superhuman powers they are believed to command.

At the heart of the oriental attitude towards other animal forms may be discerned the doctrine of reincarnation—which is incorporated in Buddhism too. According to this teaching, though human at the present time, under the influence of the good or bad karma accruing during life, an individual may be reborn in either human or non-human form. Eastern peoples subscribing to this doctrine therefore consider it wrong to treat cruelly other animals that conceivably might be reincarnations of relatives or loved ones. Similarly, they consider it natural to be compassionate and helpful to other human beings who, though strangers now, within the boundless flow of metempsychosis, could be the reborn forms of parent, sibling or spouse.

I believe that this attitude towards all forms of life is essential to modern human beings, who often tend to be excessively individualistic and self-centred.

What is your interpretation of the difference between the eastern and western attitudes towards respect for the dignity of life, and the significance of that difference?

KARAN SINGH: In September 1986, a unique interfaith meeting was held in Assisi, Italy, in which the attitude of five great world religions towards the relationship between man and nature was studied in depth. This exercise resulted in the preparation of five statements on behalf of Hinduism, Buddhism, Judaism, Christianity and Islam. Despite the sharp divergence with regard to reincarnation between the Hindu–Buddhist traditions on the one hand and the Semitic traditions on the other, it was fascinating to see the close convergence in all these declarations regarding the necessity for reverence to all living creatures, including animals and plants.

The key would seem to lie in the concept of an all-pervasive divinity, whether looked upon from the eastern standpoint as being immanent, or from the western standpoint as being part of 'God's creation'.

For those who are not particularly attached to any religious tradition, including millions of Communists, the whole question can be posed in a non-theological manner by stressing the importance of preserving the ecological balance.

Indeed, the ecology movement in the United States and the green movement in Europe, which have developed over the last few decades, show quite clearly that the western assertion that human beings enjoy absolute sovereignty over this planet is rapidly being challenged by a more caring and compassionate viewpoint. From the broader angle, it is essential that mankind move away from the obsessive anthropocentricity that has characterized western civilization over the last several centuries and adopt a wiser and more enlightened attitude towards all existence.

IKEDA: As far as reincarnation is concerned, unavailability of objective information on pre-life and post-mortem conditions hinder universal acceptance of the doctrine. But I should like to hear your opinion of ways in which we can further stimulate awareness of the dignity of all—not just human—life.

KARAN SINGH: While it is unlikely that the Semitic religions will theologically accept the concept of reincarnation, although increasing numbers of individuals are moving towards this view, it should nevertheless be possible to awaken devout Westerners to an appreciation of the dignity of non-human life forms by stressing the divine element behind creation.

Whether or not the phenomenon of reincarnation, or life after death, can be proved to the satisfaction of the doubters, the awareness of the interconnectedness of all things must grow, while the core of individuality remains intact. Thus, what is really required is a creative fusion between the best in the eastern and western traditions for the sake of a benign holism that alone can ensure the welfare of the planet Earth in this nuclear age.

9. The Wisdom of the East and the Future of Humanity

IKEDA: In the earlier phase of the modern period, developments in science and industry and great material power enabled certain European nations to subject much of the orient to the cruel sufferings of imperialism. Now, having experienced, through two global wars in the twentieth century, the horrors to which material might can lead, Europe has been reduced to a supporting player in the tragedy of conflict of power between the Soviet Union and the United States and the threat of total annihilation of the human race.

Though now independent of the European yoke of imperialistic control, all but a few of the new nations of Africa and Asia remain too economically weak and politically unstable to pursue courses of truly independent development.

It is true that the problems faced by the Soviet Union, the United States and Europe and those of the nations of Africa and Asia are different. Nonetheless, all humanity shares a common fate and must now pool its powers in the struggle to overcome the difficult problems confronting it and build a brighter future.

India and the orient in general have a spiritual culture that can contribute greatly to the future of humanity. But to enable eastern peoples to manifest their strengths in this connection, steps must be taken towards the solution of pressing issues of poverty and social unrest. The populations of China and India are far greater than those of the Soviet Union and the United States. In addition, with their thousands of years of cultural tradition, these nations could occupy positions of great leadership in the world. I am convinced that India's growth and contributions to the world could enormously influence the nations of Africa and Asia. I should like to know what future developments you foresee for your nation. Furthermore, I should like to ask you to define the kinds of efforts we, peoples of India, China, Japan and other eastern nations, should make in applying the profound wisdom of our traditions for the sake of the future of humanity.

KARAN SINGH: It is true, as I have reiterated in the course of this dialogue, that humanity today faces the gravest challenge it has ever known. The proliferation of nuclear weapons, and the continuing confrontation between the United States and the Soviet Union—not to speak of lesser conflicts in other parts of the world—pose a serious threat to the very future of the human race and indeed to all life on this planet. By its very nature the threat is such that the nations of the East, including India, China and Japan, are, willy-nilly, faced with equal danger.

This is a time when the wisdom of the East could once again give a creative turn to the human condition, and there are three major lines upon which this should proceed. Firstly, the attitudes of the Asian countries towards nuclear proliferation must be clarified. If, as seems likely, a race for nuclear weapons begins in Asia, we will hardly be in a position to lecture western nations regarding nuclear disarmament. This is an area in which public opinion must be mobilized so that the urgent problems of providing the minimum needs of our peoples are not swept aside in a renewed burst of military spending.

Secondly, regional initiatives within Asian communities must be aimed at settling bilateral issues in a peaceful manner. This will go a long way towards releasing much-needed resources for the amelioration of poverty in Asia and will greatly strengthen the Asian position vis-à-vis the western powers. Thirdly, there must be Asian initiatives—if possible supported by some western nations—to help bring about a rapprochement between the United States and the Soviet Union. The recent Six-Nation Peace Initiative is a good step in that direction.

While, essentially these three areas must be dealt with by the concerned governments, it is necessary for the peoples of all the Asian nations to rebuild among themselves those links of understanding that languished during the colonial period. As a consequence of years of foreign domination, India and Japan, for example, know much more about the United States than they do about each other. A dialogue such as the one we have undertaken can be looked upon as a small contribution to the generation of mutual knowledge and understanding.

In the final analysis, it is in the minds and hearts of human beings throughout this planet that the bulwarks of the new consciousness must be built. In concluding this dialogue, therefore, may I express the hope that the ideas we have articulated will create a ripple effect that will help in forging the new globalism to which both of us are deeply committed.

From *Humanity at the Crossroads: An Intercultural Dialogue*, 1988

On Hinduism

1

The Key Concepts

IN ADDITION TO THE VEDAS and the Upanishads, Hinduism has a vast corpus of auxiliary scriptures including the two great epics, the Ramayana and the Mahabharata. Between them they express the collective wisdom and history of the entire race, and have had a profound influence on all aspects of Hindu life and culture in India and throughout Southeast Asia for thousands of years. Then there are eighteen Puranas, rich in myth and symbol, of which the best known is the *Srimad Bhagavatam;* the Brahma Sutras which contain Vedantic philosophy in the form of aphorisms, and the tantras dealing with the esoteric aspects of the spiritual quest. There are also the codes of conduct, including the elaborate *Manu-smriti,* which seeks to relate religion to the social and individual lives of Hindus.

Embedded within the huge compass of the Mahabharata is that crest jewel of Hindu thought and one of the great religious classics of mankind, the Bhagavadgita. Before going into the teaching of the Gita, however, it will be useful to mention five sets of concepts which are an integral part of the Hindu ethos, as some understanding of these is essential if one is to grasp the main thrust of the teaching of the Gita. Briefly, the concepts are as follows.

The Four Yugas or Cycles of Time

The Hindu concept of time is cyclical, not linear. The universe is *anadi-ananta,* without beginning and without end, going through recurrent phases of manifestation and dissolution. It is quite extraordinary how the Hindu concept of time is becoming more comprehensible with recent developments in extragalactic cosmology. Each day of Brahma, the creator principle in the Hindu trinity, consists of four billion, three hundred and twenty million years, and the night of Brahma is of a similar duration. Thus, the entire universe is a process of the outbreathing and inbreathing of Brahma, corresponding to alternating periods of manifestation and dissolution. Each manifested cycle is divided into four yugas or aeons—Satya, Treta, Dvapara and Kali. In the Satya Yuga, virtue is in the ascendant, but this diminishes progressively until in the Kali Yuga it virtually disappears. At the end of each Kali Yuga, there is tremendous destruction, *pralaya*, after which the golden age appears again. The four yugas taken together form a Maha Yuga or a great cycle. We are now believed to be living in the Kali Yuga of the present cycle.

The Four Ashramas or Stages of Life

In the Hindu view human life is divided into four ashramas or stages—Brahmacharya, Grihastha, Vanaprastha and Sannyasa. As the ideal lifespan of the Hindus was a hundred years, each of these stages consists of twenty-five-year period. The first twenty-five years would be student life, when the young man is expected to spend his time and energy upon attainment of education at the feet of a qualified teacher and to observe sexual abstinence. Once this is completed, he moves on to the Grihastha ashrama, or householder stage, wherein he marries, raises a family and participates in economically productive activity for the welfare of society. By fifty, he is ready to move on to the Vanaprastha stage of semi-retirement, in which he gradually brings himself to detach himself from worldly activities and to concentrate upon the study of scriptures and meditational practices. Finally, at seventy-five, he is ready to withdraw entirely from social life and becomes a sannyasi or ascetic by renouncing the world, freeing himself from all social responsibilities and concentrating exclusively upon the spiritual quest. Sannyasa ashrama, however, can be entered into even at a younger age by a person who renounces worldly life and joins one of the many monastic orders that exist in Hinduism!

The Four *Purusharthas* or Goals of Life

According to Hindu thought, these four goals are dharma, *artha, kama* and moksha. Dharma is a word that has often been translated as 'religion', but, in fact, it is more comprehensive. It implies not only a religious and philosophical framework but a total worldview, including a scheme of right conduct under various circumstances. It comes from the root *dhri*, which means to uphold, and in the broadest sense is used for the universal laws of nature that uphold the cosmos. It also implies such concepts as justice, virtue, morality, righteousness, law and duty. It is the first of the four goals, because it is the most comprehensive and is valid throughout the life of a human being.

Artha, or wealth, is the second goal. It is interesting that Hinduism not only tolerates the importance of wealth but accepts it positively as one of the four main goals of life, provided its acquisition and utilization are in accord with the enjoyment. Here again, Hinduism gives an important place to sensual enjoyment, realising that, while renunciation may be suitable for the ascetic, it is certainly not suited to the common man. Therefore, the concept of *kama* is incorporated in the Hindu ethos, and indeed it has its own shastra in the form of the famous *Kama Sutra* by Vatsyayana. The final goal in Hindu thought is moksha, or release from suffering, old age and ultimately from death itself. As mentioned earlier, moksha is not simply a question of survival after death, which in any case is taken for granted in Hinduism: It implies transcending both life and death by the attainment of that spiritual poise whereby man is liberated from the wheel of samsara.

The Four Varnas or Castes

According to the traditional Hindu view, human beings are divided into four categories on the basis of their intrinsic qualities. The highest caste consists of Brahmin, the thinkers, philosophers, priests, whose role it is to provide spiritual guidance and intellectual sustenance to society. Next come the Kshatriyas, or warriors, whose dharma revolves around ruling the nation and defending it against aggression. Third are the Vaishyas, or traders, who are involved in agricultural and commercial operations, while all that falls within the sphere of service is the responsibility of the fourth category of Shudras, or labourers. It is interesting that the word varna also means colour, and, if one looks back over the history of early India, it is clear that the problem of colour as between the Aryans, the great existing Dravidian civilization and the numerous aboriginal tribes was a major factor in the development of this caste concept. There were certain categories beyond the pale of the caste system which were known as the outcastes, and whose ill-treatment over the centuries is a standing disgrace to the otherwise remarkable achievements of Hindu civilization.

The Four Yogas or Paths to the Divine

The word yoga is derived from the root *yuj*, meaning to join or yoke, and it involves the joining of the Atman with the Brahman, of the individual soul with the universal divine being. In the Hindu view, there are several methods of this union, and each spiritual aspirant chooses the one that is best suited to his inner and outer conditions. While the path is essentially one, it varies to the extent that emphasis is placed upon different human faculties. Over the ages, four main yogas or paths have developed—jnana, bhakti, karma and raja. Jnana is the path of intellectual discrimination, suitable for those whose intellects are highly developed and who are taught constantly to discriminate between the real and the unreal, the ephemeral and the eternal, until they reach spiritual realization. Bhakti, or the path of devotion to a personal form of God, is based on the emotional urge, and involves harnessing of the sovereign power of love to spiritual quest. In this path, there is a deep emotional relationship between the human and the divine, beautifully expressed by Arjuna in the Gita as the combined relationship of a father to a son, a friend to a dear friend and a lover to his beloved. Karma, or the way of action; is best suited for people who are particularly drawn by social service, alleviation of human suffering and organizational activity, and whose constant compulsion for work is directed towards the divine. Finally, raja yoga involves various spiritual practices, including physical and psychic exercises set out in Patanjali's classic, the *Yoga Sutras*. These paths are by no means mutually exclusive, and can, indeed, enjoy a benign symbiosis.

Another important aspect of Hindu thought is the concept of the avatar, or descent of God in human form. In keeping with its concept of cyclic time, Hinduism holds that there have been numerous such descents in the past and will be more in the future. As Krishna himself says in the Gita (4.7–8):

> Whensoever righteousness declines, O Bharata, and unrighteousness arises, then do I manifest myself upon earth. For the deliverance of the good, for the destruction of evildoers and for the re-establishment of righteousness, I am born from age to age.

With these concepts in mind, we can now turn to the Bhagavadgita. The teaching of the Upanishads is in a peaceful setting, usually in the forest ashramas or retreats of the teacher. The setting of the Bhagavadgita, however, is entirely different. Here the teacher and the disciple—Krishna and Arjuna—are placed in the very centre of the battlefield. The conches have been sounded, the flight of missiles has begun and, poised between the two armies, Arjuna suddenly suffers a failure of nerves when he sees arrayed against him, his kinsmen and teachers. He is overcome by a great wave of revulsion and at that critical juncture implores his friend and teacher to show him the correct path.

The setting of the Gita is thus similar to the present human predicament. Today, man finds himself in the midst of serious conflicts, both outer and inner; and it is on the battlefield of life that he needs correct guidance. This explains the special appeal of the Gita to modern man.

Another unique feature of the Gita is that it fuses the four paths into a single integral movement towards the divine. It deals with all the four yogas, but constantly seeks to integrate them around the overriding relationship between Arjuna and Krishna, the human and the divine. While the Brahman of the Upanishads is impersonal and is, therefore, referred to as 'That' in the Gita, Lord Krishna himself appears as the divine being that transcends both the manifest and the unmanifest in his all-encompassing consciousness. The divine in the Gita is not a non-personalized concept, but involves the personality, raised as it were to the nth degree. Thus, at the end of the teaching, Krishna instructs Arjuna in these words (18.61–2):

> The Lord, O Arjuna, is seated in the heart of all beings, causing by His divine power the entire cosmos to revolve as if mounted on a machine.
> Take refuge in Him with your entire being, O Bharata; by His Grace you will gain supreme peace and the eternal abode.

Having thus spoken of the divine in the third person, Krishna completes the teaching with the following memorable verse (18.65–6):

> Fix your mind on Me, be devoted to Me,
> Sacrifice to Me, bow to Me and to Me shall you come.
> This is My pledge to you, for you are dear to Me.
> Abandon all dharmas and take refuge in Me alone.
> Fear not, I will deliver you from all sin.

The Bhagavadgita is a remarkable fount of inspiration and power. Among its many memorable passages is the famous scene in the eleventh chapter where Krishna reveals to Arjuna his divine form which encompasses the entire cosmos and yet includes the great calm that lies behind all manifestation. It is this vision that is described as having the splendour of a thousand suns risen simultaneously in the sky. The Gita also contains the celebrated and oft-quoted statement with regard to action and its fruit. While man should work constantly for the welfare of the world, he should not be attached to the fruits of his action and should repose them in the divine. The Gita thus teaches unceasing involvement in action while retaining an inner core of detachment, and dedicating the totality of human life to the divine will. Involvement without obsession is the key concept.

While there are many avatars in the Hindu scriptures, including manifestations of Shiva in the south Indian tradition, the best-known list is a set of ten incarnations of Vishnu known as the Dashavatara. They have had a profound influence on popular Hinduism, and include two of the most popular and widely worshipped figures in the Hindu pantheon, Rama and Krishna. Interestingly, these ten incarnations represent the evolutionary iadder in a most remarkable manner. They start with Matsya, the fish; then Kurma, the amphibious tortoise; Varaha, the boar; Narasimha, the man-lion; Vamana, the dwarf; Parashurama, the wielder of the great axe; Rama, the noble hero of the Ramayana; Krishna, the divine flautist; and incarnation of this cycle yet to manifest, the Kalki avatar, depicted as a magnificent youth riding a great white horse with a meteor-like sword raining death and destruction on all sides, perhaps symbolising some cataclysmic nuclear conflict.

The inclusion of the Buddha as the ninth incarnation needs special comment, because it reveals the great capacity in Hinduism to absorb even heretical movements. Evidently the fame and influence of the Buddha were so great that he could not be ignored, and yet his teachings were in some respects antithetical to classical Hinduism. He was, therefore, absorbed into the Hindu pantheon, so that he is revered today by Hindus with no difficulty at all. Indeed, although technically the number of Buddhists in India is very small, this is partly due to the fact that many of his teachings, such as his stern condemnation of animal sacrifice, have become part of the Hindu mainstream itself. To some extent, the same can be said about Christ, and most Hindus have no difficulty in accepting him as one of the incarnations of God. What Hinduism is not able to accept is the exclusive claim of any one teacher to the monopoly of divinity and wisdom for all time to come.

From *The Sterling Book of Hinduism*, 2012

2

The Message of the Upanishads

IN THIS AGE OF TURMOIL and transition, it sometimes appears as if the human psyche itself is adrift on a vast and turbulent ocean, without any sense of direction, without any landmarks or lighthouses to show the way, buffeted by winds seen and unseen. There is turmoil in the outer world, there is violence and hatred, killing and suffering all around us, and there is also turmoil in the inner world; the deep psychological currents that rule human consciousness also seem to be disturbed. The old is dying and the new is struggling to be born, and our generation finds itself precariously poised between the past and future.

At a time like this we look towards our great spiritual traditions not to go back in time, for that is not possible; it is a common mistake for many civilizations to look back in yearning and to long for a so-called golden age that may have existed at one time, but which is no longer within the realm of possibility. Within this present space–time continuum time flows only in one direction and, therefore, there is no advantage in trying to recapture the outer structures of a bygone age. But there is great importance in trying to understand the inner spirit of a tradition.

What was it that kept India alive down through the long centuries? What was it that enabled Hinduism to survive even when it was subjected to the cruellest persecutions and invasions age after age, century after century? Why is it that whereas other great world civilizations, some of them even older than the Indian—the Egyptian, for example, Mesopotamia and

Babylon, or the great contemporary civilizations of Greece and Rome—have disappeared and live today only in the minds of research scholars or in the four walls of museums. Indian civilization remains vibrant down to the present moment? That is what we have got to try and discover, because perhaps in the recapturing of the inner spirit of the Indian civilization we will be able to derive the inspiration, the strength and the light that we require to face the problems that lie ahead; to cross this dark and stormy ocean which is before us.

When we look at the great landscape of Indian culture, we find that like the mighty Himalayas themselves from whence our culture originated stand the mighty structure of the Vedas. In flight from Delhi to Calcutta one travels parallel to the Himalayas, it is amazing to recall those great words of Kalidasa with which he opens his *Kumarasambhava: 'Astyuttarasyam disidevatatma himalayonama nagadhi-rajah, paurvaparau toyanidhi vagahya, sthitah prithivyawa manadandah'* (The Himalaya is a great *devatatma,* a great spiritual presence, stretching from the west to the eastern sea like a measuring rod to gauge the world's greatness). Kalidasa could not possibly have flown and yet such is the creativity of genius that he was able to see as a single unity this overwhelmingly powerful image of the Himalayan range.

Similarly, the Vedas stand in all their might and majesty as the very source and bedrock of Hindu civilization. The Vedas are the inspired utterances of a whole galaxy of realized souls, of spiritual geniuses, of people not merely well versed intellectually but with spiritual enlightenment. They are unique, both because of the timespan over which they were composed—the whole Vedic tradition which has come down to us must have been composed over a period of at least 1,000 to 1,500 years—and because of the scope and diversity of the people who received these great spiritual messages. And if you look upon the Vedas as the Himalayas of our cultural traditions, the Upanishads can well be described as those great peaks which are so prominent when you view the Himalayas from the air. The peaks are only a part of the entire mountain range, and yet it is they with the eternal snow upon them that draw our minds and our admiration.

The Upanishads are known as the Vedanta, both because chronologically they come at the end of the Vedas and also because philosophically they represent the noblest upshot, the highest watermark of the Vedic civilization and genius. One meaning of the word Upanishad is to sit nearby. In the Indian tradition, the guru would be seated under a tree, near a river or a lake, and one or more disciples would cluster around him to learn the wisdom. This is interesting, because it is in juxtaposition to the Greek tradition where Socrates and his disciples, including Plato, would walk up and down the corridors of their academy. Indeed, the Socratic dialogues and the Upanishads have a great deal in common; they are all dialogues between the guru and *shishya*. But the Greeks used to walk: perhaps because of climatic factors they found that the processes of thinking were stimulated by walking; hence they came to be known as the 'peripatetic' or walking philosophers.

In Sanskrit, a single word or phrase can have many shades of meaning, and they are not mutually exclusive. We do not accept the rigid diarchy whereby one word can have only one meaning. Another meaning of Upanishad is the 'secret doctrine'. In the *Mundaka Upanishad* the great householder Shaunaka goes to the sage Angiras and asks him the famous question: '*Kasmin nubhagavo vijnate sarvam idath vijnatan bhavati iti*' (Venerable sir, what is that by knowing which everything becomes known)?

And in the tenth chapter, Krishna is very clear: 'In whichever way people approach me, as long as they do it with faith, I make that resolve firm.' What an amazing assertion this is! Hinduism does not generally wish to make converts because it is aware that the divine Atman is residing in all beings. Who is it ultimately that it will convert? The universal applicability of the Gita and its wide, all-embracing doctrine is extremely important. It is not a narrow creed. Again, Krishna says that, whatever faith one may have, ultimately that worship will come to him. That is why the Gita has such a great appeal not only to Hindus but to genuine spiritual seekers whatever religion they may belong to.

Let us turn now to the content of the Gita. It is multifaceted and many-dimensional; a single sloka can be taken up and developed for days as has been done by many commentators. But, briefly, I will place before you four major aspects of the teachings of the Gita which I consider to be particularly significant. The first is the theory of correct action. I have said that the Gita is a *sangharsha* shastra and the problem in war is: what is to be done? Indeed, at any given point of time in our lives, whether we are students or in business or in politics or in any other field of life, the question always is: what is to be done, what is our *kartavyam* karma?

This is the most difficult of all questions. The Gita itself realizes this, and at one point Krishna says: '*Gahana karmano gatih*' (Thick and tangled is the way of action). The theory of correct action in the Gita revolves around a single concept; that action should not be purely for selfish purposes, although the self is obviously involved; it should not be simply as a necessary evil, because we have to act. Action must be a positive, joyous, affirmative action; it must be an offering to the divine. This is the important point. It does not really matter what it is we are doing; what is important is the psychological and spiritual input into that action. In the eighteenth chapter there is a very important sloka which says that by worshipping through one's action the divinity that pervades the entire cosmos man moves towards perfection.

So there you have the answer. It has to be an action which is skilful, which is efficient, but which tries to avoid obsession, because obsessive action can easily become self-negating. If the action is detached, there is an inner freedom and inner dedication and you do not become obsessed. I have met so many people in my life, particularly in politics, people with great gifts; but they become so obsessed with their action and the result of the actions that, ultimately, they destroy themselves as human beings. We must have involvement without attachment and commitment without obsession. It is a very difficult path. Involvement we need, but without attachment. If you do not get involved, then you are evading your responsibility; but if you get attached, you are distorting your consciousness. Similarly, commitment without obsession, that is the special type of action that the Gita gives us.

There is a story about the building of the great Brihadishvara Temple a thousand years ago by Rajaraja Chola in Tanjavur, probably the most beautiful temple in India. The king one day decided to go and inspect the work; so, he drove to the temple site, got out of his chariot and walked towards where this temple was being built. He came across a man who was cutting stones, and he asked him: 'What are you doing?'

The man said: 'Sir, I am cutting stones.'

He went a little further, and there was another man who was doing the same thing. He said: 'What are you doing?'

The man answered: 'Sir, I am earning a living.'

He went further and came to a third person who was doing exactly the same thing. He asked: 'What are you doing?'

He said: 'Sir, I am building a great temple.'

Now you will see the difference in attitude. They were doing exactly the same thing, they were getting exactly the same wages. But the first man was mechanically performing a task—he had no greater consciousness. The second one had a slightly broader vision—he had the problem of his family and was earning for them. The third one was earning for his family certainly, but he had the broad vision that he was building a great temple to Lord Shiva. That illustrates what I mean by the theory of correct action. Whatever you may be doing, it does not really matter as long as you are doing it with inner dedication and devotion, and as long as you are using action itself as a powerful means of spiritual development. This is the first major teaching of the Gita, the theory of correct action.

Secondly, there is the theory of an integrated yoga that the Gita places before us. I spoke yesterday of the four yogas, the four paths to divine union—jnana yoga, the way of wisdom, of intellectual discrimination; bhakti yoga, the way of emotional outpouring towards a personalized image of the divine; karma yoga, the way of dedicated action; and raja yoga, the way of psychic discipline, of pranayama, the discipline of breathing control, and the development of the kundalini shakti (serpent power) within us. These are the four main types of yogas that we have in our tradition, and for each there are scriptures which deal with various aspects. Thus, for the jnana yoga we have the Upanishads; for the karma yoga we have the *Karma-kanda;* for the bhakti yoga we have the *Srimad Bhagavatam*, the *Shiva Purana* and other Puranas; and for the raja yoga we have Patanjali's *Yoga Sutras* and other texts. But the Gita is unique in that, in the short compass of 700 slokas, it integrates these four yogas into a single, unified path.

The Gita points out that it is no longer enough for us to follow only one of these paths. In the old days, if you were a jnani you could go off into the mountains in Kashmir and sit there for the rest of your life meditating, but that is not good enough for the Kali Yuga. In the old days, if you were a bhakta, you could spend the whole of your life going around doing kirtan. If you were a raja yogi, you could sit in your own ashrama and develop your reply to that question the teacher expounds the theory of the two types of knowledge, the higher and the lower, the *paravidya* and the *aparavidya*.

The Upanishads deal with the higher knowledge, which is super-rational knowledge. It does not negate rationality, it transcends it, because, while the mind is a brilliant and multifaceted instrument, it is nonetheless limited by its very structure. There are ranges of knowledge and experience which do not come within the ambit of so-called rational thinking. At some point in our adventure of consciousness the mind has to be transcended, and the Upanishads deal with the higher knowledge, the super-rational realization which comes not by intellectual gymnastics but by spiritual realization. The ultimate goal of knowledge, spiritual realization, is the basis of all Upanishadic teaching.

Again, in the *Mundaka*, there are two memorable verses which describe what the Upanishads are really supposed to do. They are likened to a great bow upon which the arrow must be fastened, sharpened by meditation and sadhana. The arrow is the Atman; the target is the Brahman and the bow is aum, the sacred word. The bow has to be drawn with great attention and single-mindedness, then only do we become one with the Brahman in the same way as an arrow becomes one with its target. That is the central point of the teaching: It is a vehicle whereby the Atman becomes one with the Brahman, or, in theological terms, where the soul becomes one with God. The words 'God' and 'soul' are not really part of the Vedantic tradition and have certain connotations in the Semitic religions, which are not entirely parallel to Hinduism. The key Vedantic concepts are the Atman and the Brahman, and the merging of these two. The Upanishads as the great bow become the vehicle for this merger.

Traditionally, there are said to be 108 Upanishads, which is a sacred number. But the major Upanishads number about fourteen. Adi Shankaracharya wrote his luminous commentaries upon eleven of these Upanishads—the *Isa*, the *Kena*, the *Katha*, the *Prashna*, the *Mundaka*, the *Mandukya*, the *Aitareya*, the *Taittiriya*, the *Chandogya*, the *Brihadaranyaka*, and the *Svetashvatara*. The texts vary considerably in length. The *Isa Upanishad*, for example, has only eighteen mantras, whereas the *Brihadaranyaka*, the Upanishad of the great forest, runs into many hundreds of verses. Despite their diversity and the fact that they were composed over a vast period of time, there is an inner unity among the Upanishads which is quite extraordinary. All of the great seers seem to be talking about the same basic experience, that is, the experience of the divine, of the Brahman. So, the Upanishads can be said to be essentially the jnana-marga, the way of knowledge, and for that there are only two qualifications laid down for the teacher; he must be *srotriya* and *brahmanishtha*, well versed in the scriptures but also founded upon spiritual realization. It is important to remember that the Upanishadic teaching is not a mere academic exercise; it is a teaching for spiritual quest.

The cardinal concepts of the Upanishads can perhaps be expressed in a brief compass as being five. The first and most basic concept is the concept of the all-pervasive Brahman—'*isha vasyam idam sarvam yat kincha jagatyam jagat*' (whatever exists and wherever it exists is permeated by the same divine power and force). This is an important realization, because many philosophies have postulated dichotomies between God and the world, between matter and spirit, between good and evil, between the divine and the devil, and so on. But the Upanishadic view is that in the ultimate analysis all that exists is a manifestation of the divine. Indeed, there can be no manifestation without divinity behind it, and this, in a way, is the realization of the new science. Previously, in the classical science of Newton, there was the dichotomy between matter and spirit, matter and energy; but in the post-Einsteinian situation you find now a realization that whatever exists is really the same energy. It may appear as matter, it may appear as energy, it may appear as a particle or as a wave; it is essentially the same energy. So the unified-force theory towards which the scientists are desperately probing has its spiritual counterpart in the concept of the all-pervasive Brahman of the Upanishads. The greatest realization is to see the Brahman everywhere, wherever you look—above or below, to the right or to the left, within or without. This is the first important concept of Vedantic knowledge, the all-pervasive Brahman.

The second is that this Brahman resides within each individual consciousness, in the Atman. The Atman, as it were, is the reflection of this all-pervasive Brahman in individual consciousness. One of the examples given in the Upanishads is that, when a great fire is lighted, millions of sparks fly up out of the fire and then fall back into it, so from the Brahman arise all these millions of galaxies and into Brahman again they all ultimately disappear. The concept of '*ishvarah sarvabhutanam hriddeshe 'rjuna tishthati*', of god residing within the heart of each individual, is the second great insight of the Upanishads, and the relationship between the Atman and the Brahman is the keynote upon which the whole of Vedantic teaching revolves. All the four yogas are directed towards bringing about the union between the Atman and the Brahman. The word yoga comes from the same root as the English word 'yoke', to join. Yoga is that which joins the Atman and the Brahman. There are in our tradition four major paths of yoga—jnana yoga, the way of wisdom; bhakti yoga, the way of emotional rapport; karma yoga, the way of dedicated action; and raja yoga, the way of psychic discipline. All of them are directed towards bringing about the union between the all-pervasive Brahman without and the immortal Atman within.

Flowing from this, we come now to another important Vedantic concept, that all human beings because of their shared spirituality are members of a single, extended family. The Upanishads have an extraordinary phrase for human beings, *amritasya putrah* (children of immortality). We do not look upon human beings as essentially sinners, weak and cringing, begging and supplicating some unseen being hidden in seventh heaven. Rather, we are children of immortality because we carry the light and the power of the Brahman within our consciousness. This is within the consciousness of every human being regardless of race or colour, creed or sex, or any other differentiation. That is the basis of the concept of human beings as an extended family: *vasudhaiva kutumbakam*. A famous sloka, not from the Upanishads but from a later text, points out that the decision between 'mine' and 'yours' is a small and narrow way of looking at reality, indulged in by people with small minds. But for those of the greater consciousness, the entire world is a family. This is another great insight of the Upanishad, peculiarly relevant at this juncture in human history as I will point out later.

We come now to a fourth major philosophical concept of the Upanishads, the essential unity of all religions, of all spiritual paths—'*ekam sad viprah bahudha vadanti*' (truth is one, the wise call it by many names)—as the *Rig Veda* has it. The *Mundaka* has a beautiful mantra which says that as streams and rivulets arise in different parts of the world but ultimately flow into the same ocean, so do all creeds and castes and religious formulations arise in different times and areas, but, if they have a true aspiration, ultimately reach the same goal.

Here is a philosophy which cuts across barriers of hatred and fanaticism that have been built in the name of religion. The Vedanta is a universal religion; it accepts the infinite possibilities of movements towards the divine, it does not seek to limit or confine us to any particular formulation.

After all each one of us is different. Whether you believe in reincarnation or in genetic configuration, the fact remains that there are no two human beings who are exactly alike, and so all have to seek their own path to the divine. The Vedanta welcomes and accepts the multiplicity of paths to the divine, provided those paths are true paths towards divine realization, not merely intellectual gymnastics and disputations. It is a little like climbing a mountain. There are several different starting points, and if we keep arguing at those starting points we are miles apart. But when we start climbing and are actually moving upwards, as we come nearer and nearer to the summit, our paths will begin to converge and ultimately when we get to the top we will all meet there. Similarly, once you really start moving upwards in the field of spiritual endeavour, you will find these denominational differences gradually losing their importance, and as you rise to the summit you will realize the spiritual oneness of divinity.

A fifth Vedantic concept is that of the welfare of all beings: '*Bahujana sukhaya bahujana hitaya cha*'. The Vedanta does not seek to throw one class against another class, one caste against another caste, or one group against another group. The Vedanta seeks the welfare of all creation, not only of human beings but also of what we call the lower creatures. In our arrogance we have destroyed the environment of this planet, we have polluted the oceans, we have made the air unbreathable, we have desecrated nature and decimated wildlife. So many species have become extinct because of our ahankara as human beings. But the Vedantic seers knew that man was not something apart from nature, that human consciousness grew out of the entirety of the world situation, and, therefore, they had compassion for ail living beings. That is why the Vedanta constantly exhorts that, while we are working for our own salvation, we must also shun the path of violence, shun the path of hatred, try and develop both elements of inner and outer work: '*Atmano mokshartham jagat hitaya cha*'. Indeed, these are two sides of the same coin; we must work for our own salvation, but also for the welfare of the world. We also have a social responsibility, and as long as we are embodied we have to continue to work for the welfare of all beings.

These five concepts from the Vedanta—the all-pervasive Brahman; the Atman which resides in all beings; the concept of the human race as members of a family regardless in all differences; the idea that all religions are essentially different paths to the same goal; and the concept that we must work for the welfare of society as a whole and for the welfare of this entire ecosystem and not only for ourselves—if taken together provide us a comprehensive world view which will greatly help us in these troubled times. We are living in a very difficult age, but it is an exciting age to be alive, particularly for the younger generations. People today are often upset and worried as to why everything is so turbulent, but that is inevitable, because we are in a period of major transition. It is my belief, strengthened over the last few years by travelling extensively throughout the world, that mankind today is at a transition as important as the one many thousands of years ago from nomadic to pastoral civilization, then from pastoral to agricultural, agricultural to industrial and post-industrial civilization. Each transition is now coming quicker because of the accelerated pace of growth and development, and what is happening is that a global consciousness is beginning to emerge despite all our discords and problems.

We are too close to the event to really grasp what is happening, but what I can see is a paradigm shift, a total shift of emphasis. Whether in dress or in music, in language or in food habits or any other sphere, gradually a world civilization is being born. And it has to be born if mankind is to survive in this nuclear age. Science and technology have given us tremendous power, but that power can be used for benign or malignant purpose. We can abolish poverty and hunger, malnutrition and misery, illiteracy and unemployment from the face of this earth by the end of this century. It can be done quite easily—seven days' expenditure on world armaments can abolish hunger in Africa, ten days' expenditure on world armaments can abolish the debt of Latin America. But, instead, thousands of billions of dollars and roubles and pounds and rupees and other currencies are going into the manufacture of weapons of mass destruction every year. We must never forget that power by itself is neither good nor evil; there is the deva shakti and there is the asura shakti—the benign power and the malignant power. The worship of power, of science, is not enough. Hitler's gas chambers were an example of science and technology; the Hiroshima and Nagasaki atom bombs were an example of science and technology. We now have a single nuclear warhead packing the power of 1,000 Hiroshima bombs, and there are 50,000 such nuclear warheads on earth today. Are we not standing on the threshold of a major disaster? Are we not on the verge of the *mahapralaya* (great deluge) or *mahagni* (great fire) or whatever mode of destruction will finally develop? At such a time we can survive only if we have an alternative ideology to the present one, which has led mankind to this position. I claim that the Vedanta in fact provides such an alternative ideology. Even at this stage, even at this late hour, if we can imbibe some of the universal truths of the Vedanta we can perhaps reverse the processes of destruction.

It is a tragedy that in India, our educational system is totally devoid of any exposure to the great truths of the Vedanta. Ask young students today to name two Upanishads, and they will not be able to because they have never been exposed to them. Here we have a great heritage towards which the entire mankind is now beginning to turn, and we in India are deliberately and cold-bloodedly neglecting this heritage. Whenever one talks of the Upanishads, people think that they are something strange and bizarre, not realizing that, in fact, they provide the very foundation of the entire Indian civilization. If the whole of Western philosophy has been described as a series of footnotes to Plato, the whole of Eastern philosophy can be described as a series of footnotes to the Upanishads.

I would, therefore, urge you to go to these great and beautiful texts; do not allow yourselves to be frightened away by them, do not think that they deal with matters which you cannot grasp; open yourself to them, try and understand them. In the *Shvetashvatara Upanishad* the seer says: '*Vedaham etam purusham mahantam aditya varnam tamasah parstat*' (I know that great being, shining like the sun beyond the darkness; it is only by such knowing that you can overcome death, there is no other way to immortality). The immortality of the Upanishads is not survival after death—that is already taken for granted—it is the transcending of birth and death. The immortality of the Upanishads means that our consciousness is raised to a state where we are not obliged to be born and reborn again and again in the cycle of samsara. It does not mean that we must run away. The power of the great rishis is still there. In the Buddhist tradition we have the bodhisattvas who had attained Buddhahood but turned back in order to help the suffering humanity. In the Upanishadic tradition we have the siddhas, people who can materialize anywhere at will in order to help the suffering humanity.

So, it is not a question of being selfish but of being able to break the bonds in which we are caught. Can you imagine what it is like when a caterpillar, an ugly, land-bound worm, goes into a chrysalis and a miraculous metamorphosis takes place so that it emerges as a beautiful, radiantly coloured butterfly? That is the sort of metamorphosis that the Upanishads envisage for human consciousness. We change from our earth-bound consciousness into this bright, multi-coloured consciousness which can alight upon the ground like a caterpillar but also fly into the air which the caterpillar could not. That, as I see it, is the true message of the Upanishads, and I will end with that great and immortal Vedic prayer that seeks to lead us from the untruth of ignorance into the truth of knowledge; from the darkness within us into the light above us, and from the cycle of birth and death into immortality:

असतो मा सद्गमय ।
तमसो मा ज्योतिर्गमय ।
मृत्योर्मा अमृतं गमय ।

Asato ma sad gamaya!
Tamaso ma jyotir gamaya!
Mrityor ma amrtam gamaya!

That is the highest achievement of the Upanishads; and that is the goal towards which we all must strive.

From *Essays on Hinduism*, 2014

3

The Message of the Bhagavadgita

HUMAN CONSCIOUSNESS AS WE see it today is the result of billions of years of evolution on this plane: three billion years of pre-biological evolution; a billion years of biological evolution; perhaps five hundred thousand years of human evolution; ten or fifteen thousand years of human civilization. The juncture at which we have now arrived brings to our mind the great myth of the Samudra Manthana (the Churning of the Milky Ocean). In this great myth—and I use the term in the deeper sense of the word, meaning a powerful story which is super-rational—the devas and the asuras cooperated without any reservation. They churned for aeons, and ultimately the ocean began to throw up great gifts: Uchchaihshrava, the divine horse; Kamadhenu, the divine cow; Kalpavriksha, the wish-fulfilling tree; Airavata, the six-tusked elephant and so on. These great *ratnas* emerged from the churning, and the devas and asuras distributed them amongst each other, happy and secure in the assumption that the churning was going to continue with benign results.

Suddenly, the ocean began to boil with a totally unexpected factor; the *garala* (the terrible poison) that was hidden in the heart of this consciousness began to emerge. And when the poison emerged, the devas and the asuras fled in terror, because they had not expected this. They had assumed that they could continue to exploit and to churn ad infinitum without being forced to face the terrible reality. The poison rapidly spread through the three worlds—the earth, the water and the skies—and it was only when the great primal-divinity, Shiva Mahadeva, appeared and drank the *garala,* integrating that poison into his own being, that the danger passed; the devas and the asuras returned. The churning continued and ultimately the amrita *kalasa,* the vessel of nectar, appeared.

This myth seems, to me, to illuminate the human predicament today. Science and technology have given us tremendous gifts and unprecedented power to ameliorate the human condition. And yet, at the same time, it has thrown up this terrible poison of destruction, the destructive power that is built into the very texture of matter in the splitting of the atom. And so, here we are today; after all the great gifts, the poison has begun to emerge. And there is another story, this one from the Western civilization, the story of Atlantis which we came across first in the writings of the great Greek philosopher, Plato. This great and glorious civilization flourished where the Atlantic Ocean now holds its sway. It was unprecedented in its glory and its splendour, in its wealth and its technology. But we are told that one day it sank below the waves, unable to survive its own technological ingenuity.

It seems, to me, as I travel from land to land, and as I talk with people of different faiths and ideologies, that perhaps we are the neo-Atlantis, perhaps civilization today stands on the verge of a mighty *pralaya.* The reason our cultural tradition has come down unbroken for thousands of years is that it has the capacity for spiritual renewal from age to age. No philosophy or religion that does not have the capacity for renewal and renaissance can really meet the requirements of a changing society. It has to have the inner elasticity and breadth to cover the new developments, and there also have to be men and women who, in their own lives, live and illuminate these great truths.

When we look at the Indian civilization, we have the Upanishads and the Vedanta, representing the culmination of the Vedas both philosophically and chronologically. We have the Brahma Sutras, which give us an intellectual guide and key to the understanding of the Vedas. We have the Puranas; we have the epics, the Ramayana and the Mahabharata. I have spoken of the great Himalayan range of the Vedas and of the Upanishads as the mountain peaks. Now I will change the metaphor and talk of the starry sky at night. Nothing is more magnificent and beautiful than looking up at the sky on a moonless night, when you see thousands upon thousands of celestial bodies all glowing with inner power and light. But among these you will notice that there is one star that shines brighter than the others. It may not be bigger, it may not be closer, but it is the brightest star—what we know as the morning star or Venus. And as we look at this great galaxy of Hindu texts and scriptures, there is one star that shines brighter than the rest, and that is the Bhagavadgita.

The Gita occupies a unique place, even though it is a smriti, whereas the Vedas and the Upanishads are srutis , and the latter are considered superior in their authenticity and chronology. But the Gita has a very special position. Adi Shankaracharya, in one of his memorable slokas, says that anyone who has tasted even a drop of amrita or understood even a little of the Bhagavadgita need not have any fear of death. It has been commented upon by all the great philosophers, by Shankara and Madhva, by Ramanuja and Vallabhacharya, by Jnaneshvara, and, in our own century, by Bal Gangadhar Tilak and Sri Aurobindo, by Mahatma Gandhi and Vinoba Bhave. In my view, after Shankaracharya's commentary, Sri Aurobindo's *Essays on the Gita* is the most luminous and magnificent of modern commentaries. The whole galaxy of leaders of our freedom movement were influenced by the Gita.

What is the reason for this extraordinary popularity of the Gita and its relevance to modern times? As I see it, there are four main reasons why the Gita is so tremendously significant and relevant in this age, and why it is the best known of the Hindu scriptures—along with the Bible and the Quran, one of the three most influential religious texts in the history of mankind. The first reason is that the Gita is born in a situation of conflict—in the very midst of the great Kurukshetra war. Both armies are drawn up, the flight of missiles has begun, the conch shells have sounded, the clamour of war is tumultuous, and the hearts of the participants are torn by the conflict. It is then that the Gita teaching comes to us, it is there that Krishna calls upon Arjuna to arise, to get ready for battle. The Gita is a scripture of conflict, whereas the Upanishads are set in a very calm and peaceful atmosphere.

Let us remember that Kurukshetra is not only a plain in Haryana. The outer Kurukshetra is still there, of course, but the inner Kurukshetra is within each one of us. It is within our psyche that the asura and deva powers are drawn up in array against each other, and it is within the heart of our consciousness that this battle has constantly to be fought. Today, with the world poised on the brink of a mighty conflagration, it is a Kurukshetra situation and the Gita, a *sangharsha* shastra (scripture of conflict), is what mankind requires, a stirring call to arms, not for personal aggrandizement, not even for national glory, but for the deeper, more difficult task of becoming an instrument of the divine will, a warrior for the divine cause, a fighter for the divine consciousness. That is the battle to which Krishna calls us, and that is why man today, torn as he is in a situation of conflict, responds to the message of the Gita.

The second reason for the importance and relevance of the Gita lies in the divine personality of the teacher. Every scripture has its guru, its acharya. The *Mundaka Upanishad* has Angiras, the *Brihadaranyaka Upanishad* has Yajnavalkya, in addition to other seers and rishis. But in the Bhagavadgita it is the divine lord Himself disguised in a human form who is talking to us. Krishna can be looked upon in many different ways. In one view, he is the personification of the Brahman, the great power which, shining, causes everything else to shine, which illuminates everything that exists—'*tam eva bhantam anubhati sarvam, tasya bhasha sarvam idam vibhati*' (everything shines only after that shining light, his shining illumines all this world). In the eleventh chapter of the Gita, he appears in his great Viratasvarupa in which everything that exists is to be found, and by the glory of which Arjuna is dazzled, as if a thousand suns had risen together upon the horizon.

And yet, this very Krishna comes before us in the Gita as a charioteer, as a guide. We have God himself descended in the forms of the divine charioteer, and that is why when Krishna speaks he does so with absolute and overriding authority, not simply from the human standpoint but from the divine. That is why the Gita is so significant, because it personalizes the Parabrahman (the highest god-consciousness of the Upanishads). The Upanishads say: *Sarvam khalv idam brahma* (all this is Brahman); the Gita says: *Vasudevah sarvam iti* (all this is Vasudeva, the supreme). So, in the Gita the figure of Krishna personifies that divine splendour and power which is described so beautifully in the Upanishads, and that is why it has a unique impact upon our minds and hearts.

The third reason for the Gita's special importance lies in the relationship between the guru and the *shishya*. In the Hindu tradition this is a very intimate relationship. In the Upanishads the guru uses the term *saumaya* for disciple, meaning 'dearly beloved'; he looks upon the disciples as even more close to him than his own sons, because while the father only gives physical life, the guru makes real spiritual birth possible. But in the Bhagavadgita there is a closeness between Arjuna and Krishna which is not, as far as I am aware, to be found in any other scripture. One of the most moving verses of the Bhagavadgita is when Arjuna, after he sees the Viratasvarupa, says to Krishna: 'I bow to you, I prostrate myself before you, and I demand grace from you. Like a father to his son, like a friend to his dear friend, like a lover to his beloved, do thou bear with me.' Where else in the scriptures of the world would you get this composite relationship; the love between a father and a son, between a friend and a dear friend, between a lover and the beloved, all combined in the relationship between Krishna and Arjuna. That is what makes it so significant. It is a relationship of trust, faith and devotion; Krishna is urging his friend, not threatening him. At the end of his entire teachings, Krishna says to Arjuna: '*yathe 'cchasi tatha kuru*' (do as you please). He says, in effect: 'I am not forcing you, I am not threatening you, I am not cajoling you. You asked me a question and I have shown you the path. It is now your decision, you have to do what you like.'

It is this aspect of the Gita which makes the teaching so significant and attractive, especially for the younger generations, because the youth, not only in India but throughout the world, are not prepared to be bullied or badgered by the older generation, or accept their claim to superior wisdom or knowledge or morality. However, if we guide them with love, if we are friends with them, then perhaps we can influence them more effectively.

A fourth reason for the importance of the Gita is its universal applicability. The Gita as a doctrine does not confine itself to any particular creed. In the powers. If you were a karma yogi, you could wander around doing good deed. But it is not enough now for us to be one of these, we have to be all four. Every individual has to develop his mind, his heart, his physical capacity and his inner spiritual power, and that is the important message of the Gita. It brings us to what Sri Aurobindo calls Purna Yoga, an integrated yoga. I am often asked about caste, and I say that whatever importance caste may have had at one time, today every one of us has to have the gunas (qualities) of all the four castes.

Thirdly, there is in the Gita a repeated reassurance of divine intervention. You are familiar with the popular sloka where Krishna says that from age to age, whenever unrighteousness flourishes and dharma is about to disappear, he will assume human form for the destruction of the evil-doers and re-establishment of the dharma. This is an assurance given to all humanity, and, if we read the Gita with an open mind and have faith in it and Lord Krishna, we must accept this assurance at its face value. It is not simply hyperbole in which he was indulging. Somebody introducing me to someone mentioned that I have been a minister. As you know, when a minister makes an assurance in the House, everybody holds him to it. I think today the time has come when we have got to ask Krishna why he is not fulfilling the assurance he gave us. Surely, if we need the divine, the divine also in some way needs us. Krishna had the Sudarshana Chakra (thousand-spoked discus); he could have used it and finished the war himself. Why did he not do it? He also needed Arjuna, may be *nimit-tamatram* but he needed the *nimitta;* otherwise, he could not have won the war of Mahabharata, at least not in the way it was won.

Perhaps this is a new thought that I am putting into your mind. If we need the divine, does the divine not need us? Does the supramental power, does the greater consciousness that is seeking to descend or to emerge not need active cooperation from us? I think it does, and I make bold to say that, as Sri Aurobindo puts it, without an aspiration from below there will not be an answering call from above. And that is why it is so important that we shun the attitudes of dejection, despair and negativism that one finds so often in India; people constantly bemoaning and bewailing their lot and saying that the country is going to the dogs and that everything is breaking down. It is no use moaning and groaning like that; it will get us nowhere. We have to arise and be ready to fight the battle of existence. If our life ends before it is completed, so what? We had had thousands of lives before, and we will have thousands more. The Atman, as the Gita says, cannot be burnt, cannot be cut, cannot be drowned, cannot be cleaved.

I have spoken of the theory of correct action, of the integration of the four yogas, the four paths to spiritual development, of the repeated assurance of divine intervention. Finally, we come to the Gita's gospel of total surrender to the divine. Ultimately, at the end of the entire discourse, after Krishna has said '*yathe 'cchhasi tatha kuru*', once again he speaks; without a question this time, he speaks on his own. The rest of his speeches were in response to questions from Arjuna, but the last statement of Krishna is *suo motu.* And he says: '*Sarvadharman parityajya mam ekam* sharanam *vraja, aham tva sarvapapebhyo mokshaisyami ma suchah*'. What a beautiful sloka this is!

What is dharma? Dharma comes from the root *dhri,* that which supports. In the final analysis, what is it that supports human consciousness? It is not wealth, it is not position, it is not political power, howsoever important these may appear to us. Ultimately, it is the divine consciousness that supports us, that supports our very existence. Therefore, Krishna urges us to give up all other supports and come alone to him. Krishna speaking as the divine says … 'I will free you from all sins. Do not fear'—*ma suchah.* How much love there is in those two words 'fear not'. When a child is to go into a dark room with the parent behind, the parent says: 'Do not be afraid, I am here; go ahead.' These words *ma suchah* in a way sum up the entire message of the Gita. Let us not be afraid and let us give up all lesser supports so that, ultimately, we get the one true support, the only thing that can support the growth and development of the higher consciousness, the grace of the divine.

Krishna's flute is still playing in Vrindavan. We may not be able to hear it because our ears are so full of the clamour and noise of daily living, and the conflicts and the tensions around us, but it is still playing. And Krishna is still there as the charioteer riding with us in our own higher consciousness. We do not have to go back to Kurukshetra, we do not have to go back to Arjuna. Krishna is with us always, provided we have ears to listen, provided we have eyes to see, provided we do not get totally blinded and deafened by the outer material conflicts which surround us. The outer is also important, but ultimately it is he whose inner consciousness is firmly centred in the divine alone will be able to meet the conflicts that lie ahead.

The conflicts are there. There is no easy path to greatness or to spiritual realization, either individual or collective. We must always remember the Vedic exhortation: '*charaiveti, charaiveti*' (move on, move on). Imagine human consciousness as a great current that is flowing down through the dark channels of time. If we do not swim upwards against the stream, we will be carried down to the rapids and the waterfalls below. There can be no standing still for man. Man is a transitional being, half way between the animal and the divine. Man's destiny is to move onwards to the next stage of evolution, for then only can our divine nature be fully developed. But, in order to move upwards, we have to struggle. If we have faith and reverence, then, with the sound of the divine flute echoing in our ears and the voice of the divine charioteer resounding in our hearts, we can move resolutely onwards towards the divine destiny that awaits us. That, in essence, is the message of the Gita.

From *Essays on Hinduism*, 2014

4

The Insight of the Mystics

THE OUTSTANDING FEATURE OF the last quarter of the twentieth century is the final collapse of the materialistic paradigm that had dominated the world for many centuries. The Cartesian–Newtonian–Marxist paradigm has finally collapsed, and in the post-Einsteinian period, with quantum mechanics and Heisenberg's uncertainty principle, with Grof's extended cartography of the psyche, and so many other exciting and interesting developments, we find that the ancient vision of the mystics is again being recaptured. Humanity gropes for a new model, a new philosophy and a new paradigm to replace the old: for a new consciousness. Mankind is at a revolutionary crossroads, and it is no coincidence that this has happened when it is in supreme peril, not from another species, not from so-called 'natural' changes in the weather, not from some other world, but from itself. Deep within the human psyche has developed a terrible power that threatens not only our generation but all species of life on this planet.

Ancient myths can often illuminate the human predicament, and I want to start my presentation with a brief description of a powerful Hindu myth, the Samudra Manthana or the Churning of the Milky Ocean. In this great myth the devas and the asuras, the bright and the dark powers, both came together to churn the milky ocean. We do not have the absolutedichotomy of good and evil that is there in the Semitic tradition; the bright and the dark powers, the devas and the asuras, are, in fact, related within the whole theory of duality.

Both combine their powers to churn the milky ocean for aeons and then great gifts begin to appear. Kamadhenu, the all-giving cow; Kalpavriksha, the wish-fulfilling tree; Uchchaihshrava, the divine horse; Airavata, the divine elephant; Mahalakshmi, the goddess of wealth and prosperity. These and other great gifts appeared and were happily divided between the asuras and devas. The ultimate objective was the pot of ambrosia, the elixir of immortality, the amrita *kalasa.*

Suddenly, and without warning, the ocean started to boil with a terrible poison, the *garala*, a new and malign dimension, of which neither the devas nor the asuras had any knowledge. The poison spread throughout the three worlds; the ocean, the land and the sky. The devas and the asuras ran helter-skelter in panic, in a vain attempt to escape this terrible poison, forgetting all the gifts that they had divided, because it appeared as if the whole process of creation was coming to an end. And it was then that Shiva, the great primal divinity, aloof from the avarice and materialism of the devas and asuras, appeared. He collected the poison in a cup, and as he drank it his throat turned blue, hence one of the names of Shiva is Nilakantha, the blue-throated one. It was only when he had absorbed the poison that order was restored and the devas and the asuras returned, and the churning was resumed until finally the ambrosial pot appeared.

This is a myth of great significance. The human condition now seems to me to be very similar. Prolonged churning has given us incredible gifts. Science and technology, medicine, communications, space, the extraordinary adventure into outer space. The tremendous development of science has brought material benefits and comforts to millions upon millions of people. It gives us the capacity to abolish poverty and hunger, illiteracy and unemployment by the end of this century. We can ensure for every human being born upon this planet the necessary physical, intellectual and material inputs for a full life.

And yet, the poison is also now upon us. Thousands of billions of dollars are spent every year on monstrous weapons of unprecedented destruction. The planet is bristling with nuclear warheads, each a thousand times more powerful than the ones that demolished Hiroshima and Nagasaki, each having more than the entire explosive power used by both sides in the Second World War. With all our knowledge, with all the gifts, we have come to a single mantra—mutually assured destruction, or MAD. Five thousand years ago there was another three-letter word which, was the epitome of Vedic knowledge—AUM. In five thousand years the human race has gone from AUM to MAD.

It is not necessary to go into details of the effect of even a so-called 'limited' nuclear war which itself is a myth. *The Day After* is a film that has had a tremendous impact, though it is a gross understatement of the situation. Jonathan Schell's marvellous book *The Fate of the Earth* and its follow-up *The Abolition* give some idea of what would happen in the event of a nuclear war. The new report *The Cold and the Dark*, by Carl Sagan and others, also gives overwhelming evidence to show that any sort of nuclear war would end human civilization as we know it, poison the air and the oceans and render the planet uninhabitable.

No bomb has so far been invented that would destroy only the Russians and the Americans. All of us, whether we live in Asia or Africa, in the Arctic areas or at the ends of the earth, will be effectively eliminated. In fact, those people on whom the bombs fall may be luckier because they would go instantaneously, whereas millions of others would die lingering deaths longing to be released from their torture. And this can happen not necessarily through a political decision. A miscalculation, an accident, a flock of geese, an earthquake, a malfunctioning computer—anything can now do it.

Do we realize that we are a privileged generation, that we may be the last generation of human beings to inhabit this earth? Can we, as thinking beings, accept this situation without striving for a solution? Can we acquiesce in a situation where one-quarter of the world is overfed and three-quarters underfed? Can we live in a global village where millions die of malnutrition, stunted in body and mind, and other millions suffer from obesity and overeating? Can we live in an age where millions lack elementary medical care and other millions are overmedicated? Can we fail to heed the cry of the oppressed and the deprived and yet claim that we are on the inner path?

If the answer to these questions is in the negative, as it must be, then we must move towards a new transition. It is going to be painful as are all transitions, but they are essential for human survival. We have got to move towards complementarity in place of competition and convergence in place of conflict. We must heal the split in the human psyche. We must gather the shattered fragments of human consciousness and weld them into a glowing whole. We must affect the transition to a new global consciousness to replace the present fractured and fragmented condition of the human race.

But can this be done? Many thinkers have pointed out that, whenever there is a major transition, there is a period of reaction and crystallization. Can we afford that type of crystallization in a world bristling with nuclear weapons? Will there be a substantial enough transformation of consciousness on earth in time to prevent its destruction? Or is this particular adventure in consciousness, as Arthur Koestler has pointed out, doomed to failure? Is man a creature programmed for self-destruction, without a graceful exit like the dinosaurs but a malignant one, taking all life with it, not only collective suicide but terracide?

No one knows the answers. But the Bhagavadgita teaches that we must act in the manner we feel right and not worry about consequences.

We must act not from our inflated or deflated egos, but from the depths of our inner being. Indeed, at this juncture in planetary history, creative action is a spiritual imperative; we simply cannot accept the negative option.

And yet, with the world apparently rushing towards its doom, what is it that we can do to help the favourable resolution of this terrible conflict, to encourage a transition to the new consciousness? I have a five-point programme which could help in this process.

The first point is to work out the conceptual and theoretical philosophical underpinning of the new global consciousness. We can draw from many traditions, from science and from religion. We have inherited some astounding insights from the rishis, the great seers who lived in the Himalayas thousands of years ago. One is the unity of all existence: the fact that there is no ultimate duality whether on this planet or on the billions upon billions of galaxies. It is all the expression of a single power, of a single energy, of a single divine force. Then there is the divinity inherent in every human being. If God exists, He is divine by definition; but the concept that the human being is potentially divine, that the divine resides in every human being regardless of race or religion, caste or creed, language or ideology is of signal importance. Again, there is the vision of mankind as a family. We are all related by the fact of our humanness; we are members of the human family. Yet another Hindu concept is the harmony of religions. Religion has been a source of great art and inspiration, and also of unprecedented destruction. Even today thousands lie dead on the battlefield in the name of religion. We have got to understand that all these great religious traditions draw their sustenance from the same centre. We have got to move towards the concept of the unity of all religions. Finally, there is the concept of the welfare of all mankind, regardless of whether they live in the east or the west, the north or the south. These were some of the insights which we find in the Hindu tradition. We can go to other religious traditions and also non-religious traditions in order to develop a coherent philosophy.

This new idea should be widely spread through the media. The media today are full of violence, of negative vibrations. Why can we not use the media for something positive for a change? Why not use the tremendous power of communications, of television? Television does not have to be an 'idiot box'. It can be a box of enlightenment, but only if there are enlightened people behind it. If you have compassion and understanding behind it, this can become one of the most powerful instruments for mass enlightenment that has ever been produced.

Thirdly, we must work immediately and urgently to set up a worldwide network. There are hundreds of groups today all over the world, there are millions of people on all continents feeling the great pressure of the future. But they are disparate, not properly knit together or coordinated. They can have a symbiotic relationship with each other if there is a pooling of all this energy. Time is rushing by very fast, and we seem to be moving towards some traumatic event in human history. I commend the image of a great philharmonic orchestra in which all the creative, positive movements of the world are knit together into one tremendous power and force which has overwhelming influence upon mankind. Into the United Nations is built an incurable dichotomy which prevents it from becoming an effective organ. Why should we not set up a new United Nations of the New Consciousness to take on the task of spearheading this new movement. This might sound presumptuous, but then no great task is ever accomplished without a certain element of presumption. We must be humble, and yet our humility should not lead us into a sort of passivity, nor should we end up hypnotizing ourselves into an inability to act.

The fourth point is an immediate involvement in peace and disarmament movements. I am aware that there are political implications in this, and yet I do feel that we have to get involved in the broader anti-nuclear movements. We do not necessarily have to demonstrate on the streets, but in our own way we have to do this, first in the open societies and then in the closed societies, because no society can today remain closed howsoever much they may want to. The winds of change, the winds of awareness are blowing across the frontiers of the world. Howsoever much the United States may feel that the Soviet Union is closed, and the Soviets may feel that the United States is not open to conviction, the fact of the matter is that there is now a new awareness, a new permeability in both these great blocs. We can see that from our third vantage point, as it were.

Finally, it is not enough to be involved in a movement for outer peace; there has to be a parallel movement for inner peace within each one of us. In our own lives, we must move towards a realization of the truth at the core of our being, the higher consciousness that is the birthright of each individual born on this planet, 'the light that lighteth every man that cometh into this world'. In the crucible of our individual consciousness alone can the poison be contained, transformed into nectar and released into society and the world. In this age, it is not realistic to expect the Lord Shiva to appear once again and drink the poison for us. We have now passed that stage in evolution. Now that we have reached the stage of self-individuation, we have got to drink the poison ourselves. Each one of us has to integrate the poison within our psyches and convert it by the power of our spiritual striving into nectar.

The last point that I wish to make is that we must cooperate with the spiritual power of the earth. Every ancient tradition has known that the planet earth is not just a ball of mud, stone and lava, but a living, spiritual presence. The dramatic photograph of Earth taken from the moon shows it as it really is: a tiny, glowing jewel against the unending vastness of outer space, so fragile and yet so beautiful. In the *Atharva Veda,* composed five thousand years ago by the rishis, there is a hymn to the earth known as Bhumi Sukta. It has sixty-three verses which speak to us today with a new urgency and a resonance. I would like to read a translation of twelve of these verses to show you that the insight of the mystics is again becoming viable and important:

Truth, eternal order that is great and stern,
Consecration, Austerity, Prayer and Ritual—
these uphold the Earth.
May She, Queen of what has been and will be,
make a wide world for us.
Earth which has many heights, and slopes
and the unconfined plain that bind men together,
Earth that bears plants of various healing powers,
may she spread wide for us and thrive.
Earth, in which lie the sea, the river and other waters,
in which food and cornfields have come to be,
in which lives all that breathes and that moves,
may she confer on us the finest of her yield.
Earth, which at first was in the water of the ocean,
and which sages sought with wondrous powers,
Earth whose heart was in eternal heaven,
wrapped in Truth, immortal,
may she give us lustre and strength
in a most exalted state.
Earth, in which the waters, common to all,
moving on all sides, flow unfailingly, day and night,
may she pour on us milk in many streams,
and endow us with lustre.
Pleasant be thy hills, O Earth,
thy snow-clad mountains and thy woods!
O Earth—brown, black, red and multi-coloured
the firm Earth protected by Indra,
on this Earth may I stand—
unvanquished, unhurt, unslain.
I call to earth; the purifier,
the patient Earth, growing strong through spiritual might.
May we recline on thee, O Earth, who
bearest power and plenty,
and enjoy our share of food and molten butter.
May those that are thy eastern regions, O Earth,
and the northern and the southern and the western

be pleasant for me to tread upon.
May I not stumble while I live in the world.
Whatever I dig from thee, Earth,
may that have quick growth again.
O purifier, may we not injure thy vitals
or thy heart.
May Earth with people who speak various tongues
and those who have various religious rites
according to their places of abode,
pour for me treasure in a thousand streams
like a constant cow that never fails.
May those born of thee, O Earth,
be, for our welfare, free from sickness and waste.
Wakeful through a long life, we shall
become bearers of tribute to thee.
Earth, my mother, set me securely with bliss
in full accord with heaven.
O wise one,
uphold me in grace and splendour.

This earth, our mother, has nurtured consciousness from the slime of the primaeval ocean billions of years ago and has sustained the human race for countless centuries. Will we repay our debt to our mother by converting her into a burnt-out cinder circling the sun into eternity? Or will we so marshal our inner and outer resources that even at this late hour we succeed in making the crucial transition to the new consciousness? The answer will depend upon many factors, not the least of which is whether each one of us lives up to our ideals and our humanity, whether the transpersonal vision is translated into creative action individually and collectively.

Do we remain mired into the old consciousness or are we able to make the transition to the new? This is truly an absorbing, exciting and exhilarating challenge. Let us pray then for courage and wisdom at this crucial hour, pray to the great power that permeates the cosmos, the earth and the sky, the mountains and the rivers, the forests and the oceans, the humans and the beasts. The great power that shining causes everything else to shine; the great power that blazes like a thousand suns on the other shore beyond the darkness. The great power so beautifully symbolized by the figure of Shiva Nataraja—the dancing Shiva holding in one hand the drum, the creative sound, by which millions of galaxies spring into being, and in the other hand the eternal fire in which the cycle of regeneration is completed. Let us pray to the divine power to give mankind courage at this critical phase, so that we are able to make the transition to the new consciousness.

May that great divine power give us the strength and the courage that we need to make the transition!

From *Essays on Hinduism*, 2014

5

The Forms of the Formless

IT IS NECESSARY TO point out, however, that while learned scholars proclaimed and disputed these various schools of philosophy, for the common man, the mainstay of Hinduism has always been devotion to a deity representing some aspect or incarnation of the divine. Hinduism has a wealth of imagery, symbolism and iconography, and has produced a dazzling array of images and concepts which often baffles non-Hindus. This has led to the erroneous view, still extant in some quarters, that Hinduism is polytheistic. It certainly encourages the worship of many forms and symbols, but it must be understood that behind these myriad forms is the same all-pervasive divinity mirrored in a thousand different ways.

Very briefly, popular Hindu worship today revolves around three major deities—Shiva, Vishnu as himself and his major incarnations, and the goddess. Shiva Mahadeva is the great primaeval lord, and there is reason to believe that he is of a pre-Aryan origin because on the still undeciphered seals of the Indus Valley Civilization (c. 5000–3000 BCE), there is a figure seated cross-legged with several of the features associated with Shiva. Shiva is invariably worshipped along with a lingam, a powerful symbol representing the creative force behind all manifestation. He is generally portrayed as a resplendent ascetic sitting in meditation on a mountain peak, his body smeared with ashes, deadly snakes entwined around his neck and the sacred Ganges flowing from his matted locks.

He is also worshipped in his role as the cosmic dancer, Nataraja, whose dance symbolizes the eternal wheel of the cosmos where millions of worlds are destroyed every moment and millions other spring into existence to the best of the eternal rhythm. Indeed, the magnificent image of the dancing Shiva represents one of the high watermarks of human art.

Despite his fearsome appearance, Shiva (the word means 'auspicious') is easy to please, hence the name Ashutosha, and is generous with his boons even to the titans who often misuse them. He is neither born nor does he die, being the master of birth and death. In south India, there is a tradition in which Shiva is believed to have appeared in human form on several different occasions, either to help his devotees or to impart esoteric teachings. He is the maha yogi, the great ascetic, and the patron-saint of those practising yoga.

Shiva is the third god of the Hindu trinity—Brahma the creator, Vishnu the preserver and Shiva the destroyer—but again it must be remembered that these are not three different gods but three aspects of the same divine being. This is beautifully portrayed in the magnificent monolithic sculpture of Trimurti on the Elephanta Island, off the coast of Mumbai. One of the world's great artistic creations, this massive cave sculpture shows clearly the three aspects integrated in a single, divine entity. In fact, the great art of India provides as useful a way of approaching an understanding of the theistic concepts as the texts themselves. Apart from sculpture and painting, the great classical dance forms of India, particularly the Bharatanatyam, can bring to life concepts which may appear abstruse and unidimensional when approached purely through the written word.

Vishnu is depicted as lying on a great serpent that floats on the vast, endless ocean of milk, the Kshir Sagar. In this form he is worshipped in many temples, especially in the south, but elsewhere in India he is more widely worshipped in two of his most popular incarnations associated with the two great epics—Rama and Krishna. Indeed, these two names have carried the undying message of Hinduism to billions of men and women for thousands of years now, not only in India but wherever the Hindu cultural impact has been felt in the world. Lord Rama is depicted with a bow in hand, accompanied by his noble wife Sita, his faithful brother Lakshmana and his devoted follower, the monkey god, Hanuman. Lord Krishna is depicted in numerous forms, commencing with his early childhood as a baby, Bala Krishna, and terminating as the charioteer of

Arjuna, Parthasarathi. But his most popular and appealing form is as a beautiful cowherd youth, Gopala Krishna, dark and resplendent, standing with one foot crossed over the other and playing his magic flute. He is generally worshipped along with Radha, the shepherdess who has come to symbolize the essence of the Krishna cult of devotion. Vishnu is also worshipped in some of his lesser known incarnations such as Narasimha, the man-lion, who appeared to rid the world of the demon-king Hiranyakashipu and save his son, the great boy-devotee Prahlada.

The third major focus of devotion in India is the goddess in her numerous forms. She is worshipped as Parvati, the consort of Shiva; Lakshmi, the consort of Vishnu; Sita and Radha along with Rama and Krishna. However, and this is a point of considerable significance, she is not only worshipped as a consort, but, in her own right, as the essence of power and beauty; as Durga with eighteen arms riding a lion and scattering the demon hordes like chaff; as Kali, the fierce, naked goddess standing upon a corpse and drinking the blood of her freshly slain enemies; as Saraswati, the goddess of art, poetry and music, the patron of all learning and wisdom. The worship of the great mother is, of course, known throughout the world in one form or another, but it is in Hinduism that she appears in all her splendour.

There is a Pauranic myth about the birth of Durga which is full of symbolic significance. Once a great demon, the buffalo-headed Mahishasura, representing the evil forces of brute materialism, succeeded in defeating all the gods (devas: the shining ones) and established his supremacy over creation. The gods despaired, because, despite all their efforts, they could not vanquish this terrible monster. At last they gathered together on a mountain peak and decided to pool their divine powers. Led by the lord of the gods, Indra, each god contributed his own power symbolized by a weapon. At the end of the great ritual, when all the divine powers had been pooled, there arose a dazzling light which spread its glory throughout the three worlds. In the midst of the light appeared Durga, the great goddess, with a weapon in each of her eighteen arms, and riding a ferocious tiger. She then gave battle to Mahishasura, and after a terrible conflict lasting nine days and nine nights, she finally slew him and rid the world of this great terror. These nine nights, the Navaratri, are still celebrated every year by Hindus as symbolising the victory of divine power over the forces of evil.

An important point to remember is that the worship of the various deities in the Hindu pantheon is by no means mutually exclusive. While each Hindu usually has a special family deity—the *ishta-devata*—he often worships three or four different deities during his daily prayers and pays homage to any deity in a temple he may visit. Also, apart from anthropomorphic deities, some Hindus use certain symbols for purposes of meditation. The most important of these is the aum which is described in the scriptures as being the audio-visual symbol of Brahman itself and is endowed with a wealth of symbolism. An entire Upanishad—*Mandukya*—has been devoted to the word aum.

Meditation on the symbol and sound of aum is an important aspect of yoga, a word that has gained much currency of late throughout the world but is generally imperfectly understood. As has been mentioned earlier, yoga implies the joining or yoking of human consciousness to the divine being and, in this sense, it can be applied to the four major paths of spiritual attainment. In a more specialized sense, yoga involves physical and mental disciplines directed at control over mental and physical functions, specially breathing. The classic text of this yoga is the celebrated *Yoga Sutras* of Patanjali, one of the world's great religious classics.

The sutras, or aphorisms of Patanjali, lay down an eight-fold path, ashtanga yoga of physical, psychological and moral discipline that, if properly adhered to under the guidance of a qualified teacher, results in the consciousness of the seeker being gradually elevated until the Atman shines forth in its pristine glory as pure consciousness. This path also involves arousal of the kundalini shakti or serpent power, believed to be located at the base of the human spine. As this power rises through a series of occult centres or chakras located in various parts of the body, the consciousness is correspondingly elevated, until finally it bursts into the highest chakra at the top of the brain—the *sahasrara* or thousand-petalled lotus—where the merger between the Atman and the Brahman takes place and the seeker is plunged into the highest bliss. This elevated state, known as samadhi, is the goal of all yogic practices.

Numerous other texts on various aspects of yoga are to be found in Hindu literature, all basing themselves upon the foundations laid by Patanjali. These include the tantras or esoteric texts which deal with the various practices and techniques of kundalini arousal and acquisition of psychic powers. These miraculous powers, or siddhis, are accepted as an important aspect of yogic practices, but their misuse or even excessive demonstration is frowned upon as a hindrance to the achievement of the supreme goal. Through the ages, as today, there have been in India a fair number of persons who possess these powers, and miracle-mongering has always been an occupational hazard for yogis which it is not always easy to avoid.

An important aspect of Hinduism—whether it is yoga or any other system of philosophy, discipline or teaching—is the critical importance that is assigned to the guru or teacher. The guru in the Hindu tradition is to be venerated even more than one's parents, because while our parents give us physical life, it is the guru who brings about our spiritual rebirth, whereby man alone can fulfil his cosmic destiny. This notion, which appears to many to be somewhat exaggerated, will become clearer when it is understood that the human guru is but a symbol of the divine power that already resides within us. The word guru itself means dispeller of darkness, and by bringing the light of spiritual wisdom into the material darkness of normal human consciousness, the guru indeed performs a unique and priceless function.

Needless to say, in Hinduism, as in so many other religions, there is the usual quota of charlatans and even criminals masquerading under the guise and habit of spiritual teachers. Generally, a person gets the sort of guru he deserves, and there is a well-established tradition that when the disciple is ready, the guru will appear. In the *Mundaka Upanishad* two essential qualifications of a true guru are laid down, both of which must be fulfilled if a person is really to occupy that elevated status. The guru must be *shrotriya*, learned in the scriptures, and *brahmanishtha*, established in the Brahman or divine consciousness. Hinduism believes that spiritual attainment is not possible without a guru, although sometimes in place of a human guru, a book or scripture may suffice. There have also been instances in which people have been initiated by some high being through a dream rather than in the flesh.

From *The Sterling Book of Hinduism*, 2012

6

The Bhakti Movement

THROUGHOUT THE MIDDLE AGES there arose a series of extraordinary saint-singers who preached the gospel of divine love and ecstasy that led to a tremendous devotional revival. This has collectively come to be known as the Bhakti movement, one of the most interesting movements in the long and eventful history of Hinduism.

While previous Hindu teachings had been almost exclusively in Sanskrit, this new movement broke away from the rigid and conservative Brahmin-dominated tradition and used regional languages and dialects to propagate their message. This also involved a revolt against the rigid caste restrictions and taboos that had become a negative feature in classical Hinduism. The saint-singers not only came from all castes and communities, across religions and genders, but their message was addressed to the common people irrespective of class or creed.

In Islam also, as against the ulama or clergy, there has always been a mystical tradition of seekers intoxicated with the love of God. They were known as Sufis, and it was with the Sufi tradition that the Bhakti movement developed close affinity. The first major Sufi teacher to come to India was the great Khwaja Moinuddin Chishti (b. 1142). He arrived in Delhi towards the end of the twelfth century, and finally settled in Ajmer where he had many disciples, both Hindu and Muslim. His great shrine there, the Dargah Sharif, is today one of the most important centres of Muslim pilgrimage and draws numerous Hindu pilgrims year after year.

In Hinduism the first great figure of medieval mysticism was Ramananda (c. 1370–1440). Although a disciple of Ramanuja, Ramananda moved away from traditional orthodoxy, challenged caste divisions and began preaching in Hindi rather than Sanskrit. One of his most illustrious disciples was Guru Ravidas who was a cobbler by profession. By sheer dint of spiritual merit, he rose to become one of the most respected religious teachers of his time and still has millions of followers.

Ramananda's disciples came mainly from the lower castes, the most famous being Kabir, who is claimed both by the Hindus and the Muslims. The son of a Muslim weaver, Kabir (1440–1518) was drawn to the Bhakti movement at an early age. His songs struck at the roots of religious orthodoxy, ritualism and intolerance. Kabir combined in himself the best of the Sufi and Bhakti traditions. One of his songs (translated by Rabindranath Tagore) contains the following stanzas:

> O servant, where dost thou seek me?
> O! I am beside thee.
> I am neither in the temple nor in mosque;
> I am neither in Kaaba nor in Kailasha,
> Neither am I in rites and ceremonies,
> Nor in yoga and renunciation.
> If thou art a true seeker
> Thou shalt at once see me,
> Thou shalt meet me in a moment of time.
> Kabir says, O Sadhu, God is the breath of all breath,
> There is nothing but water at the holy bathing places,
> I know that they are useless, for I have bathed in them,
> The images are all lifeless, they cannot speak.
> I know, for I have cried aloud to them.
> The Purana and the Koran are mere words;
> Lifting up the curtain, I have seen.
> Kabir gives utterance to the words of experience;
> He knows well that all other things are untrue.

Kabir had a tremendous influence upon the India of his day. Despite the fact that he was a lowly weaver, the sheer force of his spiritual realization made him a focus of great veneration. There is an interesting, perhaps apocryphal, story about his death. Both the Hindus and the Muslims claimed his body, the former insisting that he be cremated and the latter that he be buried. When the shroud was removed, however, the body had disappeared and in its place was a heap of flowers. These were then divided between the contending parties; the Hindus carried off their share and cremated them with great devotion, while the Muslims buried their share with equal veneration. Thus, in death as in life Kabir taught the gospel of spiritual communion and brotherhood to India's two largest religious communities.

Kabir had many disciples, but two teachers who were greatly influenced by him deserve special mention. The first was Nanak (1469–1538) who went on to found the Sikh faith. He constantly emphasized that in the sight of God 'there was no Hindu and no Mussalman', and many of the hymns contained in the Granth Sahib, the sacred book of the Sikhs, echo this concept. Another of Kabir's followers was Dadu (1544–1603) who also founded a powerful movement based on his teachings known as Dadupanth. He wrote many beautiful hymns, and in one of them he says:

God is my ancestor, the creator is my kinsman,
The world-guru is my caste, I am a child of the Almighty.

The Bhakti movement produced a profusion of great literature. Two figures of particular importance in the vast Hindi-speaking Indo-Gangetic plain are Tulsidasa (1527–1623) and Suradasa (1478–1581). Tulsidasa produced the first and greatest classic in Hindi, the *Ramacharitamanasa* (Holy Lake of Rama's Deeds), which is the story of the Ramayana retold in Hindi verse with a wealth of poetry and deep devotion. There are many versions of the Ramayana, the most important ones being the original Sanskrit version of Valmiki and the Tamil version of Kamban. But the *Ramacharitamanasa* has had a unique impact. For millions of Hindus in north India, it has provided for centuries the main cultural and religious foundations, and down to this day verses from it are sung in every village and town. It was this great religious classic that the indentured labourers, who went from India to Fiji, Surinam, Mauritius and other plantations during colonial rule, took with them, and which remains their religious umbilical cord linking them to the land of their origin. Tulsidasa looks upon Rama as the supreme incarnation of the divine being, born for the salvation of mankind and worthy of total devotion and dedication.

Suradasa, considered by some critics to be an even greater poet, became blind in early childhood. Nonetheless, he composed beautiful devotional poetry directed towards Krishna. The descriptions of Krishna's childhood—his youthful pranks, his dalliance with the *gopis* (milkmaids) of Vrindavan, his magical feats, his resplendent personality epitomizing the divine lover who summons human souls to the golden notes of his eternal flute—are part of the great heritage of Hinduism. Both Tulsidasa and Suradasa, along with a number of other devotional saints including the Pathan Raskhan, another devotee of Lord Krishna, gave a tremendous boost to popular Hinduism. At a time when Muslim rule was being established over most of India, and the older, classical orthodoxy was losing its hold upon the people's minds, the Bhakti movement once again demonstrated the resilience of Hinduism and its capacity to enable its followers to restate and reinterpret the eternal verities in the light of changed circumstances.

In Karnataka, the great saint Purandaradasa (1480–1564) sang of the glory of God and won a vast following. Eastern India, particularly Bengal, has always been an important centre of Hinduism. The great eleventh-century poet-devotee Jayadeva, who composed one of the post-classical Sanskrit masterpieces in his poem *Gita Govinda,* relating the story of Krishna, had given a great fillip to Vaishnava worship in Bengal and Odisha . An extraordinary saint called Chaitanya (1485–1534), popularly known as Mahaprabhu (the Great Lord), and considered by his devotees to be an incarnation of Krishna himself, founded the Vaishnava movement in Bengal. A special feature of his ministry was the kirtans, choral singing and chanting by groups of devotees wandering from village to village and town to town. Often the men involved in chanting would be carried away by a religious frenzy, and Chaitanya himself would be thrown into a trance or fit of ecstasy as he contemplated the glory of Krishna. Although he did not write extensively, he exerted a profound influence on the subsequent development of Bengali and Oriya literature. Further east in the Brahmaputra Valley, another great teacher and reformer, Shankaradeva (1449–1568), writing in Assamese, greatly influenced the Hindus of that region. The same is true of Tukarama (1607–1649) in Maharashtra, which had earlier produced the young saint Jnaneshvara (1275–1296) whose Marathi work, *Jnaneshvari,* is one of the great classics of Hinduism.

No survey of the Bhakti movement, howsoever brief, can omit the names of two remarkable women who have left the impress of their attainment on future generations. Lalleshvari (1317–1372) was a Kashmiri saint who attained God-realization at an early age and whose life is full of legends and stories of miracles. Her utterances teach the direct path of realization through intense love of the divine, renouncing attachment to worldly possessions and family ties, and rising above the dualities of caste and creed. She writes:

Shiva abides in all that is everywhere;
Then do not discriminate
Between a Hindu and a Mussalman.
If thou art wise, know thyself;
That is the true knowledge of the Lord.
I renounced fraud, untruth, deceit;
I taught my mind to see the One
In all my fellowmen.
How could I then discriminate
Between man and man
And not accept the food
Offered to me by brother man?

The other great woman figure of the Bhakti movement was Mirabai (1450–1512), a Rajput princess who was married at an early age to the Rana of Udaipur. She was a childhood devotee of Lord Krishna and had dedicated her life to him. After her marriage, she continued to devote her entire time to the worship of Krishna, incurring the displeasure of her husband who even tried to poison her. By Krishna's grace, however, the cup of poison turned into honey as she danced in ecstasy before the image of the god. Mira subsequently renounced her worldly life and wandered through India singing her beautiful compositions, which are among the most moving devotional songs of Hinduism. One of her best loved hymns goes thus:

Tying anklets upon her feet, Mira dances in ecstasy.
People say Mira has gone mad,
Her mother-in-law says she has disgraced the clan,
The Rana sent her a cup of poison
Which Mira, laughingly, drank.
I have myself become the eternal maid-servant of

My Narayana.
Mira's God is Giridhar, lifter of the mountain.
O Indestructible One, meet me swiftly in your
Eternal embrace.

Thus, we see that in its most difficult period Hinduism produced a glittering galaxy of saint-singers drawn from all corners of the country, who inspired millions by their devotion and poetry, presented in an idiom readily understood by the masses. They were restating the great Vedantic truths—the unity of Atman and Brahman, of the human and the divine—in a new phraseology which took the message down to the humblest villages. Their songs remain to this day a major source of inspiration for Hindus, and while the sonorous Sanskrit chanting of the magnificent Vedic hymns can still be heard on special occasions, especially in south India, it is the songs of the medieval saints which reverberate in fields and forests, in villages and towns. Truly, it has been said that music has the unique capacity to carry the human consciousness out of its narrow confines towards the brimming ocean of the divine.

From *The Sterling Book of Hinduism*, 2012

7

The Modern Renaissance

THE ENTIRE HISTORY OF Hinduism, looked at from a certain angle, can be seen as a constant process of challenge and response. To each major crisis, Hinduism reacted, first by briefly withdrawing into a shell, and then, with its unparalleled capacity for assimilation and regeneration, by a new resurgence. This happened with the Jain and Buddhist movements, with the early Christian missionaries and, to a lesser extent, with the Muslim advent. But with the arrival of the British, first as traders and finally as imperial rulers, Hinduism was confronted with the most critical of all the challenges it had faced in its long and eventful history.

By the time the British arrived in India, Hinduism had reached perhaps its lowest ebb. All sorts of superstitions and undesirable practices flourished in the name of religion. Caste taboos had become so rigid that Hindu society, which a thousand years earlier had sent its great missionaries to the four corners of Asia, had begun to insist on anyone returning from abroad having to undergo purificatory rites. Women, who once enjoyed an honoured position and are found in the Upanishads conversing freely with men upon the highest philosophical topics, had become virtual slaves in the joint family. Widows were treated with great cruelty; female infanticide was rife in some castes; and compulsory immolation of widows was often enforced. Theologically also, the great Vedantic truths that lay behind Hindu thought had been obscured by the jungle growth of superstition and corruption. The inspiration of the medieval saint-singers, while still prevalent, had begun to fade in the face of the political turmoil and widespread anarchy that followed the collapse of Mughal power. Indeed, it was one of the darkest periods in Indian history, and it seemed that Hinduism had at last exhausted its spiritual reserves and would gradually fade away in the face of the new onslaught.

It was in the great movement for social reform in Hinduism that the first creative reaction to British rule manifested itself, and it was Bengal, the first province in India, to feel the brunt of British conquest that spearheaded this cultural revival. It was here that the first of a long line of great leaders of thought and action arose, a man who has often been described as the 'path-finder' of modern India. Rammohan Roy (1772–1833) was a man of unusual intellectual ability, a profound scholar of Sanskrit and Persian, as well a deep admirer of British culture. He took a leading part in starting English-medium schools in Bengal, and in 1828 founded the Brahmo Sabha, later to develop under his successor Devendranath Tagore into the Brahmo Samaj. This was the first deliberate attempt in modern India to reform Hinduism and to cleanse it of the undesirable encrustation that had developed around it over the centuries.

The Brahmo Samaj, as well as its offshoots—the Adi Brahmo Samaj, led by Devendranath Tagore; the Brahmo Samaj of India founded by Keshub Chunder Sen in 1868; and the Sadharan Brahmo Samaj founded by some of his followers in 1878—all based themselves upon the pristine authority of the Vedas, and strongly attacked idol worship and undesirable social customs such as compulsory sati, or immolation of widows upon their husbands' funeral pyres. The leaders of the movement, specially Sen, were considerably influenced by the style of Christian missionaries who had become active under British rule, and many of their prayer meetings were modelled on Christian church services.

Under the influence of the Brahmo Samaj, several such reformist movements started in other parts of India, notably the Prarthana Samaj founded in Bombay in 1867 by the great scholars M.G. Ranade and R.D. Bhandarkar. These societies, while influencing mainly the English-educated fringe, did play an important part in bringing a new intellectual awareness into Hindu society, and encouraged educated Hindus to re-examine their religious heritage in the light of changing conditions. The same is true of the Theosophical Society which was founded by Madame Blavatsky and Colonel Olcott in New York in 1875 and gained considerable popularity in India, largely through the work of Mrs Annie Besant. Simultaneously, the rediscovery of the ancient Indian texts by European scholars such as Max Muller, James Ferguson and Alexander Cunningham, and the work of Western archaeologists and linguists, which brought to light the remarkable achievements of the ancient Indian past that had been lost during the medieval period, helped to give the nineteenth-century Hindu a new awareness of his rich cultural heritage and a renewed pride in his ancient religion.

All this, however, remained largely confined to the small, educated classes, awaiting a movement that would touch the heart of traditional Hinduism. This was not long in coming. A major figure in the Hindu revival was Swami Dayananda Saraswati (1824–83) who founded the Arya Samaj in 1875. Unlike the Brahmo and its offshoots, which were considerably influenced by Christianity, the Arya Samaj was militantly Hindu. Swami Dayananda passionately advocated a return to the pristine purity of Vedic Hinduism and denounced with intolerant indignation the post-Vedic Hindu scriptures such as the Puranas. He also condemned idol worship and caste distinctions, advocated equality for women, initiated a widespread educational campaign with special emphasis on female education and launched a crusade against untouchability. Rightly described as a human dynamo, Swami Dayananda shook the structure of established Hinduism to its foundations and infused into it new blood and fresh vigour.

Numerous other reformist and educational movements in Hinduism developed in the second half of the nineteenth century. For purposes of this review, however, we shall confine ourselves to a mention of five outstanding figures who have left their indelible impress on modern Hinduism and whose tremendous personalities have gone a long way in shaping the contours of the Hindu mind in our own century. These are Ramakrishna Paramahansa, Swami Vivekananda, Ramana Maharshi, Sri Aurobindo and Mahatma Gandhi. Each of these men, drew from the very heart of the Hindu tradition and reinterpreted its eternal truths in the light of his own extraordinary attainment. Between them, they achieved nothing less than a comprehensive revival of the best in the Hindu tradition and collectively represent a major force in the contemporary religious thought of the world.

From *The Sterling Book of Hinduism*, 2012

Essays

1

A Little History*

TO WRITE ABOUT ONESELF involves, inevitably, a curious combination of egoism and introspection, especially if it covers both the inner and outer dimensions of life. I have been fortunate not only in having been actively involved from a very early age in public affairs during a turbulent and fascinating period in our history, but also in being exposed to a rich array of inner stimuli—intellectual, emotional and spiritual. These include direct contact with many of the leading figures in India's national life as well as with persons of spiritual experience and wisdom. Also, through a love of books and music, I have travelled extensively in what Keats so appropriately called 'the realms of gold'—the luminous domain of ideas as represented in their highest watermark by the Upanishads in the Indian tradition and Plato in the Western, as also by the great treasures of Eastern and Western poetry and music.

Ever since my early youth I have felt that there has to be a deeper purpose in life than simply playing out passively the hand dealt to one by destiny or fate, chance or karma—whichever term one may wish to use. Many of my political ideas and ambitions came to fruition in the period subsequent to that covered by this volume, but I also had deeper spiritual impulses which have remained with me and in fact are steadily deepening as I now enter the autumn of my life.

---

* *Originally published as the preface to the revised edition of Karan Singh's* Autobiography, *1994*

For me, writing this autobiography was a rewarding experience as it enabled me to look backwards in time and space, and inwards to myself. The material contained in this book was originally published in two separate volumes, the first twelve chapters as *Heir Apparent* in 1982 and the next twelve as *Sadar-i-Riyasat* in 1985. Though they were written three years apart, they form a continuing narrative and between them, cover the period of my life during which I was predominantly involved in the affairs of my home state of Jammu and Kashmir. In the years that have elapsed since these memoirs were published my perceptions regarding several individuals and events have changed considerably, but I have resisted the temptation to change the text which remains exactly as originally published.

Curiously, my life seems to fall neatly into eighteen-year periods. The first eighteen were spent as a student in India and a patient abroad, while no sooner had I turned eighteen than I found myself catapulted into the office of Head of State which I held under three different appellations—Regent, Sadar-i-Riyasat and Governor—for exactly eighteen years. Within a few days of my thirty-sixth birthday I was invited to join the Union council of ministers, and for the next eighteen years until 1985 I was active in national politics as a Member of Parliament [MP], including over ten years as cabinet minister. This period, and the subsequent years up to the present, have been so full of activity that it would require several volumes to cover the events in which I was involved. In this new preface all I can do is to skim lightly over some of the highlights.

One of these were four election campaigns for the Lok Sabha, all of which I won from the Udhampur parliamentary constituency. The first, in a by-election in 1967 soon after I had joined the Cabinet, was virtually a walk-over, but in the 1971 elections the BJP (then Jana Sangh) put up a strong opposition. After the cataclysmic events of the Emergency, 1977 saw the election in which Indira Gandhi and all her cabinet colleagues from north India were defeated, but miraculously I was able to retain my seat comfortably. The Janata wave which swept over the whole of north India was not able to make a major dent in Udhampur. In fact, the toughest election I fought was the one in 1980. By then the Congress had split into the Congress (I) led by Indira Gandhi and the Congress (U) led by Devaraja Urs. Indira Gandhi and Sheikh Abdullah had an electoral understanding in Jammu and Kashmir whereby the Congress (I) and the National Conference contested three seats each. The Udhampur constituency was allotted to the National Conference, which fielded one of the Sheikh's cabinet ministers, D.D. Thakur, against me. Sheikh Abdullah announced that he would not mind losing all the other five seats in the state as long as he could defeat me. I accepted the challenge—and found myself involved in an extremely difficult contest with the entire administrative machinery of the state ranged against me, with Sheikh and Begum Abdullah touring the constituency intensively. As in earlier elections, my wife was a tremendous asset; the women voters would come out to greet us which they would do for no other candidate. After a tremendous battle, I was able to win by a good margin. I was one of only five members who won on the Congress (U) ticket, and Indira Gandhi's faction emerged as the mainstream Congress thanks largely to her charisma and single-minded pursuit of power which none of her opponents were able to match.

These four elections also reflected the changing political scene in the nation. It 1967 I was the candidate of the undivided Congress, and my symbol was yoked bullocks. The party split in 1969, with one group led by Morarji Desai forming the Congress (O), and the main Congress remaining with Indira Gandhi. In 1971 and 1977, thereafter, my symbol was a cow and calf. After the 1977 debacle, the Congress split again, and Indira Gandhi formed the Congress (I) which many of us did not join. My fourth election was then fought with the symbol of a woman with a spinning wheel. Soon after the 1980 elections I realized that the two-Congress theory had collapsed, and that there was no point in belonging to a rump. I therefore resigned from the Congress (U) and sat for the remaining period of that Lok Sabha term as an independent.

Indira Gandhi had always been friendly and supportive, and was hurt that I did not support her when the second party split came. It was difficult to explain to her the twin impact of the Sanjay Gandhi and Shiekh Abdullah factors which obliged me to part company with her. While I did not join the Congress (I) as most others did, I am glad that I had a personal reconciliation with her some time before her tragic assassination. She was a remarkable woman who left a powerful impact on the Indian political scene, and my ten years as a minister in her cabinet were for me a period of valuable education and experience in administration and political life.

I had known Rajiv Gandhi since he was five, and after he became prime minister I had expected that he would invite me to return to the party and contest the 1984 elections as a Congress candidate. But a certain group, which felt threatened by my possible return, had thrown a cordon around him that I was unable to get through. After waiting almost until the last moment, I decided, for a variety of considerations, to stand as an independent candidate from Jammu. This was the other constituency in the Jammu region, and I had assumed that since it was the first time I was seeking their vote the people would support me. As it turned out, the sympathy wave for Rajiv proved too strong. The Congress (I) candidate polled 50 per cent of the votes, while the National Conference candidate and I polled about 25 per cent each. Although it was a traumatic experience at the time, in retrospect I feel that after eighteen years in the parliament it forced a much-needed break from faction-ridden politics and was a liberating event, in that it freed my time and energy for the broader areas in which I had always been interested—global consciousness, the interfaith movement, environmental concerns and the application of Vedanta to the problems and challenges of our times. In fact, this represented the conclusion of the third eighteen-year cycle in my life and the opening of the fourth, which is still in progress.

My first ministerial portfolio, tourism and civil aviation, gave me the opportunity to travel extensively in India and abroad. I was the first minister to hold this portfolio, which previously had been part of a larger ministry of transport. When I entered the scene, Indian tourism, for all practical purposes, meant the Delhi-Agra-Jaipur triangle and Kashmir. I realized immediately that India was potentially one of the world's great tourist destinations. I structured a whole new programme of tourism promotion and development of the infrastructure, along with modernization of the fleets of Air India and Indian Airlines and upgradation of airport facilities.

Having spent the earlier eighteen years as a largely ceremonial head of state, this was my first encounter with actual decision-making and implementation, and I threw myself into the task with zest and enthusiasm. I was able to draw in some of the most creative people from the private sector in the fields of design, promotion and hospitality. It was during this period that south India was placed on the tourism map and the tremendous economic potential of the industry began to enter the mainstream of public consciousness.

One of the keys to our success was an idea that came to me soon after I took over the ministry. I realized that while the tourism department had only half a dozen offices abroad, Air India over the years had built up almost a hundred offices. Falling under the same ministry, the obvious thing would be for these organizations to work in close cooperation, but I soon realized that bureaucratic procedures built up since British times worked against innovation. Nonetheless, with the support of the prime minister, I was able to bring about the needed coordination after two years, and this led to the launching of Operation Europe, a joint promotional campaign by Air India and the tourism department, which was subsequently extended to other parts of the world. This made a substantial contribution to the increase in our tourist earnings, although we still get only a tiny fraction of what has become the world's largest industry.

During this period many important political events took place. The whole controversy regarding privy purses came up soon after I joined the Cabinet. Behind the scenes I tried to work on a compromise formula whereby the privy purses would be abolished but suitable compensation in the form of bonds would be issued, which would have enabled the former princes to continue to receive adequate inputs. However, the Concord of Princes, which had been set up after the government's move, took a rigid stand claiming that the move was a blatant breach of faith in light of the solemn covenants signed by the Government of India with individual princes at the time of merger. There was high excitement when the matter came before the Lok Sabha, and I stood up to make a personal, unscheduled intervention supporting the measure. Subsequently, the bill was defeated in the Rajya Sabha by a single vote, and the whole matter had to be implemented through an ordinance.

Another major controversy during my tenure as Minister of Tourism and Civil Aviation revolved around the Avro aircraft. These were manufactured in India and were inducted into the fleet of Indian Airlines soon after I took over. Later some doubts were expressed regarding the safety of this plane, and there were heated debates in both Houses of Parliament. I defended the plane and its safety record. One day an Avro crashed killing several passengers. I felt I had a moral duty to take upon myself the responsibility, and sent in my resignation to Indira Gandhi, which created quite a sensation in and outside the parliament. On the third day the prime minister indicated that she was not going to accept the resignation. As it transpired, the crash has nothing to do with the plane but involved pilot error. Another unfortunate accident during this period was the Boeing crash in which my good friend and colleague Mohan Kumaramangalam lost his life.

Apart from the ministry, Indira Gandhi appointed me chairman of the Indian Board for Wildlife. The first thing we did was to change the national animal from lion, which is now found only in the Gir forest, to the much more widely dispersed tiger. This led to the launching of Project Tiger, which at one point was hailed as one of the most successful conservation projects in the world. I was chairman of the steering committee until Indira Gandhi lost power in 1977.

Having been a governor, virtually cocooned from the outside world, I found the challenge of the parliament stimulating. Generally, I had a friendly Lok Sabha, but in the Rajya Sabha there was a group, then known as the Young Turks, who made it a point to attack me on every possible occasion. I held my own, but it was not a particularly pleasant experience, although it did give me valuable training in dealing with hostility. It is my conviction that with the parliament one has to be absolutely honest and transparent. If a minister's bona fides are suspect, then no amount of clever rhetoric or repartee can really carry conviction. I was fortunate that during my entire tenure as minister I enjoyed a great degree of goodwill, not only from my own party but from prominent leaders of the Opposition. The parliament is a world in itself, and although one can read volumes about its procedures, it is only when one becomes a member that one realizes the true dynamics of its functioning.

The Bangladesh war, of course, was a unique event in which Indira Gandhi's capacity for leadership was displayed to a high degree. Its genesis can be traced to the whole scheme of Partition, which created a two-headed Pakistan separated not only by a thousand miles of Indian territory, but by widely differing cultural and linguistic backgrounds. Quite clearly, Sheikh Mujibur Rahman and his Awami League were the overwhelming force in east Bengal and, equally clearly, the Punjabi-dominated West Pakistan was not going to accept him as the leader of a united country. One of the proximate causes of the war was the hijacking of an Indian Airlines plane, and as aviation minister I was in close touch with that development.

Soon the exodus of refugees from East Pakistan grew to a massive torrent, and Indira Gandhi sent her ministers to the capitals of the world urging them to restrain the rulers of Pakistan from their repressive, even genocidal activities. I went to what was then the German Democratic Republic, Romania where I called on President Ceausescu, Czechoslovakia, and Yugoslavia where I spoke at length with President Tito, whom I had accompanied as minister-in-waiting when he visited India in the late sixties. I also met the Shah of Iran, who was very worried about the way President Yahya Khan of Pakistan, a fellow Shia, was mishandling the situation. In the end all diplomatic efforts proved unavailing, and the brilliantly conducted fifteen-day war resulted in an unprecedented victory for India and the emergence of Bangladesh as an independent nation. I was seated immediately behind Indira Gandhi when she announced the Dacca surrender to an ecstatic Lok Sabha. She rarely showed her emotions, but on that occasion, she could not conceal her sense of triumph and achievement. That, indeed, was her finest hour.

By 1973 I had completed six years in the ministry of tourism and civil aviation and was keen for a change. The prime minister wanted me to stay in that ministry, but at my insistence she agreed to a change in my portfolio. In November 1973, I took over the ministry of health and family planning. Almost immediately, I was hit by one of the longest medical strikes in history, when junior doctors in Delhi hospitals struck work for over a hundred days. Ultimately, we were able to work out an agreed solution whereby their most inadequate stipend was substantially increased, but no pay was given to them for the period they were on strike. The health problems of a nation like India, with one-seventh of the world's population, are staggering, and although at the apex we have some fine institutions, the base of the pyramid, which is the rural health care delivery system, is still very weak. This could only be strengthened with the full cooperation and support of the state governments, and I did my best to involve state health ministers in collective decisions.

Our major achievement during this period was the eradication of smallpox, probably the first time that a disease was actually eradicated from the face of the earth. The director general of the World Health Organization, Dr Halfdan Mahler, came to Delhi for a special function to celebrate this, which was held at the All India Institute of Medical Sciences of which I was ex-officio president. To mark the occasion, I presented him with a beautiful bronze Nataraja, which now adorns the WHO headquarters in Geneva.

However, it was family planning that really caused a major political impact. I had always been interested in the population problem and had raised it on several occasions during the governors' conferences. When I took over the ministry, I found that the whole programme was grossly inadequate compared with the requirements. The exponential rate of our population growth had already largely diluted the gains of our economic development since Independence and would surely negate all such gains in the future. I therefore took up the family planning programme in right earnest and persuaded the prime minister to include this as one of the main themes in her speeches. In 1974 I led the Indian delegation to the World Population Conference in Bucharest, where my statement that 'development is the best contraceptive' became widely known and oft quoted. I must admit that twenty years later I am inclined to reverse this, and my position now is that 'contraception is the best development'.

In April 1976, I came before the parliament with a national population policy which I wrote myself after widespread consultations with state governments, non-official agencies and experts in the field. I still hold that it was the most comprehensive and forward-looking population policy ever adopted by any country in the world, and had we followed it we could now have probably averted as many as 50 million additional births. However, the whole policy was derailed as a result of a parallel development, the imposition of the Emergency.

I can only touch here very briefly on this unfortunate chapter in Indian politics. Indira Gandhi's finest hour was during the Bangladesh crisis when she led the nation to an unprecedented victory and created not only history, but geography. After that she was at the peak of her power and, had she continued in the same fashion, the history of India might have been different. However, destiny fulfils itself in mysterious ways, and the judgement of the Allahabad High Court in 1975, which unseated her because of a technical flaw in the resignation of a member of her staff, became the occasion for the disruption of the entire political process. There was a jubilant reaction from the Opposition, which saw in it an opportunity to unseat Indira Gandhi which the normal political process was unlikely to give them. They began a programme of mass agitation with the avowed aim of forcing Indira Gandhi to resign, and this in turn touched a vein of deep-seated insecurity which she has been unable to shake off despite all her years in power. It was at this juncture that her younger son, Sanjay Gandhi, stepped more prominently into the scene and, with her blessing, became the leader of the Youth Congress.

It is amazing on what apparently trivial factors the destiny of nations depend. Indira Gandhi had earlier adopted a Twenty-Point Programme and Sanjay Gandhi had added a Four-Point Programme for the Youth Congress. This gave cynics the opportunity to call the whole programme 4-20 which, as is well known, represents a section on cheating and dishonesty in the Indian Penal Code. In order to overcome this, Sanjay decided to add one more item to his programme and that, unfortunately for all concerned, was family planning. With his characteristic energy, he threw himself into the programme to such an extent that in some north Indian states the chief ministers, who saw in him the rising star on the political horizon, unilaterally decided to raise their sterilization targets. At no point did my ministry raise these targets, and in fact I wrote letters and convened meetings of the state chief ministers and health ministers urging them that coercion should not be used. Sanjay Gandhi never directly interfered with my programme, and I do not recall a single occasion during my tenure in which we appeared on a family planning platform together, as we did not invite each other to our respective functions. However, his influence on several chief ministers was decisive. As an example, all the hospitals under the Delhi administration introduced a special fee for those who had not undergone sterilization, but those under the Government of India did not do so.

Nonetheless, the damage was done. Although sterilization figures soared in 1975–76, the post-Emergency backlash threw the programme back by at least a crucial decade. Family planning became a dirty word, and the name of the ministry itself was changed to family welfare. I was succeeded as health minister by one of the oddest politicians in post-Independence history, Raj Narain, and this compounded the disaster. It was only in the early 1990s that the government began once again to pick up the threads of the population control movement. During my tenure we had made three projections for India's population at the end of the century; the most optimistic was 900 million, the median projection 950 million and the most pessimistic one billion. Thanks largely to the Emergency and post-Emergency distortions, it is now almost certain that we will hit the billion mark by the year 2000, with all the horrendous implications that this will have for the developmental processes.

Regarding the Emergency itself, it came as a complete surprise to most members of the Cabinet. I happened to be in Delhi on 25 June when there was a knock on my bedroom door early in the morning, informing me that a cabinet meeting had been fixed at the prime minister's residence at 6 a.m. On reaching there we were told that Emergency had already been imposed, all prominent Opposition leaders arrested and censorship proclaimed. After that meeting a colleague and I took a long drive during which we discussed the situation. It was clear that we either had to support the prime minister or quit immediately; there was no third choice. Ultimately, for better or for worse, we decided to support her.

Had the Emergency lasted only six months, and elections been held as due at the end of 1976, the reaction would not have been nearly as severe. Unfortunately, extension of the parliament by a year provided the opportunity to distort many institutions and bring about fundamental changes in the Constitution. Indeed, although some of us favoured early elections, there was a school of thought which was pressing the prime minister to postpone elections further, but happily she did not accept that advice. I might also record that immediately after the Allahabad judgement I wrote Indira Gandhi a personal note suggesting that she should send in her resignation to President Fakhruddin Ali Ahmad who, in turn, could ask her to stay on until the appeal in the Supreme Court was disposed of. This would have been a graceful gesture and would have obviated much of the criticism that she subsequently had to face. But clearly, by then Sanjay and his group were calling the shots.

After the Congress defeat in 1977, a Janata government led by Morarji Desai took office. Although it called itself a single party, it was, in fact, an anti-Indira coalition of disparate and contradictory political forces. The real hero of the anti-Emergency movement was Jayaprakash Narayan, but he was by then a dying man. Instead of allowing the newly elected Janata Party to choose its leader by free election, he nominated Morarji Desai, an able but rigid and self-opinionated person. Although Chaudhri Charan Singh and Babu Jagjivan Ram joined the Desai Cabinet, both of them were deeply disgruntled. The Jana Sangh ministers Atal Behari Vajpayee and Lal Krishna Advani performed well, but the ideological differences within the anti-Indira Gandhi group were too strong and the government fell apart after barely two and a half years in office.

The actual fall came on a no-confidence motion which we in the Congress (S) had drafted, and which was put forward by our then leader Y.B. Chavan. We decided on this in the Congress parliamentary party office so as not to leave it to the Congress (I). At the time we had no idea that it would release forces that would actually topple the Janata government. With the Janata Party split, Morarji Desai was forced to resign and a coalition government between the Lok Dal led by Chaudhry Charan Singh and Congress (S) led by Y.B. Chavan assumed office in June 1979. I was allotted the ministry of education and culture, areas very close to my heart, but the new grouping was untenable, and it collapsed without even facing the parliament for a single day.

Indira Gandhi's second coming certainly represented one of the most astounding political comebacks in history. However, her last tenure lacked the clarity and decisiveness of her first two terms. Sanjay's death in an air crash was a terrible blow to her, and although she soon regained her composure, it was clear that something of her had died with her son. The crowning tragedy of this period, however, was the horrifying situation that developed in Punjab. Starting with infighting within the Congress and the Congress–Akali rivalry, it rapidly developed into a full-scale secessionist civil war with the ghastly denouement of Operation Blue Star.

I was brought up to revere the Darbar Sahib on par with my Raghunath Temple, and the bloodshed and destruction in the complex was a matter of deep sadness and shame. Surely, there could have been less lethal ways of dealing with the limited problem of flushing the militants out of the holy shrine. In fact, it was political mishandling that allowed the whole situation to deteriorate to that pass in the first instance, and the price turned out to be prohibitive. Not only did Indira Gandhi lose her life at the hands of her own bodyguards, but thousands of lives in Delhi and Punjab were lost in the decade that followed.

In Jammu and Kashmir also, Indira Gandhi's decision to unseat Farooq Abdullah and install G.M. Shah in his place set in train a sequence of events which culminated in the disastrous explosion that began in 1989 and continues down to the present day. Clearly, the calibre of advice that Indira Gandhi received during her last term as prime minister was far inferior to the earlier periods. Personally, of course, she showed tremendous courage in brushing off the trauma of defeat and overcoming personal bereavement. I was particularly pleased that she received international awards in two areas in which I was closely involved with her during her previous tenures—family planning and the environment.

From 1980 onwards, I was not involved in the government at all, but maintained a full schedule of travel within India and abroad. My wife Asha and I have travelled literally to the ends of the earth, and many of my travelogues and speeches are in books including *One Man's World* and *Essays on Hinduism*. In 1989 Rajiv Gandhi, who had succeeded his mother after her brutal assassination and the subsequent horrific anti-Sikh riots in Delhi, called for me and asked whether I would be prepared to go to Washington as ambassador with cabinet rank. I agreed to a two-year term, but events developed in such a way that Rajiv lost the general elections in 1989 and I returned much earlier. I have recorded in detail that whole episode in a book called *Brief Sojourn: Seven Months as Ambassador to the United States*. Although short, the assignment proved to be challenging and exhilarating.

The bizarre human-bomb assassination of Rajiv Gandhi in Sriperumbudur in May 1991 was a tragic event which could well have been averted. There was no good reason why he should have been dragged on an election tour through LTTE-infested areas in the middle of the night, particularly after his special security cover had been withdrawn. After five years as prime minister, and two as leader of the Opposition, Rajiv was just about ready to make his deeper contribution to public life. He and Sonia dined with us shortly before the elections, and when we spoke alone for an hour in my study he admitted that the first time he had perhaps got the prime ministership too easily.

Although Rajiv Gandhi was young and had no previous experience of politics, except his brief stint as general secretary of the Congress, and no administrative experience at all, he turned out to be a remarkably positive prime minister. On the one hand, he undertook a series of political accords—in Punjab, Assam, Jammu and Kashmir, and Sri Lanka—which required a great deal of courage and decisiveness. Not all of these accords paid off, but considering the legacy of conflict he had inherited, his initiatives in this regard have not received the credit that they deserved. In some cases, he overruled narrow party considerations in order to serve the wider national interests. On the other hand, he launched a series of technology missions covering a wide spectrum of developmental areas and brought to bear upon them fresh ideas and insights drawn from outside the rigid bureaucratic system. Here again, while the results were uneven, there were some very positive achievements such as with the National Literacy Mission. Also, by reviving and revamping the Panchayati Raj Bill, he took concrete steps to ensure that the benefits of the new liberation policy and future economic growth would go right down to the people and not get stuck at intermediate levels.

His international relations were excellent, and he emerged as one of the most popular leaders on the world scene. His several initiatives, including the Six-Nation Peace Initiative and the Delhi Declaration, were substantial achievements and, from my location in the United States, I could see how well he was regarded and how the hopes not only of Indians but of the world community for a major breakthrough in this country had begun centring on him. I do not want to comment on the Bofors affair, but it is tragic that this clouded his whole tenure and was instrumental in his not only losing the general elections but, indirectly, his life, because his successor withdrew the special security cover that was so essential for his safety.

He had learnt from his experience and was all set to lead India into the twenty-first century, of which he spoke so often. But destiny, in a cruel twist, willed otherwise. A devoted family man and a decent and dedicated human being, his assassination represented the heavy price that India had to pay for its well-intentioned efforts to help neighbouring Sri Lanka. What tragic irony that Indira Gandhi and both her sons should have met such violent deaths, two of them in the prime of their lives. Such are the inscrutable karmic patterns that govern our destinies.

The second Janata government under the erratic and unpredictable leadership of V.P. Singh, who had joined Indira Gandhi's council of ministers in the 1970s as deputy minister for commerce during my seventh year in the Cabinet, also collapsed ignominiously within 18 months. He was followed by Chandrasekhar who, like Chaudhri Charan Singh earlier, had a tenure of only about six months. It was during that period that I was offered the chairmanship of the Auroville Foundation, which had been set up by an act of the parliament in 1988. I accepted it with pleasure, as it constituted yet another link with the Sri Aurobindo movement in which I have been closely involved for three decades, particularly since his birth centenary in 1972.

Over the last few decades my interests have widened and deepened in many areas. I have found the interface between what C.P. Snow described as the 'two cultures' of science and philosophy fascinating. It enables me to continue the science–spirituality interface with some of the best minds in the world. The India International Centre has developed into a unique forum for intellectual and cultural activities. I had been associated with this remarkable institution as a trustee soon after it was founded by the late C.D. Deshmukh three decades ago. From 1992, as its president, I have been participating more intensively in its varied intellectual and cultural offerings. Membership to the fifteen-member UNESCO International Commission on Education for the Twenty-first Century has helped me to further widen my interests in reshaping education policies on a global scale. As a member of the Club of Rome, I have been pursuing my longstanding concerns about the present condition of human society and its future directions.

My interests have taken me on numerous trips within the country and, literally, to the ends of the earth. During these journeys I have had the good fortune of interacting with men and women of great intellect, varied interests and different cultural backgrounds which has enriched my own conceptualization of the global society. While I continue to speak about the Vedanta and its universal principles to audiences drawn from all parts of the world, I have taken special interest in the interfaith movement through the Temple of Understanding and the Global Forum of Spiritual and Parliamentary Leaders for Human Survival. This developing movement seeks to draw together people of different religious persuasions in a creative and harmonious dialogue. The whole series of meetings and conferences, particularly those held in Oxford, Moscow, Kyoto and Chicago, which I attended, has resulted in the movement gradually taking concrete form.

The year 1993 was a particularly significant year because it marked the centenary of events in the lives of three remarkable men who gave a new direction to our spiritual and political destiny and, as it happened, I was able to participate in all the three centenary celebrations. On 6 February 1893, Sri Aurobindo had returned to India at the age of twenty-one, after fourteen years as a student in England. He proceeded directly from Bombay to Baroda where he reached on 8 February 1893. A hundred years later, we had a big celebration there to mark this historic event, which was part of the homecoming event that lasted a whole year. On 29 May 1893, a twenty-two-year-old barrister, Mohandas Karamchand Gandhi, fresh from London's Inner Temple, landed in Durban, South Africa. I was present there a hundred years later at an impressive public function to unveil a statue of Mahatma Gandhi in Pietermaritzburg where he was unceremoniously thrown out of the train on his way to Johannesburg. On 30 June 1893, Swami Vivekananda, aged thirty, then an unknown monk, sailed to the West carrying with him the undying message of Vedanta and made a dramatic debut at the Parliament of the World's Religions in Chicago later that year. The centenary of that event was observed in 1993 with the convening of a second Parliament of the World's Religions in Chicago, which I attended and at which I spoke several times. Between them, Swami Vivekananda, Sri Aurobindo and Mahatma Gandhi represent the high watermark of modern Indian drought—spiritual and intellectual, moral and political. It is indeed India's misfortune that we are not deriving adequate inspiration from this remarkable trinity.

From the early days of Project Tiger my interest in the environment has widened. Just before the Rio Conference we set up a non-governmental organization known as the People's Commission on Environment and Development (India) which has so far held eighteen public hearings on the environment and its interface with developmental processes in different locations from Jammu in the north to Auroville in the south, and Baroda in the west to Kohima in the east. These meetings have yielded many valuable insights and perceptions from environmental groups and individual activists who are working at the grassroots. In particular, the viewpoint of rural women, which seldom gets articulation, provided an added dimension for all of us who are involved in the mighty task of saving the planet from the most destructive species it has ever harboured—the human race. At Mikhail Gorbachev's invitation, I joined the board of trustees of the Green Cross International and was present at its launching in Kyoto early in 1992.

Although I have not been directly involved in the events in Jammu and Kashmir for over a decade, the continuing tragedy there is a matter of deep anguish for me. It has now entered its fifth year, causing untold suffering, substantial loss of life, extensive migration, massive loss of property and disruption of the economy. Last October Asha and I decided, at the height of the Hazratbal crisis, that we had to worship at the holy shrine as well as the Shiva Temple at the foot of which we live in Srinagar. Our visit evoked a remarkable response not only from the militants holed up in the shrine but from the Kashmiri press as well, which is a fair mirror of Kashmiri public opinion. It received extensive television and press coverage in India and abroad, culminating in a cover story in *Sunday* magazine. It is uncanny how the visit echoed a similar one almost exactly thirty years earlier that I have recorded in this autobiography. It would seem that, though I have moved from regional to national politics and then on to wider global concerns, I still have some karmic debt to pay to this beautiful state founded by my ancestors and, in the process, perhaps to help in stabilizing relations between India and Pakistan for the greater welfare of the more than one billion people who inhabit these two countries.

It remains my conviction that despite undoubted progress since Independence, India has not really played the sort of role envisaged for it by seers like Swami Vivekananda and Sri Aurobindo. Surely, their vision of a resurgent India not merely as another nation state but as providing intellectual, moral and spiritual leadership to the human race cannot be dismissed as mere wishful thinking. And yet, as long as we remain locked in confrontational situations with our close neighbours Pakistan and China, we will not be able to play any kind of leadership role in the rapidly emerging global society. And that, in turn, revolves around a peaceful and acceptable resolution of the Jammu and Kashmir imbroglio. The Kashmir valley, particularly, has since the dawn of history absorbed a variety of religious and spiritual traditions. Vedic Hinduism, Buddhism, Kashmir Shaivism, Sufism, Sikhism, Islam and modern Hinduism have all contributed to the unique spiritual ambience of this beautiful valley. Its erosion thus represents a tragedy much deeper than mere territorial claims, and this process must be reversed before it is totally destroyed in yet another conflict which seems to be looming on the horizon. The problems of the minority regions of Jammu and Ladakh also have never received adequate attention and will need to be seriously addressed for a fair and abiding solution.

When this autobiography concludes in 1967, our little girl was in boarding school and the two boys were infants. Over the years the children have grown and married, and now have children of their own. At the time of writing Asha and I have been married for forty-four years and have six grandchildren, ranging in age from one to twelve. While it is a fascinating experience to watch one's children grow to maturity, grandchildren are in some ways even more astonishing. Talk of the twenty-first century becomes more real and meaningful when one realizes that these children will reach adulthood only after the next millennium has dawned. What sort of a world will it be, and what is the legacy that we are leaving to successive generations are questions which have concerned thinking people, but with the consequent whirlwind of change that is sweeping the world, it is becoming increasingly difficult to cope with the future. And yet cope we must, and that too not merely as wisps of straw blown about by every changing gust, but as creatures endowed with a spiritual centre towards which we must continue to grow as the years pass by.

Indeed, for me the spiritual quest is a central concern, and in whatever situation I have found myself I have tried to keep this in the forefront of my consciousness. My autobiography, apart from dealing with outer events, also seeks to give some indications of my inner development. After the passing away of Sri Krishnaprem,[1] Asha and I continued to visit Mirtola regularly, and soon thereafter we took a Vaishnava initiation from his disciple and successor Sri Madhava Ashish. This was, in fact, my second initiation, the first being a Shakta one from the late Pandit Parmanand in Kashmir in the early fifties. Later, in curious synchronicity with the end of an eighteen-year cycle, Lord Shiva's grace began to manifest and in 1965 I had an informal Shaiva initiation from the American swami Shivaya Subramaniya, who has a beautiful Nataraja temple and ashram on the island of Kauai in Hawaii. Thus, I have had the privilege of bathing in the three main streams of Hindu worship—the Shakta, the Vaishnava and the Shaiva—which together form the auspicious confluence that modern Hinduism represents.

The image of Shiva Nataraja, Lord of the Cosmic Dance, has held a special fascination for me ever since I encountered it during my visit to south India four decades ago. In the sixties I built a Nataraja shrine in the Raghunath Temple complex in Jammu, probably the first in north India. Apart from the images, I got a German friend to fabricate a thirty-inch-high lead crystal lingam which is installed there, under which in due course Asha's and my ashes will lie. Many years later I acquired through a friend a truly magnificent Nataraja standing seven feet high. I had for many years wanted to build a glass temple within which a Nataraja would actually revolve, thus enhancing the kinetic nature of this masterpiece of iconography. For over a decade I explored various possibilities, until the whole matter fell into place during my brief stint as ambassador to the United States. The temple was finally built in Swami Satchidananda's beautiful country ashram in Yogaville, West Virginia, and was consecrated in March 1991.

However glorious the outer iconography, real spiritual growth has to take place within the inner recesses of our consciousness. As the Upanishads say, 'Within the furthest golden sheath resides the immutable Brahman, the resplendent light of lights. It is this that the knowers of the Atman know.' I look upon spiritual life as the essential foundation for our outer activities, as the centre from which all our outer actions should spring, the core to which they should all be constantly referred. It is by thus centring our lives and consciousness that we can hope to move towards realization and liberation in this lifetime. It matters little what we are doing; far more significant is the inner texture of our consciousness. As the Gita says: 'It is by worshipping through one's actions the supreme power that pervades and permeates all existence, that the human being moves towards perfection.' We must all play our role in the vast cosmic dance of Shiva, astride the irreversible arrow of time which is yet a gateway to the timeless. Then perhaps we can fulfil the vision of the Tamil Shaiva saint Thiruvalluvar when he writes in *Thirumanthiram* (verse 3030):

> Entangled in crusted karma that came with their birth,
> they realized Him in the end and golden became.
> He is the spark within the spark of light, the Divine Being.
> If you reach Him, a flaming light you shall be.

From *As I See It*, 2001

2

Politics and Self

GENERAL ELECTIONS TO THE state legislature were held in the latter half of March 1957. Unfortunately, a trend was set in the Valley which remained established for several years to come. Of the 43 seats, 35 went uncontested to the National Conference, thus, pre-empting the results in the 75-member assembly. This was because the nomination papers of the Opposition candidates were in several cases rejected on flimsy grounds. Bakshi Ghulam Mohammad, with all his administrative ability, was an expert in managing elections. In the final result the Praja Parishad in Jammu led by Pandit Premnath Dogra was able to win only five seats, and the rest went to the National Conference, ensuring another five-year term for the Bakshi ministry. The pro-Abdullah forces were kept entirely out of the assembly and did not even contest the elections.

Meanwhile I had been working hard for the second part of my M.A. and in April went to Delhi to sit for the final examination. As it turned out, I did my essays even better than I had expected. When the results were announced later in the year I found that I had averaged 70 per cent in the eight papers, and had set a Delhi University record for master's in political science which still stands. It wasn't really a fair competition, because, while the other examinees had been students, I had for many years been an active participant in political affairs and constitution making. Nonetheless, I was pleased with the result, as I had put in a good deal of sustained labour despite my other preoccupations.

By the time we moved up to Srinagar for the summer the second general elections had been held, and Jawaharlal Nehru had been returned to power. There was never any doubt that the Indian National Congress under his leadership would sweep the polls, but the surprising thing was that the Congress was returned with less than 50 per cent of the total polled votes, a pattern that continued for many years. Senior colleagues who were with him earlier, including Sarder Patel, had passed away, so Govind Ballabh Pant had been brought in from Uttar Pradesh to handle the crucial ministry of home affairs and became an important figure in the Government of India.

Indira Gandhi, though not yet occupying any official position, was beginning to play a more significant role in political affairs. Having known her for several years as hostess in her father's house, I saw it as a welcome development because I could discuss problems of Jammu and Kashmir with her in much greater detail than with Jawaharlal. She was an excellent listener; and though generally she did not say very much, she absorbed information and ideas well and was becoming increasingly influential with her father. At that time few would have been able to predict her spectacular future political career, but already she was developing clear and strong views on various issues, and her unique vantage point gave her a nationwide appeal that none of the post-Jawaharlal generation of political leaders could match. Also, in refreshing contrast with the old guard of the Congress leadership, she had a modern and forward-looking attitude to national problems. She was in Srinagar that summer and I had discussed with her a question that was beginning to assume disturbing dimensions. While Bakshi's pro-India sentiments and actions were welcome, his administration was becoming more corrupt and the calibre of his ministers was generally poor. In those days, enough of the idealism of the freedom movement remained for a corrupt chief minister to be a major embarrassment. Despite my support for Bakshi I did not approve of this, and asked Indira Gandhi to convey to Jawaharlal my request that he and Pantji should intervene to improve the situation. With regard to the new cabinet I said that though Bakshi may be given a free hand in its formation, the importance of removing the abuses in his administration and party should be impressed upon him. I also urged the appointment of a chief secretary from the centre, the speeding up of the integration of state services agreed to earlier, and the revival of a post of full-time secretary for Kashmir affairs in the Government of India, so that a senior civil servant could monitor continuously the various political, financial and administrative dimensions involved in handling this most sensitive of Indian states.

Despite Indira Gandhi's importance, Jawaharlal remained the fountainhead of political power. His prestige in India and abroad was unassailable; despite the heavy pressure of administrative and parliamentary responsibilities, he retained the wider vision and depth of perception that sets a world statesman apart from his contemporaries. Always a man who combined action with deep thought, and who wrote with rare charm and elegance, Jawaharlal took to writing fortnightly letters to chief ministers, setting down his thoughts on a wide spectrum of national and international problems, probing the depths of his own mind and the dim corridors of history, to come up with fresh insights into the events of the moment. Indeed, this capacity to set India's problems in the broader perspective of world history was one of his striking achievements.

From 1956 onwards, he started sending them regularly copies of his fortnightly letters, which were an endless source of interest and inspiration. They showed how, despite his strong views, Jawaharlal steadily moved towards a rounded and more mature attitude towards life and its varied problems. In particular, I was struck by a letter he wrote on 25 October 1957 after returning from a visit to Japan, Hong Kong and Burma. In this he said, inter alia:

'We live in a country where a multitude of conflicts bear us down. Some people imagine that it is only through conflict that the right can triumph. It may be so. But the question is whether the conflict should be based on hatred and violence, or on an adherence to one's principles and, at the same time, always offering the hand of friendship … And so, I come to the conclusion that it is more important to adopt the right way, to pursue the right means, than even to have the right objectives, important as that is. No method and no way which is bound up with the creation of hatred and conflict and which bases itself on violence can ever yield right results, however good the objective. That I think should apply to our national and international policies as well as to our political and economic approaches. If it was once clear that our approach was going to be devoid of hatred and the spirit of conflict, and discarded violence, then it does not matter very much what path we pursue. The errors we make will be corrected.'

Mahatma Gandhi knew exactly what he was saying when, many years earlier in the course of the freedom struggle when Jawaharlal often differed sharply with him, he had said, 'Do not worry, when I am gone he will speak my language!' Always keenly aware of the spirit of the times, Jawaharlal was one of the first statesmen of the post-colonial era to grasp the sweeping changes that were engulfing the world. In the same letter he wrote: 'A new age and, indeed, a new world is gradually unrolling itself before our eyes. The tremendous advances of science and technology are far more revolutionary than so called revolutions in the political and economic spheres. All our past thinking is out of date, even as all past methods of warfare are completely outmoded today. Yet we think in the old way and try to solve problems of tomorrow by the methods of yesterday, which are dead and gone. We shall have to think afresh not only in India but in the rest of the world.'

Looking through the files I find that on this letter I had recorded the following note: 'This letter reveals beautifully the present political philosophy of Panditji. He seems to be mellowing and advancing spiritually, indeed to be developing into something of a sage.'

This Indian Philosophical Congress held its thirty-second annual session in Srinagar in 1957, and I was asked to inaugurate it. I had always been attracted to philosophy, not as some sort of mental gymnastics but in the more traditional Hindu sense of representing a quest for the *para-vidya*, or higher knowledge, through which alone can man move towards the fulfilment of his individual and collective destiny. In my speech I dwelt upon the unique philosophical and multi-religious tradition of Kashmir, which successively nurtured the Vedic, Buddhist, Shaiva and Sufi traditions and produced such outstanding thinkers as Acharya Abhinavagupta and mystics such as Yogin Lalleshwari and Sheikh Nooruddin. I then touched on one of my main pre-occupations, the danger caused by the sharp divergence between the exponential growth in our technological capacity for creating weapons of mass-destruction and the atrophy of our moral and spiritual faculties. 'It is indeed a tragedy,' I said, 'that while we have been able to split the atom and explore the infinitely complex structure of matter, to travel faster than the speed of sound, to explore the depths of the earth and the ocean and the infinite reaches of space, we have not been able to study our own being or grasp the true nature of the human personality.'

My own attempts to tread the inner path continued. Music remained a major interest and I had restarted my singing, this time under the guidance of the leading musician in Jammu, Pandit Uma Dutt Sharma.

Although he never became famous as a performer, he was a remarkable reservoir of classical music in every conceivable raga and tala, and I greatly expanded my repertoire by learning numerous items from him. I only regret that we did not get him to record all that he knew, which included beautiful compositions in popular as well as rare ragas. His young son, Shiv Kumar, was a brilliant tabla player, and when he was only twelve I sent him to participate in an important music conference organized every year in Bombay. He made a tremendous impression, but soon shifted to the traditional Kashmiri instrument, the santoor, which had never before been used for Hindustani classical music. Shiv excelled in it and is now globally recognized as an outstanding exponent of the santoor.

It was when I was immersed in one of the marvellous classical melodies that I would discover hitherto submerged elements in my psyche, almost as if I were a being apart, listening to my own voice. Many of Pandit Uma Dutt's pieces were from the Agra–Mathura school of Indian classical music dedicated to Lord Krishna, and, once again, the enigmatic figure of the blue god began to take predominance in my worship of the divine. That music is a potent source of spiritual inspiration is testified to by almost all the world's great religions. In Islam, the Sufis sang and danced in ecstasy as their dry orthodoxy dissolved in the crucible of divine realization.

Apart from music, I was continuing my daily puja, and a new dimension was added through a chance contact. My essays on a pilgrimage to the famous Amarnath shrine in 1953 had been published in the *Hindustan Times,* and they evoked several letters from people I had not known personally. One of these, a Ram Peare, wrote to me saying that the articles revealed that I was ready for spiritual guidance and suggesting that a person called Raushan Nath could perhaps be of help. I responded to the letter, and after a few months Raushan Nath, or Nathji as he is called among his circle, met me in Jammu. He was then of middle age, and his technique lay in a high-pitched and remarkably evocative chanting of the single syllable aum. This is par excellence the sacred word of Hinduism and receives special mention in several Upanishads and the Bhagavadgita. Interestingly, it is linked with the 'amen' of Christianity and the 'amin' of Islam, proving again that beneath the jungle of differing beliefs and rituals there is a deep underlying unity among the great world religions.

So far, I had known of 'aura' but had not realized that it could be used as a potent instrument of psychic development. Nathji would sit on the floor in my puja room and start chanting the mantra, gradually increasing in intensity until it was like a powerful jet engine ready for take-off. I would sit quietly, joining in if I felt so inclined. This contact with Nathji, which included extensive correspondence, lasted several years. Occasionally I had a curious sensation as if a fluid substance was moving at the base of my spine, and on one occasion it jumped half way up my spinal column. This was evidently a manifestation of the kundalini or the serpent power believed by yogis to reside coiled at the base of the spine.

Sir John Woodruffe (Arthur Avalon) several decades earlier, Pandit Gopi Krishna in more recent times and some others have written at length about the kundalini, its arousal and the powers it brings in its wake. The basic work on this is the celebrated *Yoga Sutras* of Patanjali, written many centuries ago. While all these texts say that the arousal of the kundalini comes as a result of prolonged discipline, including sexual abstinence, and is accompanied by ecstatic states of consciousness, I must confess that I had no such experience. Perhaps this was because I was leading a normal married life and had not undergone any penance or other discipline. However, I *did* distinctly feel the movement in the spine, rather like the column of mercury jumping up and then gradually settling down in a blood-pressure machine.

At about this time I came across another person who was clearly a man of spiritual achievement. He was Swami Ashokananda, who had, after many years of penance, set up an ashram dedicated to Ramakrishna at a beautiful spot known as Nagdandi, just beyond Achabal at the western end of the Kashmir valley. He had a gentle mien and was a man of deep learning. I began visiting him occasionally during the Kashmir season, and it was a privilege to sit in his sylvan retreat and listen to his talk of the spiritual quest in a soft Bengali voice, barely audible against the gentle laughter of the brook that flowed nearby.

The contact with Nathji and Swami Ashokananda helped to bring to the surface my desire for spiritual progress. I had begun writing poetry, and my early poems reflected this craving. I was in search of a friend, the divine friend, who would take me by the hand and lead me into new pastures. With my curious childhood and the plunge into public life at the age of eighteen I had missed an important ingredient—real friendship. My cousin Nasib remained a close confidant and had begun looking after my estates in Kashmir. Asha, of course, had shared my life since I was nineteen, and we had virtually grown up together. After Jyoti's birth there was a period which called for some mutual adjustment, but we managed this quite successfully. Nonetheless, I felt an inner void.

The temple was built almost at the top of the mountain. Our car had brought me to the village of Pannuanaula, seventeen miles beyond Almora, and from there I had walked up for about a thousand feet through the forest, aided by a stick and a servant, until I finally arrived at an idyllic spot nestling in the mountains about seven thousand feet above sea level. The temple, with its grey dome, stood in absolute silence, and the area appeared to be quite deserted, except for the chirping of birds and rustling of leaves. After a search I located a gardener who told me that Swamiji and his party were out for their evening walk. So I sat on a stone bench and, as I awaited their return, I thought about the man I had come to meet.

I had first read about him in Dilip Kumar Roy's book *Among the Great*, in which he had recorded five interviews with eminent philosophers. The one on Sri Aurobindo was particularly interesting, and not only did it whet my appetite to learn more about that extraordinary man, it also mentioned an Englishman Ronald Nixon, later renamed Sri Krishnaprem, who had come to India in search of enlightenment. On my writing to him, Dilipda sent me a book entitled *Sri Aurobindo Came to Me*, which contained a chapter on Sri Krishnaprem. I found him absolutely fascinating, and as my interest in Sri Krishnaprem grew I decided to seek him out. K.M. Munshi, a man of deep scholarship, was then governor of Uttar Pradesh, and I secured from him Sri Krishnaprem's address. Thereafter I started corresponding with him; his letters were answered on his behalf by his disciple Sri Madhava Ashish. It was after about a year's correspondence that I had decided to make a trip to Almora on 8 December 1958.

Ronald Nixon had been a fighter pilot in the Royal Air Force during the First World War. After the war he had come to India in the early twenties to teach English at the Lucknow University. By one of those strange quirks of destiny, which can be attributed either to chance or to divine dispensation depending on the predilection of the attributer, he found his guru in the saintly wife of the vice chancellor of that very university, Professor Chakravarti. Sri Yashoda Mai soon thereafter gave up the householder's life and eventually retired to the Himalayas. Sri Krishnaprem resigned from his Lucknow job and for a while moved to Banaras at less than half the salary. Thereafter he also became a sanyasi, donned the ochre robe and followed his guru to Mirtola where in the early thirties they established a Vaishnava temple dedicated to Lord Krishna. After several years they were joined by Sri Haridas Shastri and Sri Madhava Ashish, and later by several other disciples.

Sri Krishnaprem was a remarkable man, with a scintillating mind and a powerful thrust towards the divine. A brilliant Cambridge graduate, he became a serious student of Sanskrit and Pali, and could speak fluent Bengali and Hindi. He had written several books which I had read before meeting him, notably a series of articles titled *Initiation into Yoga*, a luminous commentary called *The Yoga of the Bkagawadgita* and another, *The Yoga of the Kathopanishad.* What was particularly impressive about his writings was the manner in which he drew on the Western mystical tradition—Plotinus, Hermes Trismegistus, Meister Ekhart—to show that the spiritual quest was a universal one and not confined to any particular religious tradition.

His penetrating insight was matched only by his total devotion to Lord Krishna, 'Thakur' as he called him. Dilipda was responsible for his visit to Sri Aurobindo in Pondicherry, and in a letter to him the great sage himself had written of Sri Krishnaprem: 'You know very well the value I have always put upon his insight into spiritual things, the brilliance and accuracy of his thought and vision and his expression of them. I think I described it once as *pashyanti vak.*' No wonder, then, that I awaited his return from the evening walk with keen expectation, deepened by the absolute serenity of the temple and the spiritual aura of the Himalayas in which it nestled.

After about half an hour I heard voices from afar, and then the small party emerged. Sri Madhava Ashish, a tall, handsome man looking like Gregory Peck in ochre, strode forward and greeted me. Behind him was Sri Krishnaprem, almost as tall, with short-cropped grey hair, bespectacled and with the bluest eyes I have ever seen. I bent to touch his feet and he embraced me with such affection as though we had known each other all our lives. I can still feel the coarse texture of his robe and the strength of his arms as I looked into those flashing eyes which seemed to radiate love and power.

I was lodged in a tiny cottage near the temple which had belonged to Moti Rani, Yashoda Mai's younger daughter, who, despite her chronic ill health, had accompanied them to Mirtola and had died a few years earlier.

Aarati, the evening prayer at the temple, was at seven. I stood as if in a trance while Sri Krishnaprem sang bhajans and did the kirtan in flawless Hindi, accompanied by Sri Madhava Ashish on a small double-sided drum. When the lamps were lit the third person there, a Rabindranath Banerjee, beat on the metal gong and the clear mountain air resounded with the sound of worship. I had never come across anything so simple and moving before. I just sat on the parapet, gazing at a distant star.

The temple was ingeniously constructed with a number of small rooms both on the ground and first floors, which could be kept warm during the long Kumaon winters. Sri Krishnaprem's room was on the first floor leading directly into the shrine, but visitors approached it through a flight of stone steps from the back. Here we assembled after *aarati;* Sri Krishnaprem sat in one corner next to the fire, cooking delicious potatoes and laddus, while Sri Madhava Ashish sat opposite him. I was given a seat on the cot, and we talked deep into the night. It was amazing how alert and nimble their minds were, and what a tremendous sense of humour they had. Contrary to the popular conception that gurus are sombre, rather boring fanatics, here was a pair full of fun and laughter. In one of his books Sri Krishnaprem says: 'Laughter was given by the Gods to man and it was one of their choicest gifts. No animal can laugh, nor does it need to, since it lives in the harmony of the purely instinctive life. It is only Man whose possession of an ego introduces stresses and strains which cannot be avoided and for the healing of which, therefore, the Gods gave him this supreme gift. Time and again it will save us when otherwise all would be lost. He who cannot laugh, he whose devotions are too serious for the healing waves of laughter, had better look out; there are breakers ahead.' Dilipda sent the quotation to Sri Aurobindo for his comments. Pat came the reply next morning: 'Sense of humour? It is the salt of existence. Without it the world would have got utterly out of balance—it is unbalanced enough already—and rushed to blazes long ago.'

Nonetheless, though a sense of humour helps greatly, the spiritual quest is no laughing matter. For the three days I spent there we had extended discussions about my life situation. I gained a number of valuable insights which have since stood me in good stead. He talked of how every action has the elements of light and shade, and how an inner price has to be paid for every apparent outer advance. It is the brightest light that casts the deepest shadow, and he stressed the importance of coming to terms with one's inner urges rather than brushing them under the mental carpet where they fester and finally erupt in unhealthy psychic manifestations.

At one point he said, 'I am not prepared to advise you on what to do or what not to do, but I will say one thing—do not lose the light that is within you. You have it and it is more precious than your intelligence, fame or wealth. It is the *only* thing that will last; don't lose it. Follow what seems to you to be the highest. You will never regret it.' He also stressed the importance of integrating the two halves of the human psyche—the male and the female, the emotional and the intellectual. Without this integration man remains a partial being constantly at war with himself, unable to move onward across what the *Katka Upanishad* calls the razor-edged path.

During the conversation Sri Madhava Ashish would join in from time to time in such an effortless manner that it appeared almost as if I were talking to a single mind divided into two bodies. The relationship between the guru and his disciple—'Gopalda' and 'Ashishda' as they were called—was unique. Sri Krishnaprem's words came from the depth of great spiritual achievement, the vision of a true seer. When he spoke of Krishna, his beloved, the eternal lover of all being, his eyes would glow with a strange radiance and his whole body seemed vibrant with inner joy. Never will I forget the glory of his presence when, along with Ashishda, the three of us would sit by the glowing embers in that little room in Mirtola, talking deep into the long winter nights. We talked of everything—politics, people, relationships, books, dreams. To every topic they would bring a fresh approach, constantly linking outer activity with inner aspiration. They looked upon life as a series of concentric circles, each covering different areas of activity, but all centred in the self. Here were the great teachings of the Upanishads brought alive by a pair of vibrant foreigners and raised ten thousand miles away from India. Keen intellectual perception combined with deep emotional empathy enabled them to analyse my life situation in a manner no one else had ever done, and in the process gave me a deeper awareness of my inner being. And even more eloquent than their words were their silences, when their eyes would lock into a flow of power so tangible that I hardly dared breathe lest it be disturbed.

From *As I See It*, 2001

3

'My Dear Tiger'

THE YEAR 1959 SAW the tragic denouement in Tibet which shattered the Sino–Indian friendship so laboriously nurtured by Jawaharlal Nehru and led to the debacle of 1962, a shock from which he never really recovered. Perhaps it was his idealism; perhaps inaccurate reportage from our ambassador in Peking, K.M. Panikkar, in whose insight into history Jawaharlal had great faith (he had earlier recommended *Asia and Western Dominance* as compulsory reading for senior diplomats and ministers); perhaps it was the growing influence of the ebullient but erratic Krishna Menon; perhaps it was simply the geopolitical realities of Central Asia. Whatever it was, the Tibet fiasco was the first major setback to Jawaharlal and to our hopes of a smooth upward march for the Indian nation.

For us , Indians, in particular, the Chinese subjugation of Tibet came as a rude shock. My intrepid ancestor, Maharaja Gulab Singh, and his band of remarkable generals led by Wazir Zorawar Singh, who must rank in world military history as one of the most extraordinary commanders of all times, had in the nineteenth century launched the great Central Asian campaigns that had resulted in the consolidation of India's northern frontiers and added thousands of square kilometres to its territory. After conquering Ladakh, Zorawar Singh was in fact marching on Lhasa when a particularly severe winter halted his advance and resulted in a disaster at Rupkund. Whereas other groups in India with proud martial traditions fought bravely down through the centuries, it is the Dogras alone who had the unique privilege of expanding India's national frontiers into the heart of Central Asia.

The tragedy of Tibet was felt with particular impact in the state because Ladakh was culturally very similar, and here were many religious and family bonds between that region and Tibet. About five hundred Ladakhi monks were under training in Lhasa when Chinese troops took over, including four incarnate lamas (Kushaks). Kushak Bakula flew down to Delhi to convey to the prime minister the apprehensions of the people of Ladakh about their welfare, as well as about the safety of the Dalai Lama, who was held in the deepest reverence by all Lamaistic Buddhists. Having met the Dalai Lama when he visited India a few years earlier, I too was deeply concerned for his safety. The dramatic disappearance of the Dalai Lama and his close followers from Lhasa, and their escape under a thick blanket of cloud which lasted several days until they reached Tawang, had all the elements of a classic adventure. But while it was a relief that he escaped unharmed, the destruction of the ancient Tibetan civilization by the Chinese was a source of great anguish. Whatever the military and geographical compulsions, many Indians felt hat Jawaharlal took too negative and passive a view of the whole matter. Had we moved immediately after Independence, when China was still embroiled in its terrible civil war, to ensure for Tibet the status of an independent country with a seat in the United Nations, the whole situation may well have been different. But, despite obvious difficulties, it seems that there was inadequate appreciation in those days given how important an independent Tibet was for us, which resulted in the debacle of 1962 and gravely affected India's national interest and prestige.

While relations with one mighty neighbour took a sharp nosedive, those with the others continued to improve. An official delegation from the Soviet Union led by A.A. Andriyev and N.A. Mukhitdinov visited Srinagar in March and reiterated the stand taken by Khrushchev and Bulganin three years earlier that Kashmir was an integral part of India. At my suggestion, they broke journey on their return at Jammu, where they were given a warm reception. Plans for my visit to the Soviet Union had meanwhile been settled, and on an official invitation from the Soviet government Asha and I, accompanied by Professor P.N. Chaku, paid a three-week visit to the USSR, from 23 April to 15 May 1959.

The Russians looked after us with their well-known hospitality. Our first stop was in Tashkent, which we reached on the Air India Super Constellation 'The Rani of Ayodhya' after overflying Lahore, Ghazni and Kabul. Thereafter we continued the long flight to Moscow, where we were greeted by a secretary of the Presidium of the Supreme Soviet, the minister for higher education and a battery of photographers. By the time we reached the charming wood-panelled bungalow on 13 Alexei Tolstoy Street, where we were to stay, it was quite late. During the next three weeks we went through a strenuous programme in Moscow and visited Leningrad with its great Hermitage Museum; Stalingrad, later renamed Volgograd after the de-Stalinization campaign had gathered momentum; Sochi, a Black Sea resort with impressive holiday homes for workers; Tblisi, the capital of the Georgian Republic; Tashkent, the capital of Uzbekistan; Samarkhand, with its startlingly turquoise monuments built by Timur; and finally Dushambe (then Stalinabad), the picturesque capital of Tajikistan. Our hosts had put a special plane at our disposal, so we were able to travel in comfort.

The visit was a most instructive experience. I was impressed by the warmth of the Soviet people, and the depth of their friendly sentiments towards India. Jawaharlal's policy of non-alignment had at last been appreciated by the Soviets, and from Khrushchev down to the ordinary citizen I found a sincere liking for Indians and high regard for India as a great and ancient nation. In several universities, Sanskrit, Hindi and other Indian languages were being taught, and during our visits to the Pioneer Palaces , the ubiquitous children's movement that is such a prominent feature of Soviet life, we met many children who spoke to us in Hindi. At one of these visits I responded to their cultural show by singing a lilting Dogri folk song to which they all clapped in unison.

While closely geared to the official Marxist–Leninist philosophy, the Soviet education system seemed to have a certain purposefulness and clarity of objectives which is sadly missing in India. There is no aimless drift from school to college. Only a small percentage of secondary school students, selected on the basis of carefully planned future requirements as well as aptitude tests, are allowed to enter institutions of higher education, and they are assured of employment after completing their courses. This is in sharp contrast to the appalling waste of talent and human resources that is so blatant a feature of Indian education. The total dominance of all aspects of life by the Communist Party, however, was evident. While the forms of parliamentary democracy were there—elections, secret ballots, legislatures—in practice the whole system is run by the party and there is only one candidate for each electoral seat. Whenever I gently hinted at the contradiction involved in such 'elections', I was greeted by rather embarrassed evasions from our friendly hosts.

Two aspects of the visit made a particular impact on me. With my interest in religion, I had specially asked to visit a church and a seminary. Several places were suggested, and we ultimately chose to visit Zagorsk, a small town about seventy kilometres outside Moscow, which is an important centre of the Russian Orthodox Church. We went straight to the great complex of buildings belonging to the monastery which dominates the town. As our visit was entirely unscheduled it took our hosts a few minutes to contact the local monks. A young monk, with a beard and a beautiful face, finally came out to greet us and showed us around. We first went to the church, and as it was Easter Eve the morning service was well-attended. The church was full of worshippers, mostly elderly women, who kissed the image of Jesus lying in a small sarcophagus. My wife and I lined up with the worshippers and bowed to the relics as we passed, while our interpreters looked on slightly embarrassed. Later we were taken to meet the vice patriarch, who conducted us around the Theological Institute with its museum containing a small but fine collection of religious art. Evidently, this was a training centre for monks and seemed to be supported largely by offerings from believers. Atheism is a central and essential tenet for all members of the Communist Party in the USSR, as Khrushchev himself confirmed to me in response to my query, but it seemed that religious beliefs were allowed to function through the churches, though these were strictly regulated by the State.

That evening we attended the Easter service at the Yelohovsky Cathedral in Moscow, presided over by Grand Patriarch Alexei of the Russian Orthodox Church. The huge cathedral was packed to capacity with devotees, many of whom were repeatedly crossing themselves while tears streamed down their face. The chanting of the ritual was in Old Slavonic, which sounded very much like Vedic Sanskrit, and the waving of the lighted candles and burning of incense to the accompaniment of choral singing was reminiscent of a Hindu *aarati.* Priests with flowing beards and red brocade vestments performed the solemn ritual. At quarter to twelve the patriarch asked for fifteen minutes of silence and entered the sanctum sanctorum, emerging at the stroke of midnight carrying three lighted candles in a silver stand and swinging an incense burner.

'Christ has arisen, Christ has arisen,' he intoned in his powerful voice, to which the congregation responded, 'Verily He is Resurrected.' Then the patriarch led the procession thrice around the cathedral, like the Hindu triple parikrama, where the milling crowd jostled to get a glimpse of the candelabra. It was a moving and memorable experience, this deep symbolic festival of spiritual resurgence in the land of Marxism–Leninism.

The other great experience on this trip was the glorious Russian ballet, which happily continued to receive full State patronage even after the advent of communism. We saw *Swan Lake* at the magnificent Bolshoi Theatre in Moscow, with Maya Plisetskaya dancing the twin Odette/Odile role like some ethereal creature. In Leningrad we saw *Spartak*, based on the life of the leader of the great slave revolt against the Roman tyranny, and also *Don Quixote* and *Othello*, and in Tashkent, an opera called *Din-Aram* based on a famous poem by Ali Sher Navai. Both the hero and the heroine were Kashmiri, and the scene in Kashmir had a set combining the architectural features of the Shah Hamadan Mosque in Srinagar and the Raghunath Temple in Jammu!

Politically, the highlight of our visit was a private lunch hosted by Khrushchev at the Kremlin. After a forty-minute interview in his office he walked with us to another part of the Kremlin for lunch. We had a drink in what he told us was the ante-chamber of Catherine the Great and lunched in the adjoining room. The intimate party, apart from Khrushchev and us, included Andrei Gromyko and his wife, India's ambassador K.P.S. Menon and his wife, and Mukhitdinov, the Uzbek member of the party Presidium who had visited Srinagar earlier that year. Khrushchev was a jovial host and talked a great deal. He said that he was glad to see both of us again looking so well and remarked that he thought my wife's eyes had grown darker since he had last met us. In turn, I observed him closely. He appeared to be slightly less exuberant than during this visit to India but spoke with added assurance and power. At the end of the lunch, after endless toasts in the Russian fashion, he made a speech that was reported in some detail next morning in the *Pravda*. He made friendly references to India and Indo–Soviet relations. Speaking about communism, he said:

'Some people abroad dread the word communism. Communism is a great idea and it is not abstract. Its essence is material goods; food for the people, a strong economy; a wide network of high and secondary schools and cultural institutions.' Before concluding, he observed: 'It is with pleasure that we often recall our visit to India and the hospitality accorded to us by the great Indian people, their government and in particular by the people of Kashmir and personally by you.'

I sent the prime minister a detailed note on my visit to the Soviet Union, and he circulated it to members of his cabinet for their information. I also kept in touch with him regarding political developments in Jammu and Kashmir and broader national issues. I was getting increasingly interested in national politics, and my talks with Sri Krishnaprem had revolved to a considerable extent around whether or not I should join politics. This was in the late fifties, and at the time he had advised against it because he felt that I still had important work to do where I was. However, I realized that although Kashmir was important it was only a small part of our great nation, and its problems could not in the final analysis be solved in isolation. I had no intention of spending the rest of my life as Sadar-i-Riyasat, which was one of the reasons why I had not favoured the suggestion made in 1952 that I should demand a life-term before accepting the office.

On 13 July 1958, Jawaharlal appended a seven-page note with his fortnightly letter to chief ministers in which he expressed his views, 'loud thinking' as he termed it, on a number of major problems facing the country and the world. It was a brilliant piece; the earlier vision of the *Discovery of India* has been enriched by ten years of active administration as leader of the world's largest democracy. He discussed the merits as well as weaknesses of both capitalism and communism and seemed to seek a third ground, which would be a creative synthesis between socialism and Vedanta. In fact, he mentioned the Vedantic concept several times in the note and ended by saying: 'In considering these economic aspects of our problems, we have always to remember the basic approach of peaceful means; and perhaps we might also keep in view the old Vedantic ideal of the life force which is the inner base of everything that exists.'

After reading this note I decided to write to Jawaharlal. 'Along with your letter dated 13 July', I wrote to him on 8 August, 'you attached a note in which you indulged in some "loud thinking" upon the problems that face us. The result was most thought-provoking. Belonging as I do to a much younger generation [I had just turned 27] I thought you might be interested in some random reflections that your letter induced in me, which I have set down in the enclosed note.'

I reproduce below the note in extenso, because it reflects my thinking at that time and shows that several issues—population control, nuclear disaster, corruption in public life and spiritual renaissance—which have remained important for me were already clearly formulated long before I plunged into national politics.

1. *At the outset it may be repeated, because it is not always realized by older people, that ours is what may be termed the post-Independence generation, in that our active political thinking and activity began after India had become free. Thus, even the great freedom struggle, in which you were privileged to play so distinguished a role, has not really got a deep personal significance for us and we judge men and ideas by their post rather than pre-Independence performances. This is not to say that we were indifferent to the freedom movement. On the contrary, even as teenagers, we were thrilled to the core by the great nationalist upsurge that swept the British out of the country. I still remember the feverish excitement when I first (and last) met Gandhiji here in 1947, and again when for the first time you came into my sickroom at Jammu later the same year. I recall how avidly I used to read your books in my schooldays, but surreptitiously, for fear that my father would see me and discover that I was fast becoming a youthful revolutionary, as indeed I was! But my point is that by the time we reached maturity the British had already departed, and the freedom struggle is, thus, not an integral part of our emotional make-up as it must be of older generations. Even Gandhiji is for us a somewhat shadowy figure, very great of course, but nevertheless belonging to the past rather than to the present or future.*

2. *After centuries of servitude we became free, and Mother India, though grievously amputated and bleeding, awoke to a newfound strength and vigour. India's freedom was an event of historic significance, symbolizing and heralding as it did the reawakening of Asia after a torpor of ages. A thrill of pride shot through us as we took our rightful place among*

the great nations of the world and, under your inspiring leadership, began the Herculean task of national reconstruction. In the sphere of foreign policy, we have made a creditable contribution towards the maintenance of world peace and a lessening of international tensions, and your advocacy of *Panchsheel has given the world a new philosophy of peaceful coexistence, which will have to be accepted if mankind is to survive in this nuclear age.*

3. *Internally also we embarked upon an attempt at planned economic development, and in this first decade of Independence we have made much progress on many fronts. But at the same time there is much that is unsatisfactory and indeed alarming in our present situation. The idealism that inspired public life in the half century preceding Independence appears to have largely evaporated, leaving behind a noxious residue of self-seeking opportunism. As you have so often pointed out in your speeches and writings, fissiparous tendencies seem to be growing and caste and communalism, though outlawed by our Constitution, appear to be getting more firmly entrenched. Several observers have pointed out that these forces played a much more important role in the Second than in the First General Election. Corruption has established itself at almost all levels of public life, and it is this above all that corrodes the idealism of youth. Indeed, our generation, which is always the mainstay of idealism, seems to have become largely frustrated and cynical. As you point out, this is to some extent a world phenomenon. But it is yet surprising that this should be so in India, where vast fields of constructive work have opened out before us since Independence and fresh vistas of progress lie ahead.*

4. *The older generation of national leaders no doubt retain* [sic] *their idealism, but they are necessarily fast diminishing, leaving gaps in public life which are difficult to fill. The recent demise of the Maulana is a case in point. As Sri Aurobindo wrote in 1909 on the passing away of Ramesh Chandra Dutt, 'The landmarks of the past fall one by one and none rise in their place.' I am more than forty years younger than you, and between our generations lies a vast gap, only occasionally lighted by outstanding inspiration and idealism. You stand as a titanic figure, forward-looking, young in mind and spirit, full of noble ideals allied with the constant endeavour to actualize them. But, with a*

handful of exceptions, you stand alone, though we pray that you may be spared for many more years to guide us.

5. *What is the cause of this lack of idealism in our country, even among the younger generation, as is so often reflected in our universities? I for one do not feel myself competent to offer an analysis of the complex economic, social and psychological factors that operate to shape the consciousness of our youth. But I think a fair share of responsibility must be borne by our political parties whose task it is in a democracy to infuse a spirit of hope and dedication among the people, especially the younger generation. They appear to have failed in this vital duty, and almost without exception have proved incapable of evoking in our generation genuine idealism on any substantial scale.*
6. *In your note you mention the views of a colleague: 'In our attempts to ensure the material prosperity of the country we have not paid any attention to the spiritual element in human nature. Therefore, in order to give the individual and the nation a sense of purpose, something to live for and, if necessary, to die for, we have to revive some philosophy of life to give, in the wider sense of the word, a spiritual background to our thinking.' I feel that this is a crucial point, because it is widely admitted that the general level of national character—discipline, honesty, integrity—has seriously declined and continues to do so. This is a very serious matter because without a high level of national character the new India of our dreams will remain a mirage. It is our educational institution and, perhaps, the community development organization that must spearhead this 'spiritual renaissance', if I may use the term in its broadest sense. But mere words are not enough, concrete steps are called for before it is too late. The spiritual motive has always been an important element in our past greatness—as witness the Buddha, Ashoka, Gandhi—and if our country is to achieve the pinnacle of greatness, in the future she must adhere to this ideal.*
7. *Finally, a word about our economic problems. Whether or not a spiritual motive permeates us, there is no doubt that we will be judged, and indeed our democracy itself will be judged, by the extent to which we can solve our economic problems and ensure to the people of India a reasonable minimum standard of material goods and services.*

We have of course achieved a good deal since Independence, but the expectations of our people always expand faster than our capacity to meet them, with the result that the gap remains and even grows. I am no economist and so I will not venture to say anything with regard to the method or content of our economic planning, but there is one matter which I feel bound to mention and that is the question of population. In almost all your letters you lay great stress upon the supreme importance of raising agricultural production and the need for a vigorous, sustained and coordinated drive in this direction. This is of course extremely important and must be done. But however much we may increase our food output per acre, however much we may extend our irrigation and improve our methods of production, our huge and rapidly increasing population will inexorably swallow up all that we produce, and millions will remain in economic distress. It appears that the disastrous consequences of our terrifying population growth are not really being brought home to the people. Our public leaders talk constantly on a large variety of subjects but are conspicuously silent with regard to the supreme necessity of limiting our population. It may be argued that mere words will achieve nothing unless we have the concrete means of mass birth control. This is, of course, true, but before any such campaign can be launched we must create the necessary climate of opinion in the nation, particularly in the rural areas. Are we making full use of all the modern means of publicity at our control to educate the nation with regard to this basic problem? We are spending hundreds of crores upon numerous development works, but are we spending enough upon family planning and birth-control on a mass scale? Even China, which at one time impatiently brushed aside the population problem as a 'capitalist myth' that would automatically disappear in a communist society, has now, I understand, adopted stern and active measures to limit its population growth. Unless we do the same all our plans and schemes will be gravely jeopardized, and we will never succeed in lifting the mass of our people out of the morass of poverty in which they have been sunk for so many centuries. Population control is the most fundamental and important national problem facing us today, not excepting even food production. Have we a proper awareness of this, and, if so, are we doing all we can to meet it?

After a few days, he wrote back:

My dear Tiger,

Some time ago, I received your letter of August 8th. I read your note with great interest and, I think, profit. What appealed to me especially was a young man of your generation looking at the world as it is. I wish I could enter a little more into the mind of your generation.

Yours affectionately,
Jawaharlal Nehru

From *As I See It*, 2001

4

Past, Present and Future

I FIND THAT THOSE of us who belong to the post-Independence generation, as I do, tend to take our freedom for granted. Many young people today are not aware of the sacrifices and struggles that went into the attainment of this freedom. Nothing in the world is obtained unless the price is paid, and our freedom was obtained by paying a very heavy price in service and sacrifice through long years and decades by millions of people. I think it is important that the modern generation should be fully aware of this, because then freedom will be something which will be treasured more deeply.

The fact that we live in a free, democratic society as free citizens of a free country is still a rare privilege in this world, because I think the majority of the human race does not have the freedom we have in India.

Here in this school* it is a unique occasion—a 125 years since the school was founded, a long period covering perhaps the most important years of Indian history. I think it is unique that an institution like this should have survived for so long and should have served generation after generation of people living in this country, and today should be celebrating its 125th anniversary.

I hope our friends who have come here from the United Kingdom will carry back with them my personal greetings to the old Sanawarians who

* *Sanawar School, Simla (125th Founder's Day)*

live there, because in a way Sanawar not only links the centuries, it also links nations. The old relationship between Britain and India, one of domination, has changed now to a relationship between equals. I think it is an excellent thing that a school like this is able to act as a binding force across the continents, across the oceans, because the deep link of a school is something that cuts across all barriers of race, creed and religion and even of nationality, and knits people together regardless of where they may be in the world.

As the students of any institution are its lifeblood, I will address my remarks more to the students than to the parents or the teachers. And to the students I would like to say this: Please always remember that living as we are in a vast ocean of poverty and deprivation, those of you who have the advantage of excellent education in such beautiful surroundings are a privileged few. Therefore, you must be fully aware of the responsibility that you owe to the broader community in which you live and of the fact that this rare opportunity you have been given should be utilized to its fullest.

There are four special aspects which I think need to be stressed in your education.

The first, of course, is the body. We want young people with muscles of iron and nerves of steel if a new India is to be built. Building a new country is not the work for people who are weak; I must say that I have been deeply impressed by the tattoo and the parade, which show the students' extraordinary physical skills and stamina. I think it is a very good augury for the future that our young men and women should pay such a lot of attention to physical perfection, because that to my mind is the very first prerequisite of a good education.

The second aspect is development of the mind. We live in an age of science and technology where new knowledge is pouring into the world at a fantastic rate. During the process of education your minds must be sharpened so that you can take advantage of this new knowledge and can help to yoke the power of science and technology to the chariot of India's progress. Intellectually it is tremendously important that you must develop these faculties, and along with intellectual development, you must also develop the aesthetic sensibility, the awareness of beauty, the creation of beauty, through art, music and literature. Here again, I have for the last many years been seeing your exhibitions and the work that is done in this school, and I am very happy that the all-round development of the human faculties of mind, intellect and aesthetic sensibility is being particularly looked after in this school.

Then there is the spiritual dimension. It is very difficult to talk about that, but it is, nevertheless, perhaps the single-most important dimension which differentiates the human being from many other species that live on this planet. This, of course, is a sphere in which there can be no parade and no exhibition; it is something that will develop within you because in the ultimate analysis the spiritual dimension is an inner one. I feel hopeful that, living as you do in these beautiful surroundings near nature and imbibing the beauty of the mountains around you, this aspect also will be developed in the students of this institution.

Finally, one has got to knit these various aspects into the framework of discipline and team spirit. This has been one of our national weaknesses through the centuries. We have never in this country lacked individual genius. We have produced some of the greatest scientists, artists, philosophers, and warriors. What we have lacked from time to time in our history is the capacity to knit ourselves together into a disciplined team and thereby to bring to its full power the various individual resources and faculties that we possess. One of the advantages of public-school education is the team spirit it inculcates in the students. It develops the capacity to subordinate their individual preferences to broader goals, which is a very important part of education, because when you leave this school and go out into the wider world you will invariably find that what you want to do is not always what actually happens. You have to subordinate your capacities without in any way stultifying your inner freedom and your inner independence, and you have got to knit yourselves into a broader team if this country is to become great.

And great this country will become indeed, if it is not already, because this is the destiny of India. For thousands of years, India has survived vicissitudes that would have destroyed any lesser people or country. But it has survived, and today it is the new India that you and I, and all of us, have to build. Indeed, not only a new India but a new world, because old formulations, old modes of expression are dying, disappearing, crumbling, and there is a tremendous quest for the new.

What sort of future are we going to build? This is a question I would like to pose today. It is a future in which the students of this school, I am sure, will have an important role to play. The future we are trying to build is an exciting one. The problems before us are immense—poverty, ignorance, illiteracy, disease, backwardness, superstition, narrow-thinking—these problems have to be overcome. But they can only be overcome by integrated personalities whose bodies and minds and spirits are all attuned to the new requirements. And I would venture to hope that students of this school, when they leave the portals of Sanawar will carry with them that integration which is so important in the building of the new India of our dreams.

There will be difficulties, but your motto 'never give in' provides valuable guidance for one's future life. There is a similar view which has come down the centuries to us. In the *Kathopanishad* there is a beautiful shloka, the meaning of which is exactly this: We must arise, we must awake, we must move forward boldly on the path.

Difficulties will be there, but no individual has ever become great unless he has overcome difficulty, and no nation has ever become great unless it has overcome dangers and difficulties and has thereby strengthened its own inner fibre. Therefore, difficulties should not deter us.

I call upon you, the students, our hope for the future, to gird yourselves, to integrate your personalities and to be ready when you leave this school to make your contribution towards building a new world. There is so much that needs to be done, so much suffering and misery in this world today. There are still today, as I speak here, millions of people in this country who do not even get one square meal a day, far less two; there are millions of children in India who do not get enough to eat, who never have an opportunity of going to school; there are millions who have no shelter over their heads. This is something which must be remedied. We will remedy it; we are determined to remedy it. But in order to remedy it we need young men and women who are integrated, who are aglow with power and force, whose total capacities and capabilities are attuned towards building a new India and a new world.

Therefore, my friends I will end with this great mantra of the *Kathopanishad,* which is in line with your own motto, teaching us that we must push forward. Man is an eternal pilgrim, for man there can be no waiting, there can be no tarrying on the path. Man has got a goal, and until that goal is reached one has got to move onwards despite all difficulties.

From *As I See It,* 2001

5

Three Approaches to Secularism

SECULARISM IS FUNDAMENTAL TO free India and is built into the very structure of the Constitution under which we live today as citizens of a democratic society. However, the mere fact of constitutional provisions is not enough to ensure that the concept is fully grasped, and it is necessary to constantly analyse to fully understand the importance of secularism in our life. This is particularly important where the post-Independence generation, to which I myself belong, is concerned, because for us the freedom struggle—a glorious chapter in our national history—is essentially a historical rather than a personal event. We have grown up on the assumption that India is a sovereign, independent nation, but there is also the danger of taking this for granted. The foundations of freedom and democracy have constantly to be strengthened by each successive generation, if the mighty structure of resurgent India is to grow to its full stature. In this context, I would like to analyse the concept of secularism.

There are three approaches of secularism in India, all revolving around differing conceptions of religion. The first approach is of those who look upon religion merely as an anachronism from the dark ages, as organized superstition or, at best, as an interesting sociological phenomenon, which is one of the burdens that the past has hung around the neck of the present.

In this view, the sooner all religions were consigned to the dustbin of history the better for all concerned. But this school of thought is realistic enough to appreciate the fact that Indians are on the whole a deeply religious people, and it therefore feels that secularism is the only rational and feasible approach that can be adopted. Thus, while fully committed to the concept of secularism, this commitment is based upon a rejection of religious values and can therefore be termed the anti-religious approach to secularism.

At the other end of the spectrum is what might be termed the utilitarian approach to secularism. This school of thought holds that it would have been extremely desirable if all the inhabitants of India had belonged to the Hindu faith, because in that case India could then openly become a Hindu State. However, they realize the inescapable fact that many crores of people living in this country are non-Hindus and that there is little possibility of this situation changing. As a result, they reluctantly have to accept the necessity of India being a secular state. From this point of view secularism is a necessary evil, which must be endured because of the multi-religious nature of the Indian nation.

According to the third approach, to which I personally subscribe, both these attitudes are unsatisfactory and fail to provide a dynamic and positive theory of secularism. In this view, the true sanction behind secularism is that all religions are in fact so many different approaches towards the same divine reality. As numerous streams flow from many directions to join the same ocean, as many paths ascend from different directions to the same summit, so do the various religions, which have developed among mankind through the ages, have as their goal the same divine communion. If a divine reality exists—as I firmly believe it does—it must ultimately be the same for all human beings. Howsoever deep and abrasive may be the differences that divide various religions on the sectarian and denominational level, at the level of true religious experience these must necessarily be resolved into an integral and transcendent unity.

I would submit that this view of religion alone can give us a correct approach towards the whole concept of secularism, because when we accept the basic unity of all religions we imbibe the true spirit of secularism, neither as a rejection of religious values, nor as a merely utilitarian instrument which must be accepted as a necessary evil, but as a positive and dynamic force which must remain one of the cardinal tenets of the Indian Republic.

From *As I See It*, 2001

6

Learning to Live Together

Interfaith Harmony in the Global Society

MOMENTS COME, WHICH COME but rarely in history, when, quite perceptibly, one age draws to an end and another dawns; when we stand poised between a collapsing past and an indeterminate future; when established landmarks disappear and we often seem to be adrift on a limitless ocean; when, in essence, to survive we need not merely a linear progression in thinking but a paradigm shift in consciousness. We have, in fact, reached just such a crucial crossroad in the long and tortuous history of humanity on this planet. There have been many major transitions in the past—from the caves to the forests, then to pastoral, agricultural, industrial and post-industrial civilizations. But what we are now involved in will certainly be the most crucial and difficult of all the transitions that we have encountered so far—the transition to the global society.

Impelled by science and technology, all aspects of life on our planet are undergoing a process of globalization, whether it is politics or economics, commerce or industry, environment or communications, language or music, or any other. The great religions of the world also have burnt geographical boundaries and have assumed global dimensions. While we are, thus, being irresistibly propelled towards a global society, the consciousness needed to sustain such a society is still imperfectly developed. It is this dangerous time lag which is at the root of much of the tumult and turmoil that we see around us today. If the truly religious impulse is creatively projected it can go a long way in foregoing this new consciousness that would unite rather than divide the peoples of the world. "Religion has always been a major factor in the growth of human civilization. Whether it is art or architecture, music or literature, philosophy or law, moral codes or spiritual texts, many of the glorious achievements of the human race can be traced back to the tremendous impact of religion. But let us have the courage to admit that there have also been negative contributions—mass killings, pogroms, inquisitions, torture, persecution, vandalism and bigotry have all, at some place or time, been perpetrated in the name of religion. And the crowning irony is that these have been done in the name of a divinity which every religion looks upon as being beneficent, merciful and compassionate!

We would do well to keep in mind this dual aspect of religious history, because a choice between these two paths will be absolutely vital in the decades ahead as we move into the global society. The Divine Will seems to have decreed that no one religion ever has, or ever will, dominate the entire world. And yet one thing is clear; the religious impulse is far stronger than had been generally realized. India, of course, is par excellence the land of religion, where four of the world's great faiths—Hinduism, Jainism, Buddhism and Sikhism—arose, and four others came to us from West Asia and have flourished for centuries—Judaism, Zoroastrianism, Christianity and Islam. But even in Europe it now transpires that the hold of religion remains a major factor.

The most dramatic manifestation of this has been that wherever there has been a situation of atheistic dictatorship, there has been a mass upsurge of religious activity. I was in Moscow in 1989 when the 1,000th anniversary of the advent of Christianity was being observed, and was amazed at the tremendous resilience of the faith that survived three generations of Marxist-Leninist dictatorship. There has also been a major upsurge of religious activity in Europe, West Asia and South Asia. Some of these manifestations have been disturbing, because they point to a revival of fanaticism and lead to a growth of tension. On the other hand, they also show that religion remains a major motive force for the vast majority of the six billion inhabitants of planet earth!

This being the case, the question before us is whether we are going to revert to the medieval pattern of religious wars and internecine conflict, or move onwards to a new dimension of interfaith dialogue, harmony and understanding. There are several worldwide organizations which propagate inter-religious dialogue, including the Temple of Understanding of which I am chairman.

However, unless inter-religious values are built into the education system, it will be difficult to expect the younger generation to imbibe them. They will either reject religious values altogether and fall into sterile and ultimately destructive hedonism, or they will lapse into the twenty-first century. As the great philosopher and seer Sri Aurobindo wrote, 'The conflict of religions arises because each one claims the exclusive truth and demands complete adherence to it by the method of dogma, belief, ritual, ceremony and prescribed acts. The solution would be to recognize that the real truth of religion is in the spiritual experience of which it is an outer formation.'

One of the measures necessary for this is a paradigm shift in the traditional pattern of present-day education. Instead of clinging to fixed ideas and rigid patterns, what is needed is a rediscovery of some of the insights of various religious and cultural traditions for a decisive breakthrough, a quantum leap into a new spiritual dimension. This corrective reorientation of our education systems, both their outer structure and inner content, represents one of the most exciting challenges of our times. All over the world there is a growing number of individuals and organizations who are searching for methods to expand human consciousness in order to bring about a spiritual transformation. This can be achieved through a new education based on cooperation, collaboration, reciprocal altruism and personal and social responsibility. Only a comprehensive and holistic system of education can bring about a change in our consciousness and expand our personal and global awareness so as to ensure harmony in the emerging global society.

The universal values inherent in all the great religious systems of the world need to be clearly articulated in terms of contemporary consciousness and the compulsions of the global society. For this, it is necessary to highlight the golden thread of mysticism that runs through all the great religions of the world. Whether it is the glowing vision of the great Upanishadic seers or the Jain Tirthankaras, the luminous sayings of the Buddha or the passionate outpourings of the Muslim Sufis or the noble utterances of the Sikh gurus, these and other traditions of ecstatic union with the divine represent an important dimension of religion which is often submerged under the load of ritual and theology.

It is only with such an inclusivist approach that religion will fulfil its true dual purpose—to lead us inwardly towards the spiritual light and outwardly towards peace, harmony and global consciousness. How this can be reflected in the structure of lifelong education that we envisage is an area that must involve the most creative minds in the field of educational theory and mass communication. As humanity hurtles into the future astride the irreversible arrow of time, this represents a profound challenge for those of us who propagate learning to live together.

From *As I See It*, 2001

7
A Nation's Strength

MAN IS ESSENTIALLY A social animal, and this postulates the necessity for dynamic leadership if mankind is to I move ahead. In the Bhagavadgita the importance of leadership is clearly enunciated:

> Always will people imitate a leader, following the example set by his action.

Plato's *Republic* is basically an attempt to ensure for society continued leadership of high calibre, and such examples can be multiplied from the classic literature of all lands. Today, poised precariously as mankind is between the prospect of incredible progress and the danger of utter annihilation, this question of leadership assumes added significance. With the world being rapidly knit closer together by science and technology, the effects of inadequate leadership in any one country can easily spread over vast areas, threatening a global conflagration. The importance of correct leadership is, therefore, more crucial in this nuclear age than it ever was before.

We are at present engaged in the exciting task of building a new and dynamic India. After centuries of servitude we have at last come into our own as a great unified nation, stretching thousands of miles from Kashmir in the north down to Kanyakumari in the south, and an almost equal distance from Gujarat in the west to Assam in the east. Having achieved political freedom, we are now engaged in the quest for economic betterment and social emancipation, without which freedom remains merely an empty shell. In this process of nation-building we come up against numerous difficulties. It is not easy to shake off the dead weight of centuries and surge forward into the nuclear age. Problems of economic development, political integration and social emancipation are grave and forbidding, and if we are to deal with them successfully we require leadership endowed with courage, competence and imagination.

Indeed, a nation's strength depends to a considerable extent on its leadership, not merely in politics but in all fields of national life, including commerce and industry, agriculture and administration. In all these spheres we need men and women with modern minds and a fresh vision, who can cut through the cobwebs of doubt and inefficiency and take the nation rapidly forward towards the goals of justice, equality, liberty and fraternity so eloquently affirmed in our Constitution. Political leadership, of course, is crucially important, particularly in a democracy where the government is by the consent of the people and for their benefit. It has been said that democracy is more difficult to live with than tyranny, because it requires of its citizens a constant series of decisions, whereas authoritarian regimes impose all decisions from above. It is equally true that a democracy is more difficult to lead than a dictatorship, because its leadership must constantly be responsive to the needs and aspirations of vast masses of people, to whom it must render a regular account and from whom it is periodically required to obtain a fresh mandate.

A democracy such as ours requires a broad spectrum of political leadership, covering not only the many thousand panchayats that exist in this country but also numerous other levels of public participation in the government as well as party functioning. With the massive widening of our political base, as the result of universal adult franchise, the problem arises of ensuring a high standard of political leadership. A democracy can only flourish if all those connected with representative institutions maintain at least a basic minimum standard of parliamentary decorum. Recent incidents in several of our state legislatures lead us to wonder whether this basic presumption still holds good. If it does not, then our whole fabric of democratic institutions is in danger of being destroyed. Democracy seems to be on the wane in Asia and Africa, and there is no room for complacency whatsoever. This makes the necessity for adequate political leadership even more important, and I would like to share with you some ideas as on the necessary qualities for dynamic national leadership in a democratic nation like ours.

It would seem to me that the first prerequisite for a leader is to have what I can only term a 'spiritual' commitment to democracy and public welfare. This essentially indefinable quality combines a dedication to the public good, not merely on the intellectual and emotional planes but on a higher moral and spiritual level; a commitment to the development of all that is best in our culture and heritage, and a special concern for the welfare of the backward and weaker sections of society. Without this quality, leadership is always in danger of degenerating into sheer opportunism and the quest for personal power, both of which are disastrous for democracy.

The second essential quality is the capacity to communicate, not only with colleagues and the immediate environment but in the broader context with the vast masses involved in the democratic process. In a country as large as ours, with an infinite variety of custom and tradition, language and culture, and an electorate still largely uneducated, this capacity is extremely important at the national level. A leader, though he should certainly have a strong political base in his own region, must be able to communicate with a much broader segment of the nation, not merely on the verbal plane but emotionally and intellectually. Without this his efficiency will be strictly limited.

Thirdly, it is essential that the leader should have the courage to subordinate lesser interests to the larger national good. With our broad federal structure, it is all too easy to get involved in local issues, sometimes to the detriment of that larger national integration, which is so essential if we are to develop into a truly great nation. A national leader must have the national perspective always in mind and must weigh every decision and every move against this background. This indeed is one of the important ways in which the much-talked-of national integration can be strengthened. It is true that we have emerged from the very grave crisis that confronted us last year with our unity unimpaired, even strengthened, but constant vigilance is essential, and our national leadership must remain actively dedicated to further strengthening national unity.

Fourthly, a leader must have the all-important capacity to take decisions. Decision-making is often an excruciatingly hard task, as it is seldom a question of a clear choice between right and wrong, good and evil. Rather it implies a careful weighing of various alternatives and a delicate assessment of the complex issues involved. At some stage or the other, however, a clear-cut decision must be taken, even at the risk of incurring the hostility or displeasure of a section of public opinion. This capacity to take clear decisions is one of the essential functions of a leader. Too often do we allow a policy of drift and indefinite postponement to hamstring our thrust towards progress, and it has been proved time and again that in the long run such dilly-dallying results in much more trouble than it seeks to avoid.

Fifthly, and this is closely related to the process of decision-making, the necessity to develop a clear scale of priorities regarding various issues concerned with national development, particularly economic progress. So much is desirable, and yet so little is possible. We can make the best use of our limited means only if we have a clear picture as to the ends which must receive priority, otherwise there is the danger of getting bogged down in a vast series of undertakings which fritter away our resources without achieving any substantial result. While expert advice is extremely valuable in this context, it is ultimately the task of political leadership to lay down a coherent scale of priorities which is most suited to national requirements at any given time.

Sixthly, a leader in the modern age should be aware of the mighty scientific revolution that is sweeping across the world and has begun increasingly to impinge upon our own national development. We live in an age of science and technology, in which there is an unprecedented increase in the tempo of change in almost all fields of human life and activity. It is the task of a leader to appreciate the importance of this factor and turn it wherever possible to our national advantage. This is not to say that every leader should be a scientist, although an increase in scientist-politicians would no doubt be a welcome development. It means rather that a national leader must be aware of the broad implications of the scientific revolution that is transforming the world before our very eyes, and must unreservedly accept the importance of technology in our economic development.

Seventhly, a national leader should also have a lively awareness of the world beyond the frontiers of India. It is true that we are a great nation containing almost a sixth of the entire human race, but no nation howsoever large can be an island unto itself, and we have, of necessity, to function as part of a world order. Indeed, one who knows only India lacks an important dimension which is of tremendous value in the task of providing dynamic leadership. This assumes special significance in the context of what I referred to earlier, the dire destructive potential of modern science. Willy-nilly, we are being driven to accept the concept of a world order if the future existence of mankind is to be ensured. The establishment of such an order, however, necessitates enlightened leadership in the nations of the world, and we in India must necessarily play a leading role in this process.

Having outlined what I consider to be the more important qualities which should inform our national leadership, I must mention the danger that always exists with regard to the misuse of this power. Although we can take justifiable pride in having maintained the world's largest democracy intact since independence, there is no dearth of instances in which political power has been blatantly utilized for corrupt ends. A number of institutional and procedural devices have been suggested—and several adopted—to root out corruption, but in the final analysis this can only be remedied when we develop a public morality which spurns the use of such means, for it remains true that a society gets the sort of government it deserves. Indeed, if the qualities of leadership that I have referred to in fact become widely available, this itself to a considerable extent will be an insurance against corruption and misuse of power.

Finally, there arises the question as to our leadership potential. Although the entire younger generation by very definition is a potential storehouse of leadership, I feel that our university youth provides the richest reservoir from which the future leaders of this country will be forthcoming. I have had occasion to travel fairly extensively and visit a number of university centres in the country. It is deeply encouraging to see that despite the economic and other difficulties which these young men and women face they are full of energy and idealism. The real question is whether we have the ability and imagination to tap this reservoir, to fan the sparks of youthful idealism into bright flames that would illumine the future of India—the India of our dreams for the building of which countless generations have struggled and sacrificed; an India socially emancipated, economically prosperous, politically integrated, militarily strong and spiritually dynamic.

From *As I See It*, 2001

8

Assessment of Sri Aurobindo
As a Political Thinker

HAVING SURVEYED THE POLITICAL thinking of Sri Aurobindo during the period beginning with his return from England in 1898 and ending with his departure for Chandernagore in 1910, we may now attempt a broad assessment of his contribution to modern Indian political thought. This can conveniently be done under four headings:

1. His concept of spiritual nationalism and the divinity of the motherland, which imparted an esoteric significance to the movement for India's liberation;
2. His exposition of the ideal of complete freedom from foreign rule, and his role in invigorating, inspiring and radicalizing the national movement;
3. His contribution to the theory of boycott and passive resistance, as also to the use of force, if necessary, to achieve freedom;
4. His vision of the broader role that India was destined to play in world affairs, and his enlightened ideal of human unity that must ultimately transcend mere rational development.

These aspects have been studied in some detail in the body of this work. Here it will only be necessary to sum up the notable contributions made by Sri Aurobindo.

1. We may take first his concept of spiritual nationalism and the divinity of the motherland. This is the bedrock of his political theory and underlies all his writings in this field. In the earliest religious texts, not only of India but other ancient civilizations, the earth—particularly that portion of it occupied by the tribe or society in question—was worshipped as the sustainer, nourisher and supporter of all life and prosperity. The Vedas contain numerous hymns in adoration of the earth, and the worship of *prithvi* is one of the essential rituals in Hindu religious ceremonies. This tradition continued unbroken in India right down to modern times, when Bankim Chandra Chatterjee in his *Anandamath* created the famous mantra 'Bande Mataram' glorifying the motherland. Sri Aurobindo's contribution was to take up this mystic and religious concept, adapt it to the political requirements of India at the turn of the century, and turn it into a veritable dynamo of strength and inspiration. His exposition of the religion of nationalism and the consequent necessity for self-sacrifice and immolation at the feet of Mother India was unsurpassed for its deeply felt eloquence. Brief though his political career was, he defined the essence of spiritual nationalism in a manner which for sheer power and passion has perhaps never been equalled. He thus imparted a new dimension to the national movement, lifting it above the purely material plane and placing before it an inspired and inspiring spiritual ideal. It was his *Bhawani Mandir* that became the gospel of Indian revolutionaries, and it was with a smile and the cry of 'Bande Mataram' on their lips that thousands of patriots faced repression and even death at the hands of their foreign rulers. His concept of the national movement is beautifully summed up in his own words: 'The strength of the new movement in India lies in its supreme idealism. It is not a mere economic movement, though it openly strives for the economic resurrection of the country. It is not a mere political movement, though it has boldly declared itself for absolute political independence. It is an intensely spiritual movement having for its object not simply the development of economic life or the attainment of political freedom, but really the emancipation, in every sense of the term, of the Indian manhood and womanhood.'[1] Sri Aurobindo's contribution to the creation of this 'supreme idealism' was considerable.

2. Next, we may turn to his second achievement as a political thinker, that is his exposition of the ideal of complete freedom from foreign rule and

his role in radicalizing the national movement. Despite the brevity of his political career, Sri Aurobindo did enough to infuse a new spirit into the movement and thus to help change the very complexion of politics in the country. We have seen how as early as 1893–94, in *New Lamps for Old*, he laid out a radical philosophy of politics. Later his tireless dedicated activity helped to politically galvanize the people of Bengal during the anti-partition agitation. The key to his influence upon men and events is to be found in the fact that he laid before the people a worthwhile ideal, the ideal of Purna Swaraj, or complete independence. He had the courage to demand this freedom openly, not as a favour from her alien rulers but as the inalienable birthright of India. His concept of the divinity of the motherland led directly and inevitably to the demand for her complete emancipation from foreign rule, and Sri Aurobindo preached this doctrine with immense patriotic fervour. Not only did he powerfully advocate the ideal of independence, he also effectively demolished the timid and constricted political platform of the moderates. Pouring scorn and biting sarcasm upon the 'mendicant' policies of the moderates, his writings went a long way towards isolating them from the support of public opinion and making the Indian mind receptive to a more radical political programme.

It must also be mentioned that Sri Aurobindo was one of the first Indian leaders to recognize the absolute necessity of generating mass enthusiasm and participation in the national cause, of getting the support of all the varied constituents of the Indian body politic; in other words, of democratizing the whole movement. As early as 1893 he clearly enunciated this view, and trenchantly criticized the Congress for remaining a confined and narrow organization without any mass support. He is thus one of the earliest true democrats on the modern Indian scene.

Another facet of his thought which enabled him to impart fresh spirit into the national movement was his stress on the necessity for suffering by the children before their mother could be liberated. Unlike the proper, prim and correct conservatives who thought that the British would out of their own charity and beneficence grant India the loaf of freedom crumb by crumb, Sri Aurobindo knew and stressed clearly the necessity for a 'purification by blood and fire' before the goal could be attained. His stress on the goal of complete independence, his theory of the divinity of the motherland and the almost religious character of the liberation movement, his emphasis on the necessity of suffering and sacrifice to achieve the goal, all combined to impart a revolutionary spirit to the whole struggle against British domination. His flaming advocacy of India's right to be free swept aside the more modest goals of the moderates and cut them off from the main stream of public support.

Yet another factor in his thought which helped to revitalize the spirit of India was his profound reappraisal of the true springs of Indian culture, of the true greatness of her spiritual heritage. His writings, combining as they did startling erudition with flaming patriotic fervour, caused a stir among the intelligentsia. Of all the great leaders of the radical movement, Sri Aurobindo's literary talent was by far the most impressive, and this enabled him effectively to transmit his dream of the future India to receptive and anxious minds. At the same time his forceful writing helped to break the myth of British cultural superiority so assiduously fostered by the foreign rulers. His contribution towards creating a climate of revolutionary nationalism in India directed at securing her complete independence from foreign rule was substantial. He was, indeed, as Tagore so eloquently put it, the 'voice incarnate, free, of India's soul'.

A word may here be said about a criticism levelled against Sri Aurobindo and other radical leaders that they neglected the important issue of social reform. It is true that they did not lay much emphasis on this aspect of public life, which has now assumed so much significance, but this was not because they considered social reform unimportant. It was rather because they were convinced of the primary necessity of securing political independence before a really effective scheme of social reform could be attempted with any hope of success. They recognized the importance of such reform but felt that it could not precede political independence. To attempt social reform before becoming independent would not only be to put the cart before the horse, but also to fritter away energies that could more usefully be yoked to the national movement itself. It was this view, and not any aversion to social reform per se, that led Sri Aurobindo to attack the moderate leadership for their obsession with social problems.

3. In this assessment of Sri Aurobindo as a political thinker we may turn now to his contribution to the theory of boycott and passive resistance. This has been treated at some length in this work, and we have seen how he was not only a theorist but a masterly political tactician. His

voluminous writings on boycott contain a comprehensive exposition of the theory in its many facets. At the same time, he made concrete suggestions about the positive steps that must accompany boycott if it was to be really effective. Thus, along with his theory of economic boycott he postulated the necessity of swadeshi; along with educational boycott he put forward his views of national education; along with judicial boycott he stressed the necessity for national arbitration courts; along with executive boycott he expounded the importance of national organization; and as the sanction behind the whole boycott theory he placed the concept of social boycott. Sri Aurobindo was one of those rare thinkers whose thought was not confined to the implications of a problem but who descended into the arena of life and tested his theories against the actual demands of practical politics.

A word may here be said about his advocacy of violence, if necessary, in the struggle against foreign domination. This is sometimes levelled against him as a criticism, and it is said he was an anarchist and a terrorist. As for his being an anarchist, the proposition can be dismissed out of hand as absurd. He sought to replace British rule not by anarchy but by national rule. Regarding his terrorism, there is now little doubt that he was not only closely in touch with secret revolutionary groups throughout the country but, in Bengal, was for a considerable time their secret leader and inspirer. This charge, if such it can be termed, is one which is fully in consonance with his basic political theory. Which son, if his mother was being crushed and humiliated by an alien aggressor, would hesitate to use every means including force and violence to affect her deliverance? For Sri Aurobindo the deliverance of the motherland from foreign rule was the one paramount, overriding consideration. To this end all means were admissible, including violence, especially when the foreigners themselves were in India as a result of conquest.

4. Finally, we come to his lofty ideal of human unity and of India's destined role in the international community. Although his exposition and elaboration of this concept took place mainly after 1910, and thus lies beyond the scope of this work, we have seen that even in the 1893–1910 period it is clearly brought out in his political writings. Thus, when discussing the theoretical compulsions behind Sri Aurobindo's political goal of complete independence, we saw that an important factor in his

thought was the conviction that India must be free not for herself alone, but for the benefit of entire mankind. He felt that India had a spiritual message which was urgently needed in the world of the twentieth century; in fact, that she was destined to lead mankind up the next step of spiritual evolution. One of the reasons why he was so adamant that the political goal should be nothing less than complete independence was his conviction that then alone could India fulfil her true destiny in the broader international community.

At a time when India was firmly and securely under British rule, and the prospect of her becoming free appeared extremely dim, it is Sri Aurobindo's breadth of vision that he was clearly able to foresee her destiny as a free nation and to stress the importance of the contribution that she must make to the world community. Thus, in his celebrated 'Open Letter to My Countrymen', written in 1908, he says:

> 'Our ideal of patriotism proceeds on the basis of love and brotherhood and it looks beyond the unity of the nation and envisages the ultimate unity of mankind. But it is a unity of master and serf, of devourer and devoured.'[2]

This lofty idealism in a way pre-mirrored the importance that free India has given to the maintenance of world peace, and the special role she has played therein. Sri Aurobindo's nationalism never descended into narrow chauvinism or obscurantist revivalism. It was constantly placed in a broader international context, and even in the white heat of political controversy he never lost sight of his ideal of human unity, which far transcended local problems and had for its goal the ultimate reconciliation of all conflicts in a syncretic spiritual development. This theme in fact recurs in almost all his writings, from the early passion of *Bhavani Mandir* and *Bande Mataram* to the mature reflections of his later monumental works such as *The Ideal of Human Unity*, *Essays on the Gita* and *The Life Divine*, and must be classed as one of his major contributions to modern Indian political theory. Although at the time he wrote the idea had mainly academic interest, as India was not in fact free, it had the effect of raising the whole tone of the national movement and placing before it an ideal even more elevated than that of national independence. That his ideal of human unity has to some extent been realized is a tribute to

Sri Aurobindo's wisdom; that it has still not been fully translated into action is the measure of mankind's failure to rise to its full stature.

Sri Aurobindo thus emerges as a political thinker of great importance in modern Indian political thought. He was largely responsible for imparting an esoteric and spiritual significance to the national movement, for placing before it the inspiring ideal of complete independence, for invigorating the spirit of India by a reassessment of the true basis of her great cultural heritage, for expounding a practical system whereby the goal of independence could be achieved, and for placing the whole movement in the broader context of internationalism and the ideal of human unity. For a person to have done this in the short period of hardly five years of active political life is no mean achievement. Sri Aurobindo must be counted among the great builders of modern India, as he contributed nobly towards laying the foundations for the edifice of national freedom which Mahatma Gandhi and others later reared. Even after 1910 his interest in Indian freedom remained undiminished, and he lived to see the fruition of his work when India finally achieved Independence on his seventy-fifth birthday, the fifteenth of August 1947.

From *Prophet of Indian Nationalism*, 1963

9

A Judgement for India

The ruling on the Section 377 case was grounded in logic, law and history

THE INDIAN PENAL CODE insofar as it criminalizes consensual sexual acts of adults in private is violative of Articles 14, 15 and 21 of the Constitution. These words in the Delhi High Court judgement of 1 July 2009 have stated the situation clearly and unambiguously. Indeed, it is surprising that an outmoded colonial law, introduced during Victorian times, should have remained in our statute book for so many years since Independence. Our former colonial masters' motivation for the law was clear: to prevent any physical contact between the young British civil and military officers who came out to administer India and the natives; its equivalent in the United Kingdom was repealed decades ago.

We are perhaps the last liberal, democratic country in the world to have decriminalized homosexuality, and now join 126 countries around the world that have already done so. This will come as a long-awaited relief to a particularly vulnerable section of society which, even if we accept claims that it is only 2 per cent of our population against the generally accepted figure of 10 per cent, would include over 20 million people.

The judgement has sparked off a lively debate; the media, both electronic and print, has been largely supportive. Some points need to be clarified. The judgement in no way propagates homosexuality; all it does is to ensure the fundamental right of equality, non-discrimination and personal liberty guaranteed to every Indian citizen under our Constitution. It is also important to note that it does not decriminalize non-consensual sex or paedophilia, which will remain cognizable offence subject to severe punishment.

The argument that some religious leaders are against the judgement cannot become a deciding factor. I recall that when in the early fifties, Pandit Jawaharlal Nehru and B.R. Ambedkar piloted the Hindu Code Bill through the parliament, there were a large number of Hindu leaders including some Shankaracharyas who were strongly opposed to it, as was then-president Rajendra Prasad. Nonetheless, they pushed it through, thereby ensuring that the 800 million Hindus in India today live in a much more equitable and fair society than earlier. Similarly, all Christian denominations are not against same-sex relationships. The Roman Catholic Church certainly is; they also oppose contraception, but that does not mean that we should stop our family welfare and condom distribution programmes.

As far as Muslim communities are concerned, conservative leaders might take a rigid stance, but younger people are likely to be less dogmatic. In any case, if one looks at the great Sufi tradition within Islam, we find that they celebrated love, both human and divine, in all its multifaceted glory.

The argument that this is against nature is also not viable. To begin with, for the LGBT community, their lifestyle is just as natural as heterosexual relationships. Also, this argument of nature can be pushed to extremes. It is not natural, after all, to wear clothes; or to eat cooked food. Nature is much more varied and inclusive than many realize, and varied sexuality has been found in almost all cultures, ancient and modern, around the world.

It is often forgotten that some of the greatest artists and musicians, rulers and conquerors, philosophers and poets in history have been gay or bisexual. Same-sex love was one of the bases of the ancient Greek civilization that produced such great thinkers as Socrates, Plato and Aristotle who laid the philosophical foundations of Western civilization.

In India, too, the *Kama Sutra* clearly mentions same-sex love in a very matter-of-fact manner, and the Khajuraho sculptures depict it graphically. In our magnificent iconography, the ultimate integration of the masculine and feminine archetypes is found in the concept of Ardhanarishvara;

in the broader philosophical context, the Vedanta believes that the divine resides in all human beings, in which case discrimination on any basis including sexual preference is unacceptable.

To conclude, therefore, one can say that the historic judgement of the Delhi High Court marks a positive step in widening the scope of our inclusive democratic structure and rescuing millions of citizens from the shadow of an archaic and outmoded colonial legacy.

SECTION 377 of the Indian Penal Code was introduced in 1864 during the British rule in India. Modelled on the Buggery Act of 1533, it is used to criminalize homosexual activities 'against the order of nature'.

Portions of the section were first struck down as unconstitutional with respect to homosexuality by the Delhi High Court in July 2009.

On 6 September 2018, the Supreme Court of India announced that the application of Section 377 to consensual sex between adults of the same sex was unconstitutional, 'irrational, indefensible and manifestly arbitrary' but that Section 377 remains in force relating to sex with minors, non-consensual sexual acts and bestiality.

Karan Singh was the first among the political leaders to stand in support of LGBT rights, at a time when politicians and communities were largely against the judgement. He continues to support the right to sexual preference.

Published by *The Indian Express*, 16 July 2009

Travelogues

1

Whatever Became of the Twelfth Night?

NEW YORK, OF COURSE, is unique. There may be other cities scenically more beautiful or architecturally more distinguished, but the glass and aluminium canyons of Manhattan epitomize, more than any other city, the new dimensions of twentieth century living. I spent over a year in New York two decades ago. At that time, I had flown out in a lumbering four-engine Skymaster, and it had taken almost two days from Bombay. This time, on Air India's 'Maharaja' service, the trip took only a few hours. A modern jetliner is one of the most highly researched consumer products of our age, and having taken half a dozen different airlines, on this trip I realized more than ever before the high level of technical competence that has now been built into the international tourism industry. My wife and I covered 40,000 miles around the world in twenty days, chalking up an average of 2,000 miles a day for three weeks.

On this trip I visited an exhibition of modern art at a museum in New York and had my first introduction to kinetic sculpture. The most interesting exhibit consisted of five plexiglass columns, each about eight feet high, behind which multi-coloured lights traced an intricate, ever-changing pattern of psychedelic luminosity. Sitting opposite this on a low bench, and watching it quietly for a few minutes, one feels a strange sense of unreality seeping into the mind and is transported partly out of one's self into a different dimension. I suppose this transporting quality is the real essence of any artistic work, and from that standard this 'sculpture' is indeed an artistic triumph. I also saw an unforgettable motion picture, *2001: A Space Odyssey*, in which director Stanley Kubrik has created virtually a new cinematic vocabulary to deal with the fantastic possibilities—photogenic and philosophical—of outer space. It is a film that will surely go down in history as the first really meaningful attempt to grapple with the staggering implications of outer space and its impact upon our tight little minds. The scenes of outer space can only be described as out of this world, and the theme is handled with a Vedantic nuance which made the film particularly fascinating.

From New York we took a non-stop eleven-hour flight to Buenos Aires, the huge bustling capital of Argentina. Not particularly distinguished as a city for architectural or natural beauty, Buenos Aires is nevertheless a dynamic metropolis which well reflects its role as the capital of South America's most prosperous and powerful nation. The aviation conference I attended was concerned largely with the implications of revolutionary new developments in aircraft design and performance that will be upon us in the early seventies. The meetings were held in a brand-new conference hall in the heart of the city, the marble flooring of which was as beautiful as it was treacherous. On the very first day the distinguished chief delegate from Belgium came crashing down on a glass table, narrowly escaping serious injury.

The real surprise for me in Argentina, however, was an unscheduled visit to its mountain and lake resort of Bariloche in the north-west, set in the stunning beauty of the Andes. The Andes are to South America what the Himalayas are to India, the repository alike of natural beauty and spiritual inspiration. There was something wild about the Andean lake whipped into fury by a brisk wind, on the shores of which our hotel was placed, and from our room we got a marvellous view of the surrounding snow-capped peaks. Driving through the mountains I noticed that the Andean peaks were much sharper, almost needle-like, compared with the more gradual slopes to which we in India are accustomed. The resort hotel at Llao Llao (pronounced, somewhere between '*jao jao*' and '*lao lao*'!) was closed for the winter, but another ski hotel nearby was open and packed with agile, young skiers dressed in tight-fitting ski suits and heavy, multi-coloured sweaters. Bariloche is almost the antipodes of Kashmir, and early September found the Andes deep in winter.

Perhaps the most fascinating of all our flights on this trip was the single-day journey across two continents, from Buenos Aires to San Francisco. We flew across vast, uninhabited plains, rugged mountains without any trace of vegetation, dazzling white salt flats like giant craters on the moon, occasional patches of chalky blue lake. Of habitation there were few traces apart from the capital cities, and flying, thus, one realizes how sparsely populated this great continent is. Our first stop was La Paz, capital of Bolivia and the highest international airport in the world, which bore a striking resemblance to Ladakh with its naked mountains and rarefied air. A new airport was under construction and even the workers, with whom I chatted amiably in the international language of grin and gesture, looked very Ladakhi with their high cheekbones. From La Paz we flew to Lima on the Pacific coast, then to the sweltering equatorial capital of Panama where we changed planes, then to Guatemala, then to Los Angeles, and finally, after almost 24 hours in the air, to San Francisco. The flight was a dramatic example of technological progress; a trip that would take weeks—even months—by land was covered in utmost air-conditioned comfort in less than a day. From the bottom of South America to the top of North America, spanning almost half the globe, one can jet through the air with the greatest of ease without a single bump!

San Francisco, situated on a magnificent bay opening on to the mighty Pacific, and with the great bridge standing at its Golden Gate reflecting the rays of the setting sun, is indeed beautifully set. Architecturally, however, it reflects an uneasy mixture of the old and the new. Looking at it from the bay, on which we had lunch on board a boat, one can see how attractive it must have been before the skyscrapers began reaching upwards. An attractive feature of the city, in sharp contrast to the straight lines of New York, is that it is built on a series of hills so that one is all the time driving either uphill or down, and in between catching narrow glimpses of the ocean at the end of every street.

San Francisco is the acknowledged hippy capital of the world. We drove past several hippy colonies and also visited a psychedelic discotheque. A vast hall, filled with several hundred people, resounded with the beat of some of the loudest and fastest music I had ever heard, produced by a six-man orchestra playing at one brightly illuminated end. The rest of the hall was in darkness, and on its walls a constant series of images were being projected from a sort of magic lantern, all moving steadily clockwise. Many of the symbols were Hindu, images of Krishna and Shiva; bearded yogis were interspersed with the faces and torsos of film stars and a fascinating melange of disconnected pictures. All the people in the room had long hair, and the boys invariably wore beards. It appeared as if many of the people were under the influence of some sort of drug, but what struck me most was that despite the bizarre setting there was no atmosphere of violence or tension. The hippies seem on the whole to be a surprisingly gentle race, and it was as if we were witnessing some sort of rite in an underground cave.

The whole phenomenon, set as it is in the heart of the affluent society, is strange and thought-provoking. These people have deliberately turned their backs on the norms and values of the society in which they live and are trying to create their own ethos. Despite all its aberrations, it does reflect the basic human dilemma that while man cannot live without bread, bread by itself can never satisfy him. It would appear as if a vast inner void has appeared in the heart of western youth, and they grope towards a new certitude. The old is dead and the new is yet to be born, and they find themselves suspended, as it were, in mid-air without any psychological or spiritual support.

Our next hop was from San Francisco to the islands of Hawaii, specks of land amid the liquid vastness of the Pacific Ocean. The tiny islands receive a million tourists a year, which is five times as many as we get in India. Their whole economy is based upon pineapple and tourists, and I was much impressed by the manner in which they have developed their tourism infrastructure. Sleek new hotels soar upwards into the sky, and the beautiful beaches are thronged with holidaymakers in colourful attire. The history of these Polynesian islands is a fascinating one, and there is little doubt their culture has deep roots in India although at one remove, because the islands were colonized from South East Asia. Watching the swaying Hawaiian dances one can see clearly that they are a sort of liquefied Bharatanatyam.

One of the highlights of Hawaii is its museum containing some marvellous works of Polynesian art, including the magnificent million-feathered cloak of King Kamehameha. Another is the Sea Life Park, where dolphins perform an extraordinary variety of tricks and a whale jumps twenty-three feet into the air for its lunch. The Hi Kai hotel, in which we stayed, has a glass elevator which takes one directly from the ground to the thirtieth floor. Riding it at night is a rare experience; as one rises, the lights of Honolulu emerge out of the darkness, providing an ideal setting for a Hitchcock film. The new shopping centre, with hundreds of shops within a single complex, is a paradise for tourists who come from affluent societies free from foreign-exchange restrictions. For us it is a valuable experience in spiritual discipline; as the poet Akbar Allahabadi says, '*bazaar se guzra hun, kharidddar nahin hun!*'

Life is full of odd coincidences. A quarter of a century ago I acted in Shakespeare's *Twelfth Night* at my school, and in San Francisco I met after many years a friend who had taken a leading part in this play. It so happened that on this trip I lost the twelfth night completely. We flew from Hawaii on the morning of the twelfth, but by the time we had covered the eight-hour flight to Tokyo it was already the evening of the thirteenth as we crossed the international dateline, losing one day in the process. It is an interesting philosophical conundrum as to what exactly happened to the twelfth night. How, let us say, would I have kept a New Year's resolution to have mushrooms of toast for dinner on the night of 12 October?

The beauty of Japan lies largely outside Tokyo, as I had discovered on an earlier visit. This time the most memorable part of my stay was a morning I spent in a Zen temple. For long I had wanted to make a somewhat deeper study of the relationship between Zen and Vedanta, and I was fortunate to have been put in touch with a young professor of the Tokyo University who took me to the Sojiji Temple, an hour's drive from the heart of Tokyo. An atmosphere of great calm befell us as soon as we entered the precincts of the temple. It is situated in a vast compound containing several structures, including a magnificent, wooden prayer hall where thousands can congregate, residential quarters for the monks and novices, a library and other academic buildings. We walked around the temple, and the professor—who had spent some time there as a novice—showed me the living quarters, the washrooms and the kitchens, all spotlessly clean. We finally made our way to the meditation room where we sat quietly for an hour, and I tried to absorb the living presence of Zen, to understand that which is essentially incomprehensible, to hear the voice of the silence.

The trip back from Tokyo to Delhi was one long series of boarding and disembarkation. Hong Kong, Bangkok, Singapore, Jakarta, Madras and Bombay all flashed past in the strange euphoria which prolonged jet travel induces. On the way we broke journey for a day at Jakarta. It was very warm there, but I also noticed a new warmth of feeling towards India, which is a refreshing contrast to the strange hostility evinced by the earlier regime. We finally returned to Delhi on the nineteenth morning, just in time to face the strike!

It had been a complete circumambulation of the globe, and yet with the new developments in aviation that will be upon us in the seventies this trip itself will soon appear obsolete. With our growing knowledge and technical competence, we will soon be jetting around the world faster than the speed of sound. One question, however, remains unanswered. Will mankind develop the wisdom so urgently required if his growing knowledge is to be put to constructive uses? Or, are we now witnessing the last few decades of human life on earth? Will we all disappear as in *The Twelfth Night* into a nuclear inferno, or will we hearken to the voice of the silence before it is too late?

From *Contemporary Essays*, 1971

2

Some Impressions of Japan

I HAD OCCASION RECENTLY to visit Japan for the first time. The outstanding impression that I formed during a fortnight's stay was of a people endowed with immense dynamism and vitality, enjoying all the benefits of technological affluence but retaining a distinctive quality to their life and culture.

It is common knowledge that the Japanese are economically advanced, but one is so psychologically conditioned to thinking of Asia as a poor, backward continent that it comes as a refreshing surprise to visit Japan, and actually see how an Asian nation has succeeded in breaking the shackles of poverty and taking its place among the most industrially advanced nations of the world.

This is all the more impressive when one realizes that Japan has an area of only about 142,000 square miles , and a population of almost ten crores. What is more, Japan has succeeded in establishing a democratic form of government which, along with our own, is a landmark of democratic functioning in the whole of Asia, and it has achieved all this despite a crushing and traumatic defeat hardly two decades ago. The reasons for this clearly lie deep in the history and character of the Japanese people, especially in the extraordinary phase known as the Meiji Restoration. The rule of Emperor Meiji (1867–1912) saw a complete transformation and modernization of the Japanese structure of life and economy, from the abolition of the feudal system to a restoration of the imperial powers and finally the adoption of a cabinet system of government.

It was obviously not possible for me in a short visit to study the Japanese experience in any detail, but there are some features by which even a cursory visitor to Japan cannot fail to be impressed. The first is the physical fitness, vitality and dynamism of the people. I saw hardly a local who was either overfat or emaciated, and though short of stature, the people seem to have attained a high standard of physical fitness. This is specially marked among the children who are a pleasure to behold—smiling, pink-cheeked and bursting with enthusiasm and vitality.

The second characteristic is the capacity for hard and disciplined work. I gathered that Japanese office hours are considerably longer than ours, and their discipline is visible even to the casual observer. My visit happened to coincide with the spring vacation, and there were thousands of Japanese schoolchildren in all the tourist spots. They are invariably dressed in uniform, the boys wearing black close- collar coats with metal buttons and peak caps, while the girls are in dark-blue frocks. The manner in which these children march along the streets under the guidance of a leader carrying a coloured flag is quite remarkable. When they are to cross a road they all collect in a disciplined manner, wait for the traffic to stop and then cross swiftly following their leader. This is in marked contrast to the haphazard and lackadaisical manner in which our children roam about the streets. This phenomenon is visible even in the case of groups of elderly village women who are taken around places of historic and religious interest in groups. Buses collect them from their villages, they are taken on a tour under the guidance of a young leader, and then they are escorted back to their homes. These groups of the very old and the very young were strikingly similar in the quiet and disciplined manner in which they undertook their sightseeing.

I was extremely interested to discover whether modern Japan retains a vital link with its past culture or whether defeat in war and a period of foreign occupation have caused a break in their cultural pattern. I must again admit that it was difficult for me to form any accurate impression in the space of a fortnight, but I was struck by the fact that the Japanese have retained a very distinctive pattern of culture. This is reflected in the almost exclusive use of the Japanese language at all levels of administration and life, even more so by the superb temples and shrines that are to be found throughout Japan. The two major faiths are Buddhism, which came from India via China and Korea around the middle of the sixth century, and

Shintoism, which centres on the worship of imperial and family ancestors. These two religions coexist and often overlap, with many Japanese observing Shinto rites during marriage ceremonies and Buddhist rites during funerals.

I visited a number of Buddhist and Shinto shrines in Tokyo, Kamakura, Hakone and especially Kyoto, which was the capital for a thousand years from the eighth to the eighteenth century, and the charming little town of Nara which was the first capital of Japan in the seventh century. In marked contrast to many of our own temples, specially in north India, Japanese shrines are scrupulously clean and pervaded by an aura of peace and calm. Many of these shrines are placed in huge wooded parks, or nestle on hill sides, and although they may be within some of the most highly populated cities in the world, they retain an atmosphere of absolute quiet. A striking example of this is the Meiji Shrine in the heart of Tokyo. The shrine grounds in the centre of the world's largest city occupy an area of about seven lakh square metres and contain almost one lakh trees of various kinds. Deep within this atmosphere of awe-inspiring solemnity is the main shrine and other buildings. Most Japanese shrines are constructed in wood, and in keeping with the general tradition of Japanese architecture, they merge tastefully in the surroundings. Outside every Shinto shrine there is a gate consisting of two pillars surmounted by two curved, horizontal beams, which is a symbol of purification. The idea being that by passing under them one is purified in mind and body before entering the presence of the deity. The Shinto shrines have no statues, and the sanctum sanctorum is a dimly lit room, representing the dwelling place of the deity to whom that particular shrine is dedicated.

My most memorable temple visit in Japan took place by chance. We were driving through the beautiful Fuji-Hakone-Izu National Park in fog and rain, when suddenly we came upon a lake with a thickly wooded hill rising out of it. At the foot of this was a Shinto gate standing in solitary beauty, and from there a steep flight of steps led up into the mountain. The prospect was irresistible, so I stopped the car and walked up. About a hundred stone steps led through the thick forest, and huge cedars thrust upwards into sky on either side. It was raining steadily, and a translucent fog covered the whole scene. At the top of the steps was another Shinto gate, and then I came suddenly upon a lovely wooden shrine. It was deserted but the room inside glowed with the mellow light of paper lanterns, as if the deity had just stepped out of the room and was due to return any minute. I stood quietly in front of the shrine, the rain from the roof pattering loudly on my umbrella. All around mighty trees swayed in the wind, but inside the shrine and inside my heart there was absolute peace and stillness.

The Buddhist shrines of course contain statues of the Buddha. The famous Kamakura Buddha which sits in the open looking out on to the sea is over seven hundred years old and forty-four feet high. Even more beautiful is the Todaiji Temple housing a magnificent bronze statue of the Buddha about fifty-three feet high and weighing nearly 500 tons. This temple is said to be the largest wooden structure in the world, and the statue the world's largest bronze. Apart from Buddhist and Shinto shrines, many other deities are also worshipped in Japan, including the goddess in various forms. I was particularly interested to visit the Asakusa temple near Tokyo dedicated to Kannon, the goddess of mercy, who would seem to be comparable to Mahalakshmi.

No article on Japan, howsoever brief, can fail to mention the superb gardens which are among the most beautiful in the world. The whole theory of Japanese garden architecture differs from that of the West, and for that matter from our own tradition of Mughal gardens. Whereas we strive for symmetry and geometrical lines, the Japanese gardens are superbly asymmetrical, the attempt being to interfere with nature only as little as is absolutely necessary to give the garden shape and beauty. Thus, on entering a Japanese garden one is struck by the great artistry with which the natural configuration of land, water, rock and vegetation is used, and it is only gradually that one realizes the immense effort that must have gone into creating these masterpieces of landscape architecture. The famous gardens of Kyoto are outstanding in this respect, specially the Kinkakuji (golden pavilion) and Ginkakuji (silver pavilion).

I must make special mention of the extraordinary rock garden in Kyoto's Ryoanji Temple. The main purpose of temple gardens in Japan, particularly those dedicated to various Zen sects, is to create an atmosphere of calm contemplation which finally leads to satori or enlightenment. The Ryoanji rock garden is famous in this regard, having been built at the end of the fifteenth century by the Zen master Soami. It consists of a rectangle of pure white sand carefully raked into broad parallel lines, with fifteen rocks of varying sizes placed therein. The only vegetation is a border of moss round the bigger stones and—to quote *Meet with Japan*, the superb travel book by Tosco Maraini—'... its interest lies in the harmony of its spatial relations and the significance of its tactile values. It makes no facile appeal to the senses, and ornament is totally excluded. It is a direct journey into the void from which the all is born ...'

Through the centuries, observers have claimed to read all sorts of symbolic meanings into this garden. For myself, I was immediately reminded of the photographs taken of galaxies in interstellar space. Each group of rocks appeared to symbolize these mighty galaxies whirling in outer space, and the whole garden thus became a superb symbolic representation of the vast unfathomable universe—*anadi-ananta*, without beginning or end—the eternal cosmic being and becoming.

These were my outstanding impressions; of course there were many more—the superb works of art that I saw in the museums, which clearly revealed their Indian inspiration; the dance performances expressing the colourful charm of modern Japan; the glittering variety of consumer goods in the multi-storey department stores; the friendliness of the people despite difficulties in communication; the superb roads and especially the New Tokaido Line, which is the world's fastest railway running smoothly at over 150 miles an hour; a stunning view of Mount Fujiyama from the air, its base covered in an ocean of cloud and its snowy cone glittering majestically against the blue morning sky.

I will close with one general remark. India and Japan today are the leading democracies in Asia, and it is essential that our two countries get much closer to each other than they are at present. While the original impact of India on Japan through Buddhism over a thousand years ago is important, it is not enough merely to depend upon that link. It is essential that contemporary India and contemporary Japan collaborate in a large variety of technological, economic, academic and even political undertakings. There is immense goodwill for India in Japan, but I do feel that during the eighteen years of our independence we have not fully taken advantage of this. This deficiency must now be removed, and India and Japan must play their full role in the destiny of Asia and the wider world.

From *Contemporary Essays*, 1971

3

Colombia: A Few Glimpses

SOMETIME AGO I VISITED the South American republic of Colombia; the continent's third largest nation and the only one with access both to the Atlantic and the Pacific oceans.

The capital Bogota, situated at a height of under 9,000 feet, which is about the same as Gulmarg, is a bustling city of twenty-five lakh people, set at one end of a large, rolling savannah surrounded by mountains. In between official engagements, I snatched a few hours sight-seeing and was rewarded with some memorable visits.

Upon landing at the Bogota airport, one immediately notices two landmarks on the mountains behind the city, a church and a huge statue, both of which are illuminated at night and stand over the city in dramatic configuration. On a clear morning I took the ropeway up to the church. As the glass-walled compartment started rising, the city of Bogota spread out below and in the far distance the conical peaks of the greater Andes began to appear. I was particularly struck by the symmetrical beauty of a peak called Tolima, which bears a marked resemblance to Japan's Fujiyama. The ascent of about a 1,000 feet was swiftly covered, and we stepped out on to the stone-paved courtyard of the church commanding a magnificent view of Bogota city, the valley and beyond it the great peaks covered with eternal snow.

The church itself is fairly small but contains one of the most unusual statues of Jesus that I have ever seen. He is portrayed as having stumbled while carrying the cross, bleeding profusely from the wounds inflicted upon

Him by his tormentors. The image possesses a stark realism that is startling, and apparently it is widely renowned in the area for its miraculous powers. The origins of this wooden image are unknown, but it was discovered by the natives several centuries ago on top of this mountain. Archaeologists tend to believe that it is a Spanish image which was abandoned. I will long remember the eyes of Jesus, showing acute human suffering yet endowed with a certain divine quality that renders them unforgettable.

After the church we descended the hill and visited at its foot Bolivar House, where the liberator Simon Bolivar spent many years with his favourite wife Manuelita. The small house is maintained exactly as it was in his time and is set in a garden almost Japanese in its beauty and calmness. From there we decided, on the spur of the moment, to drive up to the great statue of Virgin Mary standing on an adjoining peak even higher than the church. This is the Virgin of Guadalupe who stands with her arms outstretched, blessing the city of Bogota. The driver was not sure whether we could take the car right up to the top, but we decided to try. As it turned out, the metalled road ended about a mile short of the statue, but the car was able to negotiate the remaining fair-weather track, and we found ourselves right at the foot of the statue. The place was deserted, with the exception of a couple of dogs and some poultry, evidently belonging to the priest who looks after the tiny church nestled in the shadow of the huge image. The white plaster figure itself is tremendous, and the Virgin looks down with features at once strong and serene upon the valley beneath. Sitting at the foot of the statue and looking up at her face I could see white clouds moving against the vastness of the sky, creating the illusion that the whole image was slowly moving forward. Through a pair of binoculars, the hands stretched out in benediction appeared to be touching my head.

It was absolutely quiet up on that mountain, and I sat for quite some time looking down at the valley and ruminating upon the eternal mystery that is life; upon the divine from which creation has sprung and upon man, who has created so much that is beautiful and so much that is despicable. A curious mixture of the brute and the divine is man, truly an intermediate creature, as Sri Aurobindo has described him. Finally, after several millennia, man's ingenuity is catching up with him. In this nuclear age he has the choice either of unimagined progress or unparalleled destruction, and the die will almost certainly be cast before this century is out. Is there a divine will working behind our endless complexities, and if so, in what direction is it leading us? What role does the individual have in influencing the destiny of the race? At that height the air is thinner and clearer, and one's mind also begins to take on something of the serenity and clarity of nature. Being a mountain man myself I always cherished these moments of solitude far above the sphere of our daily activities.

In Bogota city there is the Gold Museum, which is unique in the whole world. It consists exclusively of gold artefacts created by the pre-Spanish civilizations that flourished in Colombia over the last several centuries. It is clear that these great civilizations had reached a high stage of artistic development, and they moulded gold with extraordinary facility. The pièce de résistance of the museum is right at the end when the visitor walks through heavily guarded doors into a dark room. Suddenly the lights are turned on, and one finds oneself surrounded by glass cabinets containing thousands of gold objects on display. This room contains over 9,000 exhibits, and the cumulative effect is overwhelming.

Finally, I must describe what was perhaps the most extraordinary of the sights in Colombia, the great Salt Cathedral. About 25 miles from Bogota is the town of Zipaquira, and it was here that about two decades ago a brilliant Colombian architect conceived the idea of converting an abandoned salt mine into a cathedral. One drives into the heart of a hill, the lighting and configuration of the passage reminiscent of the Jawahar Tunnel through the Banihal, except that here the road turns and twists several times. At the end of the drive, one suddenly comes into a vast, underground cavern hewn out of the salt mountain into the shape of a mighty cathedral. In the dim light one can see a wooden cross placed above the altar at one end, and in front of it rows of benches quietly await the worshippers. Although it is in the heart of the mountain, the air is fresh and sweet, and the mighty cavern produces a curious aura of mystic silence. It is an ideal place for meditation, and despite its tremendous size, it has been so designed that each person can establish a rapport with the gently luminous cross. By an act of genius, a deserted salt mine, which would otherwise have been sealed off and abandoned forever, has become a centre of pilgrimage and divine communion—a welcome change from the destruction and desecration that our generation is steadily inflicting upon nature in the name of progress!

From *Contemporary Essays*, 1971

4

The Old and The New

EVER SINCE I SAW the Elephanta Caves near Bombay first as a young boy, the great Trimurti sculpture has exerted a powerful attraction for me. I visited it again recently. This gigantic sculpture in solid rock must be among the most magnificent works of art ever produced by the human race, both in conception and execution. The concept of the trinity is well known throughout gnostic literature, and here we have the ultimate perfection of that idea, the three aspects of divinity—creation, preservation, destruction—merged in one supreme unity symbolizing the ultimate, essentially indivisible reality that pervades the cosmos. And with what superb skill and consummate art has this great idea been translated into granite. The Trimurti is almost twenty feet high, but so perfectly proportioned that it is not in the least unwieldy, the two profiles being set back from the main head in such a way that they blend into a single unified image and create a profound harmony.

As one stands inside the cave facing the great sculpture, amidst a subtle interplay of light and shadow, there are two overwhelming impressions. First is the immense calm that emanates from the Trimurti, an almost tangible 'peace that passes all understanding'. Shiva is engrossed in the mystery and wonder of his own being, yet appears to survey with a calm and timeless gaze the sea that is visible far on the horizon from within the cave. For centuries, defying the ravages of time and of human vandalism, the Trimurti has exuded an aura of peace and quiet that no sensitive observer can fail to notice. Secondly, watching the image steadily for a few minutes it appears as if it is pulsating with inner power, growing and filling all space. So skilfully has it been sculpted that the illusion of expanding form has been captured for ever, leaving one marvelling at the artistic and spiritual urge that led to the creation of this masterpiece on a tiny island, near what must then have been a comparatively deserted coast.

The cave is old, and across the bay there is the new, bustling, dynamic metropolis of Bombay. On the return trip our launch passed the Trombay nuclear energy establishment directly opposite Elephanta. Here again, there was a trinity, a modern one of concrete standing like some colossal surrealistic sculpture, formed by the huge oval Canada–India reactor, a smaller dome behind it and a graceful pylon soaring high into the air. As the launch moves they change their mutual positions, and this imparts a living fluidity and grace to their white geometrical forms. Nuclear energy is the symbol of the future; if only mankind proves wise enough to fend off a major war it can hold the key to a glorious future for the whole race, to the ushering in of a new dispensation for humanity.

Thus, the old and the new confront each other across a brief expanse of water—the ageless Trimurti of Elephanta and the new nuclear 'trinity' of Trombay. And yet is there not in fact an essential and living unity between these two? The Trimurti symbolizes the power of the divine from which modern man has tended to become increasingly alienated, and few today have the wisdom to derive power and inspiration from it; the atomic reactors symbolize nuclear power that lay dormant for all these centuries because we did not have the knowledge to utilize it. Are these not two powers in fact the same, or rather two aspects of the same supreme power that transcends all creation and yet permeates every atom of it, the power that our sages referred to when they said: '*Ishavasyam idam sarvam yatkincha jagatyam jagat*' (This whole universe and whatsoever exists in it is inhabited by the divine).

Vedanta postulates an essential unity pervading the cosmos, and modern science also appears to have rejected the duality of matter and energy and to be moving towards a non-dualistic interpretation of the universe. It is this unity that is symbolized alike in the Trimurti at Trombay and the one at Elephanta.

From *Contemporary Essays*, 1971

Poems

1

Vision

The burning splendour of an unknown world
shone from his face, and in one hand he held
aloft a mighty trident, I beheld
the glistening serpents round his forehead curled;

and then he seemed to melt with mystic change
into a boy of dark resplendent hue
who played upon a flute, on which he blew
a tune mysterious, haunting, sweet and strange;

a woman then appeared, a radiant wave
with fiery eyes that flashed with light divine
and charged with mighty power incarnadine,
one arm upraised to slay and one to save;

and then there sat, serene beneath a tree,
a figure clad in saffron robes austere,
with eyes that banished hate and lust and fear
and shed their bliss upon humanity;

and last there rose a man of gentle mien,
compassion on his face writ large and free
and eyes blue as the waters of the sea
where for mankind he preached and suffered pain;

and then these figures merged into a sea
of shining light that spread throughout all space,
and gathered in its folds the human race
and mounted upwards to Eternity.

2

The Adventurer

For I have gone where men have never been,
and wandered over countries far and near
and crossed great mountains with no trace of fear,
and gazed on many a strange and wondrous scene;

on mighty oceans have I plied my raft
where monstrous fishes close beneath me played,
and endless water heaved and lurched and swayed,
as tirelessly I hurled my lethal shaft;

and through the great primaeval forests tall
I plied the lonely furrow of my life
and slew great monsters, waged untiring strife
with creatures of the darkness, great and small;

and often as I strove with might and main,
and with each victory won far renown,
I thought that I had mown my troubles down
and conquered fear and death, old age and pain;

but ever were my hopes rudely belied,
for wander as I might throughout the world
I could not rid me of the terror curled
somewhere within my being, deep inside;

for over all our mortal hopes and gains
hovers the constant shadow of the grave,
of Time, that dims the glory of the brave
and lays at waste our labour and our pains;

and what adventure, what exploit will stay
with us beyond the folded veil of death?
and what, when we have shed our mortal breath,
will speed us on our far, eternal way.

3

Kaleidoscope

A fleeting moment,
culled from the woven web
of deep infinity;
a passing glance
pregnant with meaning,
orange with hidden fire;
a sudden thought
leaping upon the crest
of the unconscious;
a spasm of love
wrenched with cruel intensity
from our inner being;
a flash of hope
lighting the darkened comers
of dim despair;
a ray of light
seeking throughout creation
its glowing haven.

4

A Whispered Dialogue

Someone whispered in my ear
one evening,
as the setting sun set fire to the landscape;
I cannot quite recall the words
but the burden went something like this:
'Time speeds by on flying feet
and all our life is bitter-sweet
with expectations, hope and sorrow,
and we vainly seek tomorrow
what we could not find today;
for this we strive, for this we pay
with our life's blood, but then at last—
all strength expended, hoping past—
we fail and sink, and lose our breath
into the nothingness called death'
I sat quite still,
so quiet I could hear the beating of my heart,
until another whisper spoke
with somewhat firmer tone and sweeter voice:

'This is not true, the daily strife
that builds the structure of our life
need not be always fought in vain
and need not end in death and pain;
there is a path the mystics know
wherein the lights of heaven glow,
there is a path the sages tread
which leads them past the hosts of dead
and dying bodies, leads them on
to that one place where none has gone
who has not shed his mortal dross,
the rainbow bridge which all must cross
who seek in life finality,
and glowing immortality.

5

The Seminar

There sat the learned,
like rows of soda-water bottles
awaiting their turn to be drunk,
and one by one
they waddled to the mike and there unfurled
their private prejudices
garbed in the robe of reason;
one, a jaunty little cockroach,
leapt to and fro while speaking,
another stood in solemn grandeur
like a statue carved with moving lips,
a third, bearded and grim
and glaring like a hawk,
bore down in garrulous ferocity
upon the audience;
and thus it went
until, in God's own time,
their words sloshed all around the crowded hall,
they mercifully left for lunch.

6

The Conference

In trudge the white-maned elders
—some with no manes at all—
flamboyantly attired with files and briefcases
and assorted aides;
cameras clicking, movies whirling,
the all-pervasive air of tired concern,
the tinkering with this and that
lengthening into interminable hours—
statistics eddying up and down the table—
and then the exit,
not by the door wherein we went—
this one leads downstairs.

7

Quiz

What is the promise of a glowing day?
the bloom before the roses fade away;
why do the lovely flowers droop at noon?
because their beauty vanishes too soon;
what is the purpose of the flowing wind?
it seeks to emulate the human mind;
why does the rainbow sparkle bright and high?
because the earth is wedded to the sky;
why does the moon-orb change from day to day?
because what once has come must pass away;
why does the sun its fiery rays unfold?
because its heart is young, its body old;
why does the poet long to have his say?
because for him there is no other way.

8

The Tree at Night

At night the tree awakes to life
with many a murmur soft and low
as through its leaves the breezes blow
that calm the day's ignoble strife;

its branches sway in pure delight
and moonlight through them flits around
and throws upon the dewy ground
white patterns gay of dancing light;

and far away a silver flute
thrills through its being's inner reach,
as when the gift of human speech
descends on one who has been mute;

and far above a million spheres
pursue their pre-determined flight
and traverse space throughout the night;
the tree in silent wonder hears

the sonorous, deep, eternal song
that throbs within Creation's heart,
the secret longing to be part
of Nature's essence, deep and strong.

9

Stormy Night

The clouds tempestuous gather overhead
with ominous rumblings deep of distant thunder,
the brow of heaven darkens, and the bed
of the vast sky is almost rent asunder
by vivid snakes of lightning flashing
from cloud to saturnine cloud,
and suddenly with sound of cities crashing
the rain begins to fall in torrents splashing
in murky pools and on the river loud.

The wind howls like a demon, mad and screaming,
and flings the solid walls of rain
upon the cowering village which is seeming
to shrink the cruel blows with shuddering pain,
the fiery bursts of lightning grow more vivid
and deeper sound the thunderous drums of hell,
the deafening thunder and the lightning livid
transform the sky into a canopy vivid,
as through the dreadful night sharp falls the hail.

10

Winter

The bitter winds sweep down
upon us from the glittering peaks of snow
and blow,
with hectic fervour grim and obdurate
a cold and deadly chill across the land;
biting deep into our inner core
they shrivel up the senses,
and with fingers numb and aching bones
the brave sentinels stand
frozen to their appointed posts;
ah ominous silence reigns,
for far upon the distant peaks
a deadly certainty begins to grow
and menace, like a poised thunderbolt,
the placid fields and cottages below;

oh, for the sun,
the sun to leap aflame into the sky
and melt the menacing snow that chills and kills,
and fill fresh life into this drowsing land,
and strength and sinews into frozen arms,
and fire into the droop of listless hearts,
and power into eyes grown dim and cold
from watching, waiting for its fiery shaft.

11

The Living Flame

The spheres unroll their tangled trails
and sweep aloft through time and space,
and all our vaunted glory pales,
the splendours of the human race
shrink to a speck of cosmic dust
that whirls about its parent sun
and mocks our tales of love and lust
and dreams of deeds done and undone;

but yet within the human breast
there burns the mystic spark divine
that gives him neither peace nor rest
the living flame incarnadine
that ever strives to break away
and soar into the timeless light
where, luminous, the golden day
alternates with the silver night.

12

Lines Written in Milano

(after walking the streets below the great cathedral)

The stream of pavement walkers—
raincoats swishing, umbrellas dripping—
surges around me,
and the crazy roar of traffic
blares its wordy music into the grey sky,
the comic opera of modern life
grinds relentlessly along,
and yet there stirs within me
a deep, abiding peace,
born perhaps of the mighty church that stands—
a trellised curtain of living stone—
aloof amid the turbulent scene below;
how strong its grey protuberances,
how full of hope and union do they soar

into the boundless sky,
the saints stand in quick-frozen grace
pouring their permanent benediction
upon the unheeding crowd
that hurries to and fro with panic speed
unmindful of the beatitude above.

13

There Was Music

There was music and laughter and dancing galore
and couples were drifting around on the floor,
but his heart was not in it, his mind wandered wide,
for the one who adored him was not at his side.

He joked with them gaily and smiled as he spoke
but his heart deep within him was empty as smoke,
and he looked all about him for somewhere to hide
for the one who adored him was not at his side.

The tempo grew faster, and wilder the beat
of the swift throbbing dance and the quicksilver feet,
but the heart-rending rhythms he could not abide
for the one who adored him was not at his side.

Then the crashing crescendo, the zenith of sound,
the whirling of dancers around and around,
the first subtle touch of the upswelling tide—
and the one who adored him was there at his side.

14

Quest

I thought that I had found the one I sought,
deep in some inner emptiness
an echo spoke,
a flash of light burnt bright a second,
hope awoke again and rubbed its eyes:
I thought I found him
in the glimmering web of sunlight
that streamed into my bedroom—
specks of dust dancing in luminous ecstasy—
in the soft wind that blew fine patterns on the grass,
in the sea crashing for ever against the shore,
I thought that I had found him
gazing deep into the waves of time
fathoming there the spinning loom of destiny
watching—waiting;

was it me he was expecting
fresh from the throb of life
with the sweat of achievement glistening on my brow,
body glowing with restless energy
heart aflame with love, mind asparkle?
Was the one I sought
in his turn seeking me?

15

Dream

I dreamt that I was seated in the sky
upon a throne made bright with burnished gold
and rainbows all about me, far below
the azure world spun dreamily around,
the oceans and the continents beneath
were vivid patterns to my lofty gaze,
the moon a neighbour, cool and softly pink
around her parent earth did circulate
with gentle rhythm, far away the sun
aglow with fire and light sent out his rays,
the planets speeded past without a sound
muffling their music lest they wake me up,
they knew I dreamt, and in my dream I knew
their knowledge and was grateful for their love.

16

In Memoriam

(written on the passing of Jawaharlal Nehru)

Now you are gone, to join the ranks of those
whose names will ever live in every heart
with joyous fragrance, like the budding rose
that was of you so intimate a part;

you fought and strove to give our nation light,
to bring it freedom, break its binding chain,
you warred against a vast, imperial might
you suffered grief and anguish, loss and pain;

but yet you fought, and when at last we won
and took our place in freedom's glowing light
you did yourself become the nation's sun
and for her welfare laboured day and night:

Now you are gone, and we who stay behind
will cherish our sweet memories of you
and strive with every power of heart and mind
to make your dreams of glory come out true.

17

Tamas

The morbid distillation
that drugs the spirit,
quietens all our senses in the sleep of sloth,
low as the lumbering tortoise
dragging itself about the shallows of the world
in drear and meaningless languor;
the power that dims our faculties
and bids us sleep or sit around
with time a heavy burden round our necks
and life sheer boredom,
something to be borne because it's there,
devoid of sense or meaning, hope or purpose,
an interminable journey towards a non-existent goal.

18

Rajas

The spirit, fierce and fervid,
sending shafts of lightning through our brains,
urging us on to passionate action;
the sword, red in smoke and war
dripping with liquid valour,
the cannon booming,
cries of lusty men and weeping women,
bold edifices
towering heavenwards built on sweat and tears;
the veins throbbing
pulsating with fear and anger, hope and joy,
moving us to delirious action,
high achievement, lofty failings,
the spirit quivering with undone deeds and done
remembrances,
and life a seething sea of constant change
wherein we ride the ever-mounting wave
into the trough beyond.

19

Sattva

The calm dispassionate view
that looks on all creation
through lenses of equanimity,
the emotions finely balanced
lust transformed to beauty, hate to love,
anger to deep repose,
the poise whereby the world at last is held
in subtle equilibrium;
the senses calm,
not crushed and mutilated by repression
but fully rounded, free of edges, angularities;
the mind a luminous crystal
watching calm the varied show of life,
and life itself
an understanding, a fulfilment
aglow with inner wonder.

20

Hymn to Shiva

I am your plaything.
You can breathe into me
the fire of eternal life,
and make me immortal;
or You can scatter my atoms
to the far corner of the universe
so that I disappear for ever.
You can fill me with light and power
so that I shine like a meteor
against the darkness of the midnight sky;
or You can extinguish my spirit
so that I sink for ever
into the deep and fathomless ocean of time
You can set me among the eternal stars
resplendent with your divine fire;
or You can hurl me
into the abyss of darkness,
so that I can never again be visible
to mortal eyes.

You can come to me
with the glory of a thousand cupids;
or You can turn from me
and leave me stranded
in a grey and ghastly desert of despair.
You can smile at me
with the radiance that kindles the universe;
or You can open your eye of fury
and reduce me to a heap of ashes.
I am your plaything;
The choice is yours.

All poems from *Welcome the Moonrise*, 1965

Letters

Jawaharlal Nehru and Karan Singh

...... 1 ......

Srinagar
1 August 1951

My dear Panditji,

It was a great pleasure seeing you up here again. I am sure your short stay at Pahalgam gave you some much needed rest. It was a pity you could not stay on a few days longer.

You may be interested to know that I am considering donating the Gulab Mahal Palace to the University of Jammu and Kashmir. Our University, as you know, possesses no building of its own, nor has it the necessary funds to enable it to acquire or construct a suitable building. Gulab Mahal will, I am sure, be ideally suited for a university. It is a magnificent building, containing numberless rooms, several large halls and possessing lovely lawns. As a matter of fact, I am sure, with its delightful situation, it will be one of the most attractive university buildings in India. It would give me great pleasure to see it transformed into a flourishing university, and I am sure this gift will go a long way in enabling our University to achieve its lofty ambitions.

Our private property is, however, under the direct control of His Highness.[1] He has just returned from Paris and I have sent him a message requesting him to allow me to donate the building. I am expecting a reply from him soon.

We all deeply appreciate your strong and forthright stand vis-à-vis the hostile and outrageous war propaganda and hysteria which is sweeping Pakistan.[2] I sincerely hope that your clear statements[3] will make them see sense, and that your repeated declaration that India will strongly resist any aggression on her territory, including our State, will make them desist from their insane policy, which seems to have as its goal the plunging of the two countries into a tragic and disastrous war. I am sure, however, that under your leadership this danger will, in due course, be averted.

I hope this finds you very well.

With very kind regards and respects,

Yours sincerely,
Karan Singh

...... 2 ......

New Delhi
3 August 1951

My dear Tiger,

I have just received your letter of the 1st August. Thank you for it.

I am very glad to learn that you intend donating the Gulab Mahal Palace to the University of Jammu and Kashmir. That is the very best use you can put that building to and I am sure it will be greatly appreciated by the public. We have ourselves been handing over our old Government Houses to Universities and other public institutions. In Poona there was a very fine Government House with a park attached to it. This has now become the headquarters off the Poona University.

We are living in critical times and the situation vis-à-vis Pakistan difficult and delicate. I do not know how things will turn out in the end. But I doubt very much if there will be war. Yet we cannot be sure and we have to take all precautions.

Perhaps, you know that the King[1] of Nepal's daughter, Princess Vijaya Lakshmi, is going to Kashmir for a two-month stay. She has not been keeping well, although lately she has progressed greatly. I believe arrangements are being made for her stay in a house at Tangmarg. She will probably go to Kashmir on the 17th August.

The King of Nepal is coming here[2] to see her before she goes and also to have some consultations with me. There is just an odd possibility that he might like to accompany his daughter to Kashmir and stay there for about two days and then return. I am merely warning you and I am not at all sure about it.

The King is coming here with a fairly large party—his two Queens, his three daughters and a number of others.

Yours sincerely,
Jawaharlal Nehru

...... 3 ......

New Delhi
26 July 1952

My dear Tiger,

I have been wanting to write to you for some days but have been so terribly busy that I could not find the time. You have however been very much in my mind.

You must have read a report of the long speech I delivered in Parliament about Kashmir.[1] A great part of it, of course, dealt with past events. Towards the end, I indicated the broad lines of the agreement reached between us and Sheikh Abdullah and his colleagues who had come here.[2]

Our discussions were prolonged, and we sat for many hours, day after day. It was an exhausting business. We had to keep in mind all the aspects of this complicated matter. There were the legal and constitutional aspects, and there were the other aspects which were at least, if not more, important. I think that the agreement we arrived at was a satisfactory one. Apart from its contents, it brought about good feeling and put an end to the tension that has existed for some time past. The best part of this agreement was this psychological atmosphere of friendship and cooperation.

Many things were decided by this agreement which knit the Jammu and Kashmir State closer to India and which make our Constitution applicable in a greater measure to the State. At the same time, we recognized the special position of the State and gave it greater autonomy in many matters than our other States of the Indian Union possess.

You will, of course, be chiefly interested in the decisions arrived at in regard to the Head of the State.[3] Perhaps, you may not like some part of them, but I had indicated to you, in the course of our talks when you were here, that it seemed inevitable to me that some such change must take place. Circumstances had so developed, and they could not be denied without causing injury to all concerned and the cause we have at heart. I think that the decision and the form of words we have used are satisfactory and a fair compromise. Whatever the law or Constitution might say, in the last analysis, we have to pay heed to the wishes of the people. That indeed had often been declared by us in regard to the Jammu and Kashmir State. But really, the principle applies everywhere in India. When this question was raised positively, in the manner it had been raised, it became impossible to bypass it or to postpone it for long. It was better to face it and come to a decision than to leave a feeling of uncertainty and doubt in people's minds, and thus not even have the great advantage of a settlement by agreement with all the psychological consequences of friendly feeling that this produced.

In effect now, this means that at the proper moment the Constituent Assembly of Jammu and Kashmir State will make a recommendation to the President by election of a person who is to be the Head of the State. Although this is called a recommendation, the President will naturally agree. There is no doubt that your name is going to be recommended.

The period is five years. It is quite likely that at the end of the period, you might be re-elected. That is at any rate the present intention of the Kashmir leaders and, of course, we would very much welcome it. But any attempt to force the pace, or to try to have a longer period, would have defeated the real purpose in view.

As a matter of fact, in the world today, five years is a long time. Only this evening we have had the news of the sudden changes in Egypt[4] and the forcible abdication of King Farouk[5] of Egypt and his sudden departure for America. For any of us to think in static terms of continuing things as they are is to misunderstand this changing and dynamic world. We have to understand this world and adapt ourselves to it.

I am sure you will appreciate what I am writing. I need not tell you that now and later, you will be in my mind and you can always come to me for advice or any help that I can give you. The best advice is to accept cheerfully and willingly the changes suggested and thereby to put yourself in the forefront of them, instead of appearing as if you unwillingly agreed to something that you disliked. If we have to do something, we should do it gracefully and thereby gain the goodwill and respect of others.

I hope, therefore, that you will make it clear to Sheikh Abdullah and others that you willingly accept the changes suggested by agreement with the Government of India and that you will abide by any decisions that the Constituent Assembly of the Jammu and Kashmir State takes. Thus, you will strengthen not only your position but the affection that people have for you in the State.

I am feeling terribly tired after many months of continuous hard work. I want very much to go to Kashmir for a few days. It is difficult to be certain about my future programme, but I hope to be able to go to Srinagar on the 18th August or thereabouts. If I can manage it, I shall go on a short trek, probably in the Gurais Valley.

Dr Graham[6] has suggested a meeting at ministerial level at Geneva.[7] We wanted this meeting to be at Delhi, but this was not agreed to by the other people. So we have agreed to Geneva. I have suggested the date as 25 August. If this is agreed to, I am requesting Shri Gopalaswami Ayyangar to go there on our behalf. I am reluctant to give him this trouble, but he is obviously the best person to go and I am glad to say that he has agreed to do so. Probably the Geneva meeting will last about a week.

With all good wishes,

Yours sincerely,
Jawaharlal Nehru

...... 4 ......

Jammu Tawi
3 August 1952

My dear Panditji,

Thank you very much for your letter to me dated 26 July 1952.

Before I proceed, I would like to express my deep gratitude to you for the kind and sympathetic interest you have been taking in my affairs during the last three years or so since I became Regent.[1] I need hardly express how greatly I value your guidance and advice. As regards the question of whether I should or should not accept a five-year elected term as Head of State, I have—since your speech in Parliament was delivered about ten days ago[2]—been giving the matter my most thorough consideration from all its various aspects.

My highest ambition is to be able to serve effectively the people of my country, and any position which gives me that opportunity will naturally be welcomed. However, in the present circumstances, I feel that it is not possible for me to come to any decision until the new Constitution for Kashmir emerges in its final shape from the Constituent Assembly and receives the approval of the Government of India. I am sure you will appreciate that it is hardly possible for me to accept a position without knowing exactly and clearly the duties and functions which attach to it, the responsibilities which I will have to shoulder and the conditions under which I will have to work.

If the Indian Constitution was going to be accepted in toto by Kashmir, the position would have been quite clear. But as you said in your speech the situation in Kashmir differs from that which obtains in other States of the Union, and the Kashmir Consembly may draft a Constitution along lines which differ from the Indian. As a matter of fact, I do not think anyone, even Sheikh Sahib, is in a position to say definitely at this stage what exactly the new Constitution will be like.

As Head of State I will have important responsibilities to fulfil, and, as Sheikh Sahib is reported to have reiterated in some of his recent speeches, if I fail to fulfil them satisfactorily I will even be liable to impeachment.[3]

I, therefore, strongly feel that I should be very clear as to what my exact position and responsibilities are going to be, and also the nature of the Constitution over which I shall have to preside. If I accept anything without being absolutely clear, I will be being unfair not only to myself but also to all those with whom I shall have to work and come into contact and, in the larger context, to the people of the State.

Regarding my tenure of office, as I indicated to you personally, I would much prefer, if I am to serve as Head of State, to do so for more than the limited term of five years. I would be much happier if no time limit is imposed. If, however, political considerations make it imperative for a fixed term to be incorporated in the Constitution (although personally I do not think such overriding considerations exist, particularly when weighed against the political advantages flowing from the opposite course of action), I am somewhat reassured by what you say in your letter with regard to my future re-election. I am still very young, and have to plan for many years ahead, not only for five. May I feel confident that in the event of my becoming Head of State, both the Government of India and the Jammu and Kashmir Government will see that I am able to continue for much longer than just a five-year period? I need hardly add that this will be subject to the condition that I perform my duties to the satisfaction of the Government of India. All I can assure you is that if I do take up the position, I will sincerely and honestly work to the very best of my ability to make it a complete success, as I have done in the three years I have acted as Regent.

I was rather surprised at press reports which I brought to your notice when I saw you in Delhi a few days ago—that the Consembly was making preparations to swear in new Head of State within a few days. I think, to say the least, that it is rather unusual that an office is sought to be filled before it even exists constitutionally and before its duties and functions have been clearly defined. I would suggest that the matter be only taken up after the new Constitution for Kashmir has been finally prepared.

After the Constitution is finalized, and I have studied it, I will be in a position to consider acceptance. But I am sure you will appreciate my view that until that time it is not possible for me to come to any decision.

With very kind regards and respects,

Yours sincerely,
Karan Singh

...... 5 ......

Srinagar
7 August 1952

My dear Panditji,

I am sending this letter to you by hand of my ADC [aide-de-camp], Captain Kohar Singh. He is returning here on Saturday morning, and will bring back with him any reply you may be pleased to send.

By now you must have received the letter I wrote to you from Jammu on the 3rd. I was delayed en route for a day due to heavy rain and arrived here on Tuesday evening. Sheikh Sahib came to see me yesterday afternoon, and I had a long talk with him. In the course of our conversation I dwelt at some length on the two points which had formed the basis of my letter to you, namely, the question of tenure and re-election, and the fact that I could not come to any decision until the Constitution for Kashmir had been finalized. I particularly stressed the latter point which, to my mind, is the more important and significant of the two.

In reply to the question of re-election, he said that it was not possible for him to give any assurance, as he did not know what the circumstances would be after five years. To the second point he said that he could not wait until the new Constitution was finalized to elect the Head of State.[1] He did not give me any convincing reason as to why he was in such a desperate hurry, and merely said that the new Constitution might take a considerable time in the drafting and that he was not prepared to wait until then.

I tried to persuade him to understand that it was just not possible for me to say anything until the new Constitution was completed and I knew exactly what my duties and position would be, and that anyhow the question of choosing a Head of State would only arise after that. He was, however, very adamant that the matter would be taken up by the Consembly on Monday the 11th August, and asked that I should make up my mind and let him know my decision as soon as possible before that date.

I remember your saying when we met in Delhi recently that it would not be proper or possible for the Consembly to proceed in the matter until the Indian Constitution had been suitably amended, either directly or by a Presidential Order. In addition, I am sure you will appreciate the reasonableness of my point of view, and of the contention that the only proper time for the new Head of State to be chosen is after and not before the Constitution, of which he is the creation and under which he has to function, has been finalized.

Under the circumstances, I would request you to use your great influence with Sheikh Sahib and his colleagues to persuade them to take a more reasonable view of the matter and to adopt what I feel, and what I am sure you will agree, is the only logical and constitutional line of action, viz., complete the framing of the new Constitution before taking up the question of the Head of the State. If he insists on going through with his present scheme, the only answer I can give him at this juncture is to repeat that I am not able to say anything until the new Constitution is prepared in its final form.

I am sure, Panditji, you know me well enough to see that it is no outmoded conception of absolute monarchy or autocracy or anything of the sort that prompts me to take up this attitude. It is purely that I am not prepared to accept a responsible position until I know clearly what it entails, especially under the peculiarly delicate and difficult situation that exists here.

I have put my point of view frankly and clearly before you, in the earnest hope that it will meet with your sympathetic consideration. It is now entirely up to you to decide whatever action—if any—you deem it necessary to take.

With respectful regards,

Yours very sincerely,
Karan Singh

...... 6 ......

Srinagar
8 September 1952

My dear Panditji,

As you know, I have been having a series of meetings with political leaders from Jammu, mainly belonging to the Praja Parishad Party.[1] These meetings ended yesterday.

The talks were fairly comprehensive, as the invitees took the opportunity of discussing with me a range of current problems, in addition to the specific question of the Headship of the State. On the whole they did not take an entirely one-sided view, and I think my talks with them will prove to be useful.

The Jammu people do, however, feel distressed and injured for several reasons. They say that they have neither any voice in the State Assembly (which they hold they boycotted under protest, and which contains representatives of only one party), nor in the State Government and nor again in the Indian Parliament, because the members from our State were nominated and not elected.[2] They, therefore, feel extremely frustrated, as they hold that there is no one who can effectively voice their grievances and demands, and see that justice is done to them. They have several important demands—into which I need not enter here—which they strongly feel deserve sympathetic consideration. The proposed ending of the ruling dynasty has upset them immensely, not because of sentimental attachment alone but because they feel that this step will break the only link which bound them to Kashmir, and that unless it is followed by complete accession to India their position will be even more precarious than it has been for the last five years.

Their basic demand, as you know, is full accession of the whole State to India. Although I myself would very much like a closer association of this State with India, it seems clear that the Government of India is committed—at least for the time being—to limited accession, and the alternative of Jammu breaking away from Kashmir will also, at this stage, be disastrous to India, Kashmir and to Jammu itself.

Nevertheless, I feel that everything possible should be done to redress the legitimate grievances of the Jammu people, because this internal discord and disharmony is to my mind most unfortunate. It is rather tragic irony, I think, that those who want complete accession to India should be proving a source of embarrassment to India and should feel unhappy and oppressed. As I have mentioned to you personally several times, I feel that the Jammu situation has not been handled as well as it might have been. My sincere desire is that this unfortunate state of affairs should be ameliorated, and, if the State is to remain as a single unit, the maximum amount of cooperation and goodwill should be sought from all sections.

When you were here you mentioned that you would not be averse to meeting these Jammu leaders of the Praja Parishad. Maulana Sahib[3] specifically asked me to tell them that the Government of India would always be pleased to meet them and talk to them. Pandit Prem Nath and his colleagues have expressed a great desire to meet you and other concerned Ministers of India, with a view of placing before you their difficulties and demands. I would strongly urge that they be given a sympathetic hearing, as I feel that much good can come of such a meeting. Of course, you are very busy and might only be able to see them for a short while. But I feel that Maulana Sahib, Shri Ayyangar, Dr Katju and perhaps Dr Radhakrishnan could talk to them at some length. Now, I think it would be desirable if one or two members of the Kashmir Government were also present, so that controversial matters could be thrashed out on the spot, and the clouds of misunderstanding and animosity could perhaps be lifted to some extent. I do not know, however, what Sheikh Sahib's reaction to this idea will be, as I have not mentioned it to him. I thought that if you approved of the idea of a member or two of the Kashmir Government—perhaps someone like D.P. Dhar—being also present, you might drop a line or talk to Sheikh Sahib about it. I do not think he will be averse to the idea, as I am sure he is as keen as we are that the internal difficulties of the State be resolved.

I am enclosing a copy of a statement which Pandit Prem Nath Dogra issued yesterday at the conclusion of the talks, in which he sets out his Party's attitude.[4] I have decided to issue no statement yet.

I have been waiting to hear from Dr Katju as what he has settled with His Highness.[5] In the meanwhile, I saw in the papers that His Highness has sent a long memorandum to the President,[6] which is now receiving the consideration of your Government. I have not received a copy, so I do not know the contents. The papers, however, say that he has asked for a referendum in the State on the issue of the retention, or otherwise, of the dynasty.

I wonder what your view about this is. If it is possible to have a referendum—and I do not see why it should not be—I feel it would be a good thing, as it would give the people of the State a fully democratic method of expressing their decision as to whether they would like a member of the dynasty to be their Constitutional Head or would prefer to elect someone periodically. Thus, no section or group will feel that its views have been ignored in coming to a decision on this important question. I must add that from indications both in Jammu and the Valley, I feel that the result of such a referendum is by no means a foregone conclusion.

I hope this finds you very well. With warm regards and respects,

Yours very sincerely,
Karan Singh

7

New Delhi
9 September 1952

My dear Tiger,

I have just received your letter of 8 September.

I have no doubt that the Jammu people have a number of grievances and feel rather frustrated. Some of these grievances have, I believe, justification.

Indeed, both Sheikh Saheb and Bakshi Ghulam Mohammad mentioned to me some of the disabilities that Jammu province was suffering from and their desire to remove them. At the same time, they pointed out to me certain difficulties. Thus, for instance, the lack of water in Jammu is a very serious handicap.

The Praja Parishad people have largely to blame themselves for the plight they have landed themselves in. Others may also be to blame. But, consciously or unconsciously, the Praja Parishad in Jammu has acted in a manner which has been quite deplorable and excessively stupid. It is not that they have not had a chance of meeting other people and discussing affairs with them. They have met them. As you know, I met Pandit Prem Nath Dogra and had a fairly long talk with him. In the course of our talk, he agreed almost entirely with what I told him. Soon after he made public statements exactly contrary to what he had said to me and embarrassed me greatly. I found him and his companions completely irresponsible.

The kind of agitation they have been carrying on in the past in Delhi[1] itself, apart from what they have done in Jammu, has been pernicious in the extreme. They have sided with the most communal elements[2] in Delhi and attacked the Government of India in every way. If a person is to be known from his associations, then the Praja Parishad's associations were the most undesirable in Delhi or Punjab. Their activities did more harm to the Kashmir issue, from our point of view, than anything else that has happened in recent years. As a result, they received the greatest publicity in Pakistan.[3]

There is a certain looseness in the use of language in regard to accession. Kashmir has fully acceded to India. It is true that, because of international complications, there was a loophole and a vague possibility of a change, but that did not affect the fullness of the accession. There is a difference between full accession and full integration. It is that integration that has not been full, although accession has been complete.

As the position is, any attempt to give effect to their demand would not only fail in itself but might put an end to even the present accession. I explained that to you.

The Parishad people have been a disruptive influence[4] at a time when it was most important to lay stress on unity. Their influence has been disruptive not only in the Jammu and Kashmir State, but indirectly in the whole of India. The forces in India which we consider most harmful have been encouraged by the attitude of the Praja Parishad of Jammu.

I do not like being exploited and treated with discourtesy by any one in my official capacity. The Praja Parishad people have done that and, normally, they would have scant courtesy from me. But I have no objection to meeting them should you so desire. I am sure Maulana Saheb would also be prepared to meet them. So also, Dr Katju and Shri Gopalaswami Ayyangar. But it would be improper for all of us to meet them together and to hold a kind of a conference. They will have to meet people individually and separately. I do not think that Dr Radhakrishnan should be dragged into this particular picture. As a matter of fact, he is soon going away to Europe. D.P. Dhar might be present when one of us meets the Praja Parishad people. I shall mention this matter to Sheikh Saheb. He is coming here tomorrow to accompany me to our Congress meeting in Indore.

I do not like the statement issued by Prem Nath Dogra after the conclusion of his talks with you. It might, of course, have been worse. But it might have been better also. In any event, you should not issue any statement about these talks. If you see Sheikh Saheb, of course, you should tell him briefly what the nature of the talks was.

I have seen the long memorandum which your father has sent to the President. There is no reference in it to a referendum. The memorandum is rather an angry and tendentious document. Your father does not seem to realize at all that the world has changed and is changing rather rapidly. It was Dr Katju's intention to send the States Secretary, Venkatachar,[5] to Poona to see your father, but just as he was on the point of going, a telegram came that your father was not feeling quite well. So, Venkatachar's visit has been postponed for two or three days.

I am rather surprised at your reference to the referendum. This is not at all possible either from the local or from the international point of view. We have been talking about the plebiscite over other issues and even this cannot come off because there is no agreement. If the question of a referendum on a limited issue was raised, this would immediately lead to all kinds of international complications and the demand for a plebiscite immediately over the wider area. Even this referendum, it would be said, if held at all, should be over that wider area, including that part which is held by Pakistan. Within the present boundaries of the State under our control the referendum issue would naturally lead to bitterness and controversy and in effect tend to split up the State, regardless of the final issue. Indeed, I think that such a proposal is completely out of court in present circumstance. Pakistan would, no doubt, profit by it, but no one else.

I am going day after tomorrow to Indore and I shall be away for five or six days. Dr Katju is going with me. Gopalaswami Ayyangar intends returning here on the 13th or 14th of this month.

All good wishes and affection,

Yours,
Jawaharlal Nehru

...... 8 ......

New Delhi
15 November 1952

My dear Yuvaraj,

I write to congratulate you on the high honour that has been conferred upon you by the people of Jammu and Kashmir State on your election as Sadar-i-Riyasat.[1] I should like to congratulate the people of the State also on their wise choice. This puts a great responsibility upon you, for you have not merely to follow an established convention but rather to help in making conventions for the future. You know how dear the future of the State is to me. It is dear to me because of my own intimate relationship with Kashmir, and it is dear to me also because of the numerous ties that bind the State to India. Our future is linked together and we have to face good fortune and ill-fortune alike together.

A new chapter opens now in the Jammu and Kashmir State. And yet, although it is new, it is a continuation of the old but in a different form. The processes of life, whether that of an individual or of a nation, are both a continuation and a continuous change.

I earnestly hope that the changes that have been brought about in the Constitution of the Jammu and Kashmir State will lead to the greater prosperity and happiness of the people of the State and will bring them even closer to India, of which they are such an intimate part.

To you, who have to shoulder this burden and this responsibility at such an early age, I send all my good wishes and my affection.

Yours sincerely,
Jawaharlal Nehru

...... 9 ......

Srinagar
18 November 1952

My dear Panditji,

Thank you very much indeed for your kind letters in connection with my having been elected Sadar-i-Riyasat.

Since June 1949, when I first assumed the duties of Regent, down to the present day, I have been faced from time to time with several difficult situations. Without your constant help and encouragement—the appreciation and gratitude for which it is hard for me to express—I would not have been able to achieve the measure of success which had up till now crowned my efforts. Your assurance of future help and guidance gives me courage to face with confidence the new responsibilities which I have now assumed.

I am aware of the great confidence which the people of the State have reposed in me, and also of the fact that there are many difficult and serious problems which confront us. I can assure you that my efforts will always be towards serving, in whatever manner I can, the people of this State and, in the larger context, the people of the rest of our great country. With your good wishes and affectionate guidance, I feel confident that despite my youth and inexperience I will be able to successfully fulfil my responsibilities.

The oath-taking ceremony took place yesterday morning in the Rajgarh Palace. I enclose a copy of a short speech I delivered on that occasion.[1]

Thanking you again for your good wishes, and with deep respects and regards,

Yours very sincerely,
Karan Singh

...... 10 ......

Jammu
16 March 1953

My dear Panditji,

I hope you have received my letter dated the 23rd February.

In the middle of July this year quinquennial Congress of Commonwealth Universities[1] is being held in Cambridge. This will be attended by representatives from all the Universities in the Commonwealth. The Syndicate of the University of Jammu and Kashmir has requested me to represent the University on this occasion. I have talked to Sheikh Sahib about this and he is keen that I should go. I also feel that it will be a pleasant and educative opportunity for me and my wife to go abroad for a short while.

I am planning to be away for about six weeks. I will spend a fortnight in England—four days at Cambridge and the rest at London. The remaining time I wish to spend on the Continent. I am particularly keen to visit my birthplace in Cannes, in the south of France. I came back to India when I was a few weeks old and have never been able to visit there since. If, God forbid, there is another war then I may never be able to go there. I also want to spend a week or so in Switzerland as I have heard that is perhaps the only place in the world which can rival Kashmir in natural beauty, although, of course, it is incomparably better developed.

The Budget Session of the Legislative Assembly begins on the 25th, and on that day I will address the Assembly.

With respectful regards,

Yours very sincerely,
Karan Singh

...... 11 ......

Srinagar
26 June 1953

My dear Panditji,

I am sending this letter by hand of a special messenger.

I intended to be in Delhi upon your arrival, but I felt that you will be overwhelmingly busy immediately upon your return.[1] I shall come to Delhi as soon as you wish me to be there.

I hope you received the message dated 10 June which I sent through Dr Katju. Since then the situation here has become still worse, and it is now very grave. There are clear indications that unless firm and speedy action is taken very soon, the situation may well become irretrievable.

The passing away of Dr Shyama Prasad Mookerjee[2] while under detention[3] here was very sad and unfortunate indeed. Apart from its grave political repercussions[4] it came as a great shock, particularly as we were completely unaware that he had not been keeping good health for some time. I was not informed of his illness or his removal to hospital, and, most amazing of all, I only learnt of his demise several hours after the body had been flown from Srinagar, and that too from unofficial sources. There is a widespread feeling and indeed there are strong reasons which indicate that in this whole unfortunate matter, the State Government, to say the least, acted in a most questionable and incompetent manner. I shall explain further when we meet.

Regarding my proposed trip abroad, many friends feel, and I am inclined to agree with them, that under the present circumstances it would not be at all desirable for me to be away. I am therefore thinking of postponing my trip for the time being. If conditions permit, the Yuvarani and I might go on a holiday for a couple of months later on in the year. I have, however, not thought it desirable yet to give out here that I am postponing my trip. I will do finally in this matter as you advise.

I hope this finds you in very good health. With deep regards and respects,

Yours very sincerely,
Karan Singh

...... 12 ......

New Delhi
29 June 1953

My dear Tiger,

I have just received your letter of the 26th June. I returned on the 27th afternoon as my plane was held up in Bombay because of bad weather in Delhi.

Since my return I have tried to gather as much information as I could about the position in Kashmir. Dr Mookerjee's death was indeed sad, more especially, because he was under detention.

The situation in Kashmir is a bad one and has to be taken in hand. But this requires a good deal of care. I have written a long letter to Sheikh Abdullah which is quite frank.[1] I have asked him to come here with some of his colleagues on or about the 3rd July.[2]

My talks with Mohammad Ali, Prime Minister of Pakistan, were very vague and general. I am likely to meet him about the end of July.

I think you are right in postponing, for the present, your visit abroad.

Yours sincerely,
Jawaharlal Nehru

...... 13 ......

Srinagar
9 August 1953

My dear Panditji,

For several months the situation in the State has been dangerously confused, primarily as the result of a deep rift among the members of the Government. I have been watching the situation with growing concern and have been extremely distressed to see that instead of regaining harmony, the split within the Cabinet has continued to increase until it assumed critical proportions.[1]

Within the Cabinet, three Ministers including the Deputy Prime Minister were strongly opposed to the policies and actions of Sheikh

Abdullah and one of his colleagues—Mirza Afzal Beg. For some reason best known to him, Sheikh Abdullah began to publicly repudiate the policies to which he, his colleagues and the whole National Conference Party were solemnly committed. This naturally caused a great deal of confusion and distress in the minds of the people.

Yesterday matters came to a head when three out of Sheikh Abdullah's four Cabinet colleagues sent him a memorandum[2], a copy of which they sent to me, in which they openly denounced his policies and repudiated his leadership. They expressed that the policies which he was pursuing were proving disastrous to the country and that the Cabinet, lacking as it did unity of policy and action, had forfeited the confidence of the people. This represented a complete breakdown of the cabinet system and the principle of joint responsibility, which is so vital in a Parliamentary Democracy. I met Sheikh Abdullah, but he could not satisfy me regarding bringing the situation to a stable and speedy solution.[3] Naturally, this state of affairs could not be allowed to continue, as thereby the unity and stability of the State were gravely jeopardized. The continuance of such a Council of Ministers in office would have been a complete denial of constitutional and democratic principles. I had no alternative but to dissolve the Ministry forthwith. I am enclosing for your information a copy of the memorandum which Bakshi Ghulam Mohammad, Deputy Prime Minister, Pt. G.L. Dogra, Finance Minister, and Pt. S.L. Saraf,[4] Health Minister, sent to Sheikh Abdullah and also a copy of my letter to Sheikh Abdullah[5] and the order[6] regarding dismissal of his Cabinet.

It was immediately necessary, however, that a new Government be formed so as to avoid a political and administrative vacuum. Taking cognizance of the prestige and regard enjoyed by Bakshi Ghulam Mohammad among the people of the State and his position as the Deputy Leader of the majority party in the Assembly, I called upon him to aid and [advise] me in the task of forming a new Ministry. I enclose copies of letters that passed between us regarding the formation of the new Government and my order in this connection. The Council of Ministers was sworn in, as soon as possible, early this morning, as I desired to minimize the period in which the State was without a Government.[7] At present there is only one other Minister, Pt. Girdharilal Dogra, but the Cabinet will, of course, be expanded within a day or two.

The new Government will now tackle the grave issues that are before it. I am convinced that this step which we have been forced to take, grave as it is, is in the abiding interests of the people of the State. I sincerely hope that stability, unity and prosperity will soon return to our people.

As soon as conditions here permit, I propose to come over to Delhi to apprise you personally of the situation here.

With respectful regards,

Yours sincerely,
Yuvaraj,
Sadar-i-Riyasat

...... 14 ......

Srinagar
19 August 1953

My dear Panditji,

Shri A.P. Jain[1] and D.P. Dhar[2] are proceeding to Delhi in order to personally explain to you the circumstances and the situation here. I am taking this opportunity to convey to you a few salient points for your consideration.

Since the changes here last week, the political situation has begun to show definite signs of improvement. Public opinion is steadily veering round towards an understanding of the purpose and policies which animate the activities of the new regime. Several ameliorative measures [have] already been proclaimed which have favourably impressed public opinion. A considerable number of National Conference workers have been impressed by this courageous and dynamic stand and actively support and help the present administration.

Bakshi Sahib, in particular, and his colleagues have been carrying a great burden and working under conditions of great physical and mental strain. I am sure you will appreciate that at this critical juncture we must do all we can to strengthen their hands and support them. In this connection, the assurances contained in your letters gave great encouragement to all of us to work courageously and steadfastly for the welfare of the people.

While the Government was engaged in restoring peace and normalcy in the State and rallying the people round it, we were extremely perturbed to hear what Shri Jain and Vishnu Sahay[3] told us regarding your talks with Mr Mohammad Ali.[4] They informed us of the various features of the intended agreement between India and Pakistan over Kashmir, including the fixing of a date for the induction of the plebiscite administrator. This came as a great shock to all, and Bakshi Sahib and his colleagues were stunned and bewildered. They are particularly upset that a decision so vital to the very existence of the people of the State is being taken without ascertaining the viewpoint of those who at this critical juncture accepted the responsibility of Government. We all feel that before coming to any decision on this momentous matter vitally affecting our country, our views must in all fairness be taken into account.

The details of the proposed agreement came to Bakshi Sahib particularly as a grave blow. He has been under great strain, and to him this represented a complete reversal of the ideals and position which, at considerable personal risk and sacrifice, he had fought for all these years. He was very agitated and expressed to me in writing his inability to carry on the Government in these circumstances, as he feels that his position among the people will become completely untenable. Thus, it seems as if I will be faced with the unenviable task of having to find a third Prime Minister within a fortnight.

We all firmly hope and believe that the final agreement will not be [averse] to our interests and that the interests of the people of the State, which you have all along defended, will not be sacrificed at the [altar] of Pakistani communal claims. Firmness alone can save the people of Kashmir from falling prey to the frenzied and communal propaganda, which will be unleashed upon them as soon as a date for the plebiscite administrator is announced. As soon as this happens hostile elements will come into open defiance, and the administration is likely to collapse and the law and order position [to] become seriously jeopardized. To maintain peace and safeguard the minorities it may be necessary to resort to much more severe measures than have yet been used.

In view of these factors, and others that will be explained to you personally by D. P. Dhar, I would most strongly urge that the decision may in some manner be kept pending so that all its aspects concerning the situation within the State may be carefully and thoroughly examined. I would also urge that the announcement from Delhi regarding the talks be one that will strengthen and stabilize the secular and progressive forces here. I am sure you will stand by Bakshi and his colleagues who have at this critical juncture accepted the responsibility of running the Government and have never wavered in their convictions or in their faith in you.

With kindest regards,

Yours sincerely,
Karan Singh

...... 15 ......

Srinagar
25 August 1953

My dear Panditji,

Many thanks for your letter dated 21 August. You must have received my earlier letter dated 16 August which I sent by hand of Shri Vishnu Sahay.

D.P. Dhar explained the whole position to us on his return from Delhi, and we have also studied the joint statement which you and Mr Mohammad Ali issued at the conclusion of your talks. The position you have adopted and the reasons for it are now very clear, and, as you must have seen, Bakshi has issued a statement giving the joint communiqué his complete and unqualified support.[1] We never had any doubt that whatever you did would be in the highest interests of the people of the State and, in the broader context, of the people of the whole nation. Unfortunately, there seems to have been some initial misunderstanding as a result of incomplete information, which caused some flutter here.

On the whole, the repercussions of the agreement here do not seem to be unsatisfactory. It is not yet possible to say whether Pakistan and 'Azad' Kashmir will now desist from their vicious and disruptive radio and press campaign against the new regime. Pro-Pakistan elements here, however, seem to have mixed reactions. Many are dejected as they were expecting an immediate settlement. Others say that now that a date for the appointment and induction into office of the Plebiscite Administrator has been fixed, it is only a matter of time before the plebiscite is held and the State goes to Pakistan.

Bakshi and his co-workers, as is evident from their statements, are satisfied with the communiqué as it gives them some time to consolidate their position and also clearly recognizes the legal and constitutional position of the Jammu and Kashmir Government. Also, of course, such basic preliminary problems as demilitarization, the quantum and character of the 'Azad' Kashmir forces, the position of the 'Azad' Kashmir Government, refugees, regions and so on will have to be settled before the Plebiscite Administrator can be appointed, and we are confident that in these vital matters India will not compromise upon the principles she has firmly held for the last six years.

Eid day passed off peacefully in the Valley, and after the first few days there have been no more serious breaches of the peace and clashes with the police or militia. Of course, the new regime is facing an uphill task, but it has got down to work and is actively engaged in translating its new policies into action. I must admit, however, that I am not very satisfied with the present administrative mechanism which the new regime has inherited from its predecessor. In addition to its not being up to the mark in efficiency, it is also full of men whose loyalty to Bakshi is far from assured. And now the time factor has assumed great importance, as we have only about three months in which to bring concrete benefits to the people before winter sets in and the Valley is cut off from the outside world. Hence the urgency and necessity of Bakshi tightening up and vitalizing the administration cannot be over-stressed, and in this task help and guidance from the Central Government will be invaluable.

Bakshi has gone to Jammu where he received a great ovation from the people, who have a fund of goodwill for him. I feel that at this stage a goodwill gesture to the people of Ladakh, who are bitter and resentful as a result of the treatment they received from the previous regime, will be of considerable value. I have discussed with Bakshi the idea of taking a Ladakhi as Deputy Minister for Ladakh Affairs, a gesture which will not only be much appreciated by the Ladakhis but will also make the task of the administration vis-à-vis Ladakh much easier and smoother.

Before I end, I might mention another factor which deserves notice. This is that in the new set up there is a large and influential group of men whose views are reputed to lean towards the extreme left. Their support in the present context is of great value, but it is possible that problems may crop up later which we will have to face.

I understand that Bakshi has proceeded to Delhi from Jammu. I propose to visit Delhi for a few days along with my wife in the first week of September. She requires some medical treatment, and there are so many aspects of the situation here upon which I would like to seek your guidance and advice.

I hope this finds you very well. With respects and regards,

Yours sincerely,
Karan Singh

...... 16 ......

New Delhi
30 October 1953

My dear Tiger,

I am sorry for not having written to you for so long and not acknowledged your letter of the 5th October. I have been rather overwhelmed with work. We are closely following events in the Jammu and Kashmir State and are naturally gratified at the great improvement in the general situation and, especially, the economic position.[1] We are trying to help to the best of our ability, but we must not delude ourselves into thinking that the basic political problem is much easier of solution now. I am not referring to Pakistan or the UN but rather to the minds of men and women in Kashmir. I have no doubt at all that ultimately it is those people who will decide. If we win them over, well and good. Otherwise, well, we just do not succeed.

Therefore, we can never forget the political approach. Bakshi and some of his colleagues are making that political approach, in the rural areas especially, and that is good. Still we have to look ahead and not take any step now which may come in the way of a future step.

You refer to making the administration more efficient and honest. I agree and, to the extent possible, we shall help, of course. There is, however, something in what Bakshi feels. If we put Indian officers in important positions, this may be utilized by our opponents against us. We have, thus, to strike some balance between the two. But, about the necessity for an honest and efficient administration, I have not the shadow of a doubt.

In regard to Ladakh, I think, it will be a good thing for a competent officer from the Centre to be there, though, perhaps, he should go there in the capacity of an adviser rather than as the political officer in charge.

You refer to Gulab Mahal. I think, it is a great pity that this huge house should not be utilized. How it can be utilized is not clear to me. The various suggestions that you put forward, or some of them, do not seem feasible. We cannot have a Government of India office in Srinagar, at least a major one. It is difficult enough to take them out of Delhi to a nearby place, as they have to remain in constant touch with the Capital. Nor can we have a National Laboratory there. We are not having any National Laboratories in the near future.

It might be worth considering how far it could be made into a State hotel. I think, this certainly is a proposal which might work out. It will have to be a State hotel or, perhaps, while the State owns it, it may give a lease of it to some competent hotel firm. I doubt if there are any in India who are likely to take it up. There are only two such big concerns: Tatas of the Taj Mahal Hotel and Oberois. If we go to a foreign country, I would avoid the USA. Probably, a Swiss concern might consider it. We have been long thinking of a big modern hotel in Delhi situated in the Diplomatic Enclave. At long last, some decision has been more or less arrived at. This shows how long these things take.

I think, you might discuss this matter with Bakshi Saheb and find out what his reactions are.

So far as the University is concerned, you yourself point out the difficulty of having it there.

Vishnu Sahay has left today for Srinagar. You might perhaps consult him about some of these matters.

About Gulab Mahal, it might be worth considering to use it as a first-class nursing home or clinic. There is no such place in the whole of India.

Ever yours,
Jawaharlal Nehru

...... 17 ......

Jammu
2 December 1953

My dear Panditji,

Thank you very much for your letter dated the 21st November. I am fully conscious of your deep anxiety regarding matters effecting the State and your concern about Jammu. I assure you that I will do all I can do to help and facilitate the handling of problems here by Bakshi. It is a pity that he has been delayed so long in Srinagar. He is now expected here on the 5th December.

I certainly deprecate any action by the people of Jammu which may adversely affect our position in Kashmir. One does sometimes tend to lose patience with people who lack foresight and political maturity. The misfortune is that there seems to be no one here from Jammu who is in a position to guide the people along the right lines. Unfortunately, those belonging to the National Conference who represent Jammu in the Assembly and in the party grievously lack public support and confidence, and attempts to foist them upon the people only result in further ill will and disharmony. This is a very real and very knotty problem.

Whether or not the Praja Parishad will be able to retain the mass leadership, which it was able to build up during the agitation, will depend largely upon the manner in which the Government tackles the real problems facing the Jammu people. I have always held that the Praja Parishad, ironically enough, owes its following in Jammu more to the calculated policies and attitude of the previous regime than to any inherent strength. If, as I fully trust, the new Government approaches the problems here with complete honesty of purpose coupled with sympathy and understanding, then the ground will be cut away from under the feet of the Parishad and it will find it more and more difficult to mobilize mass support. This, I feel, will be the most thorough and permanent way of counter-acting the Parishad.

I am glad that Bakshi accepted my suggestion of flying the Union Flag on the Jammu Secretariat above the State Flag. This was long overdue and has had a very healthy effect on public opinion here.

I would have liked to visit Delhi earlier, but I am waiting for Bakshi to come down here as there are several matters I want to discuss with him. I expect to be able to visit Delhi by the middle of this month.

I had written a letter to Dr Rajendra Prasad suggesting that he might consider a visit to Jammu sometime this winter. He has replied saying that we might discuss the matter when I get to Delhi.

A couple of days ago I sent a copy of a book[1] by Panikkar[2]—*The Founding of the Kashmir State*—which you may find of interest. Being an eminent historian yourself, you are, of course, aware of the manner in which this State was built up. This book gives a good account of the way in which Maharaja Gulab Singh[3] and his Dogras founded this State and added vast territory to the boundaries of India.

The passing away of Sir B.N. Rau[4] was indeed very sad and a great loss to the nation. To us in Kashmir, whom he served for a while as Prime Minister, his memory will remain particularly dear.

With respects and kindest regards,

Yours very sincerely,
Karan Singh

......18......

Situation in Jammu and Kashmir[1]

1. Internal situation satisfactory—Valley/Jammu/Ladakh—perhaps better than ever since 1947.
2. However recent Pak moves have greatly disturbed us all. We feel that the main, if not the sole, motive of Pakistan in all this is to grab Kashmir.
3. This development has caused great apprehension in all pro elements. The pro-Pak elements, however, who were quite crushed, are jubilant at the move and go about saying that now it is only a matter of time before Pak shows India where it gets off and that planes will come etc.
4. In view of the fact that Pakistan has enlisted the support of a foreign imperialist power for the sole purpose of imposing its will upon India and Kashmir and coercing us. We all strongly feel that the very basis upon which the Government of India has based its policy since 1947 has changed, and hence the Government of India should consider a reconsideration of its whole policy vis-à-vis Kashmir in the light of the new developments.
5. The voluntary offer of a plebiscite by India was made under entirely different circumstances and now we feel that India need not remain bound to it.
6. You have always said that the people of Kashmir will decide their own future. Well, you have the Assembly which you have recognized as sovereign and which is engaged in framing the Constitution for the State (you recognized its competence regarding the dynasty etc. and also, to frame the Constitution).
7. Before the Constitution can be framed, naturally the first step is to decide which country we are with. Now, the Assembly will

meet in February and will pass a resolution finally and irrevocably reaffirming the accession of the State to India and also condemning a plebiscite. At that time, we would submit that the Government of India must back us up and accept that accession. If that is not done then the whole Assembly, the Delhi Agreement and so on become a complete farce.

8. (Only if necessary: there will of course be a risk of conflict, but we feel, with our very limited knowledge of international affairs, that this risk will day by day increase, as Pakistan will get stronger while we will grow weaker. And if Pakistan feels strong enough it will start trouble itself.)
9. This is the only way in which the cloud of crushing uncertainty which has plagued us for the last seven years can be removed. Of course, the negotiation with Pakistan can be delayed, but that will not be a solution. That will be condemning the people of Kashmir to a perpetual uncertainty, and if something is not done to finalize the matter soon all the wonderful work done in these four months by Bakshi and Co. will be in danger of being washed away. Again, internal dissentions will develop, pro-Pakistan intrigues will start again (many officers unreliable) and the whole internal position might once again deteriorate. Thus, we will drift from one internal crisis to another. Only a bold stand at this very opportune time can, we submit, save the situation.

...... 19 ......

Jammu
27 January 1954

My dear Panditji,

I have unofficially come across a copy of the Report of the subcommittee appointed by the Constituent Assembly Basic Principles Committee. I understand that this is being discussed with you by Bakshi and his colleagues. There are certain important points regarding that Report to which I would like to draw your attention. I feel that these points are of great importance, and that it would be most desirable that they are secured at this stage so that the possibility of difficulty or misunderstanding arising in the future is minimized:

1. Independence of the Judiciary: Whereas the necessity for the Judiciary being independent is recognized in the Report, it suggests that the appointment of the State Chief Justice and High Court Judges be made by the Sadar-i-Riyasat. As in the normal course the Sadar-i-Riyasat is expected to act on the advice of the Ministry, this will virtually mean that the appointments are made by the political party that happens to be in power at the time. It is clear that this sort of procedure will not at all ensure the true independence of the Judiciary from the Executive, which is so important if a democracy is really to function as such. Hence, I would urge that Article 217 of the Indian Constitution, whereby the appointment of the State Chief Justice and High Court Judges is made by the President, be applied to our State, also, with the modification that the word 'Sadar-i-Riyasat' be substituted instead of 'Governor' for the purpose of consultation. This will ensure the independence of the Judiciary in the State and the true interests of the people will be safeguarded ...
2. Delimitation of Constituencies: There is considerable dissatisfaction at the manner in which the previous regime carved out constituencies. It is alleged that they did so in such a manner as to keep one community in a majority wherever possible, regardless of such factors as geographical, cultural and ethnic affinities. To avoid all such controversies and to be sure that the electoral constituencies are made in an equitable manner, I would suggest that the task of delimiting our State should be entrusted to the Delimitation Commission, which has been appointed to do this job in the rest of India. The Commission consists of men of integrity and competence, and no one can question the desirability of their handling this job in the State. This will put the whole matter above controversy and criticism.
3. Sadar-i-Riyasat: Before I comment on this point, I would like to make it clear that I am not at all allowing personal considerations to affect my view. It is clear that I will not and cannot continue to be Sadar-i-Riyasat indefinitely, and any provisions made should be

such that with anyone here things should go smoothly, and India's interests should always be safeguarded.

4. In this connection, I feel that it should be made very clear that the Sadar-i-Riyasat is responsible to the President of India, in very much the same manner as is a Governor or Rajpramukh. The difference in the manner of his choice which has been allowed as a special case to Kashmir should, in no way, affect this basic responsibility, which is so important if the State is to be really, in fact as well as in theory, an integral part of India.
5. Emergency Powers of the President: It is of the utmost importance that the President's powers to declare an emergency in the State and follow that by such action as the circumstances may warrant should on no account be limited. This is very important, keeping in view the fact that we are a border State with peculiar internal and external conditions. While the special provision made in the Delhi Agreement may, if necessary, be allowed, care should be taken that this in no way binds the President down or fetters his authority.
6. Secular Character of the State: While the Report says that 'the governing features of the State Constitution would be based on democracy, equality and social and economic justice', there should be further clarification emphasizing the secular character of the State and saying that there will be equal opportunities for all regardless of their race, religion, or area of habitation. This is important to instil a sense of security in the minority communities in Jammu and Ladakh and even in the Valley.
7. Residuary Powers: Although the State has been granted a special position in the Indian Constitution, I strongly feel that the Residuary Powers must vest in the Centre. If this is not done there is always the danger of some undefined power being misinterpreted or misused by the State Government at some future date. The State has already been granted enough autonomy and there is no justification in my mind for insisting upon the retention of the Residuary Powers by the State.
8. Framing of the Constitution: Finally, when the Constitution is being actually framed many matters will come up in addition to these, which are at present being discussed with you. In all such matters, it is very important that any action the Constituent Assembly may

take should be taken in close consultation at all stages with the Government of India. This will minimize the possibility of any incorrect or undesirable steps being taken.

9. I would add that these points assume special urgency and importance in the light of local conditions and possible future developments. Today things are stable, and Bakshi is firmly in the saddle. But we cannot assume that this satisfactory situation will always continue, nor can we rule out the possibility of other less desirable elements coming into power at some future date. Hence any constitutional steps which are taken must be decided upon only after keeping such possibilities clearly in view.

With respectful regards,

Yours sincerely,
Karan Singh

...... 20 ......

Srinagar
20 July 1954

My dear Panditji,

Thank you very much for your letter of July 7th. I venture to write to you about a matter which I consider to be very important and which affects not only our State but, in the broader context, the security of the whole nation. I refer to Ladakh.

As you know there is at present no road link with Leh. The Army has constructed a road up to a few miles beyond Kargil, but that still leaves a gap of about a hundred very difficult miles to Leh, which have to be traversed on foot or by pony. The route, being slow and laborious, is not suited to carry goods and supplies in any large quantity to and from Leh. Nevertheless, it is at present the only route available.

Probably, it would be possible for the Army to complete this road from Kargil to Leh but, apart from the considerable expense that will be involved, that road will be most unsafe and precarious, passing as it will right under the enemy positions, which overlook it from the mountain tops. In the event of a renewal of hostilities, that road could be cut in half an hour by the enemy and rendered completely useless to us.

It is clear that from the political, economic and strategic points of view, it is essential that there should be a safe road linking Leh to the rest of the country. There is, of course, the Air Force, but a plane flight, apart from costing a lot of money, is also wholly dependent upon the exigencies of the weather.

Keeping these facts in view, and also keeping in mind the considerations that I shall outline below, I feel that a direct road between India and Leh deserves to be taken in hand as soon as possible. The route that immediately suggests itself is from Manali, from where a footpath to Leh already exists. As a matter of fact, it was along this path that in 1947 a gallant band of officers and men of the Indian Army pushed on to Leh by foot and reached there just in time to prevent it falling into the hands of the Pakistani invaders. Roughly, as the crow flies, the distance that will have to be covered will be only 150 miles, which will probably mean about four to five hundred miles of road. I believe that this road has actually been surveyed a few years ago, and that the approximate estimate came to between ten and twelve crores. However, keeping in view the great importance of the road, the money that is spent on it will certainly not be wasted.

I will now briefly outline the reasons why I consider this road so very important, grouping them broadly into three heads: strategic, economic, and political.

Strategic: In the event of renewed hostilities with Pakistan, or aggression from any other quarter, it will be very difficult to maintain an adequate garrison at Leh unless it can be supplied with arms, ammunition, rations etc. by road. Air supplies can at best be limited, and bad weather can prevent planes from landing there for days together.

What is more it is at present impossible to get even a jeep to Leh, far less trucks or weapon carriers, unless they are taken in pieces and flown there which is a tedious and impractical undertaking. If the Kargil route is cut—which is very likely—then our one means of supply will be cut off.

A road linking Leh with Manali, and thus with Delhi, will therefore be of great military value in the contingency of serious trouble on our northern frontiers, which I do not think we can rule out.

Economic: As you know, the economic condition of the people of Ladakh is very poor indeed. This can only really be improved if the flow of goods to and from Ladakh is greatly increased, which is not possible unless there is a road link. At present, Ladakh depends for its salt, butter, cloth and many other things on trade coming in from Tibet. This is a precarious and unsatisfactory position, as we never know when for some reason that trade might abruptly cease. The only way we can supply Leh is through Kargil or by air, both of which are most uneconomical. Under our Five Year Plan, we have some schemes and projects planned for Leh but many of them are held up because it is just not possible to get machinery or other articles to Leh except by air.

Particularly, in view of recent developments in Tibet, it is imperative that the economic condition of the Ladakhis be improved and to see that they feel clearly the advantages of their association with India. A direct road connection with the rest of India would completely change the present unsatisfactory position, and the benefits that would accrue to the economy of Ladakh would be immense.

I may also mention that Ladakh offers a vast and still unexplored field for the exploitation of mineral wealth. It is possible that those vast and inhospitable wind-swept plateaus may conceal under their forbidding exterior immense treasures, in the form of oil or even uranium, which one day may more than repay the debt that Ladakh owes to India.

Political: Addressing as I am a renowned historian, I need not dwell upon the past history of Ladakh. Suffice it is to say that until 1834 (the year of its conquest by Maharaja Gulab Singh's Dogra troops) it was an integral part of Tibet. To this day it retains its ethnic, linguistic, religious, economic and social ties with that country.

However, for over a century, Ladakh has been part of the Jammu and Kashmir State, and for about seven years part of India. I feel that its people have loyalty and affection for India, and left to themselves they will remain loyal. But in view of recent developments on the 'Roof of the World', it is most important that these ties with India must be strengthened so that they become virtually unbreakable. [Until] now, the authorities in Tibet have not shown too much interest in Ladakh, but there is no guarantee that this attitude will continue indefinitely, and after consolidation in Tibet it will be too optimistic to believe that Ladakh will escape an undue share of attention.

Our information, meagre as it is, shows that the Chinese are fast completing the road linking Lhasa with Peking, thousands of miles away, and are also engaged in constructing a network of roads within Tibet.

I can think of no one factor that will be more important in cementing the political feelings of the Ladakhis for India (and in the process turning their eyes away from Tibet) than the construction of a road directly linking Leh with India. They will then feel much closer to India than to Tibet, as it takes about four months to get from Leh to Lhasa. And after all, it must be remembered that Lord Buddha was born, lived and preached in India, not in Tibet. There is, therefore, no reason why the Ladakh Buddhists should not feel culturally and religiously as close, if not closer, to India than they do to Tibet. Indeed, I feel that instead of going to Lhasa (where reports show that they are beginning to find conditions very difficult and uninviting) lamas and monks from Leh should be encouraged to go for their higher studies to places such as Sarnath and Bodh Gaya. But all this will only be practicable if the Ladakhis can get to India directly and easily.

The road will be a lifeline linking distant Leh with the mainstream of the mother country. I may also add that if some day conditions arise in which the Government of India decides to take over directly the administration of Ladakh, the road will prove to be invaluable.

Before I close I would like to mention that if the construction of the road is taken up, either by the Army or by the civil authorities, it can hardly be completed in less than three or four years. Time, therefore, is of the essence.

I hope you will forgive me for having inflicted such a long letter upon you, but this matter had been revolving in my mind for a long time and I felt it my duty to convey my thoughts to you for what they are worth.

Yours respectfully,
Karan Singh

...... 21 ......

Jammu
11 January 1956

My dear Panditji,

Bakshi Sahib has seen me after his return from Delhi. Among other things, he mentioned that on the advice of the Government of India it has been decided to release Sheikh Abdullah towards the end of this month. No doubt this decision has been arrived at after careful consideration by all concerned, but, as this is a matter of considerable importance, I thought I should put my views before you.

Since the new regime took over on 9 August 1953, there has, as you know, been marked improvement and consolidation in many spheres, specially the economic and the constitutional. It is unnecessary to recount these achievements, and it is in no spirit of belittlement that I add that they have to be viewed in their proper perspective. Despite all that has been done, we cannot say that the political problem in the Valley has been solved. The reasons for this are primarily communal, but an important factor is that the Kashmir question still continues to be a live dispute with Pakistan and the subject of negotiations with that country. Nevertheless, the communal elements in the Valley are at the moment considerably demoralized, especially as a result of the recent statements[1] of King Saud[2] and the Russian leaders. What is more, they do not have any outstanding leader around whom they can rally their forces.

In the light of the position now obtaining, the probable repercussions of the release of Sheikh Abdullah require careful consideration. Of course, it is not possible to make precise predictions, but I feel it would not be justified to minimize the potentialities of the situation.

There is little doubt that upon his emergence from detention, he will immediately become the rallying point for all the disruptionist forces and disgruntled factions. There emerges the distinct possibility of widespread lawlessness and violent clashes between the various parties, to cope with which it may well become necessary to use forcible means. I am not suggesting that with the resources at its disposal the Government will be unable to face the situation. What I do submit is that the trouble may assume considerable proportions, necessitating measures which may expose us to severe criticism and distorted allegations in the sphere not only of local but of wider public opinion. There is no lack of those who are only too eager to exploit anything that might discredit the Government of India and the State Government, and this would be for them a heaven-sent opportunity.

It is said that if any such trouble takes place it can easily be faced, and, if necessary, Sheikh Abdullah himself can again be detained. But would not that be widely interpreted in a manner which cannot but seriously undermine the prestige and position of the present regime both within and outside the State? In such an event we will very probably have to face a situation even more difficult than the, one which confronted us in 1953[3]. Apart from the grave danger to law and order, there are three other distinct possibilities which cannot easily be ruled out. First, there is the danger that Sheikh Abdullah might be able to browbeat enough MLAs to gain a majority in the Assembly, of which he continues to be a member. This body is still functioning both in a legislative as well as a constituent capacity, and the potentialities of such an eventuality are too obvious to require any elucidation. Though Bakshi Sahib denies the possibility of any considerable defection from his ranks, I find myself, in the event of the stress of those peculiar circumstances, unable to share his optimism. Secondly, there is a section among members of the administrative services whose political bias may, in an atmosphere of communal excitement, cause large-scale desertion or even sabotage which can render any administration virtually powerless. Thirdly, there is a real danger of serious differences emerging within the ruling party itself as a result of the severe strain to which it will be subjected, and, in the present context, this would have obviously undesirable results.

One thing at least is almost certain. The atmosphere of permanence and stability which has been steadily built up will suffer a severe shock, and the whole issue will, in the minds of the people of the State, be thrown once again into the melting pot. This may lead many, who support the present situation, to reconsider their position. Fresh life will be infused into the communal movement, the immediate and cumulative impact of which can hardly fail to have serious repercussions.

It has, of course, to be considered how long he can be kept in detention.

I support the widely held view that the proper time to release him, keeping in view the security of the State which is our primary responsibility, would be only after it is found possible to declare that the Kashmir dispute is finally closed or, at the very least, until the State Constitution has been completely enacted and the Constituent Assembly dissolved, after which the situation can be reviewed. Until that time, I venture to submit, releasing him would be taking a formidable risk. Even from the wider aspect, the detention of one man is likely to be the lesser evil than having on our hands a widespread law and order problem and acute political disturbance in an area where above all stability and peace is required. Large-scale trouble may shake the faith and support even of staunch friends.

Finally, I may submit that we cannot ignore the existence of powerful forces who would be eager to support financially and otherwise any disruptive movement within the State, which would shatter its present stable and progressive association as an integral part of India. Specially, at a time when we are on the threshold of [a] new phase of substantial economic and social progress, as envisaged in the Second Five Year Plan, an essential pre-requisite for the success of which is peace and stability, we need to avoid any step which would play into the hands of such forces.

Knowing how very busy you are, I seek your indulgence for having written at such length, but in view of the consideration you have always shown me, and of the duties which you have entrusted to me, I felt that I should lay before you, in as clear and objective a manner as possible, my views on this important matter.

With respectful regards,

Yours very sincerely,
Karan Singh

...... 22......

New Delhi
11 January 1956

My dear Tiger,

Your letter of the 11th January has just reached me.

During the last year or more, the question of Sheikh Abdullah's release has often been discussed. Obviously, it is a difficult question and one has to balance various factors. So far as I am concerned, my whole mind rebels against the long detention of any person without trial. I have objected to this so often in the past that naturally I do not like it. But I realize that sometimes circumstances compel one to take action which is normally undesirable. In the balance, therefore, I left it to the judgement of the Jammu and Kashmir Government to decide what they should do in the matter.

In every such case, the advantage that one gains by the action taken gradually diminishes and the disadvantage increases. It has seemed to me that this stage was passed some time ago. It may thus become progressively more risky to release Sheikh Abdullah. Sometime or other that risk has to be taken, and it is impossible to keep him or any other person indefinitely in detention. That very detention will become an increasing factor for instability and for reactions against us in India and abroad, apart from its effect in Kashmir itself.

You say that it would be desirable to keep him in detention till it is found possible to declare that the Kashmir dispute is finally closed. That, I think, is not feasible. In fact, so long as Sheikh Abdullah is in prison, the dispute will not be finally closed. It is only when he has been released and we have faced the consequences of that release and survived them, that it will be possible for the situation to develop towards a final end.

There are the risks which you have mentioned. The question is whether the risks grow less or more by delay. The question also is as to whether internal stability in people's minds and administration will become more favourable later. These are factors which it is difficult for me to judge. But I am inclined to think that there will be no marked change for the better within some months or so, and the change might well be the other way. People in Jammu and Kashmir State are at present conscious of the considerable improvements, economic and other, in the State. They will forget them a little later.

This is my broad line of thinking. But as I have said above, I have avoided imposing my wishes on Bakshi Ghulam Mohammad or his government. If he has come to the conclusion that this is a suitable time to face the risk, I would abide by his decision and certainly not come in his way. I have no doubt that internationally speaking, the release would have powerful effect in our favour. Internally I cannot judge. But I have a very uncomfortable feeling that our position is constantly undermined by Sheikh Abdullah's detention, both internally and abroad.

I realize fully the risks involved. But one does not solve a problem or really avoid risks by running away from them. Therefore, after giving a great deal of thought to this matter, I have felt that Bakshi Ghulam Mohammad should take the action he has decided upon. This is as favourable an opportunity as is likely to occur. Of course, we should be fully prepared. Having got over this difficulty, the future of the Kashmir problem will be much simpler.

I would add that the visit of the Soviet leaders to Kashmir and its effect on the internal and external situation, which has been all to the good and has influenced many people in the right direction, is a factor to be considered. The conditions in Pakistan and in 'Azad Kashmir' are bad. Sheikh Abdullah may behave very foolishly but the effect of his behaviour is likely to be less now and can be dealt with more easily.

All these are speculations and appraisal of a difficult situation which has to be faced now or later. The question is what the most suitable time will be. It is bad to live in apprehension all the time. It is better to take the ghost out of our minds and deal with it.

Ever yours,
Jawaharlal Nehru

...... 23 ......

Jammu
19 January 1956

My dear Panditji,

Thank you for your letter of the 11th in reply to mine of the same date. It was very kind of you to have written so promptly.

I am writing this letter after studying the communiqué issued by the Government of India on 16 January in connection with the States Reorganization Commission's report.[1] Your wise and statesmanlike approach to this complex problem will, I am sure, bring about the best possible solution under the circumstances.

It appears that Jammu and Kashmir was considered by the Commission to be outside their terms of reference, for they have made no recommendations for this State. Although at present any change in the existing territorial position here is out of the question, there are some important points which do have a direct bearing upon our State and which I feel deserve serious consideration. Among these I would, at this time, like to mention the following:

1. For some reason, this State has been omitted from the list of States mentioned in the communiqué as comprising the Northern Zone. The Zonal Councils, as at present envisaged, are to be advisory and deliberative bodies, and it is difficult to see why Kashmir should be left out of them. Its exclusion will deprive the State of the benefits of coordination with adjoining States forming the Northern

zone, with which we have many matters of common concern. What is more, the omission will be exploited and misinterpreted by interested parties, while inclusion will act as a stabilizing and beneficial factor.

2. The recommendations concerning safeguards for linguistic minorities, to which the Government of India attaches great importance, is sharply relevant in our case. As you know, there are two important linguistic minorities in this State, the Dogras and the Ladakhis, and I am sure that no one will want them to be deprived of the safeguards that are to be provided for other linguistic minorities in the rest of India. Of course, as the communiqué says, this is a matter for consultation with the State Governments, but my point is that it should not be overlooked in our case on the ground that the States Reorganization Commission's recommendations do not directly pertain to us.
3. Then there is the fundamental matter of the abolition of the existing constitutional disparity between different States of the Union and equation of Part B with Part A States. Jammu and Kashmir is mentioned in the Constitution as a Part B State, though it is still governed by the Temporary Provision of Article 370. Although it may not be possible for us immediately to assume exactly the same position as other States, I feel that the question of the Headship of this State is of great importance and merits careful consideration at this stage, especially in view of the decision to abolish the institution of Rajpramukhs[2] and to bring all states under the same system of Governorship.

I may immediately submit that I am not considering this question from a personal point of view at all. It does not matter who is the Head of State here so long as we can be sure that it will always be someone who will keep the larger national interests paramount and enjoy the complete confidence of the Centre. I think, you will agree that the present arrangement does not ensure this. Although the Sadar-i-Riyasat is to be recognized by the President, this recognition is to be on the recommendation of the State Legislative Assembly, which, in turn, is through election by Assembly Members. Theoretically, it may be possible for the President to refuse recognition to a person in case he is considered undesirable, but in practice, keeping in view political and constitutional conventions, this will be very difficult. And even if it could be done, the initiative will always remain with the State Assembly.

In view of the peculiar internal, international and geographical factors that operate in this State, I feel that the importance of vesting in the President of the Republic the authority to nominate the Head of State (whatever the name of that office in Kashmir may be) can hardly be overestimated. I appreciate that this change will probably require constitutional action from our side, but this should not prove an insuperable obstacle. The importance of the matter, and the potentialities of the present situation, will amply justify any difficulty which may have to be encountered in solving it. What is more, the present phase, in which there will be far-reaching constitutional changes affecting the whole country, appears to me to be the ideal time to get over this problem also. Later, when the changes in other States have all taken place and the position in respect to the Headship here has crystallized as a result of continued usage, it will be much more difficult.

I have not discussed these points with Bakshi Sahib yet, but I trust that he will not fail to appreciate their validity and importance.

With respectful regards,

Yours very sincerely,
Karan Singh

...... 24 ......

New Delhi
20 January 1956

My dear Tiger,

Thank you for your letter of the 19th January. The question of including Jammu and Kashmir in our decisions regarding states reorganization did not arise. It is, of course, possible to include that State in the Northern Zone. But that will have to be subject to the approval of the Jammu andKashmir Government.

It would certainly be a good thing for safeguards to be given for linguistic minorities in Jammu and Kashmir. How exactly this could be done will have to be thought.

Jammu and Kashmir State may have been mentioned in the Constitution as a Part B State, but it has obviously been treated differently. In fact, it has been treated as something slightly more than a Part A State. In future, there are going to be no Part B or Part C States. There will be only one category of states. In view, however, of our special agreements with the Jammu and Kashmir State, these agreements will necessarily stand unless they are varied. They cannot be carried unilaterally.

I am sending a copy of your letter to Pantji.[1]

Ever yours,
Jawaharlal Nehru

From *Jammu and Kashmir, 1949–64*, 2006

Indira Gandhi and Karan Singh

...... 1 ......

New Delhi
17 August 1966

My dear Indiraji,

You will recall that over the last few months I have mentioned several times my desire to relinquish the office of Governor and seek a more active participation in national politics. I have been Head of the State for almost half my life since I first became Regent[1] in 1949, and I do feel that it will now be desirable for me to change my field of public activity, even though it will be a wrench for me to dissociate myself from close contact with the affairs of the State to which I belong. In view of the fact that the General Elections are approaching,[2] I write to seek your approval to my requesting the President[3] to accept my resignation[4] from the post of Governor of Jammu and Kashmir sometime next month.

With kindest regards,

Yours very sincerely,
Karan Singh

...... 2 ......

New Delhi
18 August 1966

My dear Karan Singhji,

Thank you for your letter of 17 August. We have since met and talked about the matter raised by you.

You have mentioned your desire to be relieved of your present office more than once in the past and ever since you first did so, I have been giving anxious thought to your suggestion. I fully understand and appreciate that having served as Head of State in Jammu and Kashmir for nearly two decades now, you should wish to have a change and think of more active participation in national politics. With your ability and experience you would certainly be an asset to political life. You have held the office[s] of Sadar-i-Riyasat[1] and Governor[2] with dignity and distinction in the midst of recurrent crises forced upon us largely by Pakistan's hostile and aggressive attitude. Your contribution towards the handling of this difficult problem has been invaluable.

However, as I have explained to you, we are passing through very critical times in economic and other fields. As the General Elections approach our problems will increase. The threat to our borders also continues. In these circumstances and in this delicate situation I am worried at the thought of a new person taking up your important position. That is why I should like you to agree to stay on in your present office for the time being.[3] I hope that you will find this possible.

With kind regards,

Yours sincerely,
Indira Gandhi

...... 3 ......

Srinagar
10 December 1966

My dear Indiraji,

I enclose a copy of a confidential letter[1] that I have written to Justice Kapoor,[2] Chairman of the Delimitation Commission, with regard to the delimitation of our Lok Sabha constituencies, as also a copy of the Commission's tentative proposals. I feel that it would politically be most unwise to carve out certain Muslim-majority areas from Jammu and attach them to the Valley for purpose of the election. I am also of the view that under the special circumstances of Ladakh it is only fair that it be allotted a separate parliamentary constituency. I do hope you will be able to give some thought to this matter also.

I need hardly say what a great personal joy it was to welcome you in Srinagar for the first time as Prime Minister. The general reaction to your visit here has been very favourable. I am following up actively certain important matters which I mentioned to you with Sadiq Sahib[3] and his colleagues. Incidentally, Bakshi Sahib[4] met me yesterday and complained that though he telephoned a dozen times while you were here he was not given an interview. He said that he had not gone to Delhi at all and had been in Srinagar all along. He will probably write to you about this, so I thought I should warn you in advance. He also made cautious enquiries regarding the recent investigations, to which I gave non-committal replies.

I see from the papers that your trip to Nepal has also been extremely successful.[5] It is good that our relations with this close neighbour, with which we have deep ties of culture, history and geography, are now back on a basis of full cordiality and friendship. I am sure your visit contributed substantially towards a further strengthening of these bonds.

I am planning to be in Delhi for the 14th November and hoping that J.R.D. Tata will have sent us his project report by then so that the Executive Committee can meet before the end of November to take a final decision regarding the Memorial Institute.[6] Once this is done, I can proceed with putting into motion the machinery to implement the project. Although the beginnings may be small, I am confident that one day the Teen Murti area will develop into a complex of really outstanding institutions which will be a fitting tribute to Panditji's memory.

The recent wave of student unrest is indeed a matter for grave concern. I have written an article about this for the *Indian Express*, trying to place the problem in its broader context, a copy of which I append. It is a matter which deserves the most careful consideration, as the present trend constitutes a grave threat to the very basis of our democratic structure.

Asha joins me in sending you our affectionate regards, Jyoti was thrilled to have seen you here, and Mummy[7] was touched that you dropped in to enquire after her health.

Yours as ever,
Tiger

...... 4 ......

New Delhi
10 July 1967

My dear Indiraji,

I have just returned from a two-day visit to Srinagar and hasten to write to you in order to lodge a strong protest against a further flagrant breach of trust by the ruling group in the State Congress Party.

1. You will recall that for some time I have been feeling that the present political structure of the State does not fulfil the genuine and democratic aspirations of the peoples of its three regions—Kashmir, Jammu and Ladakh. One of the approaches could be to proceed with a linguistic reorganization of the State, as has been done elsewhere in India. As this presented certain difficulties, it was suggested that a solution within the framework of the present State should be considered. I formulated some tentative proposals on these lines before the general elections when I was still Governor, and had some discussions with Shri Sadiq, Syed Mir Qasim and Shri D.P. Dhar. They agreed that the problem of fulfilling regional aspirations did exist, and solemnly promised that they would consider my proposals carefully after the elections were over.
2. I regret to say, however, that at his very first Press Conference[1] after he became Chief Minister, following the general elections, Shri Sadiq thought fit to oppose the idea of regional autonomy within the framework of the present State. Subsequently, he and the J&K Pradesh Congress Committee [PCC] President Syed Mir Qasim made public statements on several occasions reiterating their opposition to any such move. Recently, as I mentioned to you, they have also launched a vicious campaign in Jammu, spearheaded by a Governmental body

known as the Field Survey Organization in which they have tried to completely distort the whole idea of regional autonomy and arouse caste and communal prejudices against it. All this while I have scrupulously refrained from making any public statement on this matter, in deference to your wishes and in the hope that the ruling group in the State will ultimately see reason.

3. On the 7th July, however, the Executive Committee of the J&K Pradesh Congress passed a long resolution in which inter alia it openly condemned the idea of autonomy as 'part of the same shop-soiled and oft-peddled solution of fragmenting the State and thus delivering it into the hands of Pakistan on the one hand and China on the other'. The resolution added: '… in view of the sinister design concealed behind such disruptive and suicidal moves, the Executive Committee of the Pradesh Congress calls upon the people of the country in general and of the State in particular to be beware of the machination of the wider conspiracy of interested powers to drive a wedge among the people'. At a Press Conference in which this resolution was released, a report of which I enclose, Syed Mir Qasim was asked how regional autonomy within the framework of the State Constitution would lead to dismemberment. He replied that he clearly saw a foreign hand behind such a move, and added that disciplinary action was being taken against those associating with this move.
4. This statement, at a time when the Chief Minister had assured you that he would discuss the matter with me, is not only a deplorable breach of faith but can only be interpreted as direct and deliberate provocation. I may add that the present PCC is an entirely nominated body, and that the technique of labelling any idea which does not suit them as 'foreign inspired' is one which the present State Congress leaders have persistently employed, in an attempt to cast doubts upon the bona fides of those with whom they disagree.
5. Under these circumstances, you will appreciate that my political position has been gravely embarrassed. On the one hand it has been your wish that I should not say anything publicly in this matter. On the other, the ruling group in the State continues a dual policy of public denunciation and covert slander and distortion against the idea of autonomy. I am, therefore, writing to you in considerable

distress, and would request you to agree to one of the following alternatives:

(a) I may be given freedom to clearly enunciate my views at a series of public meetings which I will organize in Jammu, the Valley and Ladakh.

(b) A small Cabinet Committee is immediately set up to go into this whole issue, and a public announcement to this effect made.

6. As a Congressman, I am deeply disturbed at the fact that the Congress Party in the State—in the Valley, in Jammu as well as in Ladakh—is getting dangerously isolated from the genuine aspirations of the people. If the present situation is allowed to continue, there is danger that under stress the whole structure may collapse, thus causing a grave setback to the national interest. Meanwhile, as suggested by you when we met on an earlier occasion, I prepared a paper on this question of regional autonomy which I enclose.[2] In case you would like to circulate it to some of your Cabinet colleagues or others, I am sending separately 20 spare copies. The paper had been ready for the last few weeks, but I deliberately refrained from sending it to you as I did not wish to force the pace. The recent action by Shri Sadiq and his colleagues, however, has left me with no alternative but to take up this matter with you.
7. I will be available for further discussion at your convenience, but I thought it my duty to convey my views to you as early and as frankly as possible.

With kind regards,

Yours very sincerely,
Karan Singh

...... 5 ......

Regional Autonomy in Jammu and Kashmir[1]

1. Jammu and Kashmir is the only State in India which is bifocal by definition, the seat of Government moving between Jammu and

Srinagar for six months every year. The genesis of many fundamental political problems in the State is to be found in this peculiarity, which is the result of certain historical circumstances. Today the State comprises distinct units—Kashmir, Jammu and Ladakh. Despite its huge area, the population of Ladakh is very sparse and its requirements have to be tackled on a somewhat different basis. The main problems arise from the relations between Kashmir and Jammu provinces. Although several other States in India have regional pulls, the position of Jammu is entirely different because its separate personality forms a basic feature of the State itself. (According to the 1961 census, the population of Jammu province was 15,11,719 as against 18,83,862 of Kashmir province, while that of Ladakh district was 88,651.) In the 75-member Legislative Assembly, Jammu has 31, Kashmir 42 and Ladakh 2 seats.

2. Since the state of Jammu and Kashmir was founded in 1846, right up to Independence in 1947, Jammu had a predominant position in view of the fact that it provided the ruling class. This undemocratic situation came to an end with Independence; unfortunately, it was replaced not by a rational sharing of power between the two provinces but by the reverse domination of Kashmir over Jammu, which was as unfair and unacceptable as the earlier position. This has lasted for twenty years. The situation today is that political consciousness is steadily growing in Jammu, and with it the predominant feeling that if the State is to remain as one unit this can only be on the basis of both provinces getting a fair deal. Discontentment over the present set up has been long simmering and has erupted violently from time to time, most recently in the Jammu students' agitation last October.
3. In the recent General Elections, due to several favourable factors, Jammu emerged as one of the strongest Congress areas in the country. But this must now be consolidated by meeting the genuine political aspirations of the people; otherwise a rare opportunity for political consolidation will be lost. It is important that the Congress party itself should spearhead the demand for provincial rights rather than the movement to go into the hands of any other political group or party. Indeed, if the Congress is to function as a genuine 'people-oriented' party, this whole matter must be tackled as the result of a Congress initiative so that full political advantage is derived in the

process. It is significant that the Jana Sangh has launched a violent offensive against any move in this direction, probably because it sees in a rationalization of the present structure a grave threat to its political position in Jammu.

4. It needs to be emphasized, in view of the deliberate distortions which interested parties seek to inject into the argument, that the Jammu/Kashmir question by no means falls into neat communal divisions. It is seldom realized that fully one third of the population of Jammu province is Muslim, and that in fact the Jammu Muslim represents one of the most neglected elements in the State at present. In view of the peculiar situation in which Jammu and Kashmir was placed since 1947 there has been a reluctance to treat squarely the internal political issues involved, but twenty years and four general elections later it is now impossible to continue a policy of drift. Recent developments have presented a new opportunity for an imaginative political breakthrough.
5. There is much strength in the view that the unhappy relations between Jammu and Kashmir inter se are to a large extent responsible for the patently unsatisfactory, indeed explosive, overall political situation in the State. A bold and realistic attempt to meet the genuine aspirations of Jammu province can be expected to open up new avenues for political improvements within the Valley. It is true that we face a delicate and difficult political situation in the Valley, but a stodgy adherence to an unsatisfactory status quo will not help us in this respect. Indeed, the proposal for provincial autonomy will enable the problems of the Valley to be tackled on a more realistic basis than has been done so far. For example, this will enable Kashmiri to be increasingly introduced in the educational system as is being done with regional languages elsewhere in India. It will also help to rationalize the absurd situation which results twice every year during the en masse administrative migrations between the two capitals of the State.
6. One political fact has now to be squarely faced. If Jammu continues to feel that its legitimate rights cannot be ensured within the framework of the present State, the demand for a complete break away from Kashmir is certain to grow. There are three clear alternatives open at present:

(a) to maintain the status quo;
(b) to reorganize the State on a linguistic basis, extending to it the same principle that has been applied throughout the country;
(c) to work out a political arrangement whereby, retaining the unity of the State, each of its three regions is given political satisfaction.

The first alternative is evidently unsatisfactory, because continuance of the status quo will only lead to increasing political frustration, resulting ultimately in an explosive situation which we must seek to avoid. Statesmanship lies in meeting a genuine demand well before it reaches the point of ignition, and it will be tragic if vested interests are allowed to veto any proposal for improvement. Leaving aside the second alternative for the time being, although there are strong arguments in its favour, the attached paper attempts to explore the broad features of the third.

7. The main objectives of such a scheme must be:
   (a) to ensure that on a clear recognition of Jammu's personality and problems, its people enjoy the satisfaction of a genuine sharing of political power, a fair share of services broadly commensurate with their population within the State, and adequate attention to their economic and developmental problems—specially irrigation, power and communications.
   (b) to ensure that Kashmir benefits equally from the new changes, so that the sum total of political satisfaction in the State is substantially increased.
   (c) to ensure that Ladakh, with its peculiar geographical and strategic situation, receives the special attention that it deserves.

8. To achieve this the paper outlines a pattern of political organization which, while leaving intact the Indian Constitution in so far as it applies to Jammu and Kashmir, and the State Constitution, would superimpose upon them a system which may be defined as 'regional autonomy'. This proposal covers the more important executive, legislative and judicial aspects, and does not necessitate fresh elections because it envisages that legislators from the Jammu and Kashmir provinces would meet separately for certain specified matters, and jointly for other purposes. In view of its location and

strategic importance Ladakh is proposed to be made a special responsibility of the Governor with a local Advisory Council.

9. It needs to be stressed that the advantages of regional autonomy would under this proposal be available equally to the people of Jammu and Kashmir provinces, and that Ladakh will also be substantially benefited. Once this concept is accepted, steps for its further elaboration and implementation need to be actively pursued. The whole scheme can probably be put into effect by a simple Bill in the State Legislature, but even if an amendment of the State Constitution is legally necessary this can easily be accomplished by the overwhelming Congress legislative majority.

Paper Outlining Governance Structure

Regions

1. The State shall have three regions—Kashmir Province, Jammu Province and Ladakh District, to be demarcated on the lines of the present boundaries. The headquarters shall be the cities of Srinagar, Jammu and Leh respectively.

Ladakh Affairs

2. The affairs of Ladakh shall be the special responsibility of the Governor, who shall appoint a Chief Commissioner for this purpose. The Chief Commissioner shall be assisted by an Advisory Council whose method of appointment, powers and procedure of work shall be decided by the Governor. This Council shall include the elected MLAs [members of legislative assembly] from Ladakh, who will also participate in the meeting of the full State Legislature.

Legislature

3. There shall be a Legislature for the State which shall consist of the Government and two Houses, the Legislative Assembly and the Legislative Council.
4. The State Legislative Assembly shall for certain purposes be divided into two Provisional Legislatures of Kashmir and Jammu comprising

MLAs, including Ministers, belonging to the Province except the State Chief Minister. The Chief Minister may attend the meetings of the Provisional Legislature but shall not vote.

5. The Provisional Legislatures shall exercise powers and functions detailed in Schedule I and legislation passed by then shall go directly to the Governor for assent.
6. The Governor shall promulgate rules for regulating the procedure of the Provincial Legislatures.
7. The Provincial Legislatures shall elect Presiding Officers from among their members, and powers and functions of these officers shall be defined under rules.

Provincial Executive Councils

8. Besides the State Council of Ministers, there shall be an Executive Council for each province under a Deputy Chief Minister to aid and advise the Governor in the exercise of those functions which are delegated to the Provincial Legislatures vide Schedule I.
9. The Provincial Executive Council shall be collectively responsible to the respective Provincial Legislature.
10. The Deputy Chief Ministers and other Members of the Provincial Executive Councils shall hold office during the tenure of the Governor.
11. The Deputy Chief Ministers will be appointed by the Governor from the respective Provincial Legislatures, and Members of the Provincial Executive Councils by the Governor on their advice. They will be administered oaths of office by the Governor.

Conduct of Provincial Council's Business

12. The Governor shall make rules for the more convenient transaction of the business of the Provincial Executive Council and for the allocation among their Members of the said business.
13. It shall be duty of the Deputy Chief Ministers:
    (a) To communicate to the Governor and Chief Minister all decisions of the respective Executive Council relating to the administration of the affairs of the province and proposals for legislation;

(b) To furnish such information relating to the administration of the affairs of the province and proposals for legislation as the Governor or Chief Minister may call for; and

(c) If the Governor so requires, to submit for the consideration of the Provincial Executive Council any matter on which a decision has been taken by a Member but which has been considered by the Council.

14. All executive action of the Provincial Councils shall be expressed to be taken in the name of the Governor or of the Executive Council of the province concerned.

High Court

15. There shall be a High Court for the State, consisting of a Chief Justice and three other judges. One judge each shall form a Division Bench permanently at Jammu and Srinagar. The Chief Justice and one colleague will move between the two Benches, and with their presence each Division Bench shall be deemed as a Full Bench.

Provincial Administration

16. The two provinces shall each have a Joint Chief Secretary, and Government departments shall have provincial heads who will function under the authority of the Provincial Executive Councils.
17. Services shall be divided into two cadres: State cadre and Provincial cadre. For the former promotions and seniority shall be determined on an all-State basis and for the latter on a provincial basis.

Public Service Commission

18. The Public Service Commission shall consist of a Chairman and four Members. Two Members each shall constitute Provincial Commissions with headquarters at Srinagar and Jammu. The Chairman, who will divide his time between the two provinces, shall when present preside over the meetings of the Provincial Commissions, and in his absence the senior Member will preside.

19. Recruitment to the Provincial cadre shall be confined to residents of that respective province, and for the State cadre the competitions will be open to all permanent residents of Jammu and Kashmir State.

Deputy Advocate General

20. The Governor shall appoint two Deputy Advocates General for each province who shall work under the supervision and guidance of the State Advocate General.
21. It shall be the duty of the Deputy Advocates General to give advice to the Provincial Executive Council upon such legal matters and to perform such other duties of a legal character as may from time to time be referred or assigned to him by the Council, and to discharge the functions conferred on him by any other law for the time being in force.
22. In the performance of their duties, the Deputy Advocates General shall have the right of audience in all courts of their respective provinces.

State Planning Board

23. There shall be a State Planning Board under the chairmanship of the Chief Minister. The two Deputy Chief Ministers will be Vice Chairman of the Board, which shall include two more representatives from each province and one from Ladakh.

SCHEDULE I

Powers of the Provincial Legislatures

These subjects have been abstracted from the State list in the Constitution of India, leaving 31 subjects to the jurisdiction of the full State Legislature

1. Public order, except border security;
2. Police except border police, special police and the KAP;
3. Prisons;

4. Local government; improvement trusts etc.
5. Public health and sanitation; hospitals and dispensaries;
6. Pilgrimages, other than pilgrimages outside India;
7. Intoxicating liquors, that is to say, the production, manufacture, possession, transport, purchase and sale of intoxicating liquors;
8. Relief of the disabled and unemployed;
9. Burial and burial grounds; cremation and cremation grounds;
10. Libraries, museums; ancient and historical monuments and records other than these declared by or under law made by Parliament to be of national importance;
11. Education, except technical, professional and university education;
12. Agriculture (except agricultural education and research), protection against posts and prevention of plant diseases;
13. Preservation, protection and improvement of stock and prevention of animal diseases;
14. Pounds and prevention of cattle trespass;
15. Land improvement and agriculture loans; colonization;
16. Forests;
17. Protection of wild animals and birds;
18. Fisheries;
19. Cottage and small-scale industries;
20. Markets and fairs;
21. Theatres, dramatic performances, sports, entertainment; amusement parks and cinemas;
22. Unincorporated trading, literary, scientific, religious and other societies and associations, Co-operative Societies
23. Betting and gambling;
24. Taxes on agricultural income;

25. Duties in respect of succession to agricultural land;
26. Estate Duty in respect of agricultural land;
27. Taxes on the entry of goods into a local area for consumption, use or sale thereon.
28. Taxes on advertisements other than advertisements published in the newspapers;
29. Taxes on animals and boats;
30. Tolls;
31. Taxes on luxuries, including taxes on entertainments, amusements, betting and gambling;
32. Offences against laws with respect to any of the matters in this list;
33. Fees in respect of any of the matters in this list, but not including fees taken in any court;
34. Community Development and National Extension Services.

...... 6 ......

Preservation of Historical Legacy[1]

I understand that the NDMC [New Delhi Municipal Council] have a plan to 'improve' the Lodhi Gardens in Delhi, presumably to develop them as a greater tourist attraction. I hope the Tourism Department has been consulted by the local authorities, and nothing will be done to spoil this beautiful oasis in the Capital. Today's editorial on this subject in the *Hindustan Times*[2] makes me apprehensive. Could you look into this matter? I am sending a copy of this note to the Home Minister[3] also.

We have committees for the Buddha Jayanti Park, the Shanti Vana, etc. Could we not have a similar committee for Delhi as a whole, which could screen proposals like the one regarding Lodhi Gardens, and also prepare schemes with due regard to aesthetic values?

...... 7 ......

New Delhi
7 October 1967

My dear Indiraji,

I visited Lodhi Gardens yesterday along with Shrimati Pupul Jayakar[1] and Shri Chhabra,[2] President, NDMC. We went [a]round the Gardens, and [I] have ensured that unnecessary and unaesthetic structures and lighting will not be used. As the boundary wall on the Jor Bagh side is nearing completion it will be as well to finish it. We also impressed upon the President, NDMC, the desirability of replacing the cement roads within the gardens by grassy walks, and the question of tasteful flood-lighting of the monument will also be considered.

With kind regards,

Yours sincerely,
Karan Singh

...... 8 ......

Message for Indira Gandhi[1]

Sheikh Mohammad Abdullah met me this morning for ninety minutes. After exchanging pleasantries, we came down to political brass tacks. He started off by asking me what I thought of the present situation. I said that while it is true that the present status quo is not a very satisfactory one, the question of a 'solution' will have to be tackled with great care. Kashmir today is in actual fact a part of India, whether anyone likes it or not. It is, therefore, essential that if any steps are to be taken, the Government of India and, through them, the people of India must first be convinced. It is only after this that the question of Pakistan would arise at all.

I pointed out to him that for two decades our official policy has been an increasingly closer integration between Kashmir and the rest of India, and that a whole generation of Indians had grown up to accept this premise. Any reversal would therefore require the most delicate handling of public opinion in and outside Parliament. I added that as a first step it was necessary that the relationship between Kashmir and Jammu should be put on a fair basis, and that unless this basic problem was tackled there would be no chance of further progress.

This led us to a detailed and frank discussion regarding the whole Kashmir–Jammu problem. It soon became obvious that when he used the word 'Jammu' he meant only the predominantly Hindu-majority areas, and he specifically thought that the Doda district could not be treated as part of Jammu but would have to be placed on a separate footing. In this context, he referred more than once to Owen Dixon's[2] formula[3]. I made it quite clear to him that this was completely unacceptable, and that Jammu, Kashmir and Ladakh would have to be treated as the three units which at present comprise that State.

Although each of these did have a degree of heterogeneity, they yet formed clearly defined geographical and cultural regions and must be accepted as such. It transpired that we could come to no meeting ground regarding this basic point, and it was therefore obviously futile to discuss any of the broader issues involved. Under the circumstances, we both agreed to disagree, and I stated frankly that though I would be prepared to support the possibility of some special dispensation for Kashmir (no details were spelt out at all), I could not do so unless we were absolutely clear about the Jammu question. There the matter rests.

...... 9 ......

Note to Indira Gandhi[1]

Sheikh Mohammad Abdullah and his family lunched with me today. After lunch we had a discussion for about an hour. He began by speaking about his recent visit to Patna[2] and his meeting there with Acharya Vinoba Bhave.[3] He said that Vinoba was perhaps the only man left in India who could look upon issues from a detached moral viewpoint, and he had discussed with him a number of problems concerning the country, including language, economic development and Kashmir. He said that he had requested Vinoba to come to Delhi and convene a national convention in which all shades of opinion would be represented, where the important problems facing the country could be considered from all angles. He added that all the problems need not be taken up simultaneously but should be tackled one by one starting with the least controversial.

It was clear that this time he was trying to present Kashmir in a new perspective, as one of the many serious problems facing the country. Perhaps, he feels, with some justification, that such an approach might make it easier for the Kashmir issue to be brought up for discussion.

In the second half of our conversation he spoke at length about the utmost necessity for India and Pakistan to live in friendship, and the great political and economic advantages that would flow therefrom. I said to him that although people of goodwill in this country would certainly subscribe to his views regarding the desirability of friendship with Pakistan, he must realize that Kashmir had over the last twenty years got inextricably involved in two fundamental concepts in this country—national integrity and secularism. There was widespread apprehension that with secessionist forces active in other parts of the country any breakaway as far as Kashmir is concerned would result in disaster. Also, because Kashmir happens to be the only Muslim-majority State in India, any such breakaway would immediately upset the whole delicate balance of secularism that we have been trying to build up since partition. I told him clearly that the tremendous dangers involved in both these respects clearly outweighed the advantages that might be expected to accrue from friendship with Pakistan at this price. I also said that he should take a practical view of the situation as it was today twenty years after Independence, and that any constructive approach by him would be welcome.

In conclusion, I added that time was not necessarily on his side, and that with the reassembly of Parliament it would naturally become necessary for the Government to state its position with some firmness.

...... 10 ......

The Shahanshah of Iran: A Political Assessment[1]

16 January 1969

I had occasion to be with the Shahanshah of Iran for the full period of his twelve-day visit to India. While I did not discuss any particular political matter with him directly, I naturally had occasion in the course of this visit to converse with him on a large variety of matters. I give below some of the salient impressions that I gathered in the course of these conversations:

1. There is little doubt that the Shahanshah speaks with complete authority for his own country, and that he is a man deeply committed to the rapid economic development of Iran. The Shahanshah's pride in Iran's economic development over the last few years is unconcealed and, from all reports, well justified. His plans for the future are equally ambitious. This has led him into a feeling, perhaps slightly exaggerated, of the role that Iran has to play in the future development of mankind. His knowledge on a broad spectrum of subjects, including heavy and light industries, power generation and agriculture, education and social welfare, is indeed impressive, and he is full of statistical information with special reference to rates of growth. It is clear that his main preoccupation at present is economic development, and in this context, he was visibly impressed by what he saw in India during this visit. On several occasions he remarked on the tremendous difference that he noticed since he was here twelve years ago,[2] and after visiting some of our giant projects, such as TELCO and TISCO at Jamshedpur, Heavy Engineering at Ranchi, Integral Coach Factory at Madras and Bhabha Atomic Research Centre at Bombay, he was deeply impressed. Although he did not say so, I do feel that he was somewhat surprised at the extent of our development in the sphere of heavy engineering.
2. The Shahanshah was also obviously impressed by the warm and friendly welcome that he received wherever he went, particularly in Bombay where the Parsi community led the city in its memorable welcome.[3] On several occasions he reiterated that, despite the fact that India and Iran may be friendly with countries with which one or the other did not have good relations, this should not be allowed to come in the way of the strengthening of Indo–Iranian friendship. It is also clear that he envisaged this strengthening largely in terms of industrial collaboration.
3. Although Kashmir came up for discussion many times on a variety of matters, including food, handicrafts, winter sports etc., on no occasion did the Shahanshah say anything at all on the political

aspect, except to reiterate that the countries in this part of Asia should increasingly get together in order to counter the threat from China. However, on one occasion in a flight when I was sitting separately with the Iranian Foreign Minister, Mr Ardeshir Zahedi[4] (the playboy-turned-diplomat, who was at one time married to the Shahanshah's elder daughter Princess Shahnez), he did generally bring up the matter. From this brief conversation, as well as the longer informal talk which Mr Zahedi had with Lt Gen. Satarawala,[5] whom he had known when he was Military Attaché in Iran, it was clear that his attitude on Kashmir was entirely in favour of Pakistan. He reiterated that our claim to Kashmir was not and would never be acceptable to the Muslim countries; that it would not be possible for us to hold Kashmir indefinitely by force; and that, according to him, the only solution was to make Kashmir an independent entity, an Asian Switzerland. His mind on this matter seemed to be fully made up, and he pooh-poohed the obvious points I made to show that this was completely unacceptable to us, including the question of our national unity, secularism, the Chinese danger etc. Indeed, in his conversation with General Satarawala, Mr Zahedi went to the extent of saying that while Iran sincerely hoped that there would not be another conflict between India and Pakistan, if such an eventuality did arise we should have no illusions as to which side they would be on! It is not possible to say definitely how far these views expressed by Mr Zahedi reflect exactly the thinking of the Shahanshah. However, with the Shahanshah originating and directing all national policies, it must be assumed that they do reflect his mind. The Shahanshah himself, however, did not say anything at all, except in reply to a question at the press conference when he said that if approached by both sides he would be happy to mediate.

4. Throughout the visit I kept in various ways bringing home to the Shahanshah the multi-religious nature of our country and the extent of our efforts to build a truly free and secular nation. He seemed to be impressed by this, though Mr Zahedi once remarked that India and Ethiopia were two countries that had the reputation of being anti-Muslim. On religious matters, I found the Shahanshah to be remarkably free from fanaticism.

5. No report regarding the Shahanshah can avoid special mention of his gracious and charming consort, the Shahbanu. She is evidently a woman of deep understanding and commitment to the welfare of her people. She is genuinely interested in education, social welfare and the uplift of women, and was much impressed by her visits to some of our great artistic treasures. She and her husband thus form a highly intelligent and deeply committed royal couple, and I do feel that this visit can well mark the beginning of a new, positive chapter in the long history of Indo–Iranian relations.

...... 11 ......

New Delhi
17 August 1969

Dear Dr Karan Singh,

The Congress Party has been going through a period of anguish during the last few weeks. Senior colleagues in the Party had taken differing stands in regard to the Presidential election, leading to a good deal of confusion amongst our members.[1] It has been said that this is a struggle for power and a clash of personalities. But to my mind the differences that have arisen in the Party have much deeper significance and are based on the approaches to the problems and programmes facing the country today. These differences have existed in our organization for quite some time, and in a sense, this climaxed in the differences over the Presidential election.

I feel that the issues involved go beyond the Presidential poll. The result of the election, one way or the other, will not resolve the difference over the manner in which our basic policies of democracy, secularism, socialism and non-alignment are implemented.

I believe that there is a broad consensus in the party in regard to the future course of our economic policy. The resolution adopted at the Bangalore session[2] of the AICC [All India Congress Committee] was only a reflection of the general feeling of the large section of the members in our organization. What is now called for is for us to go through a process of heart-searching and a conscientious reappraisal of the functioning of the Party, and formulate methods for the implementation of our basic policies. I am convinced that it is not merely a matter for governmental action and legislative measures, but the Party organization at various levels should also get committed and involved in the implementation of these policies. Mere legislative enactments and administrative fiats cannot bring about social change, and what we are seeking to achieve is social change through democratic processes. Unfortunately, in the course of the years, our organization has been losing that dynamism and crusading spirit necessary to bring about a change in the attitudes and the thinking of our people. I have a feeling that as a Party we are losing contact with the vast masses of our people and especially with the youth. We do not seem to share their joys and sorrows. The real problem facing us today is how to recapture the missionary zeal which animated the organization during the days of our freedom struggle.

We took a very important step after the Bangalore session in nationalizing the 14 major banks.[3] This has kindled a sense of hope and confidence in the minds of the common man that there is now a serious intention to tackle the problems of unemployment and of the poverty affecting millions of our countrymen. But how far have we succeeded at the Party level to take advantage of this new situation, to mobilize the support of the people in order to create momentum for follow up action and the implementation of our socialist policies? The nationalization of banks was very much a part of our own programme. However, with a few exceptions, our Party has left this historic step unnoticed, whereas opposition parties have been claiming credit for this measure and organizing meetings and processions.

This has given the opportunity for some people to cloud the issues by raising the old bogey of Communism and Communist influence.[4] Other countries have had similar experiences. Any liberal, social or economic reform produces a reaction in the vested interests and conservative elements. I want to assure my Party colleagues that this has no basis whatsoever. As a Party, we are committed to democracy and the democratic way of life. We stand firmly by this basic approach.

I appeal to every Congressman to ponder over this state of affairs. How are we going to rejuvenate and galvanize the Party as a potent instrument for mobilizing public opinion and seeking its support, and at the same time create conditions in the country for speedy evolution of social change? Unless this is done, the forces of vested interests and reactionary elements in the country will take hold of the situation and obstruct our progress. The differing stands which leading Congressmen have been taking with respect to the accepted policies of our Party have brought about confusion and consequent inactivity in the organization at various levels. This situation can be improved only by a team of leaders and workers—at Government as well as Party level—who are entirely devoted and committed, who believe heart and soul in our basic policies and who will give sustained and dedicated cooperation for speedy action to translate our promises into reality. The Congress can be revitalized only by such dedicated and united leadership with a common outlook, and only a revitalized Congress can ensure the successful implementation of our social and economic policies. Experience has taught us that lack of unified thinking and outlook in the leading councils of the Party and the Government paralyses both, making them incapable of forward action.

I seek your whole-hearted cooperation in bringing about such a revitalization of the Party. Whoever be the individuals, if the Congress is to regain its position among the people, it must create a leadership which thinks, speaks and acts with unity of purpose.

The events of the last few weeks have created an atmosphere of mutual distrust and recrimination. We should make a determined effort to end this. The unity we forge has to be based on policies and programmers—and such unity should be on the basis of a commitment to the people of India. A new door has opened, and a new deal is in the offing to the toiling millions of our country. I have profound faith in the vitality of our organization and in its infinite capacity to adapt itself to meet the demands of new situations. Let us then march forward, shoulder to shoulder, towards the new goals that we have set ourselves in the service of our Nation and our people.

With good wishes,

Yours sincerely,
Indira Gandhi

...... 12 ......

Jammu and Kashmir[1]

Recent developments on the national scene, along with political turmoil in the Pakistan-occupied area of the State, have opened up new possibilities for political consolidation in Jammu and Kashmir.

However, this requires urgent and positive follow-up action on three fronts—political, economic and administrative.

Political

The Congress faces two main political challenges in the State. The first is from secessionist elements including the Plebiscite Front led by Sheikh Abdullah and Mirza Afzal Beg, and the Awami Action Committee led by Maulvi Farooq.[2] Sheikh Abdullah and his lieutenants have in their speeches made it clear that their involvement in the recent Panchayat elections[3] is with a view to wrecking the Constitution and disrupting the present relationship of the State as an integral part of India. There have been conflicting reports regarding the results of the elections, but it does seem clear that the Plebiscite Front has utilized them to spread its tentacles into the rural areas of the Valley. If so, the future consequences can be disturbing both in the event of the Front contesting the 1972 General Elections or their resorting to some form of political agitation to secure what they regard as 'the sacred right of self-determination'.

The second challenge comes from the Jana Sangh in Jammu and in a way both these challenges feed upon each other by fanning the embers of communal distrust and ill will. In Jammu, the implementation of the Gajendragadkar Commission's report[4] can set the stage for a new political consolidation, but it will have to be tackled in such a manner that the credit goes to the Congress and is not lost in a welter of confusion. In this context, the composition of the new bodies which will be created as a result of implementing the report, specially the Regional Development Boards and the University authorities, needs to be carefully worked out.

In order to meet these challenges successfully and strengthen its political position the Congress party, which is at present badly divided and poorly organized, needs urgency to consolidate its ranks. Not only have Mir Qasim and his followers virtually withdrawn from the political scene, but even in Jammu the required degree of political and organizational coordination between Sadiq Sahib and Congress workers has not been established. The Pradesh Congress Committee is in a state of suspended animation following the developments in May this year when the Qasim group was ousted from the districts. It is now necessary, at the Prime Minister's initiative, for the major political forces in the State Congress to come together in a new integration. This can be achieved either by recasting the Pradesh Congress Committee in consultation with Sadiq and myself, and persuading Mir Qasim to resume the Presidentship without insisting on the inclusion of any of his erstwhile group colleagues, or alternatively by getting the present Pradesh Congress Committee dissolved and replacing it by a five-man ad hoc Committee consisting of Sadiq Sahib, myself, Mir Qasim, Shri Girdhari Lai Dogra and Kushak Bakula. In either case it will be necessary to organize fresh party elections so that a united Congress is established as early as possible.

Economic

While the Fourth Five Year Plan has made special provision for Jammu and Kashmir, the tempo of economic development has still not gained adequate momentum. As far as the State sector is concerned, this is essentially the responsibility of Sadiq Sahib's Government. However, in the Central sector there are a number of projects which need to be expedited. The only Central projects that have been completed since the last elections are the terminal buildings at the Srinagar and Jammu airports, while the Gulmarg Winter Sports project and the Son et Lumiere at Shalimar are also actively being pursued. The Committee of Ministers of State which was set up in 1967 to ensure rapid implementation of Central schemes in Jammu and Kashmir does not seem to be functioning effectively. Prime Minister may consider the advantages of asking one of the Cabinet Ministers to preside over this Committee so that it gets a new sense of direction and dynamism.

Administration

Economic development will, of course, depend largely on the efficiency of the administration. Although several officers from the Government of India are holding key positions in the State, the general feeling is that the administrative machinery is still not functioning very effectively. The whole question of administrative cadres (IAS, IPS and KAS) needs to be looked into afresh. Also, the Governor,[5] who is an experienced civil servant, could usefully pay a little more attention to the major administrative problems of the State. In Ladakh the Gajendragadkar Commission has recommended a single line administration which is essential if the pace of progress in that incredibly remote area is ever to be substantially speeded up.

As far as law and order [are] concerned, with the activities of avowedly anti-national elements aided and abetted by Pakistan, a situation must never be allowed to develop in which the Government becomes dependent for the maintenance of law and order upon secessionist parties. The policy of liberalization can obviously not mean allowing secessionist parties to hold the Valley to ransom whenever they decide to escalate their opposition.

...... 13 ......

New Delhi
23 November 1970

My dear Indiraji,

You will recall that on several occasions recently I have put before you certain aspects relating to political developments in Jammu and Kashmir, specially this question of the Plebiscite Front's[1] possible participation in the forthcoming General Elections.[2] After your public speech in Srinagar in July this year,[3] when you unequivocally reiterated the basic policy that secessionism has no place in our country, it had been hoped that the issue would have been clarified beyond any doubt or confusion. Unfortunately, however, a situation persists in which the Plebiscite Front, which is a party clearly committed to secessionism, has stepped up its political activities with the declared intention of contesting the elections. On our part, although Sadiq Sahib has undertaken a series of political tours in the Valley, there seems to be some equivocation with regard to the basic issue. Indeed, at a press conference in Srinagar on 3 November, Sadiq Sahib is reported to have said that there was no question of banning the Plebiscite Front or taking action against its leaders, although he did characterize the party as 'extra constitutional'. The continued confusion becomes even more serious when we realize that unity in the State Congress Party is unfortunately still only skin deep, and important sections of the Party continue to have serious reservations.

With the current year rapidly running out, and hardly sixteen months left for the General Elections, I would submit that we can no longer afford the luxury of any ambiguity in regard to this question of the Plebiscite Front. While it has always been our policy to adopt a liberal attitude to political problems in the State, and even permit Sheikh Abdullah and his colleagues to hold a series of conventions in the hope that this may lead to a basic rethinking by them, it is quite a different matter when it comes to actually allowing a party like the Plebiscite Front the opportunity to capture political power. Certainly, parliamentary democracy should be strong enough to face any political challenge within its framework, but in this case, there are compelling countervailing factors that cannot be ignored, as their possible repercussions are not merely confined to the State but have important national and even international dimensions.

I would urge you to consider the following probable implications of the Plebiscite Front being allowed to contest the elections:

1. The very decision by the Election Commission to allot the Front an election symbol will give it a certain legitimacy and respectability which it has not so far been able to achieve. It is well known that the Front and its leaders are in regular receipt of lakhs of rupees every year from a neighbouring country, and with all the uproar regarding the use of foreign money in elections it would be extremely unwise to allow the Front to blatantly use this for subverting the integrity of the nation. Also, despite occasional tactical attempts to conceal its true motives, there can be no doubt that the ideology of the Front is secessionist. In this context, it does not really matter whether its leaders propagate accession to Pakistan or independence for Kashmir; the question is how far it will be wise to allow a secessionist party deriving financial aid from a foreign country to propagate its ideology in one of the most crucial and strategic areas of India. The events of 1965 are still fresh in our memory, and a recurrence of such a situation in the future cannot be ruled out.
2. Once permission to contest the elections is given, the Front will step up its political campaign. As it is, it has already started organizational work in right earnest, and my reports are that subsequent to the Panchayat election, earlier this year it has spread its tentacles far and

wide into the countryside throughout the Valley and, to some extent, in the Doda district of Jammu. Its very presence in the election campaign will inevitably involve a marked communalization of the political atmosphere in the State. The tone and context of speeches delivered by Plebiscite Front leaders over the last two or three years, within mosques and also outside, clearly reveal their political thinking. Invariably in these speeches the finality of accession is challenged, and thus the finality or otherwise of the State's accession to India, which we have always held to be a closed chapter, will become the dominant issue in the elections. This will have highly unfortunate national and international repercussions.

3. With the communalization of the atmosphere, several other baneful effects will flow. Congress workers in the Valley, already deeply disturbed, will be thoroughly demoralized, and the tiny minority community may well start migrating in considerable numbers. In Jammu communal tensions will arise, and there is a particular danger that in the Doda district, where the two communities are almost evenly matched, serious communal riots and disturbances may well be precipitated. It is significant that the President of the Plebiscite Front, Mirza Afzal Beg,[4] has recently paid a number of visits to the Doda district, and also that a Muslim Association has recently been set up in Jammu. Indeed, there are reasons to believe that a deliberate plan to foster communal disturbances at a time and place chosen by the secessionists is being hatched. Such disturbances will have counter-reactions in other parts of the State and the country, the disastrous implications of which hardly need to be spelt out. In this whole situation the Jana Sangh in Jammu is bound to emerge as the champion of Hindu interests, and there is a real danger of a complete polarization in the State on communal lines.

4. Thus, even before the date of polling, the political atmosphere in the State is likely to be thoroughly vitiated, thus creating a dangerous situation. In the elections themselves there are differing estimates of the possible results. My own feeling is that, with the situation having been thoroughly communalized, we should on no account underestimate the possibility of the Plebiscite Front winning a substantial number of seats. Whether they will get enough to form

a majority or not may be doubted by some observers, but there is every possibility that they will emerge as a major force in the State Assembly. Also, as I have said, the Jana Sangh will certainly gain considerably in Jammu. As the result, there may well emerge a deadlocked political situation in which neither the Congress, nor the Plebiscite Front nor the Jana Sangh are by themselves in a position to form the Government. The resultant political instability and its crippling effects on the economic developments that are so necessary for the welfare of the people of the State are obvious.

5. In the overall national context, a situation of this nature will cause us grave embarrassment. We will be accused of having allowed a secessionist party to emerge in a crucial border State, thousands of square miles of which are still under foreign occupation. This will be a windfall for those political elements who are opposing the Congress and may well endanger the whole strategy that we are developing for strengthening the forces of secular and democratic socialism. Indeed, a political debacle in Jammu and Kashmir can completely transform the national scene to the acute disadvantage of yourself and our party.
6. In the international field, the result of all these developments will be that far from gaining any credit the whole Kashmir issue will once again be revived. As it is, the State has been the centre of continued international intrigue and intervention ever since 1947, and the new situation will make it even more vulnerable and precarious.

Keeping all these factors in view, I would urge you to take steps to clarify and clinch this whole issue without further delay. Your speech in Srinagar should have had this effect, but evidently this has not happened. I would suggest that you may consider calling a special meeting of the Political Affairs Committee to which Sadiq Sahib and I could be invited, so that the whole matter can be thrashed out and a final decision taken within the next few weeks. It will also be useful to simultaneously call a meeting of important Congress leaders of the State at which the future political strategy can be worked out and a genuinely unified and dynamic party can emerge. Certain other points, including reports of weaknesses in the State administration and infiltration of key sectors including the police by secessionist elements, also need to be expeditiously considered.

Meanwhile, time is fast running out and the urgency of firm decisions increases day by day.

With kind regards,

Yours sincerely,
Karan Singh

…… 14 ……

New Delhi
7 December 1973

My dear Indiraji,

Soon after taking over the Ministry of Health and Family Planning, I visited the Safdarjung and Willingdon Hospitals and found that there is considerable over-crowding, particularly in Safdarjung. As against a total bed strength of 1,207 in this hospital, the normal occupancy rate is about 1,350. These hospitals are meant to cater to the general public, but a considerable portion of the beds are utilized for the hospitalization of the CGHS [Central Government Health Service] beneficiaries and, to that extent, the general public is deprived of the facilities.

1. I have given some thought as to how best the pressure on these hospitals can be relieved and at the same time the medical facilities for the general public improved. If a large percentage of the CGHS beneficiaries could be catered for in a separate hospital, the twin objective of relieving pressure on these hospitals and providing better facilities to the general public will be achieved. However, if a new hospital is to be constructed it will take many years, and the medical facilities in the capital for the general public cannot be improved in the near future.
2. I have, therefore, been exploring the possibility of starting such a hospital by utilizing some building in Delhi which can be put to that use. In this context, my attention was drawn to earlier discussions about the taking over of Dr Sen's[1] Nursing Home by the Health Ministry. I find that in the beginning of 1972 Dr Sen suggested that we might acquire the Nursing Home at a cost of Rs 60 lakhs. When this proposal was being considered, Dr Sen changed his mind and wanted that Government give financial assistance to him and that he would, in return, make all

arrangements for the treatment of the CGHS beneficiaries. This was considered by the Ministry of Health and it was felt that this suggestion would not work in practice. It was, therefore, suggested to Dr Sen that we would be interested in taking over the Nursing Home lock, stock and barrel. At that stage, Dr Sen wanted a sum of Rs 1 crore from the Ministry of Health for the purpose. The equipment, lifts and air conditioners were to be paid for separately. This matter was, however, not pursued as Dr Sen's intentions were themselves not definite.

3. Recently, from a letter that Shrimati Aruna Asaf Ali[2] had sent to me, I learnt that Dr Sen's Nursing Home would still be available for purchase. As we are in urgent need of a hospital, I requested my Deputy Minister Prof. Kisku[3] to visit the Nursing Home and have a talk with Dr Sen. He accordingly visited the Nursing Home on the 5th December and, during his talk with Dr Sen, was given to understand that the Cabinet Secretariat ha[s] offered a sum of Rs 90 lakhs for the purchase of the building for use as offices.
4. You will appreciate that Dr Sen's Nursing Home, having been designed and built as a hospital and being most centrally situated, its proper utilization should be as a hospital and not as an office building. I shall, therefore, be grateful if you will kindly allow us to negotiate with Dr Sen and purchase the building for utilizing it as a hospital. Without entering into competition with the Cabinet Secretariat, we would offer the same terms as what the Cabinet Secretariat had decided on.
5. Originally, there was no provision in the Fifth Five Year Plan for the improvement of hospital facilities in Delhi, but my Secretary, after several discussions with the Planning Commission, has succeeded in persuading them to agree to a sum of Rs 1 crore being included in the Plan for this purpose. In addition, provision has also been made for the expansion of the CGHS facilities in Delhi. Funds for the purchase of this hospital will, therefore, be available in the Fifth Five Year Plan.

I do hope you will give this matter urgent consideration. With kind regards,

Yours sincerely,
Karan Singh

...... 15 ......

New Delhi
9 December 1973

My dear Indiraji,

It is exactly a month since I took charge of this Ministry. In this period, I have adopted a dual strategy; on the one hand, I have tried to visit as many institutions under this Ministry as possible, and, on the other, I have initiated a broad review of a number of important policy matters connected with Health and Family Planning. I thought you may be interested in some details on both these accounts.

1. The institutions I have visited in Delhi include the following:
   (a) Willingdon Hospital
   (b) Safdarjung Hospital
   (c) All India Institute of Medical Sciences
   (d) National Institute of Family Planning
   (e) Central Health Research Institute
   (f) Indian Council of Medical Research
   (g) Institute of Communicable Diseases
   (h) Mass Mailing Unit
   (i) Central Health Education Bureau
   (j) National Malaria Eradication Programme
   (k) National Institute of Health, Administration & Education
   (l) Several CGHS dispensaries

I have utilized these visits not merely for formal inspections but as an opportunity to sit down with the directors and staff and discuss with them the problems of their institutions as well as their views on general matters relating to Health and Family Planning. I have found these meetings valuable and am actively following up the various issues that have emerged therefore. A pressing problem is the early improvement and expansion of medical facilities in the capital, which revolves around the acquisition of a new building for a CGHS Hospital. I have written to you separately about this and will take further action immediately on getting your clearance.

2. On the second front, I have taken a large number of meetings to deal with pressing problems of policy which need to be decided well before the Fifth Plan starts. These include:

   (a) A careful review of the figures of population growth to be included in the Plan. As a result of this, as you know, I suggested a revised set of targets which have been accepted by the Planning Commission and have been incorporated in the Plan document. According to these new targets we plan to bring down the birth rate from 35 per 1,000 at the end of the Fourth Plan to 30 per 1,000 at the end of the Fifth and 25 per 1,000 at the end of the Sixth. With the steady decline in the death rate, this would mean that the rate of population growth per annum is sought to be reduced from 2% at the end of the Fourth Plan to 1.7% at the end of the Fifth and 1.4% at the end of the sixth. The achievement of these targets, however, will require a massive and concerted effort on the part of my Ministry as well as the State Governments. Family Planning has got to become an integral part of family welfare including health and nutrition programmes and must be converted from a programme of the Government of India into a genuine mass movement.

   (b) I have initiated a wide-ranging re-examination of the question of the role of Mass Media in projecting the Family Planning programme, involving a careful reassessment of some of the existing practices to which we have been committed for many years, including such matters as monetary incentives etc. Also, in keeping with our new approach to integrate Health and Family Planning services, we are working towards a re-structuring of the basic message that has to be put across by the Mass Media. In this exercise I have associated a number of people, inducing some who have been trenchant critics of our Family Planning policies, so as to be able to get the benefit of a broad spectrum of views. The exercise will be completed by the end of this month, and I will send you a detailed report about it in due course.

(c) I am looking into the working of the Central Government Health Service, both with a view to improving its functioning as also to removing such genuine difficulties as the employees are having to face. I have closely in mind the views you have expressed for providing proper care to the ordinary beneficiary rather than only to VIP.

(d) The whole question of medical research needs a thorough review. The present position is far from satisfactory and the Indian Council for Medical Research, which should be the apex body to coordinate medical research throughout the country has, in fact, not achieved that status. As you know, a new Director General Dr C. Gopalan[1] has been appointed in place of Dr P.N. Wahi,[2] and will take over after two months. I am thinking in terms of setting up a high-level committee[3] under a very distinguished scientist like Dr D.S. Kothari[4] to look into the whole question of restructuring the ICMR [Indian Council of Medical Research]. At present, a number of medical institutes are being run directly by my Ministry, and several institutes predominantly involved in medical research are under other Ministries. The committee will examine whether it would not be desirable for all these institutes to be brought under the coordinating umbrella of the ICMR so that it fulfils the objectives that we have in mind.

(e) The Homoeopathy Bill[5] has recently been passed by Parliament. I am looking into various aspects of the development of Homoeopathy and the Indian Systems of Medicine. In the Fifth Plan an All India Institute of Indian Medicine and an All India Institute of Homoeopathy are to be set up, and I will initiate action on this shortly.

(f) At present Hindustan Latex have only one factory producing Nirodh contraceptives in Trivandrum. The requirement of Nirodh will increase sharply during the Fifth Plan, and I am actively studying the proposal to expand the Trivandrum factory as well as to set up two or three more factories in other parts of the country during the Fifth Plan period.

(g) The evil of food and drug adulteration has assumed alarming proportions over the last few years. Although we have legislation to deal with it, the actual position is most unsatisfactory mainly due to the fact that it is the local bodies that have been made responsible to deal with this matter. I have taken a high-level meeting, attended by representatives from the various local bodies in the capital as well as voluntary organizations including the Citizens Central Council, in order to evolve a coordinated strategy at least in Delhi.

(h) In my capacity as Health Minister, I am Chairman of the Governing Bodies of our two premier institutes of medical research and teaching, the All India Institute of Medical Sciences in New Delhi and the Post-Graduate Institute of Medical Sciences in Chandigarh. I have met the Directors personally and have discussed with them the problems that they face as well as their projections for the Fifth Plan. I also found to my surprise that I was President of as many as 25 other organizations. I have moved rapidly to divest myself of this unnecessary burden by passing several of these functions on to my colleagues, the Deputy Ministers for Health and Family Planning.

(i) I have personally met representatives of the various unions in our Delhi hospitals, and have started a general dialogue with the medical profession through the Delhi Medical Association whose annual function I inaugurated. There are reasons to believe that, following the unfortunate pattern of events in Maharashtra earlier this year, we may have to face certain difficulties from the medical profession in Delhi and elsewhere during 1974. I will keep the situation under careful watch.

3. I apologize for the length of this letter, but I thought you would be interested to know in some detail what I have been doing since you entrusted this portfolio to me. It is an exciting and exhilarating challenge, and the work that needs to be done is tremendous, particularly in the field of extending medical facilities to the rural areas. As soon as the Parliament session is over I intend to start touring different parts of the country, visiting Central, State and private institutions of importance in the field of Health and Family Planning, and having detailed discussions with state Chief Ministers

and Health Ministers. I am convening a meeting of Health Ministers of the States towards the end of January[6] at which all major issues relating to implementing Fifth Plan programmes will be thrashed out. I am confident that with your continued guidance we will be able in the first two years of the Plan to lay the foundation for a real breakthrough in the vital fields of Health and Family Planning.

With kind regards,

Yours sincerely,
Karan Singh

...... 16 ......

New Delhi
11 December 1973

Dear Dr Karan Singh,

I have your letter of 9 December.

I am glad to see the earnestness and enthusiasm with which you have embarked on your new assignment. It is, indeed, an enormous task. You have my good wishes.

A small point. I do not know which 25 organizations you are now delegating to the Deputy Ministers. Will they be able to handle them?

Yours sincerely,
Indira Gandhi

...... 17 ......

New Delhi
7 July 1974

My Dear Indiraji,

As I mentioned to you when we met yesterday, I have converted my mini-castle in Jammu into an institution called the Amar Mahal Museum & Library. Apart from housing my own personal library, which now comprises about 15,000 books acquired over the last 15 years, this will also display a famous series of Kangra paintings on the Nala–Damayanti theme[1], a portrait gallery, a gallery of modern art and several objects of historical interest. It is my intention over the years not only to develop the Museum & Library, but also to set up a School of Comparative Religion and Philosophy. Surprisingly enough, despite our strong emphasis on secularism there is not a single such institution anywhere in India.

The library and museum are now ready for opening, and I will be most grateful if you could spare an hour during your next visit to Jammu to inaugurate this institution. Any day in October would be suitable, as the museum is bringing out a publication on the Nala–Damayanti paintings which should also be ready for release by then. I do hope you will accept this invitation, and I will work out the details whenever your next visit to Jammu is scheduled.

With kind regards,

Yours sincerely,
Karan Singh

...... 18 ......

New Delhi
22 January 1975

My dear Indiraji,

This has reference to the meeting which you took on the 16th regarding the proposed political settlement[1] with Sheikh Abdullah. In amplification of the points that I mentioned there, I thought it would be useful if I put down in some detail my views on certain aspects. I was expecting a copy of the detailed formulations arrived at between Shri G. Parthasarathy[2] and Mirza Afzal Beg, but I have not received this yet. I will, therefore, not make any remarks on the constitutional aspects of the Centre–State relationship, except to reiterate that all matters affecting the security of the State are clarified beyond the possibility of any dispute. Also, once this agreement is finalized, there should be no question at all of its ratification by any third party.

1. The purpose of this letter is to put down for your consideration some observations on two inter-related sets of questions relating to the internal problems of Jammu and Kashmir State and the modalities of the political settlement. If the new initiative is to succeed, it will be

essential to carry the bulk of public opinion not only in the Kashmir valley but also in the two other regions of Jammu and Ladakh. This is a geopolitical reality which has to be taken into account, and is not in any way based upon communal considerations. It is true that the majority of the population in the Jammu region is Hindu and in Ladakh Buddhist, but it is also true that in both these regions there is a substantial Muslim population, which happens to be among the most economically backward in the whole state. The safeguarding of the interests of these regions, therefore, will inter alia be directly in the interests of their Muslim inhabitants.

2. It will be unrealistic to deny that the people of Jammu and Ladakh have deep reservations with regard to Sheikh Abdullah, nor is this surprising considering the historical background as well as our own public stand for 20 years after the events of 1953.[3] It will, therefore, not only be good in itself but also useful from the point of view of establishing the credibility of the new Government in these regions if certain safeguards are incorporated into the package which is being negotiated with the Sheikh. This will also make it easier for the agreement to be accepted by Parliament, the party and the country as a whole.

3. I would like to start with Ladakh, the geographical situation of which makes it one of the most highly strategic areas in the world. Its area of 95.9 thousand square kilometres is more than double the combined area of the Jammu and Kashmir regions, but its population in the 1971 census was only 1,05,291. Its sparse population, inaccessibility and strategic location make it absolutely essential in the national interest that a special administrative pattern be evolved for Ladakh to ensure its rapid economic development as well as its security. Having given this matter considerable thought I feel that the best solution would be to adopt the pattern as laid down in the VI Schedule of the Constitution for Administration of Tribal Areas in Assam. Thus, while continuing to be an integral part of Jammu and Kashmir State, this pattern of administration will place upon the Governor a special responsibility to ensure Ladakh's rapid economic development; [it] will make the people of Ladakh eligible for reservations in services, admissions etc. on a national basis from the quota set aside for

Scheduled Tribes; [it] will underline and preserve the special ethnic and political character of Ladakh. As Ladakh has only two members in the State Assembly, a special Regional Council should be set up consisting of elected representatives from Ladakh, including the Leh and Kargil tehsils. This will go a long way in meeting the aspirations of the people of Ladakh without disturbing its position as part of the Jammu and Kashmir State.

4. I turn next to the problems of the Jammu region. To effectively carry mass opinion and meet the challenge of the opposition, I would suggest five measures which could be adopted as part of the package agreement with Sheikh Abdullah. These are:

   (i) High-powered Regional Development Boards should be set up for the Jammu and Kashmir regions, which will ensure that developmental and plan expenditure is equitably distributed and there is no unfair diversion of resources from one region to the other. This was a recommendation of the Gajendragadkar Commission. In fact, Sadiq Sahib had set up such Boards, but unfortunately, they have remained virtually defunct. They need to be carefully reconstituted and made operative.

   (ii) Another recommendation of the Gajendragadkar Commission was that if the Chief Minister is from one region there should be a Deputy Chief Minister from the other. Now that a coalition is envisaged, this becomes all the more necessary.

   (iii) The Scheduled Castes population in the State is not enjoying the full benefits that are available to [them] in the rest of the country. Although they do have reservations in the State Assembly, a number of other safeguards are not available to them. The Gajendragadkar Commission recommended the extension of Article 335 of the Indian Constitution to Jammu and Kashmir. This would go a long way to safeguard the interests of the Scheduled Castes, who live only in the Jammu region.

   (iv) Gujjars and Bakkarwals[4] in the State should be included in the list of Scheduled Tribes so that their economic backwardness can be progressively overcome. They reside in both regions of the State and also lead a nomadic existence.

(v) Dogri is included in the State Constitution but not in the VIII Schedule of the Indian Constitution. The present Government has made public commitments that the State Assembly would pass a resolution urging the inclusion of Dogri in the VIII Schedule, which already includes Kashmiri. An announcement to this effect when the new Government assumes office will have a positive political impact.

5. A parallel set of problems relates to the details of the political settlement with Sheikh Abdullah in so far as the composition of the new Government is concerned. Here also it is important that details be sorted out well in advance so as to obviate misunderstanding or misinterpretation at a later stage. The following points need to be kept in view in this regard:

(i) As Sheikh Abdullah will come into power on the support of the Congress Party, the Congress should have substantial representation in the new Government. The Congress team should be headed by a Deputy Chief Minister from the Jammu region, but should also include at least one Cabinet Minister from the Kashmir valley.

(ii) The Congress team should be chosen by the Congress High Command and not by Sheikh Abdullah, otherwise the whole concept of a coalition will become meaningless.

(ii) Adequate representation should be given to Ladakh in the new Government, preferably by including a representative each from the Leh and Kargil tehsils.

(iv) Simultaneously, the entire Congress organization in the State needs to be overhauled and energized. An ad hoc Pradesh Congress Committee should be set up under the chairmanship of a senior Congress leader to revitalize and activize the organization. The importance of this in the new set up cannot be overemphasized, as the creation of a new political party by Sheikh Abdullah will almost certainly have a deeply unsettling impact upon the rank and file of the Congress, especially in the Valley.

6. I have not in this letter mentioned any specific names for governmental and party posts but will be glad to make concrete suggestions to you when you so desire. I apologize for the length of this letter, but I know that you would expect me to place before you all such points as I consider important and relevant in the new context. Indeed, the success of this experiment, as I see it, will depend largely upon absolute clarity of purpose and functioning as far as the Government of India and the Congress Party are concerned. I am always available for such further consultations as you may require. Meanwhile, I do hope that I will soon receive the terms of the agreement arrived at between Shri G. Parthasarathy and Mirza Afzal Beg so that, if necessary, I can furnish further comments.

With kind regards,

Yours sincerely,
Karan Singh

...... 19 ......

New Delhi,
13 June 1975

My dear Indiraji,

Since the news of the Allahabad judgement came in yesterday[1] I have been pondering deeply over the implications. I have not signed the reported statement[2] by some Cabinet colleagues, primarily because I was up in Srinagar but also because, as far as I am concerned, there is surely no need to reiterate support. I can never forget the affectionate guidance that I received from Panditji ever since I entered public life at the age of eighteen, nor your gesture in inducting me into national politics at the highest level at the first suitable opportunity, and your unfailing consideration thereafter. If I may say so, I have never looked upon my relationship with you in any formal terms but more as a younger brother. It is in this context that I venture to place before you my personal views on how the present crisis should be met.

The remarkable leadership you have given to the nation over the last few years will ensure for you a place in world history. In particular the

Bangladesh crisis[3]—the gravest we have faced since Independence—saw you in a truly historic role that raised India's prestige not only among the nations of the world but, more importantly, in the eyes of Indians themselves. As a nation, we tend to swing between extremes of euphoria and depression, but you have guided the destiny of India with a firm and sure hand, facing problems of incredible and unprecedented magnitude.

Clearly, the nation need[s] your leadership for many more years. Yet, it is also essential, in the wake of the Allahabad judgement, to ensure that your image in the general public is not eroded and the psychological initiative regained. The first task is to tide over the period between now and the Supreme Court verdict. In this context, it seems to me that the best course would be as follows.

When the President[4] returns from Srinagar on the 16th morning (or earlier) you call on him and give him a letter offering, in view of the judgement, to step down from office until the Supreme Court verdict. This is announced on the two o'clock news. The matter then receives the President's close consideration. In my view, the decision should be quite clear. Keeping all factors in view, including the overwhelming support you have in Parliament (which can, if necessary, be reiterated at a formal meeting of the Congress Parliamentary Party), he informs you the same evening that he does not accept the resignation. Later that night you go on the air with a special broadcast to the people of India.

This gets us over the first phase and, to an extent, takes the edge off the opposition offensive in the mind of the general public. The next stage is the Supreme Court.[5] Here I would plead that Shri Khare,[6] who has proved to be an unmitigated disaster, should no longer deal with the case. This should be handled by Palkhivala[7] and Seervai[8] in consultation with Siddhartha.[9]

I have full faith in your tremendous inner reserves to meet successfully this new challenge as you have done so often in the past. I am in Delhi and available whenever you need me. You know, of course, that my deep regard and affection will remain with you always, come what may.[10]

As ever,
Tiger

...... 20 ......

Some Aspects of Recent Affairs[1]

In view of recent developments, it is urgently necessary to take stock of the total situation in the country and devise measures to move forward rapidly in many fields so that India emerges stronger from this crisis. Placed below are some approaches which are relevant in the present context.

Economic

(a) If within the next thirty days there is a marked decrease in the price of even two or three essential commodities, there will be a favourable upsurge of public opinion and the common man will feel that the Emergency is being used directly for his benefit. This could be achieved by a combination of improving the distribution mechanism and taking deterrent action against hoarders and black marketeers dealing in essential commodities.

(b) Although we are in the second year of Fifth Plan, the plan itself has not yet been finalized. This can be turned to advantage by thoroughly revamping the Plan within the next few weeks, to make it more oriented towards meeting the minimum needs of life for the common man—food, clothing, shelter, education and health services—as well as a massive programme of employment for the educated youth. Elitist and giganticist [sic] approaches will have to give way to a new realism and pragmatism, so as to try and meet the urgent needs of the masses within the current Plan period itself.

(c) With regard to fiscal and monetary policy, it is necessary to stress increased production and productivity in every sphere as the highest priority. Various benefits to organized labour should be linked directly to production, and shortfalls by management should attract serious notice both in the public and the private sectors. A new work ethic should replace the present demand-oriented approach. Demonetization of high denomination currency notes is also likely to have a valuable fiscal and psychological impact.

(d) In the longer perspective, the burgeoning population increase must receive the highest priority with a passive programme of public education and provision of a package of health, family planning and nutrition programmes. Health problems such as malaria affecting vast masses of people must receive effective attention before they become totally uncontrollable.

Political

(a) The deeper question of evolving a constitutional structure better suited to the requirements and genius of the nation has now to be squarely faced. While many elements in our existing constitution are of tremendous and abiding value, particularly the great concepts of democracy, secularism and federalism that it enshrines, a quarter century has shown that the present structure fails in some respects to meet the dynamics of economic growth and social transformation or to prevent serious political distortions. To study this question in depth a Constitutional Commission of selected jurists, political scientists and public men of high ability and integrity should be set up to prepare a preliminary report outlining the contours of a new constitutional structure. This could become the basis of a national debate and consensus leading ultimately to the adoption of a new and improved version of our Constitution, stressing not only the rights of citizens but also their duties and responsibilities.

(b) Meanwhile, the Cabinet needs to be overhauled and restructured so as to make it a more coherent and effective instrument for facing the tremendous challenges that lie ahead. With several governorships falling vacant, a number of senior but ineffective Ministers can safely be found alternative employment, while at the lower level a good deal of dead wood can be shed and more effective persons inducted. Portfolios should be allotted on the basis of the optimum contribution that a person is best suited to make in a particular sphere.

(c) Simultaneously, the party also needs a thorough reorientation, starting with the Pradesh Congress Committees and the Working Committee itself. The tradition of mass involvement which has been the mainstay of the Congress for decades has to be revived, and special attention paid to work among women, in the co-operative movement, in the labour field and among the Scheduled Castes and Tribes. The 'Camp' approach tends to become elitist if it is not followed up by a programme of mass involvement in the rural areas as well as the urban slums.

(d) The perennial conflict between the Youth Congress and the main Party, as well as between various factions of the Youth Congress and the NSUI, needs to be firmly sorted out so that a dynamic youth movement can develop. Indeed, the mobilization of the youth is perhaps the most important single task before us, and it must receive top priority in terms of talent and financial inputs. This must include student youth, non-student youth and the younger professionals and intellectuals who play such an important role in moulding public opinion. The concrete proposals in this regard prepared recently after intensive discussion by a group of Ministers need to be vigorously implemented.

Administrative

(a) It is necessary to follow up the approaches taken by you in your two circular letters recently regarding streamlining the administrative machinery. Wherever necessary changes should be made in key positions so that a new momentum and discipline is imparted to the vast and inchoate structure that is the Government of India. In particular, the whole system of financial administration needs to be drastically reoriented so that individual Ministries are given much greater flexibility in spending the Plan funds allotted to them while at the same time being held to stricter accountability. This performance-oriented decentralization of financial and administrative authority is essential if the long tradition of conservative and status-quoist administration in this country is to be broken.

(b) The present system whereby unimportant items come to Cabinet for consideration, while major issues of policy are seldom debated, will have to change. Cabinet must be able to come to grips with the fundamental problems facing the nation, rather than spend much of its time in dealing with formal and often marginal matters.

International

(a) It is tremendously important to counteract efforts that will inevitably be made by powerful elements abroad to damage the international image of India after the recent developments. This is not a question of being hypersensitive to foreign reactions, but of taking the necessary precautions to see that a distorted picture which could lower the prestige of India in the eyes of the world does not go unchallenged. This will require a mobilization of the entire foreign service, jolting it out of its routine functioning and instilling into it an awareness of the new dimensions that have emerged. Special visits to selected countries may also be necessary to put across the correct perspective.

(b) The foreign press corps in Delhi should not be neglected. A special attempt should be made at appropriate levels to have a dialogue individually and collectively with the representatives of foreign news agencies so that, as far as possible, they do not project a one-sided and distorted picture. This is all the more necessary in view of the censorship that has been imposed, whereby all sorts of fantastic reports may gain currency abroad.

(c) A basic paper explaining in some detail the background of events leading up to the declaration of the Emergency should be rapidly prepared and cabled to our Missions abroad. This paper, which should make a logical and coherent presentation, will, when suitably expanded, be useful also in explaining the situation to intellectuals at home, sections of whom are bound to have grave reservations with regard to recent developments.

From *Kashmir and Beyond, 1966–84*, 2011

Memoir

Reminiscences of a Sovereign

A WEEK AFTER ASSUMING the office of Sadar-i-Riyasat the government moved down to Jammu for the winter. The Praja Parishad had, of course, been outraged at my acceptance of the office and had threatened a black-flag demonstration on the day I arrived in Jammu. On 24 November I flew down on an Indian Airlines plane. In sharp and poignant contrast to the earlier occasions of my return from America and marriage, when the people of Jammu gave me an enthusiastic and affectionate welcome, this time there were derisive and hostile slogans, and the city, from the airport right up to the palace gates, was a sea of black flags. Bakshi Ghulam Mohammad was with me in the open jeep; and though the National Conference had tried to lay on some kind of reception, it was swamped by the deep hostility of the Dogra masses.

I must admit that it was a rather traumatic experience, but I put up a brave front and continued to smile and greet the people. I noticed that despite themselves, many waved back. The demonstration, in fact, was not so much against me as a gesture of loyalty to and solidarity with my father. It reflected the widespread agitation launched by the Praja Parishad on 14 November against Sheikh Abdullah. Their slogan of complete integration of the state with India was expressed in the rallying cry '*Ek vidhan, ek niskan, ek pradhan*' (one constitution, one flag, one president). This agitation gathered momentum over the next few months, as it effectively capitalized upon the sense of outrage felt by the Dogras not only at having lost their predominant position in the state but also in having at one stroke been placed at the mercy of their arch enemy, Sheikh Abdullah. The Sheikh, for his part, not only made no effort to mollify the feelings of the Jammu people but continued with his hostile and aggressive attitude. An example was the question of the flag to be flown on the Jammu Secretariat. The old state flag having been hauled down, I had suggested to the government that, along with the new flag, the national flag should also be hoisted. This was sharply turned down by the Sheikh, so I in turn declined the suggestion that I should personally hoist the new flag.

After settling down in Jammu I began assessing the situation, and soon realized that the Praja Parishad agitation had spread deep and wide throughout the Jammu region. Even though I knew Jawaharlal's aversion to the Parishad, I felt it my duty to inform him about the true state of affairs. I prepared a detailed note that analysed the whole position and made certain concrete recommendations for political and economic measures, which would help to meet the genuine aspirations of the people of Jammu and Ladakh. As I put it, 'Stripped of all its nonessentials, the situation is that whereas Jammu and Ladakh strongly desire complete integration with India, Sheikh Sahib and his colleagues are extremely insistent upon the "limited" nature of the Accession and are not prepared to agree to complete integration.' This I sent to Jawaharlal with a covering letter on 22 December, following up an earlier one dated 1 December 1952. I was quite frank. 'The situation is serious', I wrote, 'not in any military sense but in the sense that an overwhelming majority of the Jammu province seem to be emphatically in sympathy with the agitation. Fundamentally responsible for this, I feel, are several deep-seated and genuine economic and psychological reasons, and I do not think it will be a correct appraisal to dismiss the whole affair as merely the creation of a reactionary clique.'

I followed this with a visit to Delhi where I talked with Jawaharlal, the home minister, Drs Katju and Rajendra Prasad, and gave them my assessment of the situation. I urged that the Government of India must intervene so that the state government reacts to the Jammu agitation not only with police repression but with concrete political, economic and administrative measures. Jawaharlal did write to Sheikh Abdullah in the same month, who replied with a long letter justifying the stand of his government and rejecting the whole Jammu problem as the work of communal organizations and a 'violent reaction on the part of Jammu landlords and other upper classes'. Jawaharlal also answered my letter, saying, 'I can quite understand your great concern over the developments in Jammu. I am naturally also very much concerned, and I have followed them closely. I entirely agree with you that while police measures are of course necessary, that is only a negative way of dealing with the situation ... The situation in Jammu is serious enough to deserve our fullest consideration and such positive action as may be necessary. At the same time, one has to view these matters, as all other important matters, coolly and dispassionately.'

Later that month I received a message from Jawaharlal saying that the president had invited me to attend the governors' and rajpramukhs' conference being held early in February and that he would like me to attend. This was my first opportunity to attend a meeting on the national level, all my previous experience having been connected only with Jammu and Kashmir. It was, therefore, with some excitement that I accepted the invitation. I arrived in Delhi on 3 February and was put up at Rashtrapati Bhavan in the Dwarika Suite reserved for visiting dignitaries. After a formal call on Dr Rajendra Prasad I turned in early. I had a curiously vivid dream that night. I was standing in a large room, and Mahatma Gandhi came in. I remember him distinctly, all his features and clothes much clearer in my memory than when I had actually seen him in Srinagar several years earlier. He walked up to me, put his left hand on my shoulder and took my right palm in his other hand. He looked at it for a moment, and then said in English, 'You will be a wise man.'

I found the two-day conference interesting, the first of a long series of fifteen such consecutive conferences that I was to attend in the future. It opened with a formal speech read out by the president, after which Jawaharlal made an hour-long intervention with a wide-ranging survey of the current national and international scene, laying emphasis on various aspects of economic development. The scholarly vice president, Dr Radhakrishnan spoke on the second day, brilliantly outlining his views on education and national development. In those days, the princely states had yet to be fully integrated into the republic and were grouped into several geographical zones, each headed by a senior prince called the rajpramukh. The conference was thus attended by the former rulers of Mysore, Nawanagar, Patiala, Travancore, Gwalior and Jaipur, apart from the governors, who included Chandulal Trivedi, K.M. Munshi, R.R. Diwakar, Jairamdas Daulatram, Fazl Ali and Pattabhi Sitaramaiyya.

At twenty-two, I was one third the age of most of the participants. After the general speeches each participant gave a brief report of the situation in his state, highlighting the main problems that they were facing. In my remarks I reviewed the important developments over the last year, and also mentioned the continuing agitation in Jammu. Apart from a formal banquet hosted by the president and attended by cabinet ministers, Jawaharlal held a dinner for the participants. He also had me over for a small, private lunch at which Indira Gandhi was hostess and Padmaja Naidu the soul of the party.

Meanwhile, the Jammu agitation showed no signs of abating and was taken up by like-minded parties in Delhi, specially the newly formed Bharatiya Jana Sangh headed by Shyama Prasad Mukherjee and N.G. Chatterjee, who decided to launch a satyagraha on an all-India level. I continued to urge that there should be a dialogue between the state government and the agitation leaders, but Sheikh Abdullah would have none of it and Jawaharlal was also averse to such talks. As he wrote in one of his letters to me (22 March 1953): 'In my view, what these people have done is little short of treason to the country and the people should realize it.' My suggestion to Sheikh Abdullah that my formal address to the legislative assembly on 25 March could be used as a good opportunity to strike a conciliating note was rejected by him.

Although Sheikh Abdullah attempted to dismiss the whole matter as the plot of 'reactionary elements', and the Government of India seemed in the beginning to support that view, I was deeply disturbed because I realized that the final chance of building a new Dogra–Kashmiri rapport, which alone could ensure the stability and welfare of the state, was being lost. I continued to dwell on this theme in my letters to Jawaharlal, even though I knew that he was allergic to the Jana Sangh and Praja Parishad leaders. In a letter of 27 March I wrote: 'What really disturbs me is the fact that the gulf between Jammu and Kashmir has widened tremendously over the last few months, and that the breach, instead of being bridged, seems to be steadily widening. Neither of the parties seems to quite realize the implications of this, and I fear that we may reap a very bitter harvest in years to come.'

At about this time Bakshi Ghulam Mohammad, who was deputy prime minister, and Girdhari Lai Dogra, the finance minister and sole representative in the cabinet from Jammu, met Jawaharlal in Delhi to discuss the whole situation. Bakshi was very different to the Sheikh: more pragmatic, a superb organizer and a man with excellent public relations with all sections of people, including many in Jammu. Although closely associated with Sheikh Abdullah and the National Conference, he never displayed the aggressive anti-Dogra attitudes of the Sheikh and M.A. Beg. His whole stance vis-à-vis the accession was also distinctly more amenable to strengthening the relationship between the state and the centre, and less charged with the Kashmiri chauvinism so sedulously fostered by Sheikh Abdullah.

Apart from the Jammu agitation, there was the broader question of implementing the Delhi Agreement on the constitutional relationship between the state and the centre, which had been worked out after prolonged negotiations between Sheikh Abdullah's team and representatives of the Government of India. While the decision regarding abolishing monarchy had been rapidly implemented because it suited the Sheikh, he had begun dragging his feet as far as the other items were concerned. It had been clear to me from the start that he was less than sincere in his professions, and that he was simply manoeuvring himself into a position of strength in relation to the central government. Had he been sincere, why the delay in implementing the rest of the agreement?

In fact, the Sheikh used one of his favourite techniques by initiating a debate within the National Conference working committee on the nature of Kashmir's relationship with India. One group, led by M.A. Beg, was vociferous in its view that the relationship should not go beyond the three subjects contained in the Instrument of Accession, while the other, led by Bakshi Ghulam Mohammad and including G.L. Dogra and D.P. Dhar, was agreeable to a more comprehensive relationship covering other vital areas, such as the judiciary, financial arrangements and so on. This tussle within the National Conference gradually assumed serious dimensions. While the Sheikh ostensibly tried to keep himself above the controversy for some time, he increasingly began throwing his weight in favour of the hardliners. It was this development, even more than the Jammu agitation, that began to disturb Jawaharlal.

I had two long meetings with him on 21 April and 23 May. At the second meeting, he opened up for the first time and expressed his deep anguish at the way the situation in the state was developing. He admitted that he had no answer when asked in Parliament or outside as to why the

Delhi Agreement had not been implemented. He said that he had written a long letter to the Sheikh pointing out that the matter had been greatly delayed and that, as he was going abroad in a few weeks, he would very much like to see the question finalized before he left for his trip. When I asked him what reply he had received, he turned to me and said in an incredulous and hurt tone, 'I received no reply at all.' He added that the Sheikh was thoroughly confused and was evidently avoiding meeting him.

I mentioned to Jawaharlal that if the state government made any move which showed that they were going back on their solemn agreements with the Government of India, my position would become impossible. It would be very difficult for me to continue to associate with them, as I would never be a party to a betrayal of India. He pondered over that for a while but did not immediately respond. When I got up to leave he turned to me and said, 'Look here, one point I quite agree on is that if our agreements are thrown overboard or something like that, your position becomes absolutely impossible.' It was clear that he was deeply disturbed, but he had not quite made up his mind how to deal with the problem. He was particularly hurt, even bewildered, at the hostile manner in which his old protégé and friend Sheikh Abdullah was acting, and he seemed to agree with me when I remarked that unlimited power seemed to have brought out the Sheikh's worst fascist and totalitarian tendencies.

Indeed, the Sheikh's attitude steadily became more and more intransigent. He made a speech at Ranbirsinghpura, a border town near Jammu, where he reacted violently against the Jammu agitation, went on to accuse India of being communal and virtually threatening that the accession of the state could not be taken for granted. I had been planning a visit to Europe around this time—and had even written formally to the president and Jawaharlal about this—but, in view of the growing tension following the Jammu agitation and the increasing schism within the National Conference, I decided against going.

The annual move to Srinagar saw further deterioration. Shyama Prasad Mukherjee, who had defied the ban on his entry to the state, had been arrested and kept in detention. On 10 June I sent a report to Jawaharlal, who was at that time on a fairly long visit to London, in which I said:

> The political situation here in the Valley continues to be extremely fluid. The division within the party is causing considerable tension.

> The pro-Indian faction continues to be determined, and claims to be strong and to have a majority both in the Working Committee and in the Assembly. Frequent meetings of the Working Committee continue.
>
> I was shocked and astounded to gather from a private meeting with Sheikh Abdullah last week that he seems to have decided to go back upon the solemn agreements which he has concluded with India and upon his clear commitments. This cannot be allowed, as it will make our position absolutely impossible and be a grave blow to our National interests and naturally to our International position also. I need not mention the grave and widespread repercussions that will result from such a development. The problem will claim your immediate attention upon your return for a final and decisive solution.

Soon thereafter came the shocking news of the death of Shyama Prasad Mukherjee while in detention. I was not informed of his illness or his removal to hospital, and only learnt of his death from unofficial sources several hours after his body had been flown out of Srinagar. The circumstances in which he died in the custody of the state government were a cause of grave resentment and suspicion. Jammu was furious because Dr Mukherjee had been martyred while fighting for the Praja Parishad cause, and there was open talk that his death had not been from natural causes. The whole of India was shocked at this event, specially the people of Bengal, who held Dr Mukherjee in the highest regard.

By now the Sheikh was clearly on the warpath. Despite repeated suggestions to visit Delhi, and an invitation from Jawaharlal to do so on 3 July, he refused to go down to the capital and discuss the whole situation. Maulana Azad came up to Srinagar for a few days, but instead of taking advantage of his visit to sort out differences, Sheikh Abdullah pointedly ignored him, and he was virtually insulted by the National Conference workers. The Sheikh's speeches became more and more strident, and it became increasingly clear that he was working on the idea of some sort of independent status for Kashmir which, inevitably, would imply a virtual negation of the accession to India. At about this time Adlai Stevenson, ambassador to the United Nations, visited Srinagar and had long talks with the Sheikh. It is not known what exactly transpired, but the general impression was that in some way the Sheikh received encouragement from these conversations for his independence theory.

Meanwhile, the rift within the National Conference had come into the open. It was common knowledge that the Sheikh was favouring the hardliners led by M.A. Beg, while most of the other senior leaders, including the two cabinet ministers G.L. Dogra and Sham Lal Saraf, and D.P. Dhar, who was deputy home minister, had rallied behind Bakshi Ghulam Mohammad. Bakshi came to my house on a few occasions in connection with meetings of the state soldiers' board, of which I was chairman, and would stay on for a few minutes after the others had left. While I was careful not to give the impression of getting involved in the controversy, I had to maintain close contact with the pro-Indian group. D.P. Dhar was a frequent visitor, and he became one of the key figures in the drama that was about to unfold. Suave and unflappable, 'D.P.' had an incisive mind and was an excellent planner. He played a significant role in keeping New Delhi informed about the inner conflicts within the National Conference. Jawaharlal liked him and had regard for his political judgement.

It was at about this time that we began to realize that unless something drastic was done to curb Sheikh Abdullah, the situation would steadily deteriorate and get completely out of hand, with grave and incalculable consequences for the entire country. The Kashmir issue was still a prominent item on the Security Council's agenda, and it would be disastrous if the Sheikh, who had twice been sent to Lake Success in New York, USA, as a member of the Indian delegation, were to do a volte-face while still prime minister of the state. I watched with increasing alarm and apprehension the trend of events, and decided that I should once more go down to Delhi and discuss the situation with Jawaharlal. This I did in the third week of July.

When I met him, I found Jawaharlal's attitude considerably changed. Not only did he not make any attempt to defend Sheikh Abdullah, he seemed to be as disturbed as I was about the way the situation was developing. It seems that, apart from my own letters, he had received detailed reports from the Intelligence Bureau (then headed by B.N. Mullick), D.P. Dhar and others from the state, as well as first-hand impressions from Maulana Azad and Jawaharlal's close political confidant, Rafi Ahmed Kidwai. He listened in grim silence to my detailed presentation, occasionally frowning and nodding agreement. I did not put any concrete proposal before him, but I did make it clear that if Sheikh Abdullah persisted in his hostile attitude a parting of the ways was inevitable. When I got up to leave he saw me to the door. As I took his leave he put his hand on my shoulder and said, 'Don't worry, do your best.'

Immediately upon my return to Srinagar I decided to break completely with the problem on hand and go off on a pilgrimage to Amarnath, the famous shrine dedicated to Lord Shiva and situated in a huge cave at an altitude of 13,000 feet. I had always wanted to go there, and felt that this was an appropriate time to do so. It would give me, hopefully, fresh strength to deal with the looming crisis. Also, as the trip would be well publicized, it would allay any suspicions that may have been raised by my air dash to Delhi. The main pilgrimage to Amarnath reaches the shrine on the full moon of Shravana, the fifth month of the Hindu calendar, which falls sometime between July and August. The July full moon was on the 26th. We therefore left Srinagar on the 23rd.

The trip was one of the most memorable I have ever made. From Pahalgam I was carried, as my leg was still not good enough to manage the steep climb, while Asha insisted on walking all the way. We camped for three nights—at Chandanwari, Sheshnag and Panchtarni—before reaching the famous cave. The scenery en route was breathtaking, specially the fabulous milky-green Sheshnag Lake set against a massive, triple-peaked glacier. Once again, I was struck by the uplifting power of natural beauty, particularly in the higher altitudes. As I wrote in a series of articles, published by the *Hindustan Times* in its Sunday supplements:

> One distinctly feels the presence of a Power greater, stronger and purer than one's own petty self. For a while I glimpse the lovely face of nature in its pure undesecrated majesty. The torrent of time slackens, the problems and strife of life pale into insignificance and I am lost in deep contemplation. I cherish a desire in the recesses of my heart to one day build myself a small ashrama in such surroundings where, with the body and mind made pure and free from the tentacles of desire and fear, ego and attachment, one can concentrate upon the unalloyed purity of Nature and thereby perhaps achieve spiritual illumination.

These articles were subsequently published in a small booklet called *The Glory of Amarnath,* which was my first literary endeavour.

The cave itself was much bigger than I had imagined, and in one corner stood the glistening ice formation about five feet high, symbolizing the creative energy of Lord Shiva. The shrine is unique in that the ice lingam forms of itself every year and is believed to wax and wane with the moon. On the journey I was reading Paul Brunton's *Search in Secret India,* and the whole experience made a deep impression upon me. I have found repeatedly that an outer crisis is an excellent time to deepen one's inner aspiration, that the thicker the battle presses the more significant becomes the voice of the inner charioteer.

I returned to Srinagar on 28 July. During my absence there had been a fresh series of meetings of the National Conference working committee at which the two sides had clashed—Sheikh Abdullah was now openly partisan in the controversy, but only one other member of his cabinet, M.A. Beg, supported him. The rift in the cabinet came to a head on 7 August when the Sheikh, using a flimsy pretext, decided to move against the opposing group by asking for the resignation of Pandit Sham Lal Saraf. On the morning of 8th Saraf sent me a copy of a long letter to the Sheikh in which he accused him of having repudiated the declared policies of the National Conference concerning the relationship of the state with the Indian Union. He refused to resign saying that 'the manner in which you have created a dangerous situation in the country by making highly inflammable speeches before the public, combined with your authoritarian attitude in the Cabinet, have convinced me that instead of helping the difficult situation my resignation will encourage you to pursue your policies unbridled. Such a course will be suicidal for the country.'

A few hours later I received a signed copy of a memorandum sent to Sheikh Abdullah by the deputy prime minister, Bakshi Ghulam Mohammad; the finance minister, G.L. Dogra; and the health minister, Pandit Sham Lal Saraf. The five-page document squarely accused the Sheikh and M.A. Beg of blatantly flouting accepted party policies. It said:

> After convening of the Constituent Assembly, certain inescapable elaborations of the State's relationship with India were defined in the Delhi Agreement, of which you were the Chief architect on our behalf. Your stand was unanimously endorsed by the Government,

> the National Conference, the Indian Parliament and the Constituent Assembly of the State. But you have not only deliberately delayed the implementation of the Agreements on these matters, which form the sheet anchor of our policy, but have purposefully and openly denounced these in public. You have thus arbitrarily sought to precipitate a rupture in the relationship of the State with India.

They added:

> Mr M.A. Beg has persistently been following policies of narrow sectarianism and communalism, which have seriously undermined the oneness of the State. Unfortunately, you have been lending your support to his policies in the Cabinet and his activities in public. This has generated bitter feelings of suspicion and doubt in the minds of the people of the various constituent units of the State. You have connived at all these unfortunate happenings and thus strengthened and encouraged the forces of disruption. The result is that unity and secular character, the two fundamental aspects of our State, stand threatened today.

Concluding, the three ministers said:

> We have been constantly urging upon you to put an end to these unhealthy tendencies and to undertake unitedly measures for restoring the morale of the people. In spite of our best intentions, we have failed in our efforts. It is, therefore, with great pain that we have to inform you of our conclusion that the Cabinet, constituted as it is at present and lacking as it does the unity of purpose and action, has lost the confidence of the people in its ability to give them a clean, efficient and healthy administration.

As soon as I received this communication, which was not entirely unexpected, the ball was squarely in my court. Legally the council of ministers held office at the pleasure of the Sadar-i-Riyasat, and as the appointing authority I also enjoyed the power of dismissal, even if this was not specifically spelt out. However, before taking any drastic action, I thought it was only appropriate that I should talk with Sheikh Abdullah.

I immediately invited him to come to see me at the earliest. He was going to Gulmarg that afternoon and came to my residence around noon. When I inquired about the situation he narrated three long, though petty, incidents regarding Sham Lal Saraf, and disclosed that he had asked him to resign. He mentioned that the Kashmir trade commissioner in Delhi had telephoned in the morning and informed him that the newspapers carried big headlines about the 'constitutional crisis' in Kashmir, and expressed surprise at the leak.

I said that I was deeply distressed and concerned at the recent trend of events, particularly the complete absence of homogeneity in the cabinet. I pointed out that it would be useful if he and his cabinet colleagues were to come to my residence that evening so that the whole matter could be discussed in depth. He side-tracked this suggestion by launching into an angry tirade against the Indian press which he accused of grossly misrepresenting and exaggerating the differences in the cabinet. He made the astonishing claim that, although there were some differences of opinion, there were no basic political or administrative differences within his cabinet. When I again stressed the necessity of doing something to rectify the situation, he stated plainly that no internal solution was possible until there was some external solution acceptable to India as well as Pakistan.

This revealed his state of mind. From a position of endorsing the accession to India as 'final and irrevocable', he had over the last few months moved into an entirely different posture. He was evidently expecting international pressure to be brought upon India to grant virtual independent status to Kashmir, and this was quite obviously the reason why he was holding up the implementation of the Delhi Agreement which would further cement the relationship between the state and the centre. In our meeting he was not only unable to give me any assurance that the internal crisis in his cabinet would be resolved, but added a new dimension of uncertainty by talking about an 'external solution'.

Our meeting lasted for about forty-five minutes, after which he left for Gulmarg for the weekend. It was clear to me that something had to be done at once if further drift was to be avoided. I summoned my political and legal advisers, including D.P. Dhar and Brigadier (later General) B.M. Kaul, who was acting as a sort of unofficial courier between us and Delhi. The Sheikh was still a popular figure in the Valley despite the fact that corruption and maladministration had to some extent eroded his stature. If we gave him an opportunity to take his case to the streets he would easily arouse acute communal and chauvinistic sentiments among the Kashmiri masses, which could result in serious and violent disturbances. Parliament was in session, and anything happening here would have its repercussions on the national scene.

We, therefore, decided that the Sheikh would have to be dismissed. While I was reluctant that he should be arrested, Bakshi Ghulam Mohammad made it quite clear that he could not undertake to run the government if the Sheikh and Beg were left free to propagate their views. Dismissing and detaining a sitting prime minister was no easy task, as all plans had to be made in absolute secrecy. The police had to be organized, the Indian Army kept discreetly informed and the media handled in an imaginative manner. Luckily, D.P. Dhar was a superb tactician who was at his best in such situations. In the three days preceding the crisis D.P. had tied up all these details.

The fact that the Sheikh decided to go up to Gulmarg, however, necessitated some last-minute change of plans. Soon after he left my house we sat down to draft the dismissal order. Along with this I dictated a covering letter to Sheikh Abdullah. The text of these documents was as follows:

SECRET

Karan Mahal, Srinagar
8 August 1953

My dear Sheikh Abdullah,

You will recall that in the course of our meeting today I conveyed to you my deep concern at the serious differences which exist in your Cabinet. I impressed upon you the immediate necessity for restoring harmony and unity of purpose among the members of the Cabinet in the execution of its policies. You were, however, unable to assure me that these acute differences could be remedied.

This conflict within the Cabinet has for a considerable time been causing great confusion and apprehension in the minds of the people of the State. The situation has reached an unprecedented crisis with the fact that three of your four Cabinet colleagues have in a Memorandum to you, a copy of which they have sent to me, expressed their complete dissatisfaction with your actions and policies, which have lost the present Cabinet the confidence of the people. This document clearly indicates that the divergence within your Cabinet has reached proportions in which the unity, prosperity and stability of the State are gravely jeopardized.

When we met today I further suggested to you that an emergent meeting of the Cabinet should be held at my residence this evening so that we could jointly explore the possibilities of securing a stable, unified and efficient Government for the country. But to my regret you evaded the issue.

Under these conditions I, as Head of the State, have been forced to the conclusion that the present Cabinet cannot continue in office any longer and hence I regret to inform you that I have dissolved the Council of Ministers headed by you. A copy of my order in this connection is attached herewith.

I need hardly add how deeply distressed I am at having to take this action, but the vital interests of the people of the State, which it is my duty to safeguard, leave me no alternative. I trust that this will in no way affect the mutual regard and cordial feelings we have for each other.

Yours sincerely,
Karan Singh
Sadar-i-Riyasat

ORDER

Whereas for some months I have been noticing with growing concern that there have existed acute differences of opinion between members of the Government on basic issues—political, economic and administrative—affecting the vital interests of the State;

And whereas members of the Government have been publicly expressing sharply conflicting points of view regarding these matters;

And whereas on these fundamental issues the views of a majority of the members of the Cabinet are sharply opposed to the view held by the Prime Minister and one of his colleagues;

And whereas efforts to work in harmony and pull together as a team having failed, and the majority in the Cabinet has expressed that, lacking as it does in unity of purpose and action, the present Cabinet has lost the confidence of the people;

And whereas the economic distress of the people has considerably increased which needs prompt and serious attention;

And whereas a stage has reached in which the very process of honest and efficient administration has become impracticable;

And whereas, finally, the functioning of the present Cabinet on the basis of joint responsibility has become impossible and the resultant conflicts have gravely jeopardized the unity, prosperity and stability of the State;

I, Karan Singh, Sadar-i-Riyasat, functioning in the interests of the people of the State who have reposed the responsibility and authority of the Headship of the State in me, do hereby dismiss Sheikh Mohammad Abdullah from the Prime Ministership of the State of Jammu and Kashmir, and consequently the Council of Ministers headed by him is dissolved forthwith.

Srinagar,
8 August 1953

Sadar-i-Riyasat
Jammu and Kashmir

By the time the documents were ready it was late evening. The weather was also in a turbulent mood; it was pouring, thunder rumbled, and jagged shafts of lightning cut through the clouds. I deputed my aide-de-camp Major B.S. Bajwa, to go to Gulmarg and deliver the letter to Sheikh Abdullah. The police also went with him, but they were delayed by the torrential rain and the bad road beyond Tangmarg. Having dispatched the documents, we all waited in Karan Mahal for word that they had been delivered. As this was delayed, tension grew. Our gamble was a risky one, for if the so-called 'Sher-e-Kashmir' got even an inkling of what was happening he would react ferociously, and our own lives may well have been in danger. However, the die was cast, and all we could do was to pray that the whole operation went off smoothly.

As it turned out, our prayers were answered. The Sheikh was totally unaware of the developments, and so arrogant in the possession of power that he could never dream that anyone would dare to challenge him. It was late at night when the ADC and the police contingent finally reached Gulmarg, and the Sheikh and Begum Abdullah were fast asleep. With some difficulty, and much knocking, he was awoken and handed the letter as well as a warrant of arrest. On reading it he flew into a rage and shouted, 'Who is the Sadar-i-Riyasat to dismiss me? *I* made that chit of a boy Sadar-i-Riyasat.' But by then his house was surrounded by the police. He was given two hours to say his namaz and pack, during which, we later learnt, he burnt a number of documents. This could have been prevented, but we had given strict instructions to the police that he and the Begum were to be treated with courtesy and not harassed in any way. In the early hours of the 9th morning they were escorted to a car and driven out of the Valley to the Tara Niwas guest house in Udhampur, where they were kept in detention. M.A. Beg and several others were also arrested that night in Srinagar and other parts of the Valley.

Meanwhile, it was my responsibility to see that there was no constitutional gap in the administration of the State. With the dismissal of Sheikh Abdullah, I wrote to Bakshi Ghulam Mohammad inviting him to meet me and discuss the formation of the new government. I ended the letter by saying that 'the continuance in office of the new Cabinet will depend upon it securing a vote of confidence from the Legislative Assembly during its coming session'. Bakshi came over and we discussed the situation. I felt that no time should be lost in swearing in the new government. We summoned the chief secretary, M.K. Kidwai, who was blissfully unaware of what was happening. When he learnt that the Sheikh had been dismissed and arrested he sank down on the steps holding his head in his hands, and was revived only after he had been plied with a couple of stiff whiskies.

In the early hours of 9 August, I administered the oath of office to Bakshi Ghulam Mohammad and G.L. Dogra, so that they would be in a position to deal with the tense situation that would inevitably develop as soon as news of the dismissal and arrests spread in the Valley. I then wrote a report to the president informing him of the entire developments, and sent a copy to Jawaharlal with a covering letter which included these two paragraphs:

> We are all acutely aware of the gravity of the step that we have been forced to take and also of the extent of its possible repercussions, both within and without the State. In this whole matter I have attempted to act in a democratic and constitutional manner, keeping especially

> in mind what you said when we met last. On the whole I feel that we have done the best that was possible under the circumstances.
> Regarding what was to be done with Sheikh Abdullah after his dismissal, this was of course a decision for the new Government to take. On my part I strongly urged them to desist from arresting him soon after the dismissal, but they were most apprehensive that with his presence in the Valley at this juncture reactions would have been greatly intensified, and there was a grave danger of the situation getting completely out of hand and even resulting in violence and bloodshed. Consequently, he has been arrested this morning at Gulmarg and is being taken to Udhampur, where he will be lodged in the State Guest House. I have stressed that he and his family be accorded all courtesy and consideration.

By the time the whole operation was over dawn had broken. The clouds and thunder of the last two days had disappeared, and the sky was clear again. I got through to Jawaharlal on the telephone just before eight, but the line was unclear. In its morning bulletin All India Radio devoted thirteen of its fifteen minutes to a detailed report on the developments in Kashmir. I had not slept a wink that night and found myself in a curiously detached and light-headed mood. I knew that what I had done was for the national good, and that all the danger and risks were worth taking if it served the country. Asha had also sat up anxiously in her room all night. Slowly I climbed up the steps and walked into her room. 'It is over,' I said, and we both smiled; she sixteen going on seventeen, I twenty-two going on twenty-three. I was asleep almost before I hit the bed.

From Karan Singh's *Autobiography*, 1994

Novella

The Mountain of Shiva

How Not to Win Friends

ASHOK SAT BACK, LETTING himself go limp against the cushioning. He breathed slowly and rhythmically for a few minutes, until his mind and body began to partake of a smoother equilibrium, a more unhurried confrontation. He tried inwardly to stand aside, to see himself as if he were a complete stranger, to watch his thoughts ebb and flow, arise and subside. After a while he began framing the question 'Who am I?', seeking to turn the searchlight of his thoughts inwards, to probe the depths of his being and discover the true centre of his consciousness. This was an exercise Swamiji had taught him several years ago, and it always gave Ashok a deepened inner poise, a curiously energizing detachment that helped him face, with greater confidence, the rush and bustle of life. Somehow, an air journey deepened his inner awareness. It was as if, in the clear atmosphere high above the humdrum of daily living, he was able to see life in a more integrated perspective and come closer to that elusive realm of heightened consciousness, which he had only been able vaguely to perceive in dreams and fragmentary recollections of early childhood.

The drone of the jet engines was soporific and reassuring. The plane was almost full except for two seats in the extreme rear, and the passengers included several foreigners—mostly Americans, guessed Ashok, from their colourful bush shirts and trademark cameras slung over their shoulders.

Two little blonde boys, about seven years old and ridiculously alike, occupied the seats across the aisle from Ashok. They kept getting up and whispering to a young couple—evidently their parents—seated in front of them. Ashok's seat was next to the window, and to his left was a small, dark, bespectacled man who was already absorbed in a paperback. Ashok glanced obliquely at the title and gave a little start: it was *How to Win Friends and Influence People.* He remembered that at school twenty years ago he and Ramesh had read it together, but in secret, because it was accepted that whoever read that book would *need* to and so would be unpopular boy. Ashok pulled a book of his own out of his briefcase—*The Ochre Robe,* written by an Austrian who had become a Hindu monk. The publishers had cleverly splashed a close-up of the robe on the cover, so that the book itself was a striking shade of ochre. He opened it to where he had left off, but Dale Carnegie had revived memories of long ago, making it impossible for him to concentrate on the book in his hands. His school days came flashing back, the bittersweet recollections of a time when joy and sorrow wove a strange tapestry in his life. Above all, and still painful, though two decades had elapsed, was the memory of Ramesh.

On the opening day at school, when the new boys were shivering with homesickness and apprehension, they had met for the first time. He still recalled vividly that first assembly, the headmaster tall and forbidding, making a stentorian speech welcoming all the new boys to the 'family of the school', 'school' drawn out so that it acquired a distinctly sinister connotation.

When the headmaster strode in and ascended the platform he had looked so overwhelming that at least one new boy had failed to suppress a little gasp, which sent a titter of amusement through the assembly hall. Then the names of the new boys were read out, and as each name was called the boy had to step forward. It was, of course, sheer torture, but well-intentioned, the idea being that each boy was individually introduced and accepted as part of the corporate life of school. 'Number thirty-six, Ashok Singh, Ashok House.' Ashok had stepped forward to a chorus of giggles. 'Number thirty-seven. Ramesh Kapur, Ashok House.'

From that inaugural day at school they became fast friends. They went through the usual first-term ragging and bullying together, deriving comfort from the fact that their misery was shared. They began the painful but exhilarating process of becoming part of a vitally pulsating institution, with its high academic standards and intense preoccupation with sports and physical fitness. Gradually they shed their shyness along with their body fat, became adjusted to their new surroundings and began talking like other schoolboys.

Despite the strict outward uniformity in dress and manner of speech, each boy soon began to develop his own distinctive personality. Ramesh grew to be a fine sportsman; even as a junior he made the school first eleven in hockey and was one of the fastest sprinters in his house. He also boxed for the school, swam like a fish, ran cross-country with credit and excelled in the gymnasium. His studies, however, were average, and he had some difficulty in getting through his examinations at the end of term.

Ashok was almost exactly the reverse. Introspective by nature, and somewhat averse to the rough and tumble of the sports ground. More cerebral than physical, from the very beginning he was a good scholar. His form master looked upon him as a model student, and his results seldom fell below the third or fourth place in class. Sports and physical training he had to do, no one in this school could possibly avoid them, but it was always with a measure of revulsion. It was not that he was a coward; in fact, when pressed he could give evidence of unusual courage. It was just that temperamentally he was much happier browsing in the liberty or in the music school. Music was his second love, his first being books, and he sang and played the flute with considerable ability.

This apparent difference between him and Ramesh only made their friendship stronger and more complete. Ashok would help Ramesh with his homework, specially solving math sums and writing essays in English, while Ramesh would instruct Ashok in the finer points of swimming and running. 'Hit the pool, Ashok, to discover yourself,' Ramesh said. Their personalities dovetailed perfectly, and as they grew older their friendship steadily grew deeper. Ashok used to be an invariable spectator whenever Ramesh was performing in an athletics or sports event, while Ramesh never missed the debating society when Ashok was speaking, or a concert in which he participated. They spent as much time together as they could manage, and found in each other's company a joy that neither experienced with anyone else.

Although Ramesh was Punjabi, his father, a senior officer of the Indian Civil Service, was for several years posted at Calcutta and it was there that he went during his holidays. Ashok's father had been in the army, and as his postings were erratic Ashok was never sure where he would have to spend his holidays. His home was in Pradhanpur, a small town in the foothills of the Himalayas, picturesquely situated amid low mountains rising in the distant north into snow-covered peaks. Once, when his father happened to be home on leave during his holidays, Ashok brought Ramesh to spend a fortnight there. Those days had been the happiest in Ashok's life. He and Ramesh would spend hours roaming the countryside around Pradhanpur, exploring the ravines and nullahs, the river and its hidden pools where the fighting mahseer grew fat and heavy. They would scramble up to one of Ashok's favourite haunts, a pool with a waterfall almost a hundred feet high which was believed to be haunted, and therefore left severely alone by the nearby villagers. There the two would sit, gazing at the water cascading over the edge and falling with abandon into the deep green pool below, causing a million glittering diamonds to fly up into the air. They had an almost psychic bond of understanding which made conversation unnecessary. Once, only once, as they were seated near the pool they saw a huge fish jump right of the water, hang for a moment with its glistening body magically suspended in mid-air, and then fall back with a mighty splash into the pool. They sat enraptured, the happiness welling through their bodies in great surges.

It was in their fifth year at school, just two terms before they were due to take the school-leaving examination, that their idyllic friendship came to a sudden, crushing end. Ramesh, always the more extroverted and adventurous of the two, was occasionally in the habit of breaking bounds from school to see a movie or have a really good tuck in one of the restaurants in town. This was a hazardous undertaking, as apprehension meant strict punishment, which could amount even to expulsion. Though he tried often, Ramesh was never able to persuade Ashok to accompany him on these escapades. Despite their deep friendship, Ashok felt that the compensations of bunking were not sufficient to justify the risk involved.

On this occasion Ramesh again urged him to come, but he declined. Ramesh then persuaded another roommate—Aftab—to accompany him. The fourth boy in the room was Anil, a quiet, inscrutable chap who secretly hero-worshipped Ramesh and was intensely jealous of his friendship with Ashok.

Ashok had remarked, half in jest, 'Look out, Ramesh, you're bound to get caught one of these days.' Ramesh had laughed in his carefree, debonair way.

Lights out was at eight-thirty, and the last show of the cinema began an hour later. As usual, Ramesh waited for fifteen minutes. Then he and Aftab crept out of bed, put on their 'home' clothes used for Saturday night dinners and slipped out of the window into the darkness. Stealthily they made their way to the back of the house, but just as the main road came in sight they froze in horror. The blinding beam of a powerful torch burst on their faces and Mr Dutta, the housemaster, clamped a firm hand on Ramesh's shoulder. As he did so, he said, 'So that note was correct after all, we caught both of you red-handed.'

So thin is the line between love and hate that in a flash of humiliation and anger Ramesh assumed that Ashok must have written the note to the headmaster. His unreasoning anger knew no limits, and his faculty for rational thought went into complete suspension. Mr Dutta told both boys sharply to go back to their room. 'See me at nine-thirty tomorrow morning,' he barked.

In a furious temper Ramesh and Aftab came back to their room. Anil was asleep—or so it seemed—but Ashok was awake. 'What happened,' he said, 'back so soon?'

Hearing his voice Ramesh's self-control completely cracked. He leapt on to Ashok's bed, pulled him up and slapped him sharply on either cheek.

'You ... You,' he hissed. 'You dirty, mean ...'

For a long moment Ashok was too stunned to speak.

Then he burst into tears and buried his face in his pillow. He did not say anything; what was there to say when his dearest friend had accused him of a treacherous betrayal? Ramesh flung himself into his own bed saying, 'If you say a single word I'll thrash the guts out of you.'

Ashok slept fitfully that night. The next morning, he had high fever and was delirious. He was removed to the school infirmary where he was confined for several days. Not once did Ramesh come to see him. Ashok was so utterly miserable that he wrote a long and passionate letter to his father asking to be withdrawn from school. Colonel Kripal Singh had just been posted to Delhi, where he had been given family accommodation after many years, and the prospect of having his only child with him was a tempting one. He wired to the headmaster requesting that Ashok be allowed to come. The headmaster had a long chat with Ashok in the hospital. Behind his forbidding exterior, he was a kind and understanding man, and finding Ashok adamant, he finally agreed to discharge him. Within a week Ashok had left the school and reached Delhi.

As for Ramesh, he had been so angry and hurt by what he considered his friend's betrayal that he felt a morbid satisfaction when Ashok was hauled off to sickbed. The housemaster had called him and Aftab to his office the next morning and given them the severest tongue-lashing they had ever received. In view of Ramesh's athletic record and the fact that it was his first offence, he said, he was being lenient and would not expel him, but he gave him a variety of other punishments, including denial of the Saturday night cinema and Tuesday tuckshop for the rest of the term.

When Ramesh learnt that Ashok had left school it confirmed his suspicion, and he assumed that his estranged friend was too scared to face him. It was only at the end of that term when he went to say goodbye to the housemaster that something prompted him to ask, 'Sir, now that it is all over, could I know what exactly was written in that note by which you caught us?' Dutta began to tell him, then stopped and said, 'Wait, I still have the note.'

He opened a drawer in his desk, rummaged around and then straightened up.

'Here it is, read it.'

The moment Ramesh saw it a shock went through his whole frame and the blood drained from his face.

'What's the matter Ramesh, are you feeling unwell?'

'N-no, Sir,' said Ramesh, 'except that this is not Ashok's handwriting.'

'Of course, it isn't,' said the housemaster. 'How could you ever think that your best friend would squeal on you? This note was from Anil.'

Ramesh's head was whirling. His eyes filled with tears, and after mumbling a hurried excuse, he rushed out of the housemaster's office and into his room. Anil was no longer there, having left a day earlier on some excuse.

Ramesh threw himself on Ashok's bed which had remained vacant since his friend had left at midterm. Great sobs racked his body as he broke under the weight of sorrow and repentance. The face of Ashok rose before his eyes, the thousand and one images of his friend in many moods and places. Of them two were unforgettable: the first when the great fish had leapt at the waterfall and they had looked at each other with wonder and inexpressible joy, the second when he had slapped Ashok that night and his friend had stared at him with an uncomprehending horror and shock which would now always haunt him.

When at last he recovered enough composure to get up he rushed straight to the headmaster's house. Not finding him there he went to the school office and got Ashok's address. At once he sat down and wrote a long letter full of remorse and tenderness, begging to be forgiven for his ghastly mistake.

He wrote again and again from home, but Ashok's father took care to see that no letter reached him. Ashok thought that Ramesh was still angry, while Ramesh assumed that his friend was too hurt and offended to reply.

The voice of the pilot over the loudspeaker snapped Ashok out of his reverie. To his own surprise his eyes were moist, and he blew his nose before looking out of the window at the great Bhakra Dam clearly visible in the foothills. He had been there once while it was being built and recalled being overwhelmed by the immensity of one of the world's great engineering feats. But from up there it looked tiny and insignificant, the great dam a mere pebble against the sweep of nature's grandeur. He decided to go to the lavatory. Pushing his book into the pocket of the seat in front, he got up and squeezed past the popularity seeker. As he turned down the aisle he tripped over a toy truck that one of the twins had put there, and stumbled straight into the arms of a man who was just coming up the aisle from the lavatory.

'Steady there,' the man said.

Ashok looked up apologetically, then stood rooted to the spot. The man before him was Ramesh.

Lovers in Kashmir

HOW LONG THE TWO stood there he did not know—a minute, an hour, eternity. It was a split second before Ramesh recognized him.

'Ashok,' he gasped, too surprised for a moment to move. His eyes filled with tears, and he pushed Ashok into the empty seat next to the window and sat down beside him.

'Where have you been, why didn't you reply to my letters?'

Ashok averted his face and gazed blindly out of the window, biting so hard into his lower lip that it began to bleed. For a few seconds he fought desperately to keep his emotion under control. Then he turned to Ramesh who was weeping openly, the tears streaming down his rugged face, wetting the lapels of his coat.

'I didn't get any letter,' he said simply.

'But I wrote so many—at least a dozen. As soon as I discovered that it was Anil and not you who had written that blasted note.'

Ashok smiled sadly. It was not the falsity of the accusation that had hurt him as much as the fact that after all those years of friendship Ramesh should have thought him capable of such an act.

'Never mind,' he said, 'that was a long time ago. We must forget the whole episode.'

'Forget it!' Ramesh almost shouted. 'How can I forget that in my blind anger and stupidity, I destroyed the love and friendship of the one person who was dearer to me than anyone else in the world? Will you, can you ever forgive me?'

Ashok was again looking out of the window. The plane was now flying over a series of mountains which grew steeper and higher as they moved north. After a long silence he said, 'Ramesh, in life one often comes up against circumstances that appear strange and tragic. But I believe deeply that whatever happens is ultimately for the best. I promise to forgive you on one condition—that you will never again mention the incident to me or anyone else.'

Ramesh had by now gained some control over himself. He took Ashok's hand in his and said, 'All right, Ashok, I accept the condition. Only remember that if ever there is anything I can do to make up for my injustice, if there is any reparation ...'

'What talk is this of reparations?' said Ashok with a smile. 'Reparations are between enemies, not friends.'

Ramesh smiled and leaned back in his seat with a deep sigh. Then he started up again. 'But how are you, my dear Ashok, where do you live, what do you do, what happened after you left school?'

A twinge of pain passed through his eyes at the last question, but he quickly suppressed it. Ashok laughed, 'One question at a time, my dear fellow.' Then he told Ramesh briefly what had happened. For a few weeks after leaving school he had been in such a state of shattered emotion that he was unable even to look at a book. It was then that he had first met Swamiji, who lived in a small cottage near Delhi. His mother went there often, and once she persuaded Ashok to come along with her. Ashok was not a particularly religious boy, but he had inherited from his mother a deep spiritual inclination.

The moment he saw Swamiji something within him seemed to give; and to his mother's astonishment, he burst into tears and fled from the room. Swamiji had told his mother to send Ashok alone the next day. That meeting had been momentous for Ashok. Swamiji, his massive head encircled by a halo of snow-white hair, had talked to the boy for three hours. He seemed to have an uncanny ability to read Ashok's mind. For the first time since he had left school, Ashok had, in tears, recounted the whole painful episode.

Swamiji had listened carefully and then said simply, stroking Ashok's hair with one hand and telling his beads with the other, 'My dear boy, whatever happens is according to God's will and therefore for the best. Always remember that, wherever you may be. Man can only shape his actions according to his best judgement. The results are beyond his control; therefore, it is futile to grieve over them. You are still young and have many creative years ahead of you. You must pull yourself together and get on with your education.'

Ashok's despair had given way to a new faith and he had decided to continue his studies. The next year he passed the school-leaving examination as a private student, getting a good second division. Then he joined one of the best colleges in Delhi, and graduated from there with a first division in economics. His father was not rich, but he managed, at considerable sacrifice, to get the necessary funds to send Ashok to England for an advanced course in business management. He returned with a diploma, and soon after had secured a position with a leading tobacco firm in India as their management adviser.

The next year tragedy had struck. His father was killed in an accident somewhere in Ladakh. The blow had come as a numbing shock to Ashok and his mother. She had immediately left Delhi for her home in Pradhanpur, and since then had not moved out of there despite Ashok's fervent entreaties. There had recently been some serious trouble at the firm. It had begun as a policy squabble at the highest level, but soon the Delhi branch manager had been sucked into the vortex of the dispute. He had involved Ashok also to back up his own view, and Ashok had consequently incurred the displeasure of the managing director. With the whole issue still hanging fire, Ashok had, in disgust, applied for a month's leave. To his surprise, it was sanctioned; perhaps the management decided that it would be a good thing to have him out of Delhi for a while. He closed down his small apartment, sent his servant on leave, and left for Pradhanpur to spend some time with his mother.

After a fortnight he began to get restive, and with her unerring instinct his mother realized this and suggested that he go and spend the second fortnight of his leave in Kashmir.

Secretly, she hoped that he might also find a girl he would like to marry. Ever since he had returned from England, she had been urging him to get married, had shown him several photographs of eligible girls from their own caste, and even arranged for him to meet two or three girls in Delhi. But he had been curiously evasive. Then his father died. Within a year his mother returned with her pleadings, only this time with more fervour.

'Your poor father is gone,' she would say, 'and I am only a guest here. Why don't you get married so that I can have the satisfaction of seeing my daughter-in-law before I die, and rocking my grandchildren to sleep, cuddling them?'

He always muttered some lame excuse and changed the topic, but in his heart, he knew that he could not delay the decision for long.

So here he was, on his way to Kashmir to spend a fortnight in the fabled vale of beauty.

'And what about you?' he asked Ramesh. 'What are you doing here?'

'Oh, I'm in the army as I always said I would be,' he grinned. 'At the moment I'm on my honeymoon, got a fortnight's leave with the greatest difficulty.'

'Congratulations!' Ashok smiled with genuine pleasure. 'Who is the lucky girl?'

'Come, I'll introduce you to her.'

The plane was flying over the Banihal pass which leads into the Kashmir valley, and it gave a sudden lurch. On either side massive snow-covered peaks jutted into the sky. Suddenly they were over the pass and into the exuberant green expanse of the Valley. It was huge, thought Ashok, much bigger than he had imagined any valley could be. Ringing its immense sweep was a series of snow-covered mountains, breathtaking in their majesty. An emerald set in a necklace of pearls was how the Kashmir valley had been poetically described, and from the plane it certainly looked spectacular. Ashok followed Ramesh to the other end. Sitting next to the window, her face glued to the pane, was a girl dressed in a pink Banarasi sari, her long hair falling in cascades over her shoulders.

'Darling,' cried Ramesh, 'what a great surprise. This is my dear school friend about whom I have spoken so much, Ashok Singh. Ashok, this is my wife, Sheila.'

The girl looked around and up at Ashok. Their eyes met for a brief instant and for the second time that morning Ashok felt that he was losing his grip on reality, that he was having a long, complicated dream. The girl raised her palms in greeting and said, 'Namaste.' Then she turned back to the window and cried, 'Look, darling, look at the Valley; how beautiful.'

Ashok also joined his palms and said, 'Namasteji.'

'The plane is preparing to land. Kindly fasten your seatbelts and observe the "No Smoking" sign. Please do not leave your seats till the plane comes to a complete halt.' The trained voice of the air hostess galvanized the passengers into waist-hugging activity. With a mumbled excuse Ashok walked unsteadily back to his seat, pushed past the intrepid Dale Carnegie fan and sat down heavily, shaking his head to make sure he was awake. He was, and the hostess, who waggled an accusing finger at his seatbelt, confirmed it. He fastened the belt and leaned against his seat, his mind racing back again across time and space.

He had not liked London, not for the first few months at least. It was cold and rainy, and the sun was seldom visible for any length of time. When it did shine it was almost apologetic, slipping behind the clouds at the first excuse. Ashok missed the fine, clear sunlight of his native land, the blue skies and, above all, Indian cuisine. He had lived in the hostel of the London School of Business Management, a dim and dreary place whose only advantage was its proximity to the school. This saved a lot of time and expense, as it was only a five-minute walk to and from the institute, morning and evening.

Once he got to grips with his studies, however, the prospect changed. Always a keen and competent student, Ashok was pleasantly surprised at the variety of courses he was expected to cover for his business management diploma—a two-year programme including advanced economic theory, econometrics, political science, outlines of chartered accountancy, labour and personnel management, the history of business administration and a special paper on the growth of the corporate sector in developing economies.

The courses were challenging, the system of teaching stimulating. In sharp contrast to the Indian method, the London School had no fixed lecture-attendance requirement. There was a variety of lectures by distinguished teachers, an excellent library and extremely competent tutors.

Ashok's tutor, Professor Harkwright, was a specialist in econometrics. He took a paternal interest in Ashok's work, conducted his tutorials and seminars with great skill and always treated Ashok as an equal. There was never any compulsion, except that born of the students' own urge for knowledge, and inside the walls of the rather forbidding stone building was a congenial intellectual atmosphere. There were about thirty students in Ashok's section, which included four other Indians, two boys—Gopal Mavlankar, G.S. Akhilan, and two girls—Savitri Gokhale and Sheila Chopra.

Ashok had never had much to do with girls. Being an only child, and not living in a joint family, he had seldom come in touch with feminine company of his own age. Of course, there had been many neighbours—in Pradhanpur a young cousin came to see his mother quite frequently and, as he later suspected, her visits grew more frequent when he was back from school for his holidays. But despite her shy encouragement, he never summoned up enough courage even to touch her. Then at school there was a cute nurse, D'Souza, with whom all the senior boys were madly in love. At college also, he had generally avoided the girls, although they seemed to find him more than a little attractive. He was tall and slim, with clean-cut features and dark luminous eyes, surmounted by a boyish shock of hair that would never for long accept the tyranny of brush and comb.

But at that stage of his life he studiously and successfully avoided any kind of emotional involvements.

In London, however, his loneliness gradually became unbearable. One afternoon after classes Sheila came up to him and said, 'You look very sad today, Mr Singh. What is the matter?'

She had said it with so much mock concern, sweet mischief dancing in her light-brown eyes, that he had been immediately captivated. She was very beautiful, her oval face classic in its configuration and her jet-black hair falling in great cascades down to her shoulders. Her body was slim and superbly proportioned, but it was her eyes, always glittering with vivacious energy, that gave her that special something which sets the beautiful woman apart from the merely attractive.

They started seeing more and more of each other, discovering rapidly how much they enjoyed being together—shopping, picnics, cinemas, theatres, lectures. By the end of term, it was becoming obvious to them both that they were falling deeply in love. With the Indian form of greeting, however, they hardly ever touched, except lightly and vicariously when Ashok would help her with her coat, or when in a cinema or theatre their hands would involuntarily brush against each other. At such moments a thrill would course through Ashok's veins, and in his room at night he would lie awake savouring the memory of that silken touch, the bittersweet texture of ecstasy and torture playing hide and seek deep within him. He had vowed to himself that the only girl he would ever marry would be Sheila, and he had decided to broach the subject just before their final examinations.

One night they went to a theatre. It was *My Fair Lady*—Ashok remembered it vividly, the colourful musical adaptation of Shaw's *Pygmalion*, which was such a smash hit that it was impossible for months to get tickets for it. With much difficulty, through the good offices of a fellow student who had contacts with the stage, Ashok had procured two tickets. He had enjoyed the play immensely with its gorgeous sets and lilting music, but he noticed that Sheila was strangely silent. After the show they emerged into the dark, depressing street. Acting on a sudden impulse Ashok took her in his arms, raised her face with his hand and gently kissed her lips, savouring the soft resilience of her body pressed against him. For a moment Sheila was yielding and responsive in his embrace, then suddenly she drew back with her eyes full of tears.

'No, Ashok, no,' she said softly. 'We cannot, we should not.'

'Why,' he pleaded, 'why can we not love each other? Neither of us is married. I will write to my parents tomorrow saying that I have found the girl who will be my wife.'

At this, to Ashok's utter amazement, Sheila broke into tears. She laid her lovely head on his shoulders, her whole body was for several minutes racked with sobs. When she had recovered some of her composure she said, 'Ashok, oh Ashok, that is not fated. My father is orthodox and will never let me marry outside our caste. This morning I got a letter from him saying my wedding has been fixed for next winter; I must return at once.'

Ashok was aghast. His whole being revolted against this system whereby a girl's future could be settled by her parents without so much as a casual reference to her.

'No,' he cried, 'this can never be. We are now living in a free country, and girls have been guaranteed their rights by law. This medieval absurdity is now dead. Write and tell your father that you are not returning home, that you will marry here in London and return only as my wife.'

'No Ashok dear, it's no use, it won't work. Since Mother died when I was a little girl, Father has pinned all his hopes on me. He did not marry again for fear a stepmother might ill-treat me. He is very unwell, and is living only for the day when I marry. Now that he has chosen—well, I am sure, according to his rights—I must agree. Much as I love you I cannot, I must not do as you say.'

Five days later she boarded the plane for India. Ashok saw her off at the airport. Just before the plane was to leave he kissed her again and they clung to each other with a desperate tenderness, struggling against their tears.

'I will always love you, Sheila, you and no one else.'

Sheila looked up at him with fear in her eyes.

'No, forget me. There will be many other girls.'

'Many others, of course, but none that I could love.'

She tore herself away from him and ran towards the plane. The last he saw of her was boarding the aircraft, clad in a plain georgette sari of light coral.

She stopped at the top step, turned and waved at him. Her sari was moulded along her figure by the brisk breeze, and her hair swept down to her shoulders. He waved back.

The plane touched down with an almost imperceptible bump. They were in Kashmir—all three of them.

Three's a Crowd

AT THE AIRPORT ASHOK tried to slip away, but as he was getting onto the airlines bus he heard the familiar voice, now matured into manhood, ring in his ears.

'Ashok, where the devil do you think you're going? I have a car here and I will drop you wherever you like.'

Ashok walked back to where Ramesh and Sheila were standing.

'Here, give me your suitcase,' said Ramesh. Taking it from Ashok he swung it up to the luggage carrier. It was by no means light, and once again, as so often in school, Ashok found himself admiring Ramesh's physical prowess.

'Now,' he said, 'where do you want to go?'

'I am booked at the Palace Hotel,' said Ashok.

Sheila, who had been studiously surveying the contents of her bag, gave a slight start.

'The Palace Hotel,' cried Ramesh, 'that's where we are staying. Come and get in. No, not here, behind—with Sheila. I'll sit in front and see that this driver fellow uses the right gears!'

Ashok protested weakly.

'Look here, two's company and three's crowd, specially on a honeymoon. I'm not going to barge in on the two of you.'

'Nonsense,' grinned Ramesh, 'we're three anyhow with this weird and wonderful driver. And, in any case,' he turned to Sheila, who blushed a deep shade of pink, 'the honeymoon doesn't really begin until one gets to the bridal suite.'

Ashok was trapped. Sheila got into the back of the car and Ashok followed her, carefully placing his briefcase on the seat between them and sitting as close to the door as possible. With a jerk the driver started off and they drove out of the airport.

Ramesh was aglow with excitement.

'I can hardly believe it's really true, Ashok, that we are together again after so many years. You haven't changed much—still the shy, slim, handsome, intellectual type.'

Ashok laughed. 'You're very much the same too, Ramesh, except a bit taller and a bit fatter!'

'A bit taller? I'm over six feet now!'

They were driving over a bare, brown hillock.

'It seems rather dry, doesn't it?' said Ashok. 'You know, emerald set in a ring of pearls and all that.'

'Wait till you get to the hotel,' said Ramesh. 'It's absolute heaven there—specially on a honeymoon. What's the matter, darling?' He suddenly turned to Sheila. 'You haven't said a single word since we landed. Are you feeling all right?'

Sheila gave a short, embarrassed laugh.

'I'm quite all right, thank you, dear. I was just thinking that one of the greatest advantages of the abolition of princely rule is that one can now live in their palaces.'

'Even though we do have to pay through our noses to do so,' added Ramesh.

They all laughed.

By now they were entering the outskirts of Srinagar city. Giant chinar trees with their thick foliage and broad green leaves stood on the roadside, massive against the light-blue sky. The first sight of Srinagar was not overly impressive, but soon they came to a newly built area of the town and the road curved inwards.

'There's the Jhelum,' said Ramesh excitedly. The driver who had so far confined his conversation to some unintelligible grunts and nods, suddenly came to life.

'This our famous river, sahib,' he said. 'Srinagar called seven-bridge city, but two new built, including one we now are driving.'

'What's this one called?' asked Sheila.

'Badshah Bridge, memsahib, after great king ruling Kashmir many years previous.'

As they drove over the bridge Ashok saw out of the window a massive and handsome white building rising from the river.

'Is that the palace?' he asked.

'That's the old palace,' said Ramesh, 'now used as offices or something.'

'Secretariat,' said the driver.

'Wherever did you learn your English?' Ashok laughed. 'You speak very well.'

'For ten years, sahib, I with British Resident, then in 1947 take job travel agency. Allow me introduce myself—Ahmed Shaikh of Fatehkadal.'

'Good heavens,' laughed Sheila, 'that sounds almost as impressive as Mountbatten of Burma. What or where is Fatehkadal?'

'Kadal is bridge, memsahib. Fatehkadal third bridge of old seven. My home there. Your good self come, have food someday.'

They were now in a modern and crowded shopping area. A number of tongas carrying tourists looking faintly ill at ease jostled each other. Two or three buses loaded with passengers honked loudly, while pedestrians hurried to and fro.

'A lot of people for office hours, don't you think?' said Ramesh.

Ahmed honked furiously. 'I will now show you my tictacs,' he shouted.

'Your what?' said Ramesh.

'He probably means tactics,' Sheila said.

'Yes, memsahib, I expert driver, use expert tictacs.'

He slowed the car down and waited till a man from the crowd stood almost against the fender. Then suddenly he accelerated just enough to push the man a couple of feet away. The unfortunate fellow shouted and shook his fist at Ahmed, the crowd parted as if by magic, and the car triumphantly sped on. Ashok was just about to make some comment when the car took a sharp right turn. He looked out of his window and there, standing in solitary beauty, was a mountain topped by a stone temple. For a moment he looked at the temple uncomprehendingly, then a flash of light shot through his brain and he felt a strange exhilaration welling up inside him. The feeling lasted only a few seconds, but it was so vivid that Ashok gave an audible gasp, which he managed to camouflage by turning it into a short cough. For a minute he was too startled to speak, and he pretended to look out of the window casually and admire the scenery.

The car was now skirting the mountain, the road running parallel to a channel of water configured like a river, but so still that it looked more like a lake. Trying to keep his voice as steady and casual as possible Ashok said:

'Ahmed, what is this mountain with the temple?'

'Your good self not know famous landmark of Kashmir, sahib,' exclaimed the driver. 'The Mountain of Shiva.'

They now sped along a delightful boulevard fringing the lake. On the right the Mountain of Shiva rose gracefully into the sky. Its slope was at first gradual, covered with a variety of shrubs and small trees. About half way up it suddenly became steeper, and a magnificent plantation of pine trees thrust their evergreen branches boldly out of the mountainside. Then there was a bare, rocky slope, and right at the top was the temple.

Ashok was astounded by his strange reaction to seeing the mountain; it was several minutes before he was calm again. Swamiji had said to him once that there was a hidden, psychic connection between each individual and certain places, especially places of religious worship. His words now flashed through Ashok's mind. That must be it, he thought. 'We are there,' said Ahmed suddenly.

The car turned right, drove up a stately road and swerved again and then came to a halt before a gracious building standing on green lawns, fountains playing.

'Maharaja's palace,' said Ahmed grandiloquently. 'Your home in Kashmir.'

They were shown to their rooms by an oleaginous young man in black.

Mercifully, thought Ashok, they were a considerable distance apart. Ramesh and Sheila had been given a suite on the first floor of the northern wing, commanding an astonishing view of the lake; while Ashok had a single room in the opposite part of the hotel, which had a clear view of the mountain with the temple.

Ashok liked the building immediately. He had been rather disturbed at the prospect of living in a Maharaja's palace, and had conjured up visions of a huge Victorian monstrosity with gilded beds. As it turned out, this palace was chaste and modern. It was a large structure, but its bulk was tastefully camouflaged by its graceful design. From a central block radiated two wings, from which two other wings extended at right angles, giving the hotel the shape of a rectangle without one of its longer sides. The whole structure was set on a large green lawn with two terraces, and it commanded a breathtaking view of Dal Lake. Behind the hotel the hill rose steeply. On the extreme left the Mountain of Shiva stood, aloof and mysterious, while in front there was a huge natural amphitheatre formed by the mountains on the north-western side of the Kashmir valley. In the foreground, near the Mountain of Shiva, was another small hill with some sort of a fort built around its top.

Ashok unpacked his suitcase as soon as he got to his room and hung his clothes in the closet. Having washed, he strolled out on to the lawn and stood admiring the view. Truly, he thought, this is the most beautiful place on earth. There was a slight breeze and Ashok savoured its gentle bite, which was in such dramatic contrast to the heat and dust of Delhi. Here the air was crystal clear, and Ashok breathed it in gratefully, filling his lungs to capacity and then gently exhaling. 'Always try and make your breathing slow and regular,' Swamiji had said, and Ashok found the practice particularly helpful whenever he faced some serious problem.

At the moment, of course, the problem uppermost on his mind was Sheila and Ramesh. He had still not fully recovered from the shock of seeing them both again in such dramatic circumstances, and he wondered whether or not he should tell Ramesh that he had known and loved Sheila in London. He was deeply devoted to his friend despite the incident at school; seeing Ramesh after all these years had only brought home to him again the depth of his feelings. He dreaded lest his saying anything upset Ramesh and ruin his honeymoon. Also, knowing his friends volcanic and suspicious nature, he feared that he might misunderstand the whole affair.

On the other hand, if he didn't say anything and Ramesh later found out that he had known Sheila, he might read non-existent motives into his silence. Also, Ashok was not sure whether Sheila would like him to tell Ramesh. He decided that when the opportunity arose he would speak to Sheila.

A hearty slap on the back jerked Ashok out of his conjectures.

'Enough nature study for the time being. Come and have a drink before lunch.'

Ashok followed Ramesh to the bar—'the most luxurious bar East of Suez'—as the hotel brochure had said. It was really a stunner—upholstered in black and maroon, one whole wall covered with mirrors which reflected a panoramic view of the lake behind. They took a high stool each.

'Beer for me,' said Ramesh to the bartender. 'What will you have?'

'A fresh lime,' said Ashok with a smile.

'Bah!' Ramesh grimaced in mock disgust. 'You are no longer at school, my dear boy, and thank heavens there is no prohibition in Kashmir.'

The drinks came, and Ramesh downed his tankard before Ashok had got through half his lime.

'Another one, bartender, and quick,' said Ramesh. 'Sheila must be waiting for us in the dining room.'

The second beer duly arrived, frothing lusciously in its broad tankard. Ramesh gulped it down and then turned to Ashok.

'Come on, let's have lunch. Don't bother,' he added, as Ashok pulled out his wallet. 'He'll put it on my account. Room number fifty-six.' The bartender nodded, and they walked out towards the dining room close by. The room was large and, like everything in the hotel, in impeccable taste. About thirty tables filled the spacious hall, each covered with fresh linen and gleaming tableware. At one end there was a raised platform about twenty-five feet wide, evidently for dancing. Above was a large, rectangular cut-glass chandelier, modern and sophisticated.

Ramesh and Ashok stopped for a moment at one of the doors and looked around the room. Sheila was sitting in a corner near the dance floor. She smiled at them and waved.

'There she is,' said Ramesh.

Wending their way between the tables they came to where Sheila was sitting.

It was a table for two, but Ramesh turned to a waiter standing nearby and told him to bring a third chair. Ashok's eyes met Sheila's for a brief, very brief, second, and he thought she gave him an almost imperceptible shake of her head. Then they sat down.

'What a delightful place,' said Sheila. She seemed to have recovered some of her vivacity, and Ashok noticed that she was looking lovelier than ever. In England she had been beautiful, but now there was a maturity about her. Also new was that golden blush of a bride. He noticed how her magnificent eyes always sought out Ramesh, and lingered on him with a tender possessiveness. As for Ramesh, it was evident that he was totally in love with her. From the deepest recesses of his heart Ashok wished them happiness.

'Now tell me about your dramatic reunion,' said Sheila. 'If you were such good friends, why did you never meet after leaving school?'

Ashok saw Ramesh's face begin to change colour, and said at once: 'Well, it so happened that since then our paths just never crossed. We wrote many letters to each other but for some reason they never reached their destination.'

Ramesh shot him a grateful glance, and added, 'Anyhow, that's all over. Now that I've found Ashok, darling, you can be sure I won't let him get lost again.'

The dining room was full to capacity by now, and a vigorous four-man orchestra was playing pop tunes with gusto. There was a tall, dark man playing the piano; a rotund drummer who performed with the elegance of a seal, and a grinning violinist whose body swayed more violently than his hand. The fourth performer was a youngster with dark, wavy hair, who held the microphone in a sadistic grip and poured into it the latest hit songs with a curious, though by no means unpleasant, Goan accent.

'Were you in the Goa operations, Ramesh?' Ashok said, as if to keep the conversation going.

'You bet I was,' Ramesh laughed. 'In fact, I was with one of the leading formations that liberated Panjim. I must say,' he added, 'the Portuguese were a pleasant surprise. We were expecting tough resistance and they collapsed like a house of cards. With China,' he rued, 'it was the opposite. But whatever made you think of Goa just before lunch?'

'Only the Goan orchestra,' Ashok laughed.

'You and your psychological motivation,' said Ramesh. Turning to Sheila he added, 'He was exactly the same at school, darling. In the middle of watching an exciting football match he would suddenly go off at a tangent and start talking about mountain flora or something equally absurd.'

The food was surprisingly good for a hotel, soup followed by delicious Kashmir trout, chicken pulao and a local vegetable. The orchestra had returned to the attack with renewed vigour after a ten-minute break. They started on a tune which jogged something in Ashok's mind, when Ramesh exclaimed suddenly, 'Darling, they're playing our favourite tune from *My Fair Lady*.'

The chicken slice in Ashok's mouth decided on the spur of the moment to go down the wrong channel. He coughed and reached for a glass of water.

He noticed that Sheila had paled almost imperceptibly, though otherwise she was completely composed.

'Yes, dear,' she said simply.

'You saw the play in England, didn't you, darling?' Then he turned to Ashok.

'When did you say you were England?'

'Nineteen fifty-nine to sixty-one.'

'Did you see this famous musical?' said Ramesh. 'I absolutely adore its music. Sheila has the long-playing record.'

'As a matter of fact, I did,' said Ashok, 'and enjoyed it immensely.'

'Weren't you there also at the same time, darling?'

'I returned to India at the end of fifty-nine,' she said.

'Don't I know it!' said Ramesh. 'We should have been married right then except for these bloody rules we have in the army. I must say, darling, it was great of you to have waited so long to marry me.'

'Well worth the wait, I'm sure,' said Ashok. Sheila blushed a deep pink.

'Sorry,' said Ashok. 'I've gone and embarrassed your wife.'

'Nonsense,' said Ramesh. 'And stop referring to her as "your wife" as if you were a bloody lawyer or something. She has a perfectly nice name—Sheila. Use it.'

The lunch finally came to an end, anticlimactically, with a pedestrian fruit salad. The waiter asked them if they wanted coffee. Ramesh and Sheila declined.

'Look here,' said Ashok, 'I'll stay on and have coffee. You two honeymooners go up and relax in your bridal suite.' He gave Ramesh an affectionate wink.

Ramesh grinned and prodded him in the ribs.

'Good idea, dear boy,' he said. He and Sheila rose. 'What are your plans for the evening?'

'*Kalah kridati, gachhati ayuh*,' said Ashok with a smile.

'You and you benighted Sanskrit. What does it mean?'

'Never mind,' said Ashok. 'The bridal suite awaits you.'

From *The Mountain of Shiva*, 2016

Farewell Speech to Rajya Sabha

'Let Us Work Together'

HALF A CENTURY AGO, I came to Delhi. After having served my home state of Jammu and Kashmir as head of the state for eighteen years, fifty years ago, at the age of thirty-six, I came to Delhi and joined Mrs (Indira) Gandhi's cabinet. Forty out of these fifty years, I have been a Member of Parliament: four times in the Lok Sabha,[1] four times in the Rajya Sabha, both in the treasury benches and in the opposition and in both houses.

It has been fascinating to see the evolution of the parliament over these years and how our Constitution gives us the flexibility to adapt to changing economic, social and political compulsions. We've witnessed an explosion in media; for example, when we started there were two channels, now there are 500. That has also changed the complexion of our politics.

Parliament has evolved over these fifty years, but not all the changes have been positive. I remember when I went to the Lok Sabha first, there were brilliant debates, with Hiren Mukherjee, with Madhu Limaye, with Nath Pai, with Atalji, and Bhupesh Gupta. Those sorts of debates now seem to be becoming rarer and the disruptions more frequent. So, I think, we need to do a little retrospection to see what we can do to ensure that the parliamentary system functions according to the rules and positively.

Looking back at this vast panorama of half a century in office, I had the privilege of interacting with a huge spectrum of political colleagues from every region, every religion, every community. I was a witness to, or participant in, every single general election since 1952, and I had the privilege of interacting, as Ghulam Nabi has said, with all the prime ministers. When I was in Jammu and Kashmir, my mentors were Pandit Jawaharlal Nehru and Lal Bahadur Shastri, and when I came to the capital, they were Indira Gandhi, Rajiv Gandhi, P.V. Narasimha Rao, Atal Bihari Vajpayee, Manmohan Singh and now Narendra Modi.

So, this has been a great experience for me and I've noticed one thing: Despite sharp differences of opinion and ideology, often expressed in intemperate language, one thing is common in all these people. They were all in their own way working for what Pandit Jawaharlal Nehru called the exciting adventure of building a new India. In their own way, every prime minister has contributed.

Ours is a unique and glorious country.

Kalidasa said:

अस्त्युत्तरस्यां दिशि देवतात्मा हिमालयो नाम नगाधिराजः ।
पुर्वापरौ तोयनिधी वगाह्य स्थितः पृथिव्या इव मानदण्डः ॥

– कालिदास, कुमारसम्भवम्, प्रथमः सर्गः १ - ८

It's a *devatatma*, a great spiritual presence. In the poem 'Tarana-i-Hindi', better known as the song 'Sare Jahan Se Achha', Allama Iqbal has said:

पर्वत वो सबसे ऊँचा, हमसाया आसमाँ का
वो संतरी हमारा, वो पासबाँ हमारा ।

That tallest of the mountains, that neighbour of the sky,
That is our sentry, that is our watchman.

The Himalayas have in a way laid down parameters of India, all the way down to Kanyakumari[2], where three great oceans meet at the feet of Mother India. And what a unique country, so much diversity of religion, of language, of custom, of food, of dress, of ideologies, but we have coped with this diversity by basing ourselves on our constitutional and civilizational values.

I would submit that if properly presented, there is no conflict between these; for example, we talk of secularism:

एकं सद्विप्रा बहुधा वदन्ति

The Truth is one, the wise call it by many names.

—The *Rig Veda*

सर्व धर्म समभाव[3]

Equal respect for all religions is our view of secularism. It's not against religious. We cannot be anti-religious in this country, except perhaps some people whose ideology may demand them to be.

ईश्वरः सर्वभूतानां हृद्देशेऽर्जुन तिष्ठति ।

The lord resides in the heart of all beings.

—The Bhagavadgita

Socialism. Again, one word, one line:

बहुजन हिताय: बहुजन सुखाये:

What better definition can there be!

सर्वे भवन्तु सुखिनः
सर्वे सन्तु निरामयाः ।
सर्वे भद्राणि पश्यन्तु
मा कश्चिद्दुःखभाग्भवेत् ।

May all beings be happy, may all be healthy,
May all beings see auspicious sights,
May no one have to undergo sorrow.

As far as freedoms are concerned:

आ नो भद्राः क्रतवो यन्तु विश्वतः

Let noble thoughts come to us from every side.

—The *Riga Veda*

We are not a closed society. We have been on the crossroads of civilizations. We've produced great ideas. We've received great ideas. That is the genius of India. That is what has kept India going.

I came to parliament fifty years ago as an idealistic young man of thirty-six. I now bid farewell as an idealistic old man, because I have implicit faith that India will overcome all its challenges as long as we remain faithful to our constitutional and civilizational values.

So, while expressing my deep gratitude for the unfailing courtesy and consideration I've always received from my parliamentary colleagues and for the kind words said by my colleagues Ghulam Nabi Azad and Ravi Shankar Prasad, the secretariat, the staff of the Rajya Sabha, I will leave you with two verses from very different sources.

The first is from Shakeel Badayuni:[4]

हर चीज़ नहीं है मरकज़ पर इक ज़र्रा इधर इक ज़र्रा उधर
नफ़रत से न देखो दुश्मन को शायद वो मोहब्बत कर बैठे।

Everything is not always perfectly centred,
There is always a slight imbalance one way or the other,
Do not look upon the enemy with hostility,
He may one day might just begin loving you.

The second is from the Upanishad:

सह नाववतु।
सह नौ भुनक्तु।
सह वीर्यं करवावहै।
तेजस्वि नावधीतमस्तु मा विद्विषावहै।[5]

Let us work together,
Let us be nourished together,
Let us achieve together,
Let there be no hatred between us.

Karan Singh delivered a version of this speech in the Rajya Sabha on 5 January 2018.

Notes

An Interview with Karan Singh

1. Head of the English department at the Doon School, Dehradun, after graduating with honours from Magdalen College, Oxford University. He was then inducted into the publicity division of the Government of India before being among the first diplomats appointed by the fledgling Government of Free India.
2. Ranbir Penal Code was introduced in 1932 during the reign of Dogra dynasty with Ranbir Singh. It is based on the Indian Penal Code with several differences that are only applicable to the state of Jammu and Kashmir.
3. India has control of 60 per cent of the area of the former princely state of Jammu and Kashmir (Jammu, Kashmir Valley, Ladakh and Siachen Glacier); Pakistan controls 30 per cent of the region (Gilgit–Baltistan and Azad Kashmir). China administers 10 per cent (Aksai Chin and Trans-Karakoram Tract) of the state since 1962.
4. Lines from *Diwan-e-Ghalib*, a well-known book of poems written by the famous Persian and Urdu poet Mirza Asadullah Khan Ghalib.

A Little History

1. Sri Krishnaprem was a British spiritual aspirant who came to India in the early twentieth century. Together with his spiritual teacher Sri Yashoda Mai (1882–1944), he founded an ashram at Mirtola, near Almora, India.

Assessment of Sri Aurobindo as a Political Thinker

1. 'The Bedrock of Indian Nationalism', *Bande Mataram*, weekly edition, 14 June 1908.
2. *Speeches*, p. 142. In his political writings, Sri Aurobindo lays great stress on this broader aspect of Indian nationalism. See, for example, editorials in the *Bande Mataram* on 'The Asiatic Role' (12 April 1948); 'The New Ideal' (12 April 1908); 'Ideals Face to Face' (3 May 1906); 'The Bedrock of Indian Nationalism' (4 June 1908).

Jawaharlal Nehru and Karan Singh

1

1. Maharaja Hari Singh (1895–1961); son of Raja Amar Singh and great grandson of Maharaja Gulab Singh; educated at Mayo College, Ajmer; received military training at Imperial Cadet Corps, Dehradun; became commander-in-chief of Jammu and Kashmir State Forces in 1915; became Maharaja on 23 September 1925; paid much attention to the promotion of agriculture, education and medical facilities; abolished forced labour, infanticide and untouchability; allowed Dalits to visit all temples; acceded Jammu and Kashmir State to the Indian Union in October 1947.
2. Propaganda against India and threats of war over Kashmir in the Pakistan press had been continuing for several months. For instance, on 10 January 1951 the *Pakistan Times* published the statement of Sardar Abdur Rab Nishtar, governor of west Punjab: 'So long as a single Pakistani is alive, nobody dare snatch Kashmir from Pakistan by force ... if the problem was not settled immediately, the whole of Asia would be engulfed in the flame of war which might lead to a world conflagration.' On 14 June 1951, the *Dawn* published the statement of Sir Muhammad Zafarulla Khan, Pakistan's foreign minister: 'I say this with full responsibility that India has now over several months taken up the attitude with regard to Kashmir which deliberately blocks progress along peaceful lines. What does India desire? It has no right to complain if it gets something else.' Similarly, on 15 July 1951, Liaquat Ali Khan, the prime minister of Pakistan, said at a press conference in Karachi that ninety per cent of the Indian army had been concentrated within striking

distance of the borders of West and East Pakistan, constituting a grave threat to Pakistan's security, the interests of neighbourly relations between the two countries and to international peace.

3. At a National Conference session on 4 June 1951 in Srinagar, Nehru said that if Pakistan 'undertake jehad, they will be answered in kind and will be defeated'. Further, he added: '[I]f there is another attack on Kashmir by Pakistan, we will not stop our armed forces once again, as we did once earlier, from crossing the border into Pakistan'. Similarly, on 16 July at a public meeting in Bangalore, he declared: 'It is intolerable for continuous propaganda for jehad to be carried out in Pakistan, month after month without check or hindrance ... we want good neighbourly relations but not at the price of aggression, insult and calumny and continuous threat of war.' He also stated that 'if Pakistan attacks any part of the Indian territory we shall repel this attack with all our strength'.

2

1. Tribhuvan Bir Bikram Shah (1906–1955); king of Nepal, 1911–50 and 1952–55.
2. King Tribhuvan was in India from 13 to 21 August 1951.

3

1. Nehru delivered this speech in the Lok Sabha on 24 July 1952. It has been reproduced in the *Selected Works of Jawaharlal Nehru* (second series) Vol. 19, pp. 219–38.
2. The agreement regarding constitutional relationship between India and Kashmir was announced on 24 July 1952. Its salient features were: (i) the head of the state of Jammu and Kashmir would be a person recommended by the state legislature and recognized by the president of India; (ii) the Indian flag would have the same status in Kashmir as in any other part of India but the Kashmir state flag would be retained; (iii) citizenship would be common in two parts of the country but the state legislature would have power to define and regulate the rights and privileges of the permanent residents in Kashmir; (iv) the fundamental rights as laid down in the Indian Constitution would be extended to Kashmir, but these would not come in the way of the

State's programme of land reforms; (v) power to reprieve or commute death sentences would belong to the president of India; (vi) the Indian president's power to declare a state of emergency in case of external danger or internal disturbances would be extended to Kashmir, but in regard to internal disturbances it would be used only at the request of the state government; (vii) residuary powers would be retained by the state but the state could transfer more rights to the Union; (viii) the Supreme Court could adjudicate in regard to disputes between the state and the central and other provincial governments and on fundamental rights agreed to by the state; and (ix) the details of the financial arrangements would be further considered.

3. According to the Delhi Agreement, the head of the state would be a person recognized by the president of the Union on the recommendation of the legislature of the state, holding office at the pleasure of the president for a term of five years.
4. In Egypt on 23 July 1952, King Farouk was forced to abdicate by General Neguib in a military coup.
5. Fouad Farouk (1920–65); last reigning king of Egypt from 1936 till his abdication in July 1952.
6. Frank P. Graham (1886–1972); president, University of North Carolina, 1930–49; appointed UN mediator for India and Pakistan in relation to the Kashmir dispute on 30 April 1951.
7. The ministerial level conference was held in Geneva from 26 August to 10 September 1952. Its object was to evolve a workable plan for demilitarization of Jammu and Kashmir and to prepare the ground for the appointment of a plebiscite administrator. India was represented by Gopalaswami Ayyangar and Pakistan by Zafrulla Khan.

4

1. Karan Singh was appointed regent by his father, Maharaja Hari Singh at the intervention of Jawaharlal Nehru on 20 June 1949.
2. On 24 July 1952, Nehru made a detailed statement in the Lok Sabha on the Delhi Agreement in regard to Jammu & Kashmir State. Among other things, he declared: '... the accession is complete in law and, in fact, Jammu & Kashmir State is a constituent unit like any other'.
3. In fact, the impeachment provision did not rest with the constitution of Kashmir, while Sheikh Abdullah wanted to include this.

5

1. On 14 November 1952, Karan Singh was elected the first head of the state and was called Sadar-i-Riyasat while the constitution of Kashmir was adopted on 17 November 1956, fixing 26 January 1957 as the date for its commencement.

6

1. The Praja Parishad Party of the Jammu Hindus was formed in November 1947. The Party gained much strength under the leadership of Prem Nath Dogra in the 1950s. Its main object was 'to achieve full integration of Jammu and Kashmir State with the rest of India like other acceding states and safeguard the legitimate democratic rights of the people of Jammu from the communist-dominated anti-Dogra Government of Sheikh Abdullah'.
2. Members of the Lok Sabha representing Jammu and Kashmir were nominated up to 1957. From 1967, election of the members started.
3. Maulana Abul Kalam Azad.
4. While reiterating the demand for complete accession, Prem Nath Dogra declared that, 'so long as the question of the Maharaja's abdication or withdrawal of his recognition as "Rajpramukh" is not finally decided by the Government of India, and till the new Constitution for the State assumes a concrete shape, it would be premature to give any definite opinion on this single issue of accepting or rejecting the office of the Head of the State by Shree Yuvaraj Bahadur'.
5. Maharaja Hari Singh.
6. Rajendra Prasad.

7

1. In the third week of June 1952, the Praja Parishad leaders submitted a memorandum to President Rajendra Prasad, in which they demanded full application of the Indian Constitution to Jammu, extension of the jurisdiction of the Supreme Court, acceptance for Jammu of the fundamental rights of the Indian Constitution and of the national flag of India. On 26 June, a big demonstration was staged outside the parliament to reinforce the Parishad demands.

2. S.P. Mookerjee, V.G. Deshpande, U.M. Trivedi and Ram Narayan Singh, members of parliament who had visited Jammu and Kashmir, said in a statement on 12 August 1952 that the people of Jammu were not prepared to be tagged on to the Kashmir valley unless the principle of full integration with India was accepted.
3. The press in Pakistan portrayed the Praja Parishad leaders as being regarded 'the Heroes of Jammu' by the Hindus.
4. Some leaders of the Praja Parishad were closed to the idea of accepting the office of elected headship of the state by Karan Singh. They opined that he should not accept Sheikh Abdullah's offer in its vague form.
5. C.S. Venkatachar (b. 1898); joined the ICS 1922; served in various capacities in the United Provinces and Central Indian States 1923–37; agent to governor general at India in British Malaysia; 1937–41, commissioner of Allahabad division, 1941–46; prime minister, Jodhpur, 1946–47; secretary, states ministry, 1951–55; secretary to the president of India, 1955–58; high commissioner to Canada, 1958–61.

8

1. On 14 November 1952, Karan Singh was elected Sadar-i-Riyasat.

9

1. In his speech Karan Singh told the gathering in the assembly hall: 'In this land of colour and beauty, men of different faiths and creeds live as common inheritors of a great past and culture. It is our task now to forge greater unity among them as joint architects of their future. Such abiding unity cannot be imposed from above but has to be based upon interests of the common man.' He described the division of Kashmir into two parts as the 'direct consequence of wanton aggression. Any attempt to impose an arbitrary solution seeking to circumvent this fundamental aspect of the situation cannot be acceptable to us.' He further said: 'Now that we are intimately associated with the Republic of India, we can look forward to a bright and prosperous future.'

10

1. The Congress of Universities of the Commonwealth was held in Cambridge from 13 to 17 July 1953. The Congress was the seventh of the series organized at quinquennial intervals since 1912 by the Association of Universities of the British Commonwealth, formerly known as the Universities Bureau of the British Empire.

11

1. Nehru was on tour from 29 May to 25 June 1953 to London, Paris, Rome, Switzerland and Cairo. He returned to Bombay on 26 June.
2. Mookerjee was kept in detention in a house near the Nishat Bagh in Srinagar, where he died on 23 June 1953.
3. Mookerjee and seven other people were arrested at Lakhanpur on 11 May 1953 under Section 3(i) of the Jammu and Kashmir Public Security Act. They had refused to comply with the warning not to remain in the state, where they had gone to support the Praja Parishad agitation.
4. On 27 June 1953, V.M. Trivedi, S.P. Mookerjee's counsel, and Guru Dutt Vaid, a co-detenu, alleged that proper medical care had not been provided to Mookerjee and this negligence of the state had hastened his death. The Jana Sangh called for a bandh on 15 July 1953 to be observed as Shyama Prasad Day and demanded a high-level impartial enquiry into the circumstances leading to Mookerjee's death. This demand was supported by various other leaders such as Purushottamdas Tandon and Jayaprakash Narayan.

12

1. In his letter of 28 June 1953 Nehru wrote, '[T]he question of Kashmir has had not only a logical appeal for me but also an emotional one ... Thus far I have proceeded on a basis of friendship and confidence in you and have been vain enough to expect the same approach from you. Whether that is justified now or not, it is for you to say. Individual relations should not count in national affairs and yet they do count and make a difference.' For full text of the letter see *Selected Works of Jawaharlal Nehru* (second series), Vol. 22, pp. 193–197.

2. Abdullah did not come to Delhi for the 3rd July meeting but sent Bakshi Ghulam Mohammad and Mirza Afzal Beg. He replied on 4 July: 'I would have certainly come down myself to Delhi but Bakshi and Beg will explain to you why it is not desirable for me to leave Srinagar at present.'

13

1. By the beginning of August 1953, the rift in Sheikh Abdullah's cabinet became more intense. In the cabinet meeting of 6 August, Sheikh Abdullah insisted that Sham Lal Saraf resign but he refused to oblige which precipitated the crisis.
2. In the memorandum of 7 August Bakshi Ghulam Mohammad, G.L. Dogra and Sham Lal Saraf charged Sheikh Abdullah with not only delaying the implementation of the Delhi Agreement but also denouncing it 'purposefully and openly'. They raised that, 'Mr Beg and you, in utter disregard of opinions of your colleagues and without their consultation, make public pronouncements which flout the principles of joint responsibility … you have frequently adopted certain arbitrary measures in complete denial of the right of expression of opinion of even your own colleagues in the handling both of external and internal affairs of the State.' They also criticized his economic policies and his support to M.A. Beg who 'has persistently been following policies of narrow sectarianism and communalism which have seriously undermined the oneness of the State'. They added: '[T]he Cabinet, constituted as it is at present and lacking as it does the unity of purpose and action, has lost the confidence of the people in its ability to give them a clean, efficient and healthy administration.'
3. On 8 August around noon Sheikh Abdullah met Karan Singh at the latter's residence. Karan Singh pointed out to him that 'it would be useful if he and his Cabinet colleagues were to come to my residence that evening so that the whole matter could be discussed in depth'. But Sheikh Abdullah side-tracked this suggestion by launching into an angry tirade against the Indian press.
4. (1904–82); businessmen and politician from Kashmir; was associated with the National Conference for many years; member, State Assembly, Jammu and Kashmir, 1951–62; minister in the Jammu and Kashmir government, 1948–62; nominated to the Lok Sabha, 1962.
5. In his letter of 8 August 1953, Karan Singh conveyed to Sheikh Abdullah that the 'conflict within the Cabinet has for a considerable time been causing great confusion and apprehension in the minds of the people of the State. The

situation has reached to an unprecedented crisis ... under these conditions I, as Head of the State, have been forced to the conclusion that the present Cabinet cannot continue in office any longer and hence I regret to inform you that I have dissolved the Council of Ministers headed by you.'

6. The order was issued on the same date.
7. Bakshi Ghulam Mohammad became the prime minister of Jammu and Kashmir on 9 August 1953 after Sheikh Abdullah was removed by the Sadar-i-Riyasat on 8 August. His cabinet colleagues included G.M. Sadiq, minister for education, health, publicity, information and jails; G.L. Dogra, finance minister; Sham Lal Saraf, minister for development, industry and local self-government; Mir Qasim, minister for agriculture, revenue, rural development and relief and rehabilitation.

14

1. Ajit Prasad Jain (1902–77); member, UP Legislative Assembly, 1937–39 and 1946–47; parliamentary secretary to Rafi Ahmad Kidwai, 1937–39; member, Constituent Assembly, 1946–50; member, Provisional Parliament and Lok Sabha, 1952–65. Union minister for relief and rehabilitations, 1950–54. Union minister for food and agriculture, 1954–59; president, UPPCC, 1961–64; governor, Kerala, 1965–66; member, Rajya Sabha, 1968–72; publications include *UP Agrarian Law* and *Rafi Ahmad Kidwai: Memoirs of His Life and Times*.
2. Durga Prasad Dhar (1918–75); deputy home minister, Kashmir government, 1948–57; minister in the Kashmir government, 1961–68; ambassador to the USSR, 1969–71; chairman, policy planning committee, ministry of external affairs, 1971–1972; union minister for planning; and deputy chairman, Planning Commission, 1972–74; member, Rajya Sabha, 1972–75.
3. (1901–1989); joined ICS, 1925; held various posts in UP up to 1941 and thereafter in the central government; secretary, ministry of food, 1947– 48; Kashmir affairs, 1949–51; ministry of food and agriculture, 1951–52, Kashmir affairs and labour, 1953–57, and of the Cabinet, 1958–62; governor of Assam, 1962–67.
4. Nehru had a two-hour talk with Mohammad Ali, the prime minister of Pakistan, on 17 August 1953 in Delhi on various issues arising from the dismissal of Sheikh Abdullah. In fact, the Pakistan government had reacted strongly over Sheikh Abdullah's dismissal and Mohammad Ali had sent a

message to Nehru suggesting an immediate meeting. Despite the latter's marked lack of enthusiasm, he finally agreed to bring forward the talks. Mohammad Ali arrived in Delhi on 16 August for talks which concluded on 20 August with a joint communiqué. For full text of the talks, see *Selected marks of Jawaharlal Nehru* (second series), Vol. 23, pp. 331–36.

15

1. On 21 August 1953, Bakshi stated that the communique was finalized 'with our concurrence and has our unqualified support'.

16

1. The Bakshi government had announced certain ameliorative measures: (i) the compulsory procurement of rice was given up and large quantities were brought from India to meet the food problem, (ii) custom duty on salt and medicines manufactured in India was lifted, (iii) education was made free, (iv) the Wazir Committee report on economic reforms which Sheikh Abdullah had pigeonholed was published and steps were taken to implement some of its recommendations. The businessmen had been assured that their capital was sacrosanct, and that the custom duty and other trade restrictions would be removed, (v) the construction of a 1.5-mile-long tunnel at an altitude of 7,200 feet under the Banihal Pass started to provide a crucial road communication between Jammu and Srinagar throughout the year.

17

1. The book was first published in 1930 (Martin Hopkinson Ltd, London) under the title *Gulab Singh 1792–1858 Founder of Kashmir.* In 1953, it was published under the title *The Founding of the Kashmir State: A Biography of Maharajah Gulab Singh 1792–1858* (George Allen & Unwin Ltd, London).
2. K.M. Panikkar (1895–1963); historian and diplomat, member of the Indian National Congress for some time; served in the princely states before Independence; ambassador to China, the United Arab Republic and France, member, States Reorganization Commission, 1953–55.
3. (1792–1858); attained eminence in the court of Ranjit Singh as a general, conquered Ladakh, Baltistan and western Tibet between 1840–42; founded

the Jammu and Kashmir State by the Treaty of Amritsar between the British government and Maharaja Gulab Singh concluded on 16 March 1846.

4. (1887–1953); member of the Indian Civil Service; judge, Calcutta High Court, 1935, chairman, Hindu Law Committee, 1941; prime minister, Jammu and Kashmir, 1945, constitutional adviser to the Constituent Assembly, 1946–49; India's representative and later leader of India's delegation to the UN, 1949–52; judge, International Court of Justice at the Hague, 1952–53.

18

1. Note to Jawaharlal Nehru, Srinagar, 18 December 1953.

21

1. King Saud Ibn Abdul Aziz in a statement on 10 December 1955 in Bombay said: 'The fate of Indians Muslims is in safe hands as Mr Nehru is bravely, determinedly executing a wide policy of affection and neighbourliness to all Indians irrespective of creed.' He also advised the Indian Muslims to preserve the unity of the country and 'to be true to your country and good to your neighbours, your national duties must be executed with sincerity and straight forwardness'. The King had declined an invitation from the Kashmir government to include Kashmir in his tour.
2. Saud Ibn Abdul Aziz (1902–1969); second son of Ibn Saud, the founder of Saudi Arabia and its first king; became king on 9 November 1953; visited India from 27 November to 13 December 1955; deposed in November 1964.
3. When S.M. Abdullah was removed and arrested.

23

1. In a communiqué issued by the home ministry on 16 January 1956, the government announced its acceptance of most of the recommendations of the States Reorganization Commission. But it was decided to divide the Bombay region into Maharashtra including Vidarbha, Gujarat including Saurashtra and Kutch, and a centrally administered Bombay city including some surrounding villages. Decisions on the future of the Punjab and Telengana area of Hyderabad were still under consideration.
2. Abolished in November 1956.

24

1. G.B. Pant (1887–1961); eminent Congressman from UP; member, Kashipur Municipal Board; leader of the Swaraj Party, UP Legislative Council, 1923–30; president, UPPCC, 1927–30; took part in the Congress movements, 1930, 1940 and 1942 and was imprisoned several times; member, Central Legislative Assembly, 1934–36; leader of Congress party, UP Legislative Assembly, and premier, 1937–39; chief minister, UP, 1946–55; member, Rajya Sabha, 1955–61; Union minister of home affairs, 1955–61; awarded Bharat Ratna, 1957.

Indira Gandhi and Karan Singh

1

1. Karan Singh became regent on 20 June 1949 and continued in this post up to 13 November 1952.
2. The fourth general elections were held from 15 February to 1 March 1967.
3. Sarvepalli Radhakrishnan (1888–1975); eminent educationist and statesman; taught philosophy at Calcutta University, 1921–41, and Eastern Religions at Oxford, 1936–52; vice-chancellor, Banaras Hindu University, 1939–48; ambassador to the Soviet Union, 1949–52; vice president of India, 1952–62; and president, 1962–67. His works include *Indian Philosophy* (two volumes, 1923 and 1927); *East and West in Religion* (1933) and *Religion and Society* (1944).
4. Karan Singh wanted to join active politics and had hence sent his resignation to the president on 16 August 1966.

2

1. Karan Singh was elected Sadar-i-Riyasat of Jammu and Kashmir on 14 November 1952 and served in this position up to 9 April 1965.
2. He served as governor of the state from 10 April 1965 to 15 March 1967.
3. In deference to Prime Minister Indira Gandhi's wishes, Karan Singh withdrew his resignation and agreed to continue in the office for the 'time being'.

3

1. Not traceable.
2. Malik Jeevan Lal Kapoor (1897–1982); eminent barrister of Punjab, practised law, Lahore High Court, 1922–47; vice president, All India Postmen's Union, 1926–47; judge, Punjab High Court, 1949–57; judge, Supreme Court of India, 1957–62; chairman, Delimitation Commission, 1963.
3. Ghulam Mohammed Sadiq was the prime minister of Jammu & Kashmir from 1964 to 1965, till the position was renamed. He became the first chief minister and served out his term till 1971.
4. Bakshi Ghulam Mohammad of the National Conference served as the deputy prime minister of Jammu & Kashmir from 1947–53 and as the prime minister from 1953–64.
5. Indira Gandhi was on a four-day visit to Nepal from 4 to 7 October 1966. She discussed the international situation and matters of mutual interest with King Mahendra and chairman of the Council of Ministers, Surya Bahadur Thapa. She also announced Indian aid of Rs 40 crores for Nepal's Third Plan. In a joint communique issued on 7 October, the two countries reaffirmed their faith in non-alignment and called for immediate cessation of the American bombing of North Vietnam as an essential first step to peace talks for a political settlement of the Vietnam problem.
6. The idea of setting up a research institute in memory of Jawaharlal Nehru was conceived by Karan Singh after Nehru's death in 1964. In order to craft it he took up the issue with Indira Gandhi, J.R.D. Tata and other trustees of the Jawaharlal Nehru Memorial Fund. Karan Singh considered Nehru his political guru, role model and infallible guide. To him Nehru possessed extraordinary intellectual brilliance and political acumen. Hence, he campaigned for years to launch a research institute at the Teen Murti House where Jawaharlal Nehru lived for seventeen years, and thereby wanted to offer a befitting tribute to the memory of his mentor. Finally, Indira Gandhi laid the foundation stone of the building of Nehru Memorial Library on 27 May 1969 at a special function at the Teen Murti House. B.R. Nanda, a civil servant and an accomplished historian, was appointed its founder-director who nurtured the institution in a scholarly fashion. According to the expectation of Karan Singh, NML today really is one of India's leading research institutions.

7. Maharani Tara Devi (1910–67), fourth wife of Maharaja Hari Singh, originally hailed from a Katoch family of Kangra district, Himachal Pradesh. A deeply religious and generous lady, she had great concern for the poor; her work for War Aid during the Second World War earned her the coveted title 'crown of India'.

4

1. At a press conference on 26 June in Srinagar, Ghulam Mohammad Sadiq expressed that, '... the idea of regional autonomy is completely against the interest of the State. It is rather a mischievous move.'
2. See the succeeding item.

5

1. Note for Indira Gandhi, New Delhi, 10 July 1967.

6

1. Indira Gandhi sent this note to Karan Singh on 25 September 1967.
2. In its editorial of 25 September the *Hindustan Times* wrote, 'The gardens, which have grown around the tombs of the later Lodi Kings, are perhaps the best example of a natural, well-wooded park existing anywhere in the country today. They have served as lungs of fresh air for the town in a part where increasing urbanization has done away all together with the concept of a green belt.' It further noted: 'The NDMC seems bent now on doing to death the nature-based charm and character of this beautiful park. There are plans to build a restaurant and a 'fun corner' for children. The suggestion has also been put out that a part of it will be developed as a site for garden parties, by which, no doubt, is meant those loud, garish weddings with their attendant horrors.' It concluded that 'the country's natural beauty being destroyed by the heavy touch of an unimaginative bureaucracy'. The *Patriot* also reported in a similar manner.
3. Y.B. Chavan.

7

1. Pupul Jayakar (1915–97); cultural activist and writer; worked for the revival of traditional and village arts, handlooms and handicrafts; organized a series of

Indian art festivals in the 1980s in France, US and Japan to popularize Indian artistic achievements in the West; a close friend of Indira Gandhi; served as cultural adviser to Indira Gandhi and Rajiv Gandhi; founded the National Crafts Museum in 1956, the Indian National Trust for Art and Cultural Heritage in 1984; founder trustee, Indira Gandhi National Centre for Arts; wrote biographies of Indira Gandhi and philosopher Jiddu Krishnamurti.

2. S.C. Chhabra was the president of New Delhi Municipal Corporation (NDMC) from 1 November 1966 to 16 October 1970.

8

1. This note was sent on 3 January 1968.
2. Owen Dixon (1886–1972); judge, High Court of Australia, 1929–52, and chief justice, 1952–64; United Nations mediator in the Kashmir dispute.
3. Owen Dixon, in order to bridge differences with regard to the plebiscite between India and Pakistan and to find possibilities of solving the problem, had put forward the following proposals in August 1950: (1) Withdrawal of forces by both Pakistan and India, followed by the appointment of political agents by the United Nations to administer and guard through the local officers the northern approaches to the Valley; (2) replacement of the regular government of Kashmir and that of 'Azad Kashmir' by an administrative body consisting of officers of the United Nations; and (3) plebiscites in place of an overall plebiscite. Though these proposals enabled Pakistan to retain some of the advantages of her aggression, India was willing to consider the proposals, but Pakistan showed no willingness to think in terms of any settlement.

9

1. This note was sent on 30 January 1968.
2. Sheikh Abdullah visited Patna on 15 January 1968 where he met Jayaprakash Narayan and Vinoba Bhave. In his meeting with them, Abdullah sought a peaceful solution to the Kashmir issue to save the Valley from further trouble.
3. Acharya Vinoba Bhave (1895–1982); joined Sabarmati Ashram in 1916; was named by Gandhi as his first satyagrahi to offer individual civil disobedience in 1940; launched the Bhoodan movement after Independence and covered on foot more than 40,000 miles; undertook peace missions in the dacoit-infested areas of Bhind and Morena in Madhya Pradesh, 1960; toured Rangpur

and Dinajpur districts of East Pakistan in connection with the Bhoodan movement, 1962.

10

1. Note to Indira Gandhi 16 January 1969.
2. Mohammad Reza Pahlavi and his second wife Queen Soraiya were in India from 16 February to 8 March 1956.
3. The Parsis of Bombay had beautifully decorated part of the city and accorded a warm welcome to the Shahanshah and the queen. Overwhelmed by such reception the shah reciprocated in a befitting matter by extending sincere and heartfelt thanks.
4. Ardeshir Zahedi (b. 1928); educated at the American University of Beirut and State University of Utah; took part in the revolution led by General Zahedi which overthrew Mossadegh, 1953; adjutant to Shahanshah of Iran, 1954–59; head of Iranian Students Programme, 1959–60; ambassador of Iran in USA, 1960–62, and to the United Kingdom, 1962–66; foreign minister of Iran, 1966–73; ambassador to USA, 1973–79.
5. Lieutenant General J.T. Satarawala (1917–86); commissioned in 1939; lieutenant colonel, 1947–56; brigadier, 1957–60; major general, 1961–66; lieutenant general, 1967–72.

11

1. An open conflict between the Congress left and the Congress right appeared at the party conclave in Bangalore from 10 to 13 July 1969 when Indira Gandhi suggested radical changes in the economic policies presented by the rightists, including nationalization of banks, general insurance, state trading in import and export, curbs on business monopolies and rapid implementation of land reforms. Furthermore, nominations of N. Sanjiva Reddy on 13 July, despite Indira Gandhi's opposition, by the Congress Parliamentary Board (where the Congress right enjoyed majority) as the party's candidate for the presidential election created a grave crisis in the Congress party. It was the death of President Zakir Hussain in May 1969 that precipitated the events leading to the long-awaited split in the Congress. On 13 July, V.V. Giri, vice president and acting president, also announced his candidature for the presidential election as an independent candidate, supported by the Communist Party

of India and Communist Party of India (Marxist), Samyukta Socialist Party, Dravida Munnetra Kazhagam, Muslim League and a section of the Akali Dal. Both Reddy and V.V. Giri filed their nomination on 21 July. To ensure Reddy's election, S. Nijalingappa, the Congress president, leaned towards an understanding with the right-wing Swatantra Party and Jana Sangh. Fakhruddin Ali Ahmad and Jagjivan Ram on 11 August wrote to S. Nijalingappa criticizing his understanding with the Jana Sangh and Swatantra Party on a 'personal level'. Indira Gandhi also accused him of having struck a secret deal with communal and reactionary forces. She and her two colleagues, Fakhruddin Ali Ahmad and Jagjivan Ram, demanded the right to a 'free vote' in the presidential election. Nijalingappa opposed this move and urged Indira Gandhi to issue a whip to party members. Indira Gandhi refused to issue a whip in favour of Reddy and asked the Congress MPs and MLAs to vote freely according to their conscience. Indira Gandhi by then, more or less openly, supported V.V. Giri.

2. The AICC met in Bangalore on 10, 11, 12 and 13 July 1969 and took certain decisions on economic policy. Prime Minister Indira Gandhi prepared a note on the subject and placed it before the Working Committee. It evoked considerable discussion, and a brief resolution was drafted by C. Subramaniam and Sadiq Ali, with Mrs Gandhi's note appended to it, and placed before the AICC. On 10 July Morarji Desai moved the resolution, which ran: 'There has been a good deal of discussion in the Congress organization regarding the economic and social policy and the direction to be given in the economy to reach the socialist goal which the Congress is pledged to achieve. The note by the Prime Minister sets out the policies to be pursued and steps to be taken for the purpose of improving the performance of our economy in industry and agriculture and, at the same time, ensure that the process of economic development does not lead to concentration of wealth and economic power in a few hands.' In her note Indira Gandhi observed: 'The time has come to restate our economic policy and set the direction in which we have to move to achieve our social goal ... The Congress has always championed the cause of the weaker sections, minorities and the underprivileged. This should continue to be the policy of the Congress.' The resolution was passed after two days of discussion on 12 July.
3. On 19 July 1969, Indira Gandhi announced the nationalization of fourteen major banks which controlled 85 per cent of the total bank deposits in the country. The bill to nationalize the banks was introduced in Parliament on 25 July and was passed. On 9 August it received the president's assent.

4. The Congress rightist leaders such as S. Nijalingappa and Morarji Desai considered the nationalization of banks to have happened under the influence of the communists and charged Indira Gandhi and her supporters, the Congress left, of cooperating with the communists and other Left parties.

12

1. Note for Indira Gandhi, 28 August 1969.
2. Maulvi Farooq was the Mirwaiz of his time in Kashmir and chairman of the Awami Action Committee, a coalition of disparate political parties in Jammu and Kashmir. He was the chief preacher at the Jama Masjid in Srinagar and had considerable influence in the state. He was assassinated on 21 May 1990 at his home, and after his death his son Mirwaiz Umar Farooq took over.
3. The first panchayat elections on the basis of adult suffrage were held in Jammu and Kashmir in August 1969.
4. The Gajendragadkar Commission was appointed on 6 November 1967 to enquire into complaints of regional imbalances in Jammu & Kashmir. In the report submitted on 6 December 1968, it suggested that equitable share in government employment, educational facilities and in judicial system be granted to various regions and communities. The report was released on 19 January 1969.
5. Bhagwan Sahay was the governor of Jammu and Kashmir at this time.

13

1. The Plebiscite Front, founded by Mirza Afzal Beg in August 1955, worked to popularize the demand of a plebiscite in Kashmir under the auspices of the UN. It was a subversive organization, and on 12 January 1971 it was banned. Finally, on 5 January 1975, Sheikh Abdullah dissolved the Plebiscite Front and allowed it to merge with the National Conference.
2. Mid-term elections for the fifth Lok Sabha were held all over the country, except in Mandi, Ladakh and Nagpur constituencies.
3. Addressing a public meeting at the Polo ground in Srinagar on 15 July 1970, Indira Gandhi categorically stated that the Kashmir issue had been settled once and for all, and there would be no reopening of it. She declared that the course of Kashmir's history could not be changed, and no prime minister who compromised on the integrity of the country would last. She also pointed out

that some people with vested interests wanted to reopen issues settled twenty-three years ago. But it was difficult to undo the commitments, promises and pledges given by the people.

4. Mirza Mohammad Afzal Beg (1908–82); arrested for taking part in the Quit Kashmir agitation, 1946; minister in Sheikh Abdullah's Cabinet, 1948; founded the Jammu and Kashmir Plebiscite Front, 1955; accused in the Kashmir conspiracy case, 1964; arrested with Sheikh Abdullah and detained at Ootacamund, 1965; released in 1967; externed from Kashmir, 1971; allowed to re-enter, 1972; minister for revenue, industry and commerce, 1975–77; deputy chief minister, 1977–78.

14

1. Santosh K. Sen was a famous physician of Delhi during the 1960s and 1970s. His nursing home was located on Tilak Marg.
2. Aruna Asaf Ali (1909–96); earlier Aruna Ganguli; married in 1928 to Asaf Ali, a distinguished Congress leader from Delhi; participated in the Civil Disobedience movement, 1930, and was imprisoned for one year; imprisoned again in 1932 for six months, and for one year in connection with individual satyagraha, 1940; took active part in the Quit India movement, hoisted the Indian tricolour at Gwalia Tank Grounds, Bombay, 8 August 1942; remained underground till 1946; president, Delhi Provincial Congress Committee, 1947–48; joined the Socialist Party, 1948; left the Socialist Party and formed Left Socialist Group, 1950; member, CPI, 1955–58; mayor of Delhi, 1958–59; rejoined Congress, 1964; president. National Federation of Indian Women and All India Women Conference; one of the founders of *Link*, a news magazine and *Patriot*, a daily; received the Lenin Peace Prize, 1965, and the Jawaharlal Nehru Award for International Understanding, 1991; publications include: *Travel Talk, Socialist Party: Its Rejection of Marxism, Fragment from the Past, Private Face of a Public Person: A Study of Jawaharlal Nehru*, and *Resurgence of Indian Women*; awarded the Bharat Rama posthumously in 1997.
3. Amiya Kumar Kisku (b. 1923); educated at Calcutta and California Universities; worked for the upliftment of scheduled castes and scheduled tribes in West Bengal, Bihar, Odisha and Assam; taught for some years at the Union Christian Training College, Berhampore ; minister for education, social and tribal welfare, government of West Bengal, 1967–68; elected to

the Lok Sabha, 1967 and 1971; union deputy minister of education, 1970–71; and deputy minister, health and family planning, 1971–74.

15

1. Colunthur Gopalan (1918–98); physician and noted researcher in nutrition; director, National Institute of Nutrition, Hyderabad, for several years; vice-president, International Union of Nutritional Sciences; chairman, Indian National Commission for Nutrition; director, Indian Council of Medical Research, 1974–77.
2. Prem Nath Wahi (1908–97); renowned pathologist from Uttar Pradesh; educated in Lucknow and London; professor and head of department of pathology, S.N. Medical College, Agra, 1941–60; its principal, 1960–68; vice chancellor, Agra University 1968–69; director general, ICMR, 1969–74.
3. Finally no such committee was appointed.
4. Daulat Singh Kothari (1906–93); taught physics at Allahabad University, 1928–34; Delhi University, 1934–71; professor emeritus, Delhi University; scientific adviser to the ministry of defence, 1948–61; chairman, University Grants Commission, 1961–73, committee of scientific and technical terminology, 1960–65; education committee, Government of India, 1964–66; president, Indian Science Congress, 1964; president, Indian National Science Academy, 1973–74.
5. The Homeopathy Central Council Bill, 1971, was passed by the Rajya Sabha on 23 July and by the Lok Sabha on 19 November 1973. The president gave his assent on 19 December 1973. It provided for the constitution of a Central Council of Homeopathy and the maintenance of a Central Registrar of Homeopathy.
6. On 28 January 1974, a conference of the health ministers of the states was held in New Delhi.

17

1. A famous story from the Mahabharata on the theme of which there are forty-seven paintings in the museum.

18

1. Following over two years of talks between the Indian government and Sheikh Mohammad Abdullah, an agreement on relations between India and Kashmir was reached on 17 January 1975. In fact, final negotiations began on 2 July 1974 between Mirza Afzal Beg, representing Sheikh Abdullah and G. Parthasarathy representing Indira Gandhi. After a series of talks they signed an aide-memoire stating the points of agreement which had, emerged from their discussions. The final round of talks between Beg and Parthasarathy took place on January 12–17, 1975. The agreed conclusions of their emissaries were accepted by Sheikh Abdullah and Indira Gandhi. It was approved by the Political Affairs Committee of the Union cabinet on 18 January and by the executive committee of the Kashmir Congress on 21 January. The details of the agreement were announced by Indira Gandhi on 24 February 1975 in the parliament. It included, among other things, that, 'The State of Jammu and Kashmir, which is a constituent unit of the Union of India, shall in its relations with the Union continue to be governed by Article 370 of the Constitution of India.' And that, 'The residuary powers of legislation shall remain with the state, however, Parliament will continue to have power to make laws relating to the prevention of activities, directed towards disclaiming, questioning or disrupting the sovereignty and territorial integrity of India or bringing about cession of a part of the territory of India or secession of a part of territory of India from the Union or causing insult to the Indian Flag, the Indian National Anthem and the constitution.' The parliament approved this accord on 13 March 1975.
2. G. Parthasarathy (1912–95); diplomat and administrator; assistant editor, *The Hindu,* 1936–49; chief editor of PTI Bombay, 1952–54; chairman, International Commission for Supervision and Control, Cambodia and later Vietnam, 1954–57 and 1961–62; ambassador to Indonesia, 1957–58, and to China, 1958–61; high commissioner to Pakistan, 1962–65; permanent representative to the UN, 1965–69; founding vice-chancellor, Jawaharlal Nehru University, 1969–74; chairman, policy planning committee, ministry of external affairs, 1975–77 and 1984; chairman, Indian Council for Social Science Research, 1980–90; political adviser to Prime Minister Indira Gandhi, 1981; chairman, policy advisory committee, cabinet secretariat, 1986.

3. Since May 1953, the situation in Jammu and Kashmir had been dangerously confused, primarily as the result of a deep rift among the members of the cabinet of Sheikh Abdullah. And by the beginning of August 1953, the rift became more intense. In the cabinet meeting of 6 August, Sheikh Abdullah insisted that Sham Lal Saraf should resign, but he refused to oblige, which precipitated the crisis. On 7 August, three of four ministers of Sheikh Abdullah—Bakshi Ghulam Mohammad, G.L. Dogra and Sham Lal Saraf—sent a memorandum to him in which they openly denounced his policies and repudiated his leadership. They sent a copy of the memorandum to Karan Singh on the same date. Karan Singh met Sheikh Abdullah on 8 August, but the Sheikh could not satisfy him 'regarding bringing the situation to a stable and speedy solution'. Karan Singh considered this conflict within the cabinet a complete breakdown of the cabinet system and on the same date in the capacity of Sadar-i-Riyasat he dissolved the council of ministers. Sheikh Abdullah was arrested on 9 August and the new ministry headed by Bakshi Ghulam Mohammad was sworn in.
4. Bakkarwals are a nomadic and shelterless scheduled tribe in Jammu and Kashmir. They are concentrated mainly in the Pir Panchal region, a far-flung and difficult area of the state.

19

1. On 12 June 1975 at the Allahabad High Court, Justice Jagmohan Lal Sinha delivered his momentous judgement on Raj Narain's election petition filed in April 1971 against Indira Gandhi, challenging her election from Rae Bareli on various grounds. He not only set aside her election from Rae Bareli but also debarred her from elective office for six years.
2. In a signed statement, some 125 Congress MPs and several members of the council of ministers said, 'The Party and people have immense faith and confidence in your leadership and hence urge upon you to lead and guide the country as Prime Minister.'
3. By 1970 Sheikh Mujibur Rahman and his Awami League had emerged as a dominant force in East Pakistan, but the Punjab-dominated West Pakistan did not accept him as the leader of a united country. They adopted repressive actions against the supporters of Mujibur Rahman. As a result of it, refugees from East Pakistan began to enter into India on a large scale. Indira Gandhi

tried to solve it diplomatically, but her efforts went in vain. Finally, the fifteen-day war resulted in the victory of India and the emergence of Bangladesh as an independent nation.

4. Fakhruddin Ali Ahmed was the president of India at this time.
5. On 20 June 1975 Indira Gandhi filed an application in the Supreme Court seeking an absolute and unconditional stay on the operation of the Allahabad High Court judgement.
6. S.C. Khare was an eminent lawyer of the Supreme Court.
7. Nani Ardeshir Palkhivala (1920–2002); eminent constitutional lawyer and businessman from Bombay; senior advocate, Supreme Court of India; ambassador to USA, 1977–79; served as chairman, various units of Tatas; publications include, *Taxation in India* (1960), *Our Constitution Defaced and Defiled* (1975), *India's Priceless Heritage* (1980), *We, the People* (1984).
8. H.M. Seervai (1906–90); eminent lawyer from Maharashtra; advocate, Supreme Court, since 1957; advocate general of Maharashtra, 1957–67; publications include: *Constitutional law of India, The Position of Judiciary in India, Federalism in India.*
9. Siddhartha Shanker Ray (1920–2010); politician and eminent lawyer from West Bengal; member, West Bengal Legislative Assembly, 1957–71, 1972–77, 1991–92; member, Lok Sabha, 1971–72; minister of law and tribal welfare, government of West Bengal, 1957–58; leader of the opposition, West Bengal Assembly, 1969–67, 1971–92; union minister for education, culture, social welfare, 1971–72; chief minister of West Bengal 1972–77; governor of Punjab, 1986–89; ambassador to USA, 1992–96.
10. On 7 November 1975 the Supreme Court upheld the election of Indira Gandhi to Lok Sabha from Rae Bareli in 1971 and set aside the judgement of the Allahabad High Court.

20

1. Note for Indira Gandhi, New Delhi, 28 June 1975

Farewell Speech in Rajya Sabha

1. The Lok Sabha is the lower house of India's bicameral parliament, with the upper house being the Rajya Sabha.
2. A coastal town in India's southernmost tip.

3. '*Sarva dharma, sama bhava*' is a concept embodying the equality of the destination of the path's followed by all religions, although the paths themselves may be different. The concept was embraced by Ramakrishna and Vivekenanda, as well as Mahatma Gandhi.
4. Shakeel Badayuni (1916–1970) was in Indian Urdu poet, lyricist and songwriter.
5. The Sahanavavatu Mantra is one of the shanti mantras which has its origins in the *Taittiriya Upanishad*. It is often used as a 'universal' prayer to send the message of peace and prosperity.

Acknowledgements

I AM INDEBTED TO Dr Karan Singh who shared his vast world of knowledge and experiences with me over the last two years. I am thankful for his trust, kindness and mentorship that will remain with me forever.

I am grateful to Dr Jyotsna Singh for the generous access to the historical archives and artifacts at Amar Mahal Palace and Museum, and for the support of research stay at Hari Niwas Palace.

My humble gratitude to Drs Manmohan Singh and Shashi Tharoor for bringing light to this work.

Profs Ashis Nandy, Gopalkrishna Gandhi and Pratap Bhanu Mehta for being the first readers of this book and for their precious remarks and suggestions.

Dr Prasanta Chakravarty for his guidance on the structure of the interview, and Priya Thuvassery and Amita Rana for recording it.

Rimina Mohapatra, my philosopher friend, who was by me when I took on this journey and carried it with me along the way.

Nidhi and Ashok Rai for the unconditional warmth and joys shared during the years past.

Anuj Bahri and Krishan Chopra for believing in the project and bringing it out to the world. Thanks to Himani Arora, Siddhesh Inamdar, Bonita Shimray, and the brilliant team at HarperCollins which made it all possible.

Raghav Verma

About the Author

KARAN SINGH ENTERED POLITICAL life at the young age of eighteen, when he was appointed regent of Jammu and Kashmir in 1949. He remained the elected head of state for eighteen years as Sadar-i-Riyasat for three terms and later as governor. In 1967, he was inducted into the Union cabinet by Indira Gandhi. He held the portfolios of tourism and civil aviation, health and family planning, and education and culture for the next eighteen years. He was also India's ambassador to the United States during the conclusion of the Cold War.

Dr Singh is the only former ruler of a princely state to voluntarily surrender his privy purse. He served as chancellor of Jammu and Kashmir University, Banaras Hindu University and Jawaharlal Nehru University; chairman of the Central Sanskrit Board; and president of the Authors Guild of India, the Commonwealth Society of India and the Delhi Music Society. He was president of the India International Centre, chairman of the Auroville Foundation and member of UNESCO's International Commission on Education for the Twenty-first Century, vice chairman of the Jawaharlal Nehru Memorial Fund and chairman of the Temple of Understanding, a major global interfaith association.

List of Original Publications

'I Believe'

I Believe: A Philosophy for the Global Society, Rajpal and Sons Publishing; 2012

Dialogue with Daisaku Ikeda

Humanity at the Crossroads: An Intercultural Dialogue, Oxford University Press India, 1988

On Hinduism

Sterling Book of Hinduism, Sterling Publications 2012

- The Key Concepts
- The Bhakti Movement
- The Modern Renaissance
- The Forms of the Formless

Essays on Hinduism, Third Edition, Primus Books 2014

- The Insight of the Mystics
- The Message of the Upanishads
- The Message of the Bhagavadgita

Essays

As I See it, Full Circle Publishing Ltd, 2001

- A Little History
- Politics and Self
- 'My Dear Tiger'
- Past, Present and Future
- Learning to Live Together
- A Nation's Strength

Prophet of Indian Nationalism, Allen & Unwin, 1963

- Assessment of Sri Aurobindo as a Political Thinker

The Indian Express, 16 July 2009

- A Judgement for India

Travelogues:

Contemporary Essays, Bharatiya Vidya Bhavan, 1971

- Whatever Became of the Twelfth Night?
- Some Impressions of Japan
- Colombia: A Few Glimpses
- Three Approaches to Secularism
- The Old and The New

Poems

Welcome the Moonrise, Asia Publishing House, 1965

Letters

Jammu and Kashmir, 1949–64, Penguin Books, 2006

- Letters between Jawaharlal Nehru and Karan Singh

Kashmir and Beyond 1966–84, Penguin India, 2011

- Letters between Indira Gandhi and Karan Singh

Memoir

Karan Singh's *Autobiography*, Oxford University Press, 1994

Novella

The Mountain of Shiva, Palimpsest Publisher, 2016